NEW YORK CITY
SHSAT

SPECIALIZED HIGH SCHOOLS ADMISSIONS TEST

Patrick Honner, M.S.Ed.
Brooklyn Technical High School

Young Kim, M.A.
Bronx High School of Science

T0116649

About the Authors

Patrick Honner has been teaching mathematics for over 20 years, and he has spent the past 15 at New York City's specialized high schools teaching everything from introductory algebra to linear algebra and multivariable calculus. He is a recipient of the Presidential Award for Excellence in Mathematics and Science Teaching (PAEMST), a four-time Math for America Master Teacher, a New York State Master Teacher, and a National STEM Teacher Ambassador.

Patrick writes a column for Quanta Magazine where he connects active mathematical research to classrooms and curricula, and his work also appears in the New York Times, WIRED, and in a variety of other publications. You can find out more at *PatrickHonner.com*.

Young Kim holds a Master of Arts in the Teaching of English from Columbia University Teachers College. Currently, he teaches 11th grade AP English Language and Composition at the Bronx High School of Science and the Junior Seminar at Mercy College. In addition to his classroom teaching, he has taught in the DREAM SHSI program.

*The views expressed in this book are those of the authors and not necessarily those of the City of New York (NYC).

Copyright © 2019 by Kaplan North America, LLC d/b/a Barron's Educational Series

All rights reserved. No part of this publication may be reproduced or distributed in any form or by any means without the written permission of the copyright owner.

Published by Kaplan North America, LLC d/b/a Barron's Educational Series
1515 West Cypress Creek Road
Fort Lauderdale, Florida 33309
www.barronseduc.com

ISBN: 978-1-4380-1236-0

10 9 8 7 6 5 4 3

Kaplan North America, LLC d/b/a Barron's Educational Series print books are available at special quantity discounts to use for sales promotions, employee premiums, or educational purposes. For more information or to purchase books, please call the Simon & Schuster special sales department at 866-506-1949.

Contents

MATHEMATICS

Introduction to the SHSAT

AN OVERVIEW

The specialized high schools of New York City offer a wide range of excellent academic programs and extracurricular activities. While some of the schools are STEM-focused (Science, Technology, Engineering, Mathematics), others emphasize humanities and the arts.

Admission to these schools is based entirely on one single exam—the New York City Specialized High School Admissions Test, often referred to as the SHSAT. Since this exam is the only admission criterion, performing well on the SHSAT is the only way to secure one of the limited spots in New York City's specialized high schools. And with nearly 30,000 students taking the exam each year, every bit of preparation counts.

Regardless of where you go to school, what grades you earn, or how you usually perform on tests, you can significantly enhance your chances of success on the SHSAT, and thus your chances of admission to the school of your choice, with good test prep, guided practice, and review.

When Should You Begin to Prepare?

The sooner you begin to prepare, the better: the more time you have to learn, practice, and review, the better you will do on test day. Some students begin a year or more in advance. This book allows you to proceed at your own pace and provides you with all the material you need to perform well on the exam.

What's on the Test?

The test consists of two major sections.

English Language Arts (three parts)	Mathematics (two parts)
Stand-alone Revising/Editing	Grid-in Questions
Passage-based Revising/Editing	Multiple-choice Questions
Reading Comprehension	

All questions are worth the same number of raw points. No one question is worth more than another. There is a time limit of 180 minutes, with no break. It is recommended that you allow 90 minutes for each of the two sections, but you are permitted to allocate the time however you wish. There is no penalty for wrong answers or omissions (questions left blank), so it is to your advantage to bubble in an answer to every question, even if you must guess.

When Is the Test Administered?

The SHSAT is administered to current eighth graders seeking admission to the ninth grade, and another version of the test is given to current ninth graders seeking admission to the tenth grade. The vast majority of test-takers are eighth graders. Test dates have varied in recent years, so be sure to verify this year's test dates and locations with your guidance counselor or on the Department of Education website.

How and When Do I Obtain Information and Application Forms?

You must get information regarding applications and test sites from your school guidance counselor. Do this early in September. In addition, you should obtain a copy of the *Specialized High Schools Student Handbook*, which is available from your guidance counselor or online from the Department of Education website. The handbook contains additional current information regarding the test sites and any special rules that may apply.

All procedures and dates are subject to change. Be sure to obtain the most current information from your counselor or the handbook.

What Decisions Do I Have to Make?

You have to decide, in advance, which of the specialized schools will be your first choice, second choice, etc. Where you actually take the exam does not affect your indicated choice of schools. You may take the exam only once in any given year. Violation of this rule will disqualify you from attending any of the specialized schools.

What Score Do I Need?

Your total number of correct answers is your raw score. Your raw score becomes a scaled score by means of a special formula that converts your raw score into a number between 200 and 800. The Department of Education does not publicly release the conversion formulas, but the scale does not convert scores in a uniform manner. For example, at the middle range of scores, a difference of one correct answer may change the scaled score by only a few points, whereas at the higher and lower extremes of the score range, one correct answer may translate to 10 or 20 scaled points.

The cutoff score for a specialized school is the minimum scaled score needed to gain admission to that school. Each school's cutoff score is determined by how many seats the school has available and how many students select that school as one of their choices.

Although it may be possible to find out a school's cutoff score from previous years, you can't predict future cutoff scores nor can you predict how many questions you need to answer correctly to achieve them. With that in mind, your goal should simply be to earn as many points as possible on the SHSAT.

The Summer Discovery Program

Certain applicants whose scores are just short of the cutoff score may qualify for the Summer Discovery Program. Successful completion of this program allows qualifying students to gain admission. The eligibility requirements for admission to this program include:

- Scoring just below the cutoff score
- Recommendation from the current school as having high potential for the program
- Have listed a specialized high school participating in the Discovery Program
- Certified as disadvantaged by current school

When students are informed of their eligibility, they should consult their guidance counselor about applying for the program. Once enrolled into the program, students must complete the program successfully to gain admission into the specialized high school.

THE SPECIALIZED HIGH SCHOOLS

Bronx High School of Science

75 West 205th Street, Bronx, New York 10468

Telephone: (718) 817-7700 Website: *www.bxscience.edu*

Brooklyn Latin School

325 Graham Avenue, Brooklyn, New York 11206

Telephone: (718) 366-0154 Website: *www.brooklynlatin.org*

Brooklyn Technical High School

29 Fort Greene Place, Brooklyn, New York 11217

Telephone: (718) 804-6400 Website: *www.bths.edu*

High School for Mathematics, Science and Engineering at City College

240 Convent Avenue, New York, New York 10031

Telephone: (212) 281-6490 Website: *www.hsmse.org*

High School of American Studies at Lehman College

2925 Goulden Avenue, Bronx, New York 10468

Telephone: (718) 329-2144 Website: *www.hsas-lehman.org*

Queens High School for the Sciences at York College

94-50 159th Street, Jamaica, New York 11451

Telephone: (718) 657-3181 Website: *www.qhss.org*

Staten Island Technical High School

485 Clawson Street, Staten Island, New York 10306

Telephone: (718) 667-3222 Website: *www.siths.org*

Stuyvesant High School

345 Chambers Street, New York, New York 10282-1099

Telephone: (212) 312-4800 Website: *www.stuy.enschool.org*

THE TEST: A DETAILED DESCRIPTION

The SHSAT consists of two sections: English Language Arts and Mathematics. The time limit is 180 minutes total for both sections with no break. The suggested time is 90 minutes for each section.

English Language Arts Section 57 multiple-choice questions

- Revising/Editing questions
  - Up to 4 Stand-alone Revising/Editing questions
  - Up to 7 Passage-based Revising/Editing questions
- Reading Comprehension
  - Up to 4 informational texts followed by 6 to 10 questions
  - Up to 2 literary prose texts followed by 6 to 10 questions
  - One poem followed by 6 to 10 questions

Mathematics Section 5 grid-in questions and 52 multiple-choice questions

- Total of 57 questions covering a range of topics and testing a variety of skills and abilities

English Language Arts

STAND-ALONE REVISING/EDITING

Part A of the Revising/Editing section includes up to eight questions, each of which is based on its own sentence or paragraph and measures your ability to identify an error, correct an error, or improve the quality of a given text.

Each question directs you to read a sentence, a list of sentences, or a paragraph with numbered sentences. Then you must address issues associated with language or punctuation.

Directions

The usual directions instruct you to read the sentence or paragraph and identify an error or to select an option that fixes an existing error.

➡ Example _____

1. Read this paragraph.

> (1) People often associate monosodium glutamate, or better known as MSG, with headaches and nausea, but there was no evidence to substantiate that link. (2) In fact, the compounds associated with MSG are commonly found in beef, pork, or chicken. (3) Scientists believe the sicknesses might be the result of a "nocebo effect." (4) The nocebo effect, like the placebo effect, isn't caused by an actual substance, but merely by suggestion.

Which sentence in this paragraph contains an error and should be revised?

- (A) sentence 1
- (B) sentence 2
- (C) sentence 3
- (D) sentence 4

Answer

1. **(A)** The paragraph is written in present verb tense; however, the use of *was* in sentence 1 is past tense.

PASSAGE-BASED REVISING/EDITING

Part B includes questions that are based on one or two passages. Each Revising/Editing passage may have up to eight questions. Revising/Editing items assess students' ability to recognize and correct language errors and to improve the overall quality of a piece of writing. The passages are approximately 400 words long and may be either informative or argumentative. An argument presents evidence to persuade the reader of its claim, while an informative passage introduces an idea and presents supporting examples to illustrate that idea. Subjects range from history to the sciences. Passages may contain errors that are typical in student writing, such as errors in language usage, irrelevant or insufficient details, inappropriate transitions, and problematic introductory/concluding statements. Each sentence is numbered for reference.

Directions

The usual directions instruct you to read the passage and identify an error or to select an option that fixes an existing error from a given sentence.

 **Example**

The Harmful Effects of Acid Rain

(1) An ecosystem is a community of plants, animals, and other organisms along with their environment, including the air, water, and soil. (2) Everything in an ecosystem is connected. (3) The ecological effects of acid rain are most clearly seen in aquatic environments, such as streams, lakes, and marshes, where it can be harmful to fish and other wildlife. (4) As it flows through the soil, acidic rainwater can be harmful to the environment. (5) The more acid that is introduced to the ecosystem, the more aluminum is released. (6) Some types of plants and animals are able to tolerate acidic waters and moderate amounts of aluminum. (7) Others are acid-sensitive and will be lost as the pH declines. (8) Generally, the young of most species are more sensitive to environmental conditions than adults. (9) At pH 5, most fish eggs cannot hatch, while at lower pH levels, some adult fish die. (10) Even if a species of fish or animal can tolerate moderately acidic water, the animals or plants it eats might not. (11) For example, frogs have a critical pH around 4, but the mayflies they eat are more sensitive and may not survive pH below 5.5.

1. Which sentence can best follow and support sentence 2?

   (A) If something harms one part of an ecosystem—one species of plant or animal, the soil, or the water—it can have an impact on everything else.

   (B) Likewise, humans create connections primarily through technology, such as telephones and the Internet.

   (C) The government currently manages 58 national parks around the country, each with its unique needs.

   (D) The consequences of overdevelopment and pollution are apparently manageable precisely because of the redundancies built into these interconnections.

Answer

1. **(A)** This sentence best explains how an ecosystem can be connected, which supports sentence 2.

READING

The Reading section tests your ability to read carefully and understand what you have read. This is gauged by how well you distinguish between stated fact and implication, as well as your ability to draw valid inferences based on the passage.

You are presented with a reading passage of about 350 to 1,000 words in length. The subject matter of informational texts may include descriptions of historical events, information about natural or scientific phenomena, or discussions of topics relating to music, art, or sports. The literary texts may feature adventure stories, historical fiction, mysteries, myths, science fiction, realistic fiction, allegories, parodies, or satire. One poem will also be included. In each passage, there is a central unifying theme, and points of view are often expressed or implied. Following each passage, there is a set of six to ten multiple-choice questions. The first question asks you to identify the central theme or main idea of the passage. Other questions pertain to factual information contained in the passage, inferences that may be drawn, the meaning of words and phrases, points of view expressed or implied, and more.

Directions

The usual directions instruct you to read the passage and answer the six to ten questions following that passage. You are cautioned to base your answers only on what is contained in the passage. Choose, from among the answer choices, the best answer for each question.

➡ Example _____

Antonio Stradivari was born in 1644 in Cremona, Italy, a town noted for the production of excellent violins. Although Stradivari made cellos and violas as well as violins, it is violins for which he is renowned. His teacher, Nicolo Amati, passed on to him the techniques of violin making as these were practiced in Cremona. The pupil Stradivari employed these techniques but went on to surpass his teacher, making violins whose excellence has never been exceeded or even fully understood.

What makes a Stradivarius such a fine instrument? Stradivari did alter the proportions of the violin, but this change alone does not explain their superiority. Some think that the special varnish he used is responsible for the wonderful sound of the instruments, but not every expert agrees with this idea. A relatively recent theory concerns the unusually cold weather in Europe during this period of history. Lower-than-usual temperatures would have slowed the growth rate of the trees whose wood was used in the violins, resulting in a very dense wood. Perhaps the magnificent Stradivarius sound derives from the density of the wood rather than from the composition of the varnish.

The only violin maker whose instruments rival those of Antonio Stradivari is Giuseppe Antonio Guarneri, who lived at the same time. This fact does not give conclusive proof, but it does seem to bolster the cold-weather theory of the secret of the Stradivarius.

21. Which of the following best expresses the purpose of the author of the passage?
    (A) To discuss the excellence of the violins produced by Stradivari
    (B) To indicate a surprising result of climate change
    (C) To explain what makes a violin superior
    (D) To compare the violins of Stradivari and Guarneri

22. Which of the following is not mentioned as a possible factor influencing the quality of a Stradi-varius violin?

    (E) Special varnish
    (F) Dense wood
    (G) Experience gained through making violas and cellos
    (H) Changes in proportions

Answers

21. **(A)** The passage primarily focuses on the excellence of the violins made by Antonio Stradivari, so choice A is the correct answer. Although weather is discussed as a potential factor in Stadi-vari's unique violins, the passage does not address climate change. This rules out choice B. The passage only talks about violins made by Stradivari, and it does not talk about the traits that make violins in general superior. Therefore, choice C is incorrect. Lastly, although the passage mentions a competing violin maker, Giuseppe Antonio Guarneri, it does not compare the violins of the Stradivari and Guarneri. So choice D is not correct.

22. **(G)** The question asks which of the choices is *not* mentioned as a factor that influenced the quality of Stradivari's violins. The passage mentions the varnish, wood density, and proportions as factors that affect the quality of Stradivari's violins. Although the passage addresses Stradivari's experience making violas and cellos, it does not cite this as a factor in the quality of his violins. Therefore, choice G is not a factor, so it is the correct answer.

Mathematics

There are 52 multiple-choice questions and 5 grid-in questions covering a broad range of topics and assessing a wide range of abilities. The mathematical content of the exam is representative of what is covered in the curriculum of New York City middle schools.

Students are expected to solve problems involving arithmetic, basic algebra, geometry, ratios and proportions, and probability and statistics. Students are also be expected to perform computations involving addition, subtraction, multiplication, and division on integers, fractions, and decimals, without the use of a calculator.

Many questions assess your knowledge of basic concepts. Others ask you to interpret and apply these basic concepts in novel and possibly unfamiliar situations.

IMPORTANT!
- **Calculators are not permitted on the SHSAT.**
- **No formulas are provided on the SHSAT.**

Of the 57 questions on the Mathematics section, only 47 preselected questions will actually be scored. Ten unidentified "field test items" on the test will not be scored. You will not know which questions are field items, so you should do your best to answer all questions correctly.

Formulas and definitions of technical terms will not be provided. Geometric diagrams are not necessarily drawn to scale, but graphs and charts can be assumed to be drawn to scale. Answers involving fractions will be given in *lowest terms*: for example, $\frac{1}{2}$ instead of $\frac{3}{6}$.

MULTIPLE-CHOICE QUESTIONS

Multiple-choice questions on the SHSAT have four answer choices. After solving the problem, choose the **best** answer from among the given choices. There is no penalty for a wrong answer—a wrong answer is scored exactly the same as no answer. Thus, you should never leave an answer blank, even if your answer is a **guess**.

➡ Examples

63. On the number line below, point A is located at -4 and point B is located at 20. AQ is $\frac{3}{8}$ of the distance from A to B, while BR is $\frac{3}{8}$ of the distance from B to A. Find the length of QR.

    (A) 6
    (B) 9
    (C) 12
    (D) 15

64. If $x < x^3 < x^2$, which of the following could be a possible value for x?

    (E) $-\frac{1}{2}$

    (F) 0.1

    (G) 0.5

    (H) $\frac{2}{3}$

Answers

63. **(A)** We can compute the distance from A to B by subtracting their respective coordinates, so $AB = 20 - (-4) = 24$. Since AQ is $\frac{3}{8}$ of AB, we can compute $AQ = \left(\frac{3}{8}\right)(24) = 9$. Similarly, $BR = \left(\frac{3}{8}\right)(24) = 9$. Finally, since $AB = AQ + QR + RB$, we can find the length of QR: $QR = AB - AQ - BR = 24 - 9 - 9 = 6$. Notice how we cannot assume the diagram is drawn to scale.

64. **(E)** Here we will use the **strategy** of trying each answer choice by plugging it in. Since $-\frac{1}{2} < -\frac{1}{8} < \frac{1}{4}$ is true, we know choice E is correct. In a similar manner, we can see that the other choices are wrong: $0.1 > (0.1)^3 = 0.001$, so choice F is not correct; $0.5 > (0.5)^2 = 0.25$, so choice G is not correct; and $\frac{2}{3} > \left(\frac{2}{3}\right)^2 = \frac{4}{9}$, so choice H is not correct.

GRID-IN QUESTIONS

A **grid-in question** requires that you solve a problem by computing a numerical answer and then entering the answer into a grid. This is different from a **multiple-choice question**, in which you select the most correct answer from among a given set of choices.

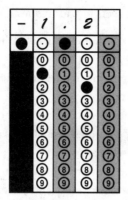

For example, if a problem asks you to compute the product -3×0.4, then the answer, -1.2, would be correctly entered as shown on the grid at the right.

The official directions that you will see on the actual exam appear as follows:

Directions: Solve each problem. On the answer sheet, write your answer in the boxes at the top of the grid. Start on the left side of each grid. Print only one number or symbol in each box. **DO NOT LEAVE A BOX BLANK IN THE MIDDLE OF AN ANSWER.** Under each box, fill in the circle that matches the number or symbol you wrote above. **DO NOT FILL IN A CIRCLE UNDER AN UNUSED BOX.**

Here is an example grid-in question and solution.

58. $\dfrac{3.6}{0.2} \times 0.32 =$

Answer

58. **(5.76)** Notice that $\dfrac{3.6}{0.2} = \dfrac{36}{2} = 18$ and $0.32 = \dfrac{32}{100}$. So $\dfrac{3.6}{0.2} \times 0.32 = 18 \times \dfrac{32}{100}$. Since $18 \times 32 = 576$, we have that $18 \times \dfrac{32}{100} = \dfrac{576}{100} = 5.76$.

And here's the correct gridding for this answer.

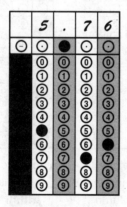

Here are some tips for entering the answers to grid-in questions:

- Immediately after solving and checking a problem, enter the answer in the boxes in the top line of the grid.
- When entering your answer in the top line of the grid, note that the first box is used **only** if the answer begins with a minus (−) sign.
- Always start entering the numeric part of your answer at the second box.
- Every box after the first should only get a digit (from 0 to 9) or a decimal point (.).
- Do not leave any blank boxes **within** the answer.
- Fill in the circles **after** you enter your answer in the boxes in the top line.
- If you change the top boxes later, be sure to erase and correct the filled-in circles below.
- If you skip a problem, be sure to also skip the grid for that problem.

Samples of Correct and Incorrect Gridding

Suppose the answer is –3.2.

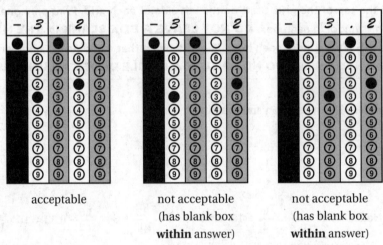

| acceptable | not acceptable (has blank box **within** answer) | not acceptable (has blank box **within** answer) |

Suppose the answer is 602.

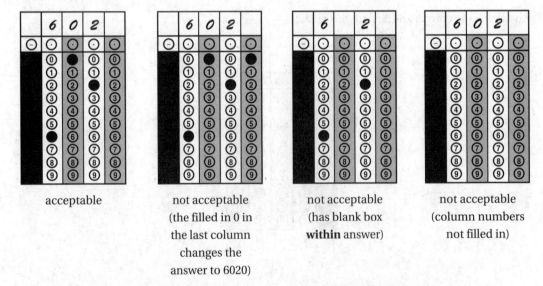

| acceptable | not acceptable (the filled in 0 in the last column changes the answer to 6020) | not acceptable (has blank box **within** answer) | not acceptable (column numbers not filled in) |

The Department of Education may make additional revisions regarding "acceptable" and "not acceptable" answers. Be sure to obtain the latest copy of the DOE Handbook.

Summary of the Number and Types of Questions on the SHSAT

The ELA and Mathematics sections of the test will each contain 57 questions, distributed as follows.

English Language Arts Section	
Stand-alone Revising/Editing	Up to 4 questions
Passage-based Revising/Editing	Up to 7 questions
Reading Comprehension	Up to 48 questions

Mathematics Section	
Grid-in Questions	5 questions
Multiple-choice Questions	52 questions

Marking the Answer Sheet

Bring to the test three to five well-sharpened #2 pencils, a good eraser, and a non–calculator/non–smart watch to keep track of time.

When solving problems or computing answers, do all your work in the test booklet. Do not do any such work on the answer sheet. When you bubble in an answer on the answer sheet, make sure your mark is clear and dark and completely fills the circle. Do not bubble in more than one answer to a problem, or no credit will be given for either answer. If you change an answer, erase the old mark completely.

Be very careful where you bubble in each answer. If you make a mistake, the process of erasing and re-entering your answers later will cost you valuable test-taking time. Make it a habit to double-check the number of the question each and every time you bubble in an answer. Check the number in the test booklet with the number in the grid. These few seconds could save you several minutes later on. More important, it could save you several points! This is especially important if you intend to skip questions and return to them later.

Make sure there are no stray marks on the answer sheet. Do not fold or tear the answer sheet.

HOW TO USE THIS BOOK

This book is designed to help you by providing:

- Focused exercises that target specific skills required for success on the exam
- Review of essential content and techniques
- Sample tests in the style and structure, and at the level, of the actual test with detailed solutions
- Test-taking strategies and suggestions to improve your performance

To be a successful test-taker, keep the following principles in mind as you prepare.

The Basics

You already have the basic math and verbal skills, but keep practicing them! Practice will keep those skills sharp, allowing you to execute the basics with speed and accuracy.

Test Format

Familiarize yourself with the types of questions you'll see, the time limits you'll need to observe, and the directions and gridding procedures you'll need to follow.

Strategies

Throughout this book, you will be presented with general test-taking techniques as well as strategies that are specific to each type of question. Applying these will give you the advantage you need.

Practice!

Preparing for the SHSAT is just like preparing for a big game or an important performance, and a good performance is a result of good rehearsals. Practice thoughtfully and consistently to be ready for test day. Upon completion of this book, make sure to take the practice test materials in the *SHSAT Handbook* published by the NYC Department of Education.

SUGGESTED PLAN OF STUDY

Here is a suggested plan of study using this book.

General Preparation

First, make sure you are familiar with the structure and scope of the SHSAT as presented here in this chapter. Then read the next chapter, "General Test-taking Strategies," to get a general overview of how to approach the test.

Once you are ready, begin the content sections.

ELA

1. Start with the Revising/Editing section. Complete each section in sequence. Even if you are familiar with the material, review each section to gain a strong grasp on the question types.
2. Upon completion of the review sections, complete the practice tests at the end of the Revising/Editing sections.
3. Move on to the Reading Comprehension review sections, and do all problems in the practice test.

Mathematics

1. Start with Chapter 9, "Taking a Math Test," to familiarize yourself with basic math test-taking strategies. Read the example problems and the solutions closely, and look for opportunities to apply these strategies as you work through the remaining chapters.
2. Work through each of the content chapters ("Numbers and Arithmetic"; "Equations and Inequalities"; "Ratios and Proportions"; "Counting, Probability, and Statistics"; and "Geometry") slowly and thoroughly. Review the content and carefully read the problems and worked solutions. Complete the exercises at the end of each chapter.

It is NOT recommended that you speed through the review sections. Take your time and think about the questions. Speed comes with mastery. On the model tests, however, complete each test in actual testing conditions.

Practice Tests

When you have completed both the ELA and Mathematics review sections, take the first practice test. Be sure to take the practice test under strict testing conditions. Do the entire test in one three-hour block, just like you will have to do on test day. Use this as an opportunity to prepare yourself for the experience of the test, as well as the content.

After you complete the first practice test, review the answers. Read the detailed answer explanations carefully, even the explanations of the questions you got correct. The answer explanations often offer alternative approaches, ones that may work better or faster for you next time.

After you have finished reviewing the first practice test, go back and reread the review sections, especially the sections where you performed the weakest on the practice test. Look for tips and strategies that could have helped you.

After some time has passed, take the following practice tests under the same conditions, and repeat the above process. If you have enough time, wait a while and retake the practice tests again at a later date.

General Test-taking Strategies

The suggestions in the section apply to the test in general. Specific skills and tips that apply to particular content on the test will be offered in the review chapters.

Know the Test Site

Be sure you know where you are taking the test and how to get there. It's a good idea to visit the site before test day to make sure you are familiar with the area and the commute.

Know the Test Directions

Look over the practice tests in this book. Familiarize yourself with the directions for each section of the test. Reading the directions on test day will cost you valuable time that could otherwise be used for answering questions. On test day, make sure to take a quick look at the directions to be sure there are no changes, but be prepared to start answering questions right away.

Remember, for the Mathematics section, no reference formulas are given and calculators are **not** permitted.

Develop a Plan

You have 180 minutes, or three hours, to complete the entire SHSAT. The two sections—ELA and Mathematics—are not individually timed. This means you have to decide how you will allocate your time on the two sections. You are also free to choose to start with either section.

Since each section is worth the same amount of points, it is recommended that you plan to spend an equal amount of time, 90 minutes, on each section. But you may wish to start with the section you feel more comfortable with. Here are a few examples:

- If you are especially good at English, choose Revising/Editing, Reading, Mathematics.
- If you are especially good at Math, choose Mathematics, Revising/Editing, Reading.

Just remember to give yourself enough time for each section. Every question contributes equally to your final score.

Pace Yourself

Time management is very important in test taking. You have 180 minutes to answer 114 questions on the SHSAT. That means that, on average, you have about 90 seconds to answer each question. It is important not to spend too much time on any one question. Spending five minutes on one question may mean you won't get to answer two other questions later. Maybe those later questions are easier or more familiar to you, but you'll never know if you don't get to them.

Remember that all the questions are worth an equal number of points. The ELA questions are worth the same as the Mathematics questions. The questions at the end of a section are worth the same as those in the beginning. On the Math section, a grid-in question is worth the same amount of points as a multiple-choice question. There is no reason to spend more time on any one section or question type than another.

Use a watch when you take the practice tests. Time yourself on the various sections. Develop a sense of how long it takes you to read a passage and then answer the related questions or how long it takes you to multiply numbers involving decimals or to solve a ratios problem, etc. Use this information to help plan your strategy.

Practice with your watch so you are ready to use it on test day. Pay attention to your pace during testing. You don't need to time every question, but you should be getting through about ten questions every 15 minutes. If you're not answering questions at this rate, you should pick up the pace so you can be sure to at least see all the problems.

Keeping a quick pace on the test is very important. But, of course, if you rush through problems too quickly, you are likely to make more mistakes. So what can you do?

The answer is to make good strategic decisions about which problems to invest your time in. Give yourself a few seconds to read and think about a question. If you can solve it, do it. If you are unsure, take a guess or mark it, move on, and come back to it later. Using this strategy appropriately will give you extra time to review those questions later, after you have made your way through the entire test. Knowing which problems you should solve right away and which problems should you skip and come back to later is a part of knowing your own strengths and weaknesses. It takes time and practice to master this, but it can make a big difference in your test performance.

Leave Nothing Blank

You should answer every question on the SHSAT. There is no additional penalty for a wrong answer—a wrong answer and a blank answer both earn zero points. Do your best to solve each problem using appropriate techniques, but if you have no idea what the answer is, take a guess and write it down.

Do not feel bad about guessing if you don't know the answer. It is a good test-taking strategy and the best test-takers all do it. On a multiple-choice question with four options, a guess has a 25 percent chance of being the right answer. This means that if there are four questions you can't answer and you guess on all of them, on average you will get one of them right. That one extra correct answer just might make the difference in your final score!

But remember, guessing is only a good strategy on problems you can't solve. The best strategy is to know the material and to use your expertise to answer the question. Even if you don't end up getting the answer, your work can still be valuable. You might be able to eliminate one or more of the answer choices and improve your chances of guessing correctly. But make sure you leave nothing blank. A blank answer is the only one that guarantees no points.

Mark Questions

As you go through the test, you may find some questions that you are unsure of and some that you cannot solve at all. When this happens, mark questions with either a question mark (?) or an X. This will help you keep track of these questions so you can easily find them and return to them later. When using this strategy, remember to put these marks only in your test booklet, never on the answer sheet.

1. If you try a question but you are not sure if you have the correct answer, then put a question mark next to the question number in your test booklet. Because you have already spent some time analyzing the problem, choose an answer now and mark it on the answer sheet, even if it is a guess. You will go back to these questions later.

2. If you have no idea how to solve a question, put an X next to the question number in your test booklet. You can make a guess now or wait until you revisit the problem later. However, if you aren't sure that you will have enough time to come back to the question, then make a guess. Remember, never leave a question blank.

3. When you finish the test, go back to all of the question mark problems. That mark in your test booklet will make them easy to locate. You may find that you now remember things that will help you answer these questions.

4. When you finish looking over the question mark problems, try the X problems. You may not be able to find the correct answer, but for multiple-choice questions, first try to eliminate choices and narrow down the potential answers. Since there is no penalty for guessing, make sure you enter an answer for every question, even if it has to be a random guess!

ELIMINATING CHOICES: If you must guess at an answer, try to reduce the number of choices first. If you can eliminate choices that are obviously wrong, your chances of guessing correctly are improved. Lightly cross out the choices that you eliminate. That way, when you return to the problem later, you need only concentrate on the reduced set of choices.

Read the Questions with Focus and Purpose

Read each question carefully. Always determine precisely what is being asked for. Answering a question that is not being asked will almost certainly lead to a wrong answer, especially since multiple-choice questions often anticipate student reading errors by providing related options among the answer choices.

Rehearse for the Test

Take the practice tests in this book under the same time limits and test conditions that you will face on exam day. Use the practice tests as an opportunity to get familiar with not only the content of the test, but also the *experience* of the test. What will it feel like to work on the test for three straight hours? How long will it take you to work through the different sections? How will you react when you encounter a problem you don't know how to solve?

One of the hardest things to prepare for is the length of the test. Staying intellectually focused and active for three hours is not easy. But with preparation and training, you can get better at it. When you take the practice tests in this book, push yourself to be active for the full three hours. Train yourself to have the necessary test-taking stamina. Use every available minute to maximize your score. If you finish the test and still have time left, use it! Make sure you've answered every question. Review your marked questions. Double-check your answers to easy questions to make sure you didn't make any silly mistakes.

Each year, hundreds of students miss the cutoff for their school of choice by one or two questions. Every point you can earn on the SHSAT is important, so make sure to take full advantage of all your time to maximize your score.

On the test, you will likely encounter problems you haven't seen before or problems you aren't sure how to solve. Don't panic! The test is designed to challenge you. You are not expected to get every question correct. Just focus on getting as many correct answers as you can. Do this by properly managing your time so you see every question. This will allow you to apply the skills you have spent so much time developing. And make your best guess when appropriate. If you start to get anxious during the test, pause for a moment, take a deep breath, and try to relax your mind. Then, turn the page and focus on the next question.

Use the Test Booklet and Scratch Paper Wisely

Work in the test booklet and on scratch paper if provided. Mark the test booklet in any way you are comfortable with: underline or circle words, make marks on diagrams or charts, or perform arithmetic in the margins of problems. But remember to always bubble in your answers on the answer sheet—only your answer sheet will be graded. Do not make any stray marks or do any work on the answer sheet.

Be neat and organized in your work. If working on scrap paper, write the question number next to your work so you can find it later if necessary. Organized work will help you focus your efforts, and it will be easier to check and correct if necessary.

The Night and Morning before the Test

- Make sure you know how to get to the test site and when you need to be there.
- Prepare your supplies the night before: your admission ticket, three to five well-sharpened #2 pencils, a good eraser, and a non–calculator/non–smart watch.
- Get a good night's sleep.
- Get up early and have a good breakfast.
- Bring everything you need.
- Plan on arriving to the test site early so you do not feel rushed or anxious.

Feel free to review your practice materials the night before, but don't overdo it. Cramming the night before is not an effective test preparation technique, and it can often do more harm than good. It can heighten anxiety and prevent you from getting the rest you need to perform your best on test day.

Some Additional Ideas and Suggestions

READ

Read regularly and read a wide variety of works: books, articles, current events, short stories, poetry, etc. Be a mindful, alert reader. When you read, try to process both the content of the text and the purpose and tone of the author. Look up and learn new words to improve your vocabulary. Try to increase your reading speed, but not at the expense of comprehension.

WRITE

Practice writing often, such as with a daily journal. Incorporate the writing rules from the content reviewed in the Revising/Editing sections.

DO CHALLENGING MATH PROBLEMS

Practice the math problems in this book and study the solutions carefully. The more you practice, the sharper your math skills will be. Practice math every day, like you would a sport or an instrument. Find challenging problems that will push the limits of what you know and force you to learn new content and techniques.

WRITE YOUR OWN PROBLEMS

Try writing your own test questions. Mimic the types of questions you see in your preparation materials and create problems in your own style. Take passages from books or articles you have read and write related questions. Write new math questions based on those you see in this book or in your classes or textbooks.

Practice writing *good* multiple-choice questions with answer choices. When you write a multiple-choice question, make sure you include the correct answer and good wrong answers. Anticipate the mistakes test-takers are likely to make when solving such a problem. Doing this will help *you* anticipate and avoid those errors. It will also give you extra insight into what test questions are asking for.

DON'T CRAM

The best strategy for preparing for an exam is to consistently work a little each day for an extended period of time. Develop a plan that spreads out your practice in the weeks or months leading up to the exam. Cramming the night before the exam is very unlikely to improve your score, and in fact it may have a negative impact on your performance.

PART ONE
English Language Arts

Revising/Editing Overview 1

The SHSAT introduces you to the test with a section called Revising and Editing. The section tests your understanding of standard written English, which is, in many ways, very different from spoken English.

There are a total of nine questions divided into two sections. The first section, called Revising/Editing Part A, tests your ability either to detect errors or to propose an improvement. The second section, called Revising/Editing Part B, contains an essay, either informative or argumentative. You will have to read the entire passage, and then do everything that you did in Part A, as well as modify, by adding or deleting, given sentences to enhance the organization of the essay.

Given the wide array of problems and the finer nuances of the English language, it is virtually impossible to go over every grammatical rule. However, there are several frequently appearing errors on the SHSAT. Learning how to identify these error types can help you hone your skills on this test.

Tips:

- The following chapters in this book will help you develop the skills to answer the frequently appearing errors on the SHSAT. Although each chapter deals with a specific skill set, *it is highly recommended that you do ALL the exercises in order.* Jumping from chapter to chapter may not be that helpful because there are key terms, ideas, and strategies that the chapters cumulatively build upon.

- As a native English speaker or someone just learning the language, the rules and conventions in this chapter might seem either odd or foreign. Even if you understand the concepts in spoken English, you might not recognize the logic in written English. This can be as incredibly frustrating to a native speaker as it is to a student who is just learning the language. Rather than just using your "ear" to sound out the right answer, try to approach these problems like video games. They are merely reflections of reality, and, accordingly, they operate with their own rules and system. You need to understand the system, and you only get better at a game through practice.

- Eliminate wrong answer choices where you can. You will cover this a bit more in the Math section, but remember that if you can eliminate one answer choice, the probability of guessing the correct answer jumps from 25 to 33 percent. Eliminate two answer choices and the probability jumps from 25 to 50 percent. That's better odds than winning a prize from a cereal box.

Grammatical Agreements 2

In the Revising and Editing section, four types of problems require the use of an agreement strategy, where you are asked to find the "partner" of a given word. Once you find this partner, you must select the answer that correctly accompanies the relationship. It's similar to playing a game of connect-the-dots, but the difference is that you need to know how to identify the dots.

There are four different grammatical rules you need to understand in order to play this "game": subject-verb agreement, pronoun agreement, verb tense agreement, and modifier placement. In this chapter, we will go over the nature of these rules and demonstrate a strategy to connect the elements for each of these games. Keep in mind that, like video games, you only improve with practice. Make sure to complete the practice sections to master this section.

SUBJECT-VERB AGREEMENT

Every sentence contains something called a **subject noun** and a **predicate verb**. These two words always share a relationship, where if the noun is singular or plural, then the predicate verb must also agree in its form. The subject noun is in parentheses, and the predicate verb is underlined:

> The (dog) is barking.
> The (dog) bites the shoe.

Notice that if you change *the dog* into *dogs*, the verbs *is* and *bites* must change as well:

> The (dogs) are barking.
> The (dogs) bite the shoe.

Now, the SHSAT won't make it this easy. To make it more difficult, the SHSAT includes a series of filler words between the subject noun and the predicate verb. This makes it more likely that you will lose track of the original subject noun and choose the answer that seems correct but is not. Examine the following incorrectly constructed sentence:

> The books is not on sale.

Set this way, you should be able to see that the verb *is* is clearly wrong. However, the SHSAT will insert words in between the subject noun and the predicate. Consider the following sentence:

> **Incorrect:** The books, written by Mr. Monkey, is not on sale.

Notice that there is a singular noun, *Mr. Monkey*, placed right next to the singular verb *is*. Because of its location, your brain really shouldn't register an error because it processes the singular noun with a singular verb. However, this sentence is wrong, because the thing that accompanies the verb *is* is not Mr. Monkey, but *the books*.

Correct: The **books**, written by Mr. Monkey, **are** not on sale.

Examine the following examples:

Incorrect: My friend, who is commended by all the teachers, are working hard.
Correct: My **friend**, who is commended by all the teachers, **is** working hard.

Incorrect: The angry group of students were thinking about escaping school.
Correct: The angry **group** of students **was** thinking about escaping school.

Hint 1: If you see an auxiliary verb (is/was, are/were, has/have) in the answer choice, always trace it back to the subject noun.

Hint 2: Prepositions are words that typically indicate position (hence the word pre*position*). If you see a preposition followed by a series of words, it's almost *never* the subject. It's placed between the subject noun and the predicate verb to trick you. Prepositions to look out for are as follows:

of, at, in, for, on, with, by, from, to, about, over, below, above, between

If you see prepositions, follow these steps:

1. Cross out the prepositions and all the words that appear after them *up* to the verb.
2. Underline the subject noun and the predicate verb.
3. Change subject noun or predicate verb.

➡ Example _____

The dogs in the house of my brothers bark really loud.
Step 1: The dog ~~in the house of my brothers~~ bark really loud.
Step 2: The **dog** ~~in the house of my brothers~~ **bark** really loud.
Step 3: The **dogs** ~~in the house of my brothers~~ **bark** really loud.

OR

Step 3: The **dog** ~~in the house of my brothers~~ **barks** really loud.

Hint 3: If you see a comma to the left of the predicate verb, cross out all the words in between that comma and the other comma. You should be able to connect the subject nouns and the predicate verbs.

➡ Example _____

My four yachts, which were developed by my dad, travels very slowly.
Step 1: My four yachts, ~~which were developed by my dad,~~ travels very slowly.
Step 2: My four **yachts**, ~~which were developed by my dad,~~ **travels** very slowly.
Step 3: My four **yachts**, ~~which were developed by my dad,~~ **travel** very slowly.

Some Other Things to Know

Here are some things you should know:

Each and *every* take singular verbs, even if they are followed by plural nouns.

Each of the boys **was** absent.
Every man, woman, and child **is** alive.

Neither and *either* take singular verbs.

> **Neither** of the boys **is** here.
>
> **Either** the dog or the cat **was** in my room.

Verbs that end in *-ing* can sometimes be used as nouns. These are called gerunds.

> **Jogging is** a fun activity.
>
> **Studying** every day **was** not what I had in mind.

When in doubt about whether a word is singular or plural, just add the word *is* or *are* right after it. If it sounds correct with *is*, then it is singular. If *are* sounds better, then it is plural.

Subject-Verb Agreement Exercise 1

Choose the correct verb.

1. The biggest problem with math problems (is/are) that they involve unknown variables.
2. John and my pet iguana (has/have) one thing in common: a mouth.
3. People who are suspected of a crime in our country (has/have) the right to a speedy trial.
4. Remembering all the people from my past (is/are) a daunting task.
5. Every man, woman, and child (is/are) related to each other in some way.
6. One of the things I learned from life (is/are) that life is neither easy nor hard.
7. Each of the men (has/have) already made up his mind on the issue.
8. Many students who want to go to a good college (develops/develop) consistent and intensive study habits.
9. No two of the creatures (was/were) considered unique organisms unto themselves.
10. Some of the most important lessons we gain in life (reveals/reveal) themselves in moments of quiet reflection.
11. Neither of the girls (wants/want) to be a part of the choir.
12. One of my best students always (completes/complete) the assigned work on time to perfection.
13. The fear of numbers, such as 4 or 13, (originates/originate) from cultural beliefs whose meanings are often shrouded in mystery.
14. There (is/are) many people in the room.
15. There (is/are) in our deepest nightmares a silent monster waiting for its next victim.
16. There (is/are) within our vast universe a dizzying complex of stars, whose number can never be comprehended by our limited minds.
17. In the New York school system, students from different countries and backgrounds (learns/ learn) things from each other.
18. The wooly mammoth, an enormous hairy pachyderm with long tusks, (was/were) once common in North America.
19. Maple syrup, normally made from the sap of red or black maple trees, (is/are) used in numerous baked goods.
20. The rise of online video games that are free for all people (has/have) reduced the number of children playing outside with their friends.

(Answers are on page 18.)

Subject-Verb Agreement Exercise 2

1. Read this sentence.

   > In the fourth century, jobs in farming was abundant, because the bubonic plague drastically reduced the labor supply.

   Which edit should be made to correct this sentence?

   (A) Change *farming* to *farmings*.
   (B) Change *jobs* to *job*.
   (C) Change *was abundant* to *were abundant*.
   (D) Change *reduced* to *reduce*.

2. Read this sentence.

   > A distinguished and respected organization of students and teachers have met with the administration to voice concerns about plans for the new program.

   Which edit should be made to correct this sentence?

   (E) Change *organization* to *organizations*.
   (F) Change *have* to *has*.
   (G) Change *met* to *meetings*.
   (H) Change *voice* to *voices*.

3. Read this sentence.

   > Studying the effects of different types of poisons help toxicologists understand how different combinations of molecules can lead to deadly, yet interesting, outcomes.

   Which edit should be made to correct this sentence?

   (A) Change *Studying* to *To study*.
   (B) Change *effects* to *affects*.
   (C) Change *help* to *helps*.
   (D) Change *understand* to *understanding*.

4. Read this sentence.

   > Many readers in today's society consider complex intricacy to be the hallmark of quality writing, but the most sophisticated writings by Ernest Hemingway is marked by an austere simplicity.

   Which edit should be made to correct this sentence?

   (E) Change *readers* to *reader*.
   (F) Change *society* to *societies*.
   (G) Change *consider* to *considers*.
   (H) Change *is* to *are*.

(Answers are on page 19.)

PRONOUN AGREEMENT

Pronouns are a class of words that almost everyone knows and uses. You learn to use pronouns before you learn to form sentences. Here's a list of pronouns:

I, me, mine, my, you, your, yours, he, him, his, she, her, hers, we, us, our, ours, they, them, their, it, its, that, this, these, those, who, whom, one

To solve **pronoun antecedent** problems, you must trace the pronoun's antecedent. **Antecedent** is a fancy term for the word the pronoun is replacing. Examine the following sentence:

The book was so popular that **it** was turned into a movie.

The pronoun **it** replaces the word book, so the antecedent to **it** is book.

Now this is what an error looks like:

The book was so popular that **they were** turned into a movie.

You can see here that the plural pronoun **they** replaces the singular noun book. This is wrong because a plural pronoun cannot replace a singular noun.

To make this more difficult, the SHSAT may ask you to find a "vague pronoun." The word *vague* simply means unclear. A vague pronoun question is a sentence in which the antecedent cannot be identified. For instance, if I were to tell you "Give me that," you would be confused. In real life, I can point to something or we might have been talking about something to help you know what "that" is. In text, however, pronouns are difficult to identify unless there are clues.

To solve the vague pronoun problems, first apply the same method. Trace the pronoun to its antecedent. Unlike the pronoun antecedent agreement question types, you will find either TWO equally acceptable antecedents or none at all. Examine the following sentence:

Charlie and Robert both swore to be best friends forever, but **he** changed his mind after graduating college.

The pronoun here is **he**, and the antecedent is Charlie and Robert. The problem here is that **he** can refer to either Charlie OR Robert. Therefore, the pronoun is vague.

There will also be times when there is no antecedent. Examine the following sentence:

Charlie took the train to see the movie, but the instructions **they** gave **him** were unclear.

In this sentence, there are two pronouns. The antecedent to the pronoun **him** can be traced to Charlie, but what about the pronoun **they**? We can assume many things, but unless the sentence clearly contains an antecedent, this pronoun remains a problem and, therefore, would be committing a vague pronoun error.

Pronoun Exercise 1

Identify the pronoun antecedent of the bolded pronoun. Then, correct the pronoun.

1. My school has always been committed to assisting **their** students in their academic goals.
2. The agency, upon review of its scholarship policies, decided that **they** would give authority to only the most qualified individuals.
3. After the contest began, each of the boys wanted **their** idea for the school mascot.
4. Although you shouldn't be completely lazy, **one** shouldn't be completely work crazy either.
5. Students sometimes are not ready to handle the extra work when **his or her** classwork becomes too difficult.
6. Everybody is expected to do **their** part in the project.

7. The museum received so many visitors that **they** had to turn some people away.

8. Some plants are connected to other plants through chemical networks that enable **it** to detect intruders.

9. When one is in a community with different cultural backgrounds, it is important that **we** keep an open mind.

10. The poodles drew a large crowd of concerned citizens because **it** was the biggest the world had ever seen.

11. The survey indicated that students in the United States hope that **his or her** tuition for college will remain affordable.

12. For the American public, access to information is an important aspect of participating in government, for without **them**, people would not be able to make informed choices.

13. Oil is a finite resource, which will soon become depleted, and we must find ways to replace **them**.

14. Because celebrities are in the public spotlight, **he or she** often prefer to celebrate personal events with friends and family.

15. Throughout the centuries, men have always endeavored to allow destruction of everything, including **his** own creations.

16. Although the group of students did not want to break into a dance, **they** had no choice, for the music was too irresistible.

17. The citizens of a democratic country must recognize that **he or she** is not just passive members but active participants in shaping the values and the policies of the country.

18. The country and its citizens share a responsibility to ensure that both of **its** interests are met.

19. The gang of monsters decided on calling a truce with mankind, for **they** ran out of ammunition to fight.

20. Many people believe that trigonometry exercises are useless, but studies show that **it** can actually enhance a person's ability to think logically.

(Answers are on page 19.)

Pronoun Exercise 2

1. Read this paragraph.

> (1) In 1692, the people in the town of Salem, Massachusetts, were wracked by a fear and paranoia that paralyzed them to the very core. (2) Both poor and wealthy people alike were accused of witchcraft, regardless of how many times they protested. (3) Two of the more affluent men were John Proctor and Giles Corey. (4) He was executed by "pressing," which involved the placement of heavy weights on top of a person.

Which sentence should be revised to correct a vague pronoun?

(A) sentence 1
(B) sentence 2
(C) sentence 3
(D) sentence 4

2. Read this paragraph.

> (1) Many people are growing alarmed about conventionally grown food products and believe that organic food is better for their health. (2) However, studies show that their fears may be unwarranted. (3) If Betty ate organic apples while Jody ate conventionally grown apples, she would have to eat 700 more apples to exceed the EPA safety limit on harmful chemicals. (4) For some reason, though, organic fruits seem to taste better, possibly because people believe they are better.

Which sentence should be revised to correct a vague pronoun?

(E) sentence 1
(F) sentence 2
(G) sentence 3
(H) sentence 4

3. Read this paragraph.

> (1) My mother was looking over a lamp and a table from the yard sale and praised their beauty. (2) Although the lamp was chipped and the table was splintered, she said that they reminded her of her happy childhood home. (3) When she brought them home, my father was less than excited. (4) In fact, he examined the cracked lamp and the splintered table and exclaimed that it was filled with bedbugs.

Which sentence should be revised to correct a vague pronoun?

(A) sentence 1
(B) sentence 2
(C) sentence 3
(D) sentence 4

4. Read this paragraph.

> (1) The Loch Ness Monster, an aquatic creature allegedly living in the Scottish Highlands, resembles a brontosaurus, but many claim that its neck is a lot longer. (2) Photographs suggest that the monster's neck reaches a maximum length of about 6 to 10 feet long, while that of the brontosaurus reaches about 70. (3) While there is no doubt that Nessie is no brontosaurus, Loch Ness specialists claim that Nessie's size is due to the size of its environment. (4) The smaller the area in which an organism lives, the smaller it gets.

Which sentence should be revised to correct a vague pronoun?

(E) sentence 1
(F) sentence 2
(G) sentence 3
(H) sentence 4

(Answers are on page 20.)

VERB TENSE AGREEMENT

There are three basic tenses: the past, the present, and the future. As a general rule on the exam, all predicate verbs should be in the same tense. If three sentences contain past tense verbs and one uses a present tense verb, then that will usually be the incorrect verb.

To identify the incorrect verb usage, identify all the predicate verbs then select the one that doesn't look like the others.

➥ Example

(1) Prairie dogs **are named** dogs because their warning calls **resemble** a dog's bark. (2) However, the prairie dog **is** not really a dog. (3) In fact, it **was** more a squirrel than a dog. (4) It **belongs** to the Sciuridae family, which **includes** squirrels, chipmunks, and marmots.

The list of predicate verbs in the sentences above is as follows:

1. are named (always use the helping verb rather than the verb that follows to determine tense)
2. resemble
3. is
4. was
5. belongs
6. includes

All verbs are in the present tense, except the verb **was**, which is in the past tense. Therefore, **was** is used incorrectly. It should be **is**.

Hint: Watch out for participles and gerunds. They should NOT be used to identify the tense of the sentence. Participles are verbs that end with *-ed* or *-ing*. Participles are more like adjectives than they are verbs. Gerunds are verbs that are transformed into nouns by adding *-ing* to the end of the verb.

Examine the sentence below:

John, tired of running the race, went home.

You'll notice three verbs here: *tired*, *running*, and *went*. The word *tired* describes John, while the word *running* is a gerund. The verb *went* is the predicate verb.

Verb Tense Exercise 1

Correct the tense of the **bolded** verb to connect it to the other verb in the sentence.

1. Although we never made it to the finals, we **will have** a lot of fun.
2. It is common knowledge that many high-quality songs, books, or poems rarely see commercial success because they **had never been** marketed correctly.
3. A jet flying at the speed of sound was never a reality until Captain Chuck Yeager **pilots** the first supersonic jet.
4. The belief that each snowflake **was** special and different has been debunked by science numerous times.
5. My sister and I can play video games together, and rarely **did** we lose our temper.
6. People tend to perform better on certain tasks when others **were** watching.
7. The latest generation has never known a world without the Internet, and this **had made** it difficult for parents to understand why kids refuse to go out and play.

8. Despite the pressure of high expectations, Jonathan managed to overcome the workload and pass the class because his faith in himself **is** unshakeable.

9. Wildfires may appear to move slowly, but with wind blowing at top speeds, they **clocked** in at over 14 miles per hour.

10. Some argue that Alexander the Great was one of the greatest figures in military history, but others **claimed** that he was one of the most arrogant fools.

11. Dogs have an amazing ability to identify their owners, even if their owners **were** a half a mile away.

12. One of the ways in which Japan rose to power was through the early adoption of Western technology, which **enables** it to develop a formidable military.

13. Some of the earliest weapons used by 19th-century Japanese armies were canons and rifles. Despite their strength, these weapons **take** a very long time to load, allowing enemies to strike during reload.

14. Most "fruit juices" aren't made from fruit juices but **were** instead with chemicals designed to mimic the flavor of fruit.

15. Although we **did** not know for sure who Colonel Sanders is, we do know that his chicken is definitely delicious.

16. I find it strange that in the old days people went inside booths to call other people. What **do** they do when they **don't** have those booths around?

17. People seem to believe that hunters and gatherers, prior to the emergence of agriculture, did not have much food. However, analysis of archaeological evidence **suggested** that people ate much better before agriculture arrived.

18. The earthquake shook the land, but the buildings **continues** to stand tall.

19. In ancient times, people celebrated the winter solstice by having wild, raucous parties. Today, people **did** the same.

20. Although we like to think that modern society is more cruel, calculating, and corrupt, studies show that hunter and gatherer societies in ancient times **are** far more brutal.

(Answers are on page 21.)

Verb Tense Exercise 2

1. Read this sentence.

> After the air force destroyed the critical infrastructure, the rebels decided to retreat to their bunkers because there is nowhere to go.

Which edit should be made to correct this sentence?

(A) Change *destroyed* to *destroys*.
(B) Change *decided* to *will decide*.
(C) Change *retreat* to *retreated*.
(D) Change *is* to *was*.

2. Read this sentence.

> Although doctors recommend a minimum of seven hours of sleep per day, many people believed that they can operate with less sleep and neglect the advice.

Which edit should be made to correct this sentence?

- (E) Change *recommend* to *recommending*.
- (F) Change *believed* to *believe*.
- (G) Change *operate* to *operated*.
- (H) Change *neglect* to *will neglect*.

3. Read this sentence.

> In the 1860s, George Washington Carver was born into slavery, but he goes on to become one of the greatest scientists, devising over 100 products through the humble peanut.

Which edit should be made to correct this sentence?

- (A) Change *was* to *is*.
- (B) Change *goes* to *went*.
- (C) Change *become* to *becoming*.
- (D) Change *devising* to *devises*.

4. Read this sentence.

> The biggest problem I faced when I took the test is identifying verb tenses.

Which edit should be made to correct this sentence?

- (E) Change *faced* to *face*.
- (F) Change *took* to *take*.
- (G) Change *is* to *was*.
- (H) Change *identifying* to *identified*.

(Answers are on page 23.)

MODIFIER AGREEMENT

Modifiers are words that add more information to another word. They can be a single word or a group of words, but generally, they are placed right next to the word that is being modified. Examine the modifiers added to each sentence below and notice how each modifier adds more information to the first sentence. Modifiers will be <u>underlined</u>.

> The dog barked at Joey.
> The <u>ugly</u> dog barked at Joey.
> The <u>very ugly</u> dog barked at Joey.
> The <u>very ugly</u> dog barked <u>loudly</u> at Joey.
> <u>Louder than thunder</u>, the <u>really ugly</u> dog barked at Joey.

It is very important to note that the modifiers typically have to be adjacent (next to) the word that they are modifying (object modified).

The SHSAT will rearrange the words so that the object modified is placed away from the modifier. Examine the following sentence:

Louder than thunder, Joey was barked at by the really ugly dog.

In this sentence, the modifier *Louder than thunder* is placed next to *Joey*, so the sentence suggests that Joey is louder than thunder. To fix this, *the really ugly dog* should be placed right next to the modifier *Louder than thunder*.

A lot of times, the misplaced modifiers are quite comical if you imagine them. Try to imagine how the modifiers add information to the **modified object** in the following sentences.

The rat was chased by **mom** hiding behind a box of cereal.
Having cheated on the test, **the teacher** punished Jimmy.
The magician amazed **the crowd** wearing a mysterious, shape-shifting cape.

In the incorrect sentences below, the modifiers appear in the beginning of the sentence right before the comma and the **modified object** appears in the wrong position. The correct sentences place the modifiers and **modified objects** next to each other.

Incorrect: Located deep in the Amazonian jungles, the explorers found **the Lost City**.
Correct: Located deep in the Amazonian jungles, **the Lost City** was discovered by the explorers.

Incorrect: Eating millions of slices every year, pizza is loved by **Americans**.
Correct: Eating millions of slices every year, **Americans** love pizza.

Incorrect: A woman of many talents, the trombone can be played masterfully by **Kimberly**.
Correct: A woman of many talents, **Kimberly** can play the trombone masterfully.

Incorrect: Dried up and brown, we decided to throw away the **Christmas tree**.
Correct: Dried up and brown, **the Christmas tree** was thrown away.

Misplaced Modifiers Exercise 1

Find the word or phrase that should be placed next to the underlined modifier.

1. Hoping for a victory, many days were spent practicing by the basketball team.
2. Looking for a way to escape, the prisoner's spoon was used to dig a hole.
3. Worn as a traditional dress, many Korean women wear the *hanbok* during holidays.
4. A celebrated poet, the sonnet "New Colossus" was written by Emma Lazarus.
5. Translated in over 200 languages, F. Scott Fitzgerald wrote *The Great Gatsby*.
6. Beaten and battered by the wind, my grandmother cut down the old oak tree.
7. Known for its amazing views, thousands of tourists visit Niagara Falls.
8. To meet the school's requirement for community service, five hours a week was what Jimmy spent at the hospital.
9. Looking down at the aquarium's glass floor, the shark was found to be the students' most interesting animal.
10. One of the most popular singers of her time, various instruments and singing techniques were used by Diana Ross.
11. Spread by Europeans, many Native Americans died from small pox.
12. Hidden from daylight, the average person rarely gets to see the wild and crazy life of green fungal mold.

13. Dressed like a cute potato, the costume was perfectly worn by my brother.
14. After failing the exam, the park was the only place Larry could find comfort.
15. Flying high above the sky, Matt always viewed the pigeons with reverence and awe.
16. Celebrated by people all over the world, Johnny's favorite holiday was Christmas.
17. Modified by a home-made hacking technique, Johnny manipulated the graphics on the billboard.
18. Going from rags to riches, fried dumplings is what made Colonel Blanders the legend that he is today.
19. Respected by all the animals in the forest, the humble mouse saved the kingly lion.
20. Valued for its medicinal properties, my grandmother always uses ginger in her food.

(Answers are on page 23.)

Misplaced Modifiers Exercises 2

1. Read this paragraph.

(1) The Bronx High School of Science was a product of its time founded in 1938. (2) Considered unfit for rigorous academic programs, girls were excluded from specialized high schools. (3) In 1946, the school's principal, Dr. Morrie Meister, and the Parents Association spearheaded the efforts to open the school to girls. (4) Stuyvesant and Brooklyn Tech soon followed suit, making their programs accessible to both boys and girls.

Which sentence should be revised to correct a misplaced modifier?

(A) sentence 1
(B) sentence 2
(C) sentence 3
(D) sentence 4

2. Read this paragraph.

(1) In the early 19th century, rivers served as primary conduits that linked the major hubs in interstate commerce. (2) Dewitt Clinton, governor of New York, played an instrumental role by securing $7 million, equivalent to $100 billion today, to develop the Erie Canal. (3) Reducing the cost of shipping from $100 a ton to $8, creating jobs for thousands, and providing revenue for the state government, New Yorkers received many economic benefits of the Erie Canal. (4) Soon, however, the canal gave way to the railroad, which made the glorious canal obsolete.

Which sentence should be revised to correct a misplaced modifier?

(E) sentence 1
(F) sentence 2
(G) sentence 3
(H) sentence 4

3. Read this paragraph.

> (1) While money may not grow on trees, scientists have found that gold does. (2) Examining eucalyptus trees near gold prospecting sites, scientists observed that gold gets sucked up with other nutrients in the soil. (3) As a dissolved mineral, the tree transports the element throughout its leaves. (4) Trace amounts of the mineral found on leaves is not enough to make anyone rich, but it does provide a new way to find hidden sources of gold.

Which sentence should be revised to correct a misplaced modifier?

(A) sentence 1
(B) sentence 2
(C) sentence 3
(D) sentence 4

4. Read this paragraph.

> (1) To improve upon a skill, people typically train one skill at a time. (2) It would make sense that one should learn to walk before learning to run to someone who is learning a new skill. (3) Psychologists, however, are finding that this is not always the case. (4) Practicing several skills together, a process called interleaving, produces much better results than working one skill at a time.

Which sentence should be revised to correct a misplaced modifier?

(E) sentence 1
(F) sentence 2
(G) sentence 3
(H) sentence 4

(Answers are on page 25.)

Answers for Subject-Verb Agreement Exercise 1 (page 7)

The subject noun or nouns and correct predicate verb are in **bold**.

1. The biggest **problem** with math problems (**is**/are) that they involve unknown variables.

2. **John and my pet iguana** (has/**have**) one thing in common: a mouth.

3. **People** who are suspected of a crime in our country (has/**have**) the right to a speedy trial.

4. **Remembering** all the people from my past (**is**/are) a daunting task.

5. **Every man**, woman, and child (**is**/are) related to each other in some way.

   When a series of nouns begin with the word *every*, the predicate verb is singular.

6. **One** of the things I learned from life (**is**/are) that life is neither easy nor hard.

7. **Each** of the men (**has**/have) already made up his mind on the issue.

   Each is always singular, so it takes a singular verb.

8. Many **students** who want to go to a good college (develops/**develop**) consistent and intensive study habits.

9. No **two** of the creatures (was/**were**) considered unique organisms unto themselves.

10. **Some** of the most important lessons we gain in life (reveals/**reveal**) themselves in moments of quiet reflection.

11. **Neither** of the girls (**wants**/want) to be a part of the choir.

    As a general rule on the test, *neither* or *either* will always be singular.

12. **One** of my best students always (**completes**/complete) the assigned work on time to perfection.

13. **The fear** of numbers, such as 4 or 13, (**originates**/originate) from cultural beliefs whose meanings are often shrouded in mystery.

14. There (is/**are**) many **people** in the room.

    There is not a subject. When a sentence begins with *There is/are*, flip it around. You will then be able to identify the subject. The original sentence can be rewritten as "Many people in the room are there." Cross out the prepositional phrases as you normally would. Then you can identify the subject more easily.

15. There (**is**/are) in our deepest nightmares a silent **monster** waiting for its next victim.

16. There (**is**/are) within our vast universe a dizzying **complex** of stars, whose number can never be comprehended by our limited minds.

17. In the New York school system, **students** from different countries and backgrounds (learns/**learn**) things from each other.

18. The wooly **mammoth**, an enormous hairy pachyderm with long tusks, (**was**/were) once common in North America.

19. **Maple syrup**, normally made from the sap of red or black maple trees, (**is**/are) used in numerous baked goods.

20. The **rise** of online video games that are free for all people (**has**/have) reduced the number of children playing outside with their friends.

Answers for Subject-Verb Agreement Exercise 2 (page 8)

1. **(C)** Choice C correctly changes the predicate verb *was* to *were* so that the predicate verb agrees with the subject noun *jobs*.

   ~~In the fourth century,~~ **jobs** ~~in farming~~ **was** abundant, because the bubonic plague drastically reduced the labor supply.

2. **(F)** Choice E makes the subject noun *organizations* agree with the verb *have*, but the phrase *A . . . organizations* is incorrect. Choice F correctly changes the plural predicate verb *have* to *has* so that it agrees with the singular subject noun *organization*.

   A distinguished and respected **organization** ~~of students and teachers~~ **have** met with the administration to voice concerns about plans for the new program.

3. **(C)** Choice C correctly changes the predicate verb *help* to *helps* so that the predicate verb agrees with the subject noun *Studying*.

   Studying ~~the effects of different types of poisons~~ **help** toxicologists understand how different combinations of molecules can lead to deadly, yet interesting, outcomes.

4. **(H)** The incorrect pairing is *italicized*.

   Many **readers** ~~in today's society~~ **consider** complex intricacy to be the hallmark of quality writing, but the most sophisticated *writings* ~~by Ernest Hemingway~~ *is* marked by an austere simplicity.

   The subject noun *readers* correctly agrees with the predicate verb *consider*. The subject noun *writings* does not agree with the predicate verb *is*.

Answers for Pronoun Exercise 1 (pages 9–10)

The antecedent is underlined, and the correct pronoun is in (parentheses) next to the ~~incorrect pronoun~~.

1. My school has always been committed to assisting ~~their~~ (its) students in their academic goals.

2. The agency, upon review of its scholarship policies, decided that ~~they~~ (it) would give authority to only the most qualified individuals.

3. After the contest began, each of the boys wanted ~~their~~ (his) idea for the school mascot.

4. Although you shouldn't be completely lazy, ~~one~~ (you) shouldn't be completely work crazy either.

5. Students sometimes are not ready to handle the extra work when ~~his or her~~ (their) classwork becomes too difficult.

6. Everybody is expected to do ~~their~~ (his or her) part in the project.

7. The museum received so many visitors that ~~they~~ (it) had to turn some people away.

8. Some plants are connected to other plants through chemical networks that enable ~~it~~ (them) to detect intruders.

9. When one is in a community with different cultural backgrounds, it is important that ~~we~~ (one) keep an open mind.

10. The poodles drew a large crowd of concerned citizens because ~~it was~~ (they were) the biggest the world had ever seen.

11. The survey indicated that <u>students</u> in the United States hope that ~~his or her~~ (their) tuition for college will remain affordable.

12. For the American public, <u>access</u> to information is an important aspect of participating in government, for without ~~them~~ (it), people would not be able to make informed choices.

13. <u>Oil</u> is a finite resource, which will soon become depleted, and we must find ways to replace ~~them~~ (it).

14. Because <u>celebrities</u> are in the public spotlight, ~~he or she~~ (they) often prefer to celebrate personal events with friends and family.

15. Throughout the centuries, <u>men</u> have always endeavored to allow destruction of everything, including ~~his~~ (their) own creations.

16. Although the <u>group</u> of students did not want to break into a dance, ~~they~~ (it) had no choice, for the music was too irresistible.

17. The <u>citizens</u> of a democratic country must recognize that ~~he or she is~~ (they are) not just passive members but active participants in shaping the values and the policies of the country.

18. <u>The country and its citizens</u> share a responsibility to ensure that both of ~~its~~ (their) interests are met.

19. The <u>gang</u> of monsters decided on calling a truce with mankind, for ~~they~~ (it) ran out of ammunition to fight.

20. Many people believe that trigonometry <u>exercises</u> are useless, but studies show that ~~it~~ (they) can actually enhance a person's ability to think logically.

Answers for Pronoun Exercise 2 (pages 10–11)

1. **(D)** Examine the pairings of <u>antecedents</u> and **pronouns** below.

   (1) In 1692, the <u>people</u> in the town of Salem, Massachusetts, were wracked by a fear and paranoia that paralyzed **them** to the very core. (2) <u>Both poor and wealthy people</u> alike were accused of witchcraft, regardless of how many times **they** protested. (3) Two of the more affluent men were <u>John Proctor and Giles Corey</u>. (4) **He** was executed by "pressing," which involved the placement of heavy weights on top of a person.

   Sentence 1: The correct antecedent to **them** is <u>people</u>.

   Sentence 2: The correct antecedent to **they** is <u>Both poor and wealthy people</u>.

   Sentence 3: There is no pronoun, but <u>John Proctor and Giles Corey</u> serve as the antecedent to the pronoun in Sentence 4.

   Sentence 4: The pronoun **He** indicates a singular antecedent, but it is impossible to determine whether the pronoun replaces <u>John Proctor</u> or <u>Giles Corey</u>. Therefore, the pronoun should be revised to **John Proctor** or **Giles Corey** to clearly indicate who was executed.

2. **(G)** Examine the pairings of <u>antecedents</u> and **pronouns** below.

   (1) Many <u>people</u> are growing alarmed about conventionally grown food products and believe that organic food is better for **their** health. (2) However, studies show that **their** fears may be unwarranted. (3) If <u>Betty</u> ate organic apples while <u>Jody</u> ate conventionally grown apples, **she** would have to eat 700 more apples to exceed the EPA safety limit on harmful chemicals. (4) For some reason though, <u>organic fruits</u> seem to taste better, possibly because people believe **they** are better.

Sentence 1: The correct antecedent to the plural pronoun **their** is <u>people</u>.

Sentence 2: The correct antecedent to the plural pronoun **their** is <u>people</u> from sentence 1 (yes, this is allowed).

Sentence 3: The pronoun **she** indicates a singular antecedent, but it is impossible to determine whether the pronoun replaces <u>Betty</u> or <u>Jody</u>. Therefore, the pronoun **she** should be revised to either **Betty** or **Jody** in order to indicate who would have to eat 700 more apples.

Sentence 4: The correct antecedent to the plural pronoun **they** is <u>organic fruits</u>.

3. **(D)** Examine the pairings of <u>antecedents</u> and **pronouns** below.

(1) My mother was looking over <u>a lamp and a table</u> from the yard sale and praised **their** beauty. (2) Although the <u>lamp</u> was chipped and the <u>table</u> was splintered, she said that **they** reminded her of her happy childhood home. (3) When she brought **them** home, my father was less than excited. (4) In fact, he examined <u>the cracked lamp and the splintered table</u> and exclaimed that **it** was filled with bedbugs.

Sentence 1: The correct antecedent to the plural pronoun **their** is <u>a lamp and a table</u>.

Sentence 2: The correct antecedent to the plural pronoun **they** is <u>lamp</u> and <u>table</u>.

Sentence 3: The plural pronoun **them** can be traced back to the two items, <u>lamp</u> and <u>table</u>, in sentence 2.

Sentence 4: The pronoun **it** indicates a singular antecedent, but it is impossible to determine whether the pronoun replaces the <u>lamp</u> or the <u>table</u>. Therefore, the pronoun **it** should be revised to **the lamp** or **the table** to indicate which object was filled with bedbugs.

4. **(E)** Examine the pairings of <u>antecedents</u> and **pronouns** below.

(1) The <u>Loch Ness Monster</u>, an aquatic creature allegedly living in the Scottish Highlands, resembles a <u>brontosaurus</u>, but many claim that **its** neck is a lot longer. (2) Photographs suggest that the monster's <u>neck</u> reaches a maximum length of about 6 to 10 feet long, while **that** of the brontosaurus reaches about 70. (3) While there is no doubt that <u>Nessie</u> is no brontosaurus, Loch Ness specialists claim that Nessie's size is due to the size of **its** environment. (4) The smaller the area in which an <u>organism</u> lives, the smaller **it** gets.

Sentence 1: The antecedent to the pronoun **it** can refer to <u>brontosaurus</u> or the <u>Loch Ness Monster</u>. Therefore, the pronoun **it** should be revised to **the brontosaurus** to indicate which creature possessed a longer neck.

Sentence 2: The antecedent to the pronoun **that** is <u>neck</u>. The phrasing "that of" indicates possession in the same way "the monster's" indicates possession.

Sentence 3: The correct antecedent to the pronoun **it** is <u>Nessie</u>.

Sentence 4: The correct antecedent to the pronoun **it** is <u>organism</u>.

Answers for Verb Tense Exercise 1 (pages 12–13)

The clue verb is <u>underlined</u> and the correct (verb tense) is located next to the incorrect **bolded** verbs.

1. Although we never <u>made</u> it to the finals, we **will have** (had) a lot of fun.

2. It is common knowledge that many high-quality songs, books, or poems rarely <u>see</u> commercial success because they **had never been** (are not) marketed correctly.

3. A jet flying at the speed of sound <u>was</u> never a reality until Captain Chuck Yeager **pilots** (piloted) the first supersonic jet.

4. The belief that each snowflake **was** (is) special and different <u>has</u> been debunked by science numerous times.

5. My sister and I <u>can</u> play video games together, and rarely **did** (do) we lose our temper.

6. People <u>tend</u> to perform better on certain tasks when others **were** (are) watching.

7. The latest generation <u>has</u> never known a world without the Internet, and this **had made** (makes) it difficult for parents to understand why kids refuse to go out and play.

8. Despite the pressure of high expectations, Jonathan <u>managed</u> to overcome the workload and pass the class because his faith in himself **is** (was) unshakeable.

9. Wildfires may <u>appear</u> to move slowly, but with wind blowing at top speeds, they **clocked** (clock) in at over 14 miles per hour.

10. Some <u>argue</u> that Alexander the Great was one of the greatest figures in military history, but others **claimed** (claim) that he was one of the most arrogant fools.

11. Dogs <u>have</u> an amazing ability to identify their owners, even if their owners **were** (are) a half a mile away.

12. One of the ways in which Japan rose to power <u>was</u> through the early adoption of Western technology, which **enables** (enabled) it to develop a formidable military.

13. Some of the earliest weapons used by 19th-century Japanese armies <u>were</u> canons and rifles. Despite their strength, these weapons **take** (took) a very long time to load, allowing enemies to strike during reload.

14. Most "fruit juices" <u>aren't</u> made from fruit juices but **were** (are) instead with chemicals designed to mimic the flavor of fruit.

15. Although we **did** (do) not know for sure who Colonel Sanders is, we <u>do</u> know that his chicken is definitely delicious.

16. I find it strange that in the old days people <u>went</u> inside booths to call other people. What **do** (did) they do when they **don't** (didn't) have those booths around?

17. People <u>seem</u> to believe that hunters and gatherers, prior to the emergence of agriculture, did not have much food. However, analysis of archaeological evidence **suggested** (suggests) that people ate much better before agriculture arrived.

18. The earthquake <u>shook</u> the land, but the buildings **continues** (continued) to stand tall.

19. In ancient times, people celebrated the winter solstice by having wild, raucous parties. <u>Today,</u> people **did** (do) the same.

    Watch out for key words or phrases like *today* and *now*. They indicate present tense, so present tense verbs are necessary.

20. Although we like to think that modern society is more cruel, calculating, and corrupt, studies show that hunter and gatherer societies <u>in ancient times</u> **are** (were) far more brutal.

Answers for Verb Tense Exercise 2 (pages 13-14)

1. **(D)** Examine all the predicate verbs underlined below.

   After the air force <u>destroyed</u> the critical infrastructure, the rebels <u>decided</u> to retreat to their bunkers because there <u>is</u> nowhere to go.

   All predicate verbs are in the past tense except *is*. Choice D correctly revises the predicate verb to the past tense.

2. **(F)** Examine all the predicate verbs underlined below.

   Although doctors <u>recommend</u> a minimum of seven hours of sleep per day, many people <u>believed</u> that they <u>can</u> operate with less sleep and neglect the advice.

   All predicate verbs are in the present tense except *believed*. Choice F correctly revises the predicate verb to the present tense.

3. **(B)** Examine all the predicate verbs underlined below.

   In the 1860s, George Washington Carver <u>was</u> born into slavery, but he <u>goes</u> on to become one of the greatest scientists, devising over 100 products through the humble peanut.

   Choice B correctly revises the verb to the appropriate past tense. The verb *to become* is an infinitive and *devising* is a gerund. Neither is a predicate verb so they do not need to be changed.

4. **(G)** Examine all the predicate verbs underlined below.

   The biggest problem I <u>faced</u> when I <u>took</u> the test <u>is</u> identifying verb tenses.

   The first two verb tenses in this sentence are in the past tense. The verb *is* should be changed to the past tense. The verb *identifying* is a gerund, so it should not be changed.

Answers for Misplaced Modifiers Exercise 1 (pages 15-16)

The word that should be placed next to the <u>modifier</u> is in **bold**. Then a corrected version of the sentence is written below.

1. <u>Hoping for a victory</u>, many days were spent practicing by **the basketball team**.

   <u>Hoping for a victory</u>, **the basketball team** spent many days practicing.

2. <u>Looking for a way to escape</u>, **the prisoner**'s spoon was used to dig a hole.

   <u>Looking for a way to escape</u>, **the prisoner** used a spoon to dig a hole.

3. <u>Worn as a traditional dress</u>, many Korean women wear **the *hanbok*** during holidays.

   <u>Worn as a traditional dress</u>, **the *hanbok*** is worn by many Korean women during holidays.

4. <u>A celebrated poet</u>, the sonnet "New Colossus" was written by **Emma Lazarus**.

   <u>A celebrated poet</u>, **Emma Lazarus** wrote the sonnet "New Colossus."

5. <u>Translated into over 200 languages</u>, F. Scott Fitzgerald wrote ***The Great Gatsby***.

   <u>Translated into over 200 languages</u>, ***The Great Gatsby*** was written by F. Scott Fitzgerald.

6. <u>Beaten and battered by the wind</u>, my grandmother cut down **the old oak tree**.

   <u>Beaten and battered by the wind</u>, **the old oak tree** was cut down by my grandmother.

7. <u>Known for its amazing views</u>, thousands of tourists visit **Niagara Falls**.

   <u>Known for its amazing views</u>, **Niagara Falls** is visited by thousands of tourists.

8. To meet the school's requirement for community service, five hours a week was what **Jimmy** spent at the hospital.

   To meet the school's requirement for community service, **Jimmy** spent five hours a week at the hospital.

9. Looking down at the aquarium's glass floor, the shark was found to be **the students**' most interesting animal.

   Looking down at the aquarium's glass floor, **the students** found the shark to be the most interesting animal.

10. One of the most popular singers of her time, various instruments and singing techniques were used by **Diana Ross**.

    One of the most popular singers of her time, **Diana Ross** used various instruments and singing techniques.

11. Spread by Europeans, many Native Americans died from **small pox**.

    Spread by Europeans, **small pox** killed many Native Americans.

12. Hidden from daylight, the average person rarely gets to see the wild and crazy life of **green fungal mold**.

    Hidden from daylight, **green fungal mold** has a wild and crazy life, which the average person rarely gets to see.

13. Dressed like a cute potato, the costume was perfectly worn by **my brother**.

    Dressed like a cute potato, **my brother** wore the costume perfectly.

14. After failing the exam, the park was the only place **Larry** could find comfort.

    After failing the exam, **Larry** could find comfort only in the park.

15. Flying high above the sky, Matt always viewed **the pigeons** with reverence and awe.

    Flying high above the sky, **the pigeons** were always looked upon by Matt with reverence and awe.

16. Celebrated by people all over the world, Johnny's favorite holiday was **Christmas**.

    Celebrated by people all over the world, **Christmas** was Johnny's favorite holiday.

17. Modified by a home-made hacking technique, Johnny manipulated **the graphics on the billboard**.

    Modified by a home-made hacking technique, **the graphics on the billboard** were manipulated by Johnny.

18. Going from rags to riches, fried dumplings is what made **Colonel Blanders** the legend that he is today.

    Going from rags to riches, **Colonel Blanders** became the legend that he is today through fried dumplings.

19. Respected by all the animals in the forest, the humble mouse saved **the kingly lion**.

    Respected by all the animals in the forest, **the kingly lion** was saved by the humble mouse.

20. Valued for its medicinal properties, my grandmother always uses **ginger** in her food.

    Valued for its medicinal properties, **ginger** is always used in my grandmother's food.

Answers for Misplaced Modifiers Exercise 2 (pages 16–17)

1. **(A)** Examine the pairings of <u>modifiers</u> and **modified objects** below.

   Incorrect: The Bronx High School of Science was a product of its time <u>founded in 1938</u>.

   Correct: <u>Founded in 1938</u>, **the Bronx High School of Science** was a product of its time.

2. **(G)** Examine the pairings of <u>modifiers</u> and **modified objects** below.

   Incorrect: <u>Reducing the cost of shipping from $100 a ton to $8, creating jobs for thousands, and providing revenue for the state government</u>, New Yorkers received many economic benefits of **the Erie Canal**.

   Correct: <u>Reducing the cost of shipping from $100 a ton to $8, creating jobs for thousands, and providing revenue for the state government</u>, **the Erie Canal** provided many economic benefits for New Yorkers.

3. **(C)** Examine the pairings of <u>modifiers</u> and **modified objects** below.

   Incorrect: <u>As a dissolved mineral</u>, the tree transports **the element** throughout its leaves.

   Correct: <u>As a dissolved mineral</u>, **the element** is transported by the tree throughout its leaves.

4. **(F)** Examine the pairings of <u>modifiers</u> and **modified objects** below.

   Incorrect: It would make **sense** that one should learn to walk before learning to run <u>to someone who is learning a new skill</u>.

   Correct: It would make **sense** <u>to someone who is learning a new skill</u> that one should learn to walk before learning to run.

Punctuation

3

Punctuation marks are the traffic lights and stop signs of the language world. They tell you when to pause, to stop, or to slow down. Now, it's impossible to cover all the rules of punctuation, but the one punctuation mark that the SHSAT will, without fail, test is the comma. This chapter tells you the basic scenarios you need to know about commas.

COORDINATE ADJECTIVES

Adjectives are a class of words that describe nouns. A noun can take an infinite number of adjectives, but for convenience's sake we normally use one or two, or a maximum of three, adjectives to describe a noun. When we use two or more adjectives to modify one noun, we are using **coordinate adjectives**. Examine the adjectives in the sentences below:

> We want **passionate** and **talented** people to sing *Mary Had a Little Lamb.*
> In writing, we can also replace the *and* with a comma, like so:
> We want **passionate, talented** people to sing *Mary Had a Little Lamb.*

> **Incorrect:** Jill bought a **trendy expensive** sweater.
> **Correct:** Jill bought a **trendy, expensive** sweater.

> **Incorrect:** The president flew to Davos in a **fast reliable** jet.
> **Correct:** The president flew to Davos in a **fast, reliable** jet.

> **Incorrect:** The **terrified angry** bear fought back.
> **Correct:** The **terrified, angry** bear fought back.

To test whether two adjectives need a comma in between, switch the order of the adjectives and insert the word *and* in between the adjectives. If it makes sense, then they are coordinate adjectives, and the commas should be used. If it doesn't make sense and distorts the meaning, then it is called a **cumulative adjective**, and a comma should not be used. Examine the following sentences:

> **Incorrect:** Jill bought a **pink, polyester** sweater.
> **Correct:** Jill bought a **pink polyester** sweater.

> **Incorrect:** The president flew to Davos in an **expensive, supersonic** jet.
> **Correct:** The president flew to Davos in an **expensive supersonic** jet.

> **Incorrect:** The **terrified, grizzly** bear fought back.
> **Correct:** The **terrified grizzly** bear fought back.

Coordinate Adjectives Exercise

Read the following sentences and add a comma between the **coordinate adjectives** if necessary. To test them, remember the rule: Reverse the order of the adjectives and insert the word *and*. If it makes sense, then commas are necessary.

1. We enjoyed the **fresh clean** taste of the fish tacos.

2. Our teacher assigned a very **difficult final** test, but we were more than prepared.

3. Even if snow doesn't accumulate much in the **mild winter** storms, salt trucks stand by in case the situation changes.

4. My great-grandmother had a reputation for being a **brave honest** woman.

5. The **aggressive overgrown** bully of a pig was feared by all the farm animals.

6. My mother thought the **moldy cheddar** cheese was her pet rat.

7. My father often gets aggravated by the **loud dance** music that our neighbors love to play at night.

8. The replica of the **ancient Chinese** artifact appeared so authentic that one of the greatest museum curators thought it worthy of its own display.

9. The **biggest kindest most lovable** ogre is probably not the easiest creature to find in these parts.

10. The **smooth silk** sheets were the only items not on sale at the store.

11. The **angry tenth** grader erupted into laughter as he realized that he was in a dream.

12. No one would have ever guessed that the treasure was hidden in a **humble wooden box**.

13. Success favors not the **hasty impatient** rusher but the **slow deliberate** planner.

14. The **withering neglected** tree eventually collapsed on top of a lonely tomato.

15. The **destructive black** hole remains a mystery on various levels.

16. It's important to water the **young spring** flowers on a daily basis.

17. In contrast, **old desert** cacti need very little water.

18. Hockey is typically played during the **cold winter** seasons.

19. The **foolish ignorant** clown received a beatdown for his antics.

20. Aside from its oddly **large marsupial** pouch, the kangaroo also walks on its hind legs.

(Answers are on page 32.)

MODIFIERS

Remember that a modifier is a word or group of words that provides extra information about the word next to it. If the modifier appears at the beginning of the sentence, then place a comma right before the object being modified. If the modifier appears after the word being modified, then it needs a comma around it. Here are some examples:

The skinny man, **an intimidating figure on his own,** picked up a stick.

Using nothing but a stick, the man beat the bear.

The bear, **beaten by the man,** retaliated.

Afraid of retaliation, the man ran away.

The bear **watching the man run,** laughed.

Modifiers Exercise

Add commas in the appropriate places.

1. Alexander Hamilton a man born in poverty soon rose to become one of the founding fathers.

2. A man of unyielding beliefs Diogenes the Cynic was known to be a grumpy man.

3. Wearing nothing but a ribbon the teddy bear needed more clothes.

4. According to legend Excalibur could only be removed from the stone by a worthy person.

5. We watched the parade a celebration of unity and love on television.

6. After training for seven years the expert dog whisperer can then move on to dog yelling.

7. The statue of David by far one of the best known of Michelangelo's works is on display at the Accademia Gallery in Italy.

8. Aquaculture or fish farming promises to provide enough seafood for the world.

9. Martians believed to be little green men were popularized by several science fiction novels.

10. Hoping to win the championship Jimmy practiced every day to become the best tennis player in his school.

(Answers are on page 33.)

SERIAL COMMAS AND PREPOSITIONAL PHRASES

Serial Commas

If there is a list of more than two words or phrases, the items in the list need to be separated by a comma. This is called an oxford or a serial comma. Your teacher may have told you that you do not need a comma before the *and*. On the SHSAT, the commas are necessary.

Incorrect: The dog ate a shoe, a pie and a peach.
Correct: The dog ate a shoe, a pie, and a peach.

Incorrect: Jill found that the key to life consisted of taking long walks finding close friends, and making good dinners.
Correct: Jill found that the key to life consisted of taking long walks, finding close friends, and making good dinners.

Incorrect: Teachers and psychologists have both found that successful students make concerted efforts to create a routine, stick to their schedule and approach difficulties with a good attitude.
Correct: Teachers and psychologists have both found that successful students make concerted efforts to create a routine, stick to their schedule, and approach difficulties with a good attitude.

Commas and Prepositional Phrases

Commas should not be placed before prepositional phrases.

> **Incorrect:** The king, of the jungle, is the lion.
> **Correct:** The king of the jungle is the lion.
>
> **Incorrect:** We stayed at my grandma's house, in Miami.
> **Correct:** We stayed at my grandma's house in Miami.
>
> **Incorrect:** I went to school, with the actress, in that movie.
> **Correct:** I went to school with the actress in that movie.

Punctuation Exercise 1

Examine each sentence and add or delete commas where necessary. If it contains no error, then mark *No error* after the sentence.

1. The hardest, math problems are often the ones that appear obvious.

2. Studying six hours a day, Joey, the top student in class, had a nervous breakdown.

3. We took the boat for our trip to the tropical island forests of Tahiti.

4. The raccoon broke into my home, ate everything in the fridge and pooped everywhere.

5. The chicken, the turtle, and the rabbit fell down the endless mysterious hole.

6. Although we were not happy, with the results, we knew that the contest was judged fairly.

7. Late, night television shows are becoming more popular amongst the younger generation.

8. Some of the most interesting people, in the world today, still have no idea what they want to be.

9. One of the oldest surviving predators today the shark boasts amazing agility, razor sharp senses, and powerful jaws.

10. My sister and I bought an amazing, remote-controlled drone.

11. We bought the toy, by using a gift card, and the money in our piggy bank.

12. Children who are given responsibilities at a young age develop good, work habits that contribute to their success later in their lives.

13. Working with the right tools and the right attitude we can overcome any obstacle that comes our way.

14. Some of the strongest indicators of future success are patience, and hard work.

15. Roller coasters, Ferris wheels, and cotton candy are some of the most memorable, satisfying, and enjoyable things at an amusement park.

16. The golden, metal box was shrouded in mystery.

17. An engineer, physician, and teacher, Mae Jemison became the first African American woman to travel in space.

18. Picked from the best of the best, the champion of foosball is no mere mortal.

19. Instant noodles and chicken noodle soup remain the key mode of sustenance, for the poor college student.

20. Hamburgers, hot dogs, and pretzels are the reasons why I love going to baseball games, with my friends and family.

(Answers are on page 33.)

Punctuation Exercise 2

1. Read this sentence.

> John Brown, an ardent abolitionist launched an attack on Harper's Ferry, West Virginia.

Which edit should be made to correct this sentence?

(A) Delete the comma after *Brown*.
(B) Insert a comma after *abolitionist*.
(C) Insert a comma after *attack*.
(D) Delete the comma after *Ferry*.

2. Read this sentence.

> After poring over the problem John felt that his spirit, body, and mind were frazzled with all the energy spent on thinking.

Which edit should be made to correct this sentence?

(E) Insert a comma after *problem*.
(F) Delete the comma after *spirit*.
(G) Delete the comma after *body*.
(H) Insert a comma after *spent*.

3. Read this sentence.

> Jerry, unfazed by anything, jumped headlong into the messy, formidable task of cleaning his bedroom, and the kitchen.

Which edit should be made to correct this sentence?

(A) Delete a comma after *Jerry*.
(B) Delete a comma after *anything*.
(C) Delete a comma after *messy*.
(D) Delete a comma after *bedroom*.

4. Read this sentence.

> Traveling at a slow and deliberate pace, massive alien, spaceships hovered over the Pentagon, the White House, and the Empire State Building.

Which edit should be made to correct this sentence?

(E) Delete a comma after *pace*.
(F) Insert a comma after *massive*.
(G) Delete a comma after *alien*.
(H) Insert a comma after *spaceships*.

(Answers are on page 34.)

Answers for Coordinate Adjectives Exercise (page 28)

Coordinate adjectives require a comma. *Cumulative* adjectives do not.

1. We enjoyed the **fresh, clean** taste of the fish tacos. *Coordinate*

2. Our teacher assigned a very **difficult final** test, but we were more than prepared. *Cumulative*

3. Even if snow doesn't accumulate much in the **mild winter** storms, salt trucks stand by in case the situation changes. *Cumulative*

4. My great-grandmother had a reputation for being a **brave, honest** woman. *Coordinate*

5. The **aggressive, overgrown** bully of a pig was feared by all the farm animals. *Coordinate*

6. My mother thought the **moldy cheddar** cheese was her pet rat. *Cumulative*

7. My father often gets aggravated by the **loud dance** music that our neighbors love to play at night. *Cumulative*

8. The replica of the **ancient Chinese** artifact appeared so authentic that one of the greatest museum curators thought it worthy of its own display. *Cumulative*

9. The **biggest, kindest, most lovable** ogre is probably not the easiest creature to find in these parts. *Coordinate*

10. The **smooth silk** sheets were the only items not on sale at the store. *Cumulative*

11. The **angry tenth** grader erupted into laughter as he realized that he was in a dream. *Cumulative*

12. No one would have ever guessed that the treasure was hidden in a **humble wooden box**. *Cumulative*

13. Success favors not the **hasty, impatient** rusher but the **slow, deliberate** planner. *Coordinate*

14. The **withering, neglected** tree eventually collapsed on top of a lonely tomato. *Coordinate*

15. The **destructive black** hole remains a mystery on various levels. *Cumulative*

16. It's important to water the **young spring** flowers on a daily basis. *Cumulative*

17. In contrast, **old desert** cacti need very little water. *Cumulative*

18. Hockey is typically played during the **cold winter** seasons. *Cumulative*

19. The **foolish, ignorant** clown received a beatdown for his antics. *Coordinate*

20. Aside from its oddly **large marsupial** pouch, the kangaroo also walks on its hind legs. *Cumulative*

Answers for Modifiers Exercise (page 29)

The modifying element is in **bold**. The commas have been added in the appropriate places.

1. Alexander Hamilton, **a man born in poverty,** soon rose to become one of the founding fathers.

2. **A man of unyielding beliefs,** Diogenes the Cynic was known to be a grumpy man.

3. **Wearing nothing but a ribbon,** the teddy bear needed more clothes.

4. **According to legend,** Excalibur could only be removed from the stone by a worthy person.

5. We watched the parade, **a celebration of unity and love,** on television.

6. **After training for seven years,** the expert dog whisperer can then move on to dog yelling.

7. The statue of David, **by far one of the best known of Michelangelo's works,** is on display at the Accademia Gallery in Italy.

8. Aquaculture, **or fish farming,** promises to provide enough seafood for the world.

9. Martians, **believed to be little green men,** were popularized by several science fiction novels.

10. **Hoping to win the championship,** Jimmy practiced every day to become the best tennis player in his school.

Answers for Punctuation Exercise 1 (pages 30–31)

The location in which the comma needs to be added or deleted is **bolded**. A reason for the modification follows the sentence in *italics*.

1. The **hardest math** problems are often the ones that appear obvious. *Remove comma on cumulative adjective.*

2. Studying six hours a day, Joey, the top student in class, had a nervous breakdown. *No error.*

3. We took the boat for our trip to the tropical island forests of Tahiti. *No error.*

4. The raccoon broke into my home, ate everything in the **fridge, and** pooped everywhere. *Serial comma necessary.*

5. The chicken, the turtle, and the rabbit fell down the **endless, mysterious** hole. *Coordinate adjective requires comma.*

6. Although we were not **happy with** the results, we knew that the contest was judged fairly. *Prepositional phrase does not need a comma.*

7. **Late night** television shows are becoming more popular amongst the younger generation. *Remove comma on cumulative adjective.*

8. Some of the most interesting **people in** the world **today still** have no idea what they want to be. *Prepositional phrase does not need a comma.*

9. One of the oldest surviving predators **today, the** shark boasts amazing agility, razor sharp senses, and powerful jaws. *Modifying phrase before **the shark** requires a comma.*

10. My sister and I bought an **amazing remote-controlled** drone. *Remove comma on cumulative adjective.*

11. We bought the **toy by** using a gift **card and** the money in our piggy bank. *Remove commas. Prepositional phrase does not need commas.*

12. Children who are given responsibilities at a young age develop **good work** habits that contribute to their success later in their lives. *Remove comma on cumulative adjective.*

13. Working with the right tools and the right **attitude, we** can overcome any obstacle that comes our way. *Modifying phrase before **we** requires a comma.*

14. Some of the strongest indicators of future success are **patience and** hard work. *Remove comma. There are only two items in the list, so comma is unnecessary.*

15. Roller coasters, Ferris wheels, and cotton candy are some of the most memorable, satisfying, and enjoyable things at an amusement park. *No error. The first series properly uses commas, and the series of adjectives are coordinate adjectives.*

16. The **golden metal** box was shrouded in mystery. *Remove comma on cumulative adjectives.*

17. An engineer, physician, and teacher, Mae Jemison became the first African American woman to travel in space. *No error. Serial commas used correctly.*

18. Picked from the best of the best, the champion of foosball is no mere mortal. *No error. Modifying phrase is followed by a comma.*

19. Instant noodles and chicken noodle soup remain the key mode of **sustenance for** the poor college student. *Remove commas. Prepositional phrase does not need commas.*

20. Hamburgers, hot dogs, and pretzels are the reasons why I love going to baseball **games with** my friends and family. *Remove commas. Prepositional phrase does not need commas.*

Answers for Punctuation Exercise 2 (pages 31–32)

1. **(B)** The phrase *an ardent abolitionist* is a noun phrase modifier that provides more information about John Brown. Commas around the phrase are necessary.

   John Brown☉ *an ardent abolitionist*☉ launched an attack on Harper's Ferry, West Virginia.

   Choice C is wrong because violates the rule about prepositions. Choice D is wrong because a comma is necessary to separate a city and state.

2. **(E)** *After poring over the problem* is a participle phrase that modifies *John*. A comma right after the phrase is necessary.

   After poring over the problem☉ John felt that his spirit, body, and mind were frazzled with all the energy spent on thinking.

   Choice F is wrong because the comma is necessary for the list. Choice G is wrong because the serial comma is necessary before the word *and*. Choice H is wrong because a comma is not necessary before a preposition.

3. **(D)** There are only two places he needs to clean: *his bedroom* and *the kitchen*. If there are two objects, then you do not need to insert a serial comma.

Jerry, unfazed by anything, jumped headlong into the messy, formidable task of cleaning his *bedroom and* the kitchen.

Choices A and B are wrong because *unfazed by anything* is a participle phrase that modifies *Jerry*. It appears to the right of *Jerry*, so the phrase needs commas around it. Choice C is wrong because *messy* and *formidable* are coordinate adjectives. You can say *formidable and messy kitchen*. Therefore, the comma is necessary.

4. **(G)** A comma is never placed between a noun and the adjective right next to it. You would rarely say *the happy, boy*.

Traveling at a slow and deliberate pace, massive *alien spaceships* hovered over the Pentagon, the White House, and the Empire State Building.

Choice E is wrong because *Traveling at a slow and deliberate pace* is a participle phrase that modifies *massive alien spaceships* and therefore needs the comma to break it off from the modified object. Choice F is wrong because the words *massive alien* are not coordinate adjectives. They cannot be used interchangeably. You cannot say *alien and massive spaceships*. Choice H is wrong because *spaceships* is the subject and *hovered* the predicate verb. You cannot separate those two with a comma when they are directly next to each other. For example, *John, walks* would be wrong because a comma is between the subject noun and predicate verb.

Clauses

4

INDEPENDENT AND DEPENDENT CLAUSES

A clause, at its most basic form, is a subject noun and a predicate verb. A clause can be independent, meaning it can stand by itself independently as a sentence. Or, it can be dependent, meaning it cannot stand by itself as a sentence. Aside from using your intuition and basic knowledge of the English language, you can identify a dependent clause by looking for a conjunction before the subject. Conjunctions are words that connect two clauses. The two types of conjunctions you will need to know are coordinate and subordinate conjunctions. Coordinate conjunctions are known by their acronym FANBOYS: *For, And, Nor, But, Or, Yet, So*. Subordinate conjunctions don't have a neat acronym, but you use them in your speech all the time. They are words like *although, because, if, before/after, that, which, until, while, since, who/what/when/where/why*.

Independent and Dependent Clauses Exercise

Read each sentence and mark whether the *italicized* section is an independent clause or a dependent clause.

1. The happiest day of my life was my birthday last year *because I won the lotto.*

2. *The day after the Twin Towers fell*, my father joined the army.

3. *My brother and I love going to the beach*, but my mother and my father do not.

4. *Typically, humans have 23 pairs of chromosomes* while apes have 24 pairs.

5. My group suffered from fatigue, *for we worked 30 hours without sleep.*

6. Instead of going to the park, we decided to go to the playground, since we knew that *monsters were allergic to seesaws.*

7. *My three dogs and two cats seem to bother my upstairs neighbor*, but her loud music and dance parties bother me more.

8. *Although Jonas never expected to achieve success*, his hard work and determination did not go unnoticed by his supervisors.

9. *Seeing themselves on the top of the leaderboard, the school of fish thought they won the tournament*, but the school of students cooked and ate them.

10. *According to the ancient Greeks, the two happiest days of a man's life are when a marriage begins and ends*, so it's probably a good idea to get married several times.

(Answers are on page 45.)

PUNCTUATING CLAUSES

Now that you know the difference between independent and dependent clauses, you need to know the difference between coordinate and subordinate conjunctions. The rules for punctuating the two clauses are different.

Here are the rules:

1. When you see two clauses (what look like two sentences) separated by FANBOYS (*For, And, Nor, But, Or, Yet, So*), then a comma needs to be inserted before the FANBOYS. Examine how the comma and FANBOYS separate the two clauses in the following:

John drank the dirty water, **for** he was thirsty.

John drank the dirty water, **and** he got sick.

John didn't take medicine, **nor** did he go to the doctor.

John stayed home, **but** he got better.

He knew he had to leave, **or** he would go crazy.

He was feeling better, **yet** he wasn't well enough to run.

John wasn't strong enough, **so** he stayed home.

2. Beware of FANBOYS connecting two phrases. A sentence that uses a FANBOYS conjunction to connect two different phrases does NOT take a comma before FANBOYS. In the following, the series of words after the FANBOYS is a phrase and cannot stand alone as a sentence:

John drank the dirty water **and** got sick.

John stayed home **but** got better.

He knew he had to leave **or** would go crazy.

He was feeling better **yet** wasn't well enough to run.

3. When you see two clauses separated by subordinate conjunctions (*because, while, when, after, if, since, that, though*), they do not take a comma. Examine how the non-FANBOYS subordinate conjunctions separate the two clauses in the following:

John drank the dirty water **because** he was thirsty.

John drank the dirty water **when** he got sick.

John didn't take the medicine **while** he was sick.

John stayed home **after** he got sick.

John was feeling better **since** he took some medicine.

4. If a sentence with a subordinate clause begins with a subordinate conjunction, then it must take a comma before the beginning of a new clause. Examine the following:

Because he was thirsty, John drank the dirty water.

When he got sick, John drank the dirty water.

While he was sick, John didn't take the medicine.

After he got sick, John stayed home.

Since he took some medicine, John was feeling better.

Punctuating Clauses Exercise

Examine the **bolded** words, and insert or remove a comma if necessary. If the sentence is correct, write *No error*.

1. We did not want to go to **school for** the weatherman predicted eight inches of frog.
2. Although we did not plan to go to school, our parents forced us to **go, because** they said that the weatherman was crazy.
3. As we walked to our bus **stop, we** noticed the pitter patter of frog bodies plopping on the ground.
4. Some kids were **ecstatic but** we were terrified.
5. Since the frogs from the sky were getting **bigger we** thought that the best thing to do was to hide under a tree.
6. It was probably the right **choice and** the safe one as well.
7. If we didn't get protection from the **tree, we** would have surely been crushed by the eight-foot frog that fell right in front of the bus stop.
8. We were **safe yet** others were not so lucky.
9. They were drenched in frog **slime so** they had to return home.
10. My parents need to watch who they call **crazy, because** that frog storm was crazy.

(Answers are on page 46.)

RUN-ONS

Note: It is very important that you complete both Clauses and Punctuating Clauses exercises to understand the terminology in the following Run-ons section.

A run-on is a sentence that connects two clauses *without* a conjunction. For example:

1. Although it was feared that the storm might persist until dawn, a time understood as the time of the leprechauns, the rain, as fierce as it was, stopped at the witching hour, reassuring those of us who feared the worst.

2. I walked, John ran.

To the untrained eye, Example 1 would seem to run on, drawing out a lot of information (running on and on and on). Example 2, in contrast, appears short, direct, and to the point. However, Example 1 properly uses conjunctions and supporting phrases to connect different ideas. In contrast, Example 2 connects two ideas with nothing but a comma. A conjunction like *but, and, because,* or *while* is necessary to correct the sentence. Therefore, Example 2 commits the run-on error.

Identifying Run-ons

To identify run-ons, you must learn to identify independent clauses, dependent clauses, and phrases/modifiers. Independent clauses look like sentences. They can stand by themselves. Dependent clauses begin with a FANBOYS or subordinate conjunction or relative pronoun (*who, when, which, whose*). Phrases or modifiers are a group of words that do not complete a full thought.

Examine the following sentences, which contain mixtures of independent clauses, dependent clauses, and phrases/modifiers. Conjunctions are shown in boldface.

I walked,	**and** John ran.
Independent Clause	Independent Clause

While I walked,	John ran.
Dependent Clause	Independent Clause

One of the fastest kids in class,	John ran	**because** he could.
Noun Phrase (Modifier)	Independent	Dependent Clause

One of the fastest kids in class,	John ran to his home in Elmhurst	**because** he could run like the wind.
Noun Phrase (Modifier)	Independent	Dependent Clause

If a sentence has two independent clauses that are combined without a conjunction, then it is a run-on. For the following example:

1. Add a set of parentheses around the clauses, both dependent and independent.
2. Correct the sentence by inserting an appropriate conjunction OR by replacing a word with a relative pronoun (*who, which, that, when, where, whom, whoever, whose*).

➡ Example _____

The doctor, fearful of a mass epidemic, decided to place her patient under quarantine it would stop the spread of the disease.

(The doctor, fearful of a mass epidemic, decided to place her patient under quarantine) **because** (it would stop the spread of the disease.)

OR

(The doctor, fearful of a mass epidemic, decided to place her patient under quarantine) (~~it~~, **which** would stop the spread of the disease.)

Run-ons Exercise 1

Add a set of parentheses around the clauses, both dependent and independent. If two independent clauses are combined in one sentence, then correct the sentence by inserting an appropriate conjunction or relative pronoun.

1. During the 1980s, personal computers were never expected to change the world, they did.

2. When I was a child, I believed in Santa, he would bring me presents.

3. With nothing but a hammer, Abraham Lincoln nailed down an entire house it stayed erect for centuries.

4. George Washington, one of the richest men of the American colonies, had a very strong interest in leading a military, he became a general during the fateful war.

5. The incessant rain, unforgiving in its intensity, saw to it that I would be drenched, I was waiting for the bus.

6. Before President Truman met Joseph Stalin, he believed that the two countries would cooperate, their relationship soon led to the beginning of the Cold War.

7. As more people "cut the cord" and turned to the Internet for entertainment, the format of entertainment changed people who has less time didn't have to sit through a 30-minute episode.

8. John Quincy Adams was forced to take a trip with his father, his mother, sensing his unhappiness, wrote a letter to inspire him.

(Answers are on page 47.)

Run-ons Exercise 2

1. Read this paragraph.

> (1) Never the one to back down, Harry fought against the crowd full of people from all walks of life. (2) These people, who existed solely to put Harry down, couldn't accept the fact that he was different. (3) Because he was so filled with rage, he never considered the possibility that it might be all in his head, it could have been a dream. (4) Then in the blink of an eye, Harry woke up, and it was, indeed, a dream.

Which sentence should be revised to correct a run-on?

(A) sentence 1
(B) sentence 2
(C) sentence 3
(D) sentence 4

2. Read this paragraph.

> (1) Thomas Jefferson was a polymath, a man skilled in numerous subjects. (2) A philosopher, artist, scientist, and architect, Jefferson represented the ideal academic in a New World filled with possibilities. (3) Accordingly, it seemed fitting that Jefferson should draft the Declaration of Independence because he was the right man for the job. (4) His words laid the foundation for a nation, they were the foundation for the future as well.

Which sentence should be revised to correct a run-on?

(E) sentence 1
(F) sentence 2
(G) sentence 3
(H) sentence 4

3. Read this paragraph.

> (1) When Jimmy Johnson decided to run for class president, he knew that it would be a long shot. (2) Not many people knew what he was about, nor did many people believe that he could make a difference. (3) However, his mother believed in Jimmy, Jimmy could make a difference. (4) She urged him to run, and he ran because he had a person who believed in him.

Which sentence should be revised to correct a run-on?

(A) sentence 1
(B) sentence 2
(C) sentence 3
(D) sentence 4

4. Read this paragraph.

> (1) Hidden deep in the farthest reaches of Edwards Air Force Base, Area 51 is one of the most intriguing military bases in the United States. (2) Many UFO enthusiasts believe the base to be a secret labyrinth, storing secret alien spaceships. (3) Others believe that the base is a communications lab it has been in contact with aliens since the 1950s. (4) Whatever it may be, it serves as an important source of stories in the public imagination.

Which sentence should be revised to correct a run-on?

(E) sentence 1
(F) sentence 2
(G) sentence 3
(H) sentence 4

(Answers are on page 47.)

TRANSITIONS

There are five basic categories of logical transitions you need to be familiar with: causal, additive, contrasting, illustrative, and intensifying transitions.

Causal Transitions

This transition shows causal relationships between two sentences. Examine the following sentences:

1. My dog Max barked very loudly.
2. He woke up the neighbors.

The list of causal transition words below can be used to connect the two sentences:

as a result, for this reason, therefore, thus, because, due to the fact, consequently, hence, accordingly, since

Additive Transitions

This transition is used to link information with additional or similar information. Examine the following sentences:

1. The SHSAT is a difficult exam for middle school students.
2. The SAT is a difficult exam for high school students.

The list of additive transition words below can be used to link a sentence that provides more information:

and, also, furthermore, moreover, in addition, additionally, similarly, in the same way, by the same token, likewise

Contrasting Transitions

This transition is used between sentences that suggest contrary or conflicting ideas. Examine the following sentences:

1. My sister loves school.
2. I hate school.

The list of contrasting transition words below can be used to emphasize the contrast between the two sentences:

but, in contrast, conversely, however, still, nevertheless, nonetheless, yet, on the other hand, on the contrary, in spite of this, actually, notwithstanding, although, despite, while, regardless

Illustrative Transitions

This transition is used to link a general statement with an example or detail that supports it. Examine the following sentences:

1. Specialized high schools are notorious for the amount of work assigned.
2. Students for the High School for Specialized Programs typically spend three to four hours on their homework each day.

The list of illustrative transition words below can be used to support the claim in sentence 1:

for example, for instance, in particular, to illustrate, to be specific, specifically, such as, in this case, for this reason, for one thing

Intensifying Transitions

This transition is used to emphasize a certain aspect of a given sentence. Examine the following sentences:

1. Americans are in a love-hate relationship with debt.
2. The average American household carries over $120,000 in debt.

The list of intensifying transition words below can be used for emphasis between sentences:

indeed, of course, without a doubt, in fact, surely, more importantly, as a matter of fact, in other words, in short

To tackle these problems, DO NOT plug in each of the transition words to "see if it makes sense." Doing so can actually work against you. Your brain is designed to make sense of any relationship, so this method will work about half of the time. Instead, read the two sentences without looking at the transitions. Then, identify the relationship before selecting the transition word.

Transitions Exercise

> (1) Prior to the 20th century, most people believed that germs arose from a theory called "spontaneous generation." (2) Louis Pasteur felt that the idea was absurd and that attributing life to such random speculation was tantamount to superstition. (3) He began a series of experiments that would conclusively explain the process of putrefaction.

1. Which transition should be added to the beginning of sentence 2?

   (A) In addition,
   (B) Therefore,
   (C) However,
   (D) For example,

> (1) The r/K selection theory attempts to describe two modes of evolutionary strategies. (2) The theory holds that "r-selected" organisms produce numerous offspring expecting only a few to survive into adulthood. (3) Spiders lay from 100 to 200 eggs but only a few survive the first week.

2. Which transition should be added to the beginning of sentence 3?

   (E) In fact,
   (F) For example,
   (G) Likewise,
   (H) Thus,

> (1) High school is a time marked by notable changes. (2) Changes in location, friends, beliefs, and value systems, as well as one's own physical self, lead to a considerable amount of stress that some adolescents are unprepared to handle. (3) Many high schools provide both teachers and guidance counselors with training to ensure that they can help when students are overwhelmed.

3. Which transition should be added to the beginning of sentence 3?

   (A) In particular,
   (B) On the other hand,
   (C) Indeed,
   (D) Due to this fact,

> (1) As long as our society remains technology reliant, the demand for energy will continue to soar unabated. (2) Due to this trend, job prospects in the energy sector are promising. (3) Job prospects for petroleum engineers are anticipated to be three times the average rate of all other jobs.

4. Which transition should be added to the beginning of sentence 3?

   (E) In particular,
   (F) Conversely,
   (G) Similarly,
   (H) Thus,

(Answers are on page 50.)

Answers for Independent and Dependent Clauses Exercise (page 37)

The answer follows the sentence.

1. The happiest day of my life was my birthday last year *because I won the lotto.* Dependent clause—conjunction *because.*

2. *The day after the Twin Towers fell,* my father joined the army. Dependent clause—conjunction *after.*

3. *My brother and I love going to the beach,* but my mother and my father do not. Independent clause.

4. *Typically, humans have 23 pairs of chromosomes* while apes have 24 pairs. Independent clause—*typically* is not a conjunction but an adverb.

5. My group suffered from fatigue, *for we worked 30 hours without sleep.* Dependent clause—conjunction *for.*

6. Instead of going to the park, we decided to go to the playground, since we knew that *monsters were allergic to seesaws.* Independent clause. The word *that* is not italicized. If it were italicized, then it would be a dependent clause.

7. *My three dogs and two cats seem to bother my upstairs neighbor,* but her loud music and dance parties bother me more. Independent clause.

8. *Although Jonas never expected to achieve success,* his hard work and determination did not go unnoticed by his supervisors. Dependent clause—conjunction *although.*

9. *Seeing themselves on the top of the leaderboard, the school of fish thought they won the tournament,* but the school of students cooked and ate them. Independent clause—the clause begins with a modifier and not a conjunction.

10. *According to the ancient Greeks, the two happiest days of a man's life are when a marriage begins and ends,* so it's probably a good idea to get married several times. Independent clause. The word *according* is an adverb.

Answers for Punctuating Clauses Exercise (page 39)

A short explanation follows each sentence.

1. We did not want to go to **school, for** the weatherman predicted eight inches of frog. *Comma added. Rule 1.*

2. Although we did not plan to go to school, our parents forced us to **go because** they said that the weatherman was crazy. *Comma removed. Rule 3.*

3. As we walked to our bus **stop, we** noticed the pitter patter of frog bodies plopping on the ground. *No error. Rule 4.*

4. Some kids were **ecstatic, but** we were terrified. *Comma added. Rule 1.*

5. Since the frogs from the sky were getting **bigger, we** thought that the best thing to do was to hide under a tree. *Comma added. Rule 4.*

6. It was probably the right **choice and** the safe one as well. *No error. Rule 2.*

7. If we didn't get protection from the **tree, we** would have surely been crushed by the eight-foot frog that fell right in front of the bus stop. *No error. Rule 4.*

8. We were **safe, yet** others were not so lucky. *Comma added. Rule 1.*

9. They were drenched in frog **slime, so** they had to return home. *Comma added. Rule 1.*

10. My parents need to watch who they call **crazy because** that frog storm was crazy. *Comma removed. Rule 3.*

Answers for Run-ons Exercise 1 (page 41)

1. (During the 1980s, personal computers were never expected to change the world), **but** (they did.)

2. (When I was a child), (I believed in Santa), (~~he~~ **who** would bring me presents.)

3. (With nothing but a hammer, Abraham Lincoln nailed down an entire house)**, (which** ~~it~~ stayed erect for centuries.)

4. (George Washington, one of the richest men of the American colonies, had a very strong interest in leading a military), **and** (he became a general during the fateful war.)

5. (The incessant rain, unforgiving in its intensity, saw to it that I would be drenched)~~,~~ **while (**I was waiting for the bus.)

6. (Before President Truman met Joseph Stalin), (he believed that the two countries would cooperate), **but** (their relationship soon led to the beginning of the Cold War.)

7. (As more people "cut the cord" and turned to the Internet for entertainment), (the format of entertainment changed), **so** (people who had less time didn't have to sit through a 30-minute episode.)

8. **When** (John Quincy Adams was forced to take a trip with his father,) (his mother, sensing his unhappiness, wrote a letter to inspire him.)

Answers for Run-ons Exercise 2 (pages 41–42)

1. **(C)** Sentence 1 contains a modifier and an independent clause. This is not a run-on.

Never the one to back down,	Harry fought against the crowd full of people from all walks of life.
Phrase	Independent Clause

Sentence 2 contains an independent clause and a dependent clause. This is not a run-on.

These **people** *who existed solely to put Harry down* **couldn't** accept the fact	that he was different.
Independent clause with a *relative clause* inserted in between the **subject noun** and the ***predicate***.	Dependent Clause

Sentence 3 contains an independent clause at the end of the sentence. The independent clause requires a conjunction to correct it. This is a run-on.

Because he was so filled with rage,	he never considered the possibility	that it might be all in his head	it could have been a dream.
Dependent Clause	Independent Clause	Dependent Clause	Independent Clause

Correction: Because he was so filled with rage, he never considered the possibility that it might be all in his head ***and that*** it could have been a dream.

Sentence 4 contains a modifier, an independent clause, and an independent clause. This is not a run-on.

Then in the blink of an eye,	Harry woke up,	and it was, indeed, a dream.
Modifier	Independent Clause	Independent Clause

2. **(H)** Sentence 1 contains an independent clause and a modifier. This is not a run-on.

Thomas Jefferson was a polymath,	a man skilled in numerous subjects.
Independent Clause	Modifier

Sentence 2 contains a modifier and an independent clause. This is not a run-on.

A philosopher, artist, scientist and architect,	Jefferson represented the ideal academic in a New World filled with possibilities.
Modifier	Independent Clause

Sentence 3 contains an independent clause, a dependent clause, and a dependent clause.

This is not a run-on.

Accordingly, it seemed fitting	that Jefferson should draft the Declaration of Independence	because he was the right man for the job.
Independent Clause	Dependent Clause	Dependent Clause

Sentence 4 contains two independent clauses. This is a run-on.

His words laid the foundation for a nation	they were the foundation for the future as well.
Independent Clause	Independent Clause

Correction: His words laid the foundation for a nation, **and** they were the foundation for the future as well.

3. **(C)** Sentence 1 contains a dependent clause and an independent clause. This is not a run-on.

When Jimmy Johnson decided to run for class president,	he knew that it would be a long shot.
Dependent Clause	Independent Clause

Sentence 2 contains an independent clause followed by two dependent clauses. This is not a run-on.

Not many people knew what he was about,	nor did many people believe	that he could make a difference.
Independent Clause	Dependent Clause	Dependent Clause

Sentence 3 contains two independent clauses. *However* is not a conjunction. It is instead called a *conjunctive adverb*. Conjunctive adverbs are used to connect two sentences and not two clauses. Here is an example:

John likes cheese. However, Jill likes apples.

This is, therefore, a run-on.

However, his mother believed in Jimmy,	Jimmy could make a difference.
Independent Clause	Independent Clause

Correction: However, his mother believed in Jimmy, *who* could make a difference.

Sentence 4 contains an independent clause followed by three dependent clauses. This is not a run-on.

She urged him to run,	and he ran	because he had a person	who believed in him.
Independent Clause	Independent Clause	Dependent Clause	Dependent Clause

4. **(G)** Sentence 1 contains a modifier and an independent clause. This is not a run-on.

Hidden deep in the farthest reaches of Edwards Air Force Base,	Area 51 is one of the most intriguing military bases in the United States.
Modifier	Independent Clause

Sentence 2 contains an independent clause and a modifier. This is not a run-on.

Many UFO enthusiasts believe the base to be a secret labyrinth,	storing secret alien spaceships.
Independent Clause	Modifier

Sentence 3 contains an independent clause, a dependent clause, and an independent clause. This is a run-on.

Others believe	that the base is a communications lab	it has been in contact with aliens since the 1950s.
Independent Clause	Dependent Clause	Independent Clause

Correction: Others believe that the base is a communications lab **and that** it has been in contact with aliens since the 1950s.

Sentence 4 contains a dependent clause and an independent clause. This is not a run-on.

Whatever it may be,	it serves as an important source of stories in the public imagination.
Dependent Clause	Independent Clause

Answers for Transitions Exercise (pages 44–45)

1. **(C)** Louis Pasteur's belief stands in contrast to what most people believed, so a contrasting transition best introduces his belief.

   (A) In addition, (Additive)
   (B) Therefore, (Causal)
   (C) However, (Contrasting)
   (D) For example, (Illustrative)

2. **(F)** Spiders are an example of an "r-selected organism," so an illustrative transition best introduces the example.

   (E) In fact, (Intensifying)
   (F) For example, (Illustrative)
   (G) Likewise, (Additive)
   (H) Thus, (Causal)

3. **(D)** Sentence 2 discusses a cause (*considerable amount of stress*) that leads to the effect in sentence 3 (*schools provide both teachers and guidance counselors with training*).

   (A) In particular, (Illustrative)
   (B) On the other hand, (Contrasting)
   (C) Indeed, (Intensifying)
   (D) Due to this fact, (Causal)

4. **(E)** Sentence 2 introduces the idea that job prospects are promising. Sentence 3 provides an illustrative example of such jobs (petroleum engineers). Choice G is a tempting choice, but the specificity of petroleum engineers makes E the better choice.

   (E) In particular, (Illustrative)
   (F) Conversely, (Contrasting)
   (G) Similarly, (Additional)
   (H) Thus, (Causal)

Precision and Relevance 5

As humans, we love to categorize the world. Open up this book, and you'll see that it is divided into different topics, which are categorized by units, which are then categorized into chapters, and so on. Now, let's take a look at the way you fall into a category in the world. Start with the category that contains the greatest number of things: the world. From the world, let's narrow it down to living organisms, then to humans, then to adolescents, and finally to you.

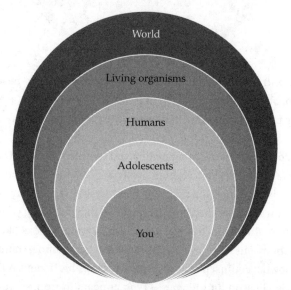

We see such forms of categorization everywhere. Think about your local supermarket. You'll no doubt recall that the store is divided and not just one place with a giant pile of food and supplies. The food and supplies are categorized into different aisles that are then sorted into more specific types of items. You'll find aisles for juices, pasta, dairy, snacks, or pet food. It doesn't end there. Once you enter the aisles, the categories are sorted into even more specific sections. For example, the pasta aisle would contain a pasta section, a pasta sauce section, and a canned tomato section. Look even closer and you'll find the pasta section sorted even further by specific brands of pastas or pasta types.

So what's the point? In this chapter, you are asked to organize sentences based on their relationships. Understanding the supermarket metaphor will allow you to better navigate these relationships, which rely on precision, supporting details, and main ideas. This chapter will focus on these skills.

PRECISION

Let's go back to the supermarket metaphor and visualize the categorization.

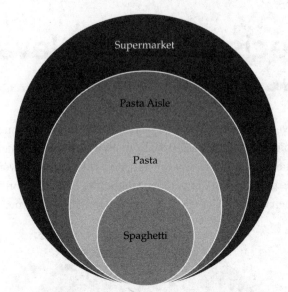

Categorizing the world through such circles can be described as a "nested hierarchy." In this form of categorization, objects are categorized from the most general to the most specific. And just why do we need to be precise? Can you imagine the frustration if you were told to get the "thing" from the pasta aisle?

Or consider the following scenario: Imagine that you're walking home. On the street is a golden magic lamp. You pick it up and open it. A genie slowly appears and he promises to make one wish come true. You could wish for anything that your heart desires (except anything illegal of course). That's easy of course. You've always had your heart set on that one thing your parents never got for you. You don't remember the name, but you know exactly what it looks like. Unable to hold back your excitement, you blurt out "the toy," hoping that the genie understands what you're talking about. The genie, somewhat confused at your response, snaps his fingers. A DVD of the 1982 movie *The Toy*, starring Jackie Gleason and Richard Pryor, appears in front of you, and then the genie quickly disappears back into the lamp. What was the problem? You weren't precise in your definition of what you had wanted. Now if you had been precise and told him that you wanted a teddy bear, a GI Joe, or a Barbie, then the precision of your word choice would have made your request clearer, and you'd be holding that toy you've always wanted. Unfortunately, now you're stuck with a DVD, and you don't even have a DVD player.

Fortunately, now you know why precision is important and you can use this knowledge to answer the "precise revision" questions on the SHSAT.

Precision Exercise 1

For each question, rank the answer choices from the least to the most precise.

1. Least Precise _____

   _____

   _____

   Most Precise _____

   (A) Animal
   (B) Dog
   (C) Chihuahua
   (D) Small animal

2. Least Precise _____

   _____

   _____

   Most Precise _____

   (E) Polynomials
   (F) Subject
   (G) Math
   (H) Algebra

3. Least Precise _____

   _____

   _____

   Most Precise _____

   (A) Head chef
   (B) Kitchen staff
   (C) Worker
   (D) Chef

4. Least Precise _____

   _____

   _____

   Most Precise _____

   (E) High school
   (F) Stuyvesant
   (G) School
   (H) Specialized high school

5. Least Precise _____

   _____

   _____

   Most Precise _____

   (A) House
   (B) Room
   (C) The smallest seat at the dining table
   (D) Dining room

6. Least Precise _____

   _____

   _____

   Most Precise _____

   (E) Person
   (F) Student
   (G) Star student
   (H) Valedictorian

7. Least Precise _____

   _____

   _____

   Most Precise _____

   (A) Electrical engineers
   (B) People who work
   (C) Professionals
   (D) Engineers

8. Least Precise _____

   _____

   _____

   Most Precise _____

   (E) Place
   (F) City
   (G) Very large city
   (H) New York City

9. Least Precise _____

_____

_____

Most Precise _____

(A) SHSAT

(B) Test

(C) Test for 8th and 9th grade students

(D) Verbal section of the SHSAT

10. Least Precise _____

_____

_____

Most Precise _____

(E) Animal

(F) Animal in the zoo

(G) Gorilla in the zoo

(H) Harambe the Gorilla in the zoo

11. Least Precise _____

_____

_____

Most Precise _____

(A) Meme

(B) *It's None of My Business* meme

(C) Picture

(D) Picture with words

12. Least Precise _____

_____

_____

Most Precise _____

(E) Ice cream

(F) Food

(G) Dessert

(H) Vanilla ice cream

(Answers are on page 71.)

Process of Elimination in Precise Language Questions

Using the process of elimination is one of the most powerful ways to reduce the options that are designed to confuse you. Here is an example of a precise language question you will encounter on the SHSAT.

➡ **Example** _____

Read this sentence.

> During the YouTube interview about cosplay, the host spoke to the three people who were dressed as comic book characters.

Which of these is the most precise revision for the words *spoke to the three people who were dressed as comic book characters*?

(A) chatted with some people who were dressed up as comic book characters
(B) talked with three people dressed up as comic book characters
(C) discussed the costumes with some of the people
(D) interviewed three Captain Americas

PROCESS OF ELIMINATION

First, look at all the answers and notice patterns, similarities, and differences. The best way to approach the precise revision questions is to divide the answer choices into two segments. For each segment, eliminate the answer choice that comparatively contains the least precise element. For example, look at the following sentence, and find the best revision for the words in italics:

The subway is a *good way for people to get to places*.

(A) great option for New Yorkers to get to where they need to go
(B) superior method of transportation for people to get to places
(C) speedy form of transportation for New Yorkers
(D) great method for people to get to places where they need to go

Here are the steps:

1. Look for common elements and compare them.

Least Precise (cross out)	Most Precise
great option	superior method of transportation
great method	speedy form of transportation
people	New Yorkers

2. Eliminate the choices that contain the least precise information.

(A) ~~great option~~ for ~~people~~ to get to where they need to go
(B) superior method of transportation for ~~people~~ to get to places
(C) speedy form of transportation for New Yorkers
(D) ~~great method~~ for ~~people~~ to get to places where they need to go

3. Select the remaining answer.

Precision Exercise 2

1. Read this sentence.

> During the winter break, my family decided to do something that was interesting in the community.

Which of these is the most precise revision for the words *do something that was interesting in the community*?

(A) engage in a community activity that was interesting
(B) participate in something that's interesting
(C) volunteer for an interesting community activity
(D) do an interesting community activity

2. Read this sentence.

> Our class felt that it was important to work very hard for the test that was coming up.

Which of these is the most precise revision for the words *work very hard for the test that was coming up*?

(E) study all day for the upcoming test
(F) make sure that the test coming up was studied very hard for
(G) review the chapter for the upcoming test
(H) do our best for the future test

3. Read this sentence.

> In light of a possible epidemic, the scientists made recommendations in order to prevent the disease from spreading further.

Which of these is the most precise revision for the words *the scientists made recommendations*?

(A) the scientists told people about the virus
(B) the scientists cautioned against sharing glasses
(C) the scientists shared their thoughts
(D) the scientists brought up their ideas for consideration to the public

4. Read this sentence.

> Anthropologists believe that culture is one of the reasons that make humans different from other types of life.

Which of these is the most precise revision for the words *is one of the reasons that make humans different from other types of life*?

(E) differentiates humans from other animals
(F) is a reason that makes humans different from other types of life
(G) makes humans different from other types of life
(H) is precisely the reason which makes humans different from other animals

5. Read this sentence.

> Due to the rising cost of materials, people interested in arts and crafts get their supplies from other countries.

Which of these is the most precise revision for the words *people interested in arts and crafts get their supplies*?

(A) people interested in arts and crafts obtain resources
(B) people who are interested in arts and crafts purchase fabrics and wood
(C) arts and crafts enthusiasts get fabrics and wood
(D) arts and crafts enthusiasts purchase fabrics and wood

6. Read this sentence.

> Anyone who is serious about losing weight should consider both physical activities and eating right.

Which of these is the most precise revision for the words *physical activities and eating right*?

(E) physical activities and limiting their caloric intake
(F) cardio exercises and eating right
(G) physical activities and dieting
(H) cardio exercises and limiting their caloric intake

(Answers are on page 71.)

IRRELEVANT SENTENCES

Using your abilities to identify the most precise elements, you need to now do the opposite in order to identify irrelevant sentences. Irrelevant sentences are simply sentences that shouldn't be in the nested hierarchy. Here, we're not talking about the least precise but about the worst possible addition you can make to a series of ideas. It's as if you were teaching your friend about algebra by frying an egg. It can be done if you explain it right, but the lack of relevance makes it the least effective way to develop ideas on algebraic equations.

In irrelevant sentence questions, you are asked to identify a sentence that seems out of place within a paragraph. You can often tell that a sentence is out of place because it does not follow the sequence or purpose of the paragraph. Examine the following:

1. Dolphins are remarkably intelligent creatures, whose intelligence "mirrors" that of our own.
2. Researchers devised an experiment in which dolphins demonstrated the ability to recognize the concept of themselves.
3. Dolphins also possess a blowhole and sonar-like abilities.
4. By identifying themselves in the mirror, dolphins revealed that they possess the advanced cognitive ability of self-awareness.

In these four sentences, the main purpose is to explain a dolphin's intellect. Sentence 3 discusses other physical characteristics, so it should be deleted.

Another way to identify the irrelevant sentence is to use transition words, pronouns, and key words. Examine the following sentences:

1. The white-nose syndrome poses a major threat to bat populations, killing off more than five million bats within the first year of its discovery.
2. Scientists and government agencies have both made a concerted effort to stem the catastrophic disease.
3. White-nose syndrome is a fungal disease that causes eccentric behavior.
4. They have worked with the public to raise awareness of the issues so that tourists would minimize behaviors that could harm their environment.

Sentence 4 contains the pronoun *they*. The antecedent to the pronoun is *scientists and government agencies* located in sentence 2. Although sentence 3 might be relevant, it is irrelevant at that location. Therefore, it should be deleted so that the word *they* can be placed adjacent to the antecedent *scientists and government agencies*. The same principle applies to sentences containing transitions.

1. The sharing economy refers to peer-to-peer based sharing of goods and services through advances in technology.
2. Various industries have emerged within the last ten years, capitalizing on the capacities of mobile technology.
3. It is becoming increasingly more difficult to subsist on one job, so people use sharing economies to supplement their income.
4. Ride-share companies, for example, use GPS and a mobile app platform to help riders connect with drivers who are willing to share their cars.

Sentence 4 contains the transition words *for example*, which introduce an example of a company that uses mobile technology mentioned in sentence 2. Sentence 3 breaks the connection between the sentences linked by the transition *for example*. Removing sentence 3 would help sentence 2 link with sentence 4. Sentence 3 is therefore irrelevant.

Irrelevant Sentences Exercise

(1) The tin can for preserving food was a revolutionary invention of the early eighteenth century. (2) For more than a hundred years, however, it was difficult and sometimes even dangerous to get at the stored food. (3) In 1930, an efficient and convenient can opener became available, and this design continues to be used today. (4) Meats, vegetables, and fruit retain their flavor and nutrients through the canning process. (5) This useful machine has a sharp circular blade that cuts into the lid of the can as a toothed wheel under the lip of the can moves the can around in a smooth, continuous cut.

1. Which sentence is irrelevant to the argument presented in the passage and should be deleted?
   (A) sentence 1
   (B) sentence 2
   (C) sentence 3
   (D) sentence 4

(1) The "Rails to Trails" movement has become an influential force in many communities. (2) The purpose of the movement is to transform useless eyesores into useful and attractive spaces. (3) The amount of trash in the world has been accumulating to unsustainable levels. (4) The transformation requires an initial investment to pay for the removal of unused railroad tracks. (5) Then, only minimal maintenance is required to ensure a useable pathway for hiking, running, or biking.

2. Which sentence is irrelevant to the argument presented in the passage and should be deleted?

   (E) sentence 1

   (F) sentence 2

   (G) sentence 3

   (H) sentence 4

(1) Ranging in length from 18 to 25 inches and with a wingspread of 36 to 60 inches, the great horned owl is indeed one of the "greatest" North American owls. (2) The North American owl is a highly adaptive species whose population has stabilized. (3) However, while the greatness might be justified, the "horned" is not, for the bird's head bears not horns, but prominent ear tufts. (4) These giant appendages give it a fearsome appearance that is not at all deceiving, as this species is one of the most ferocious predators of the bird world. (5) Aided by its size and strength, extremely acute hearing, and flying speeds of up to 40 miles per hour, this owl preys not only on small animals but also larger ones.

3. Which sentence is irrelevant to the argument presented in the passage and should be deleted?

   (A) sentence 1

   (B) sentence 2

   (C) sentence 3

   (D) sentence 4

(1) The main function of leaves is photosynthesis, which takes place in a leaf tissue called mesophyll, where cells absorb carbon dioxide from air in the surrounding spaces, replacing it with expelled oxygen. (2) Food produced by this process is circulated to other parts of the plant by a vascular system, which also transports water to the leaf. (3) Some plants have modified leaves that help the plant in special ways. (4) Many gardeners prefer cactus to leafy plants. (5) Some plants use leaves to trap insects, while others use them to deter predators.

4. Which sentence is irrelevant to the argument presented in the passage and should be deleted?

   (E) sentence 1

   (F) sentence 2

   (G) sentence 3

   (H) sentence 4

(1) Walter McCrone, an American chemist, was the leading expert in microscopy. (2) For years, he published articles, advancing the usefulness of microscopes. (3) Microscopes are, however, being increasingly produced in poor quality. (4) His work, recognized by many experts, led him to the examination of the Shroud of Turin, a revered Christian relic. (5) His findings about the nature of the shroud were disputed by his own team members, and eventually, McCrone resigned.

5. Which sentence is irrelevant to the argument presented in the passage and should be deleted?

   (A) sentence 1

   (B) sentence 2

   (C) sentence 3

   (D) sentence 4

(1) The wakes week is an English and Scottish holiday that has its roots in religious celebration. (2) Religious celebrations are often rooted in nonreligious events. (3) Originally, every church celebrated a patron saint at a church service that began at sunset on Saturday. (4) Wakes gradually grew in popularity as each town added its own event or activity. (5) Soon, the religious aspect of the celebration disappeared, and businesses closed to accommodate the wakes holidays as unpaid holidays.

6. Which sentence is irrelevant to the argument presented in the passage and should be deleted?

   (E) sentence 2
   (F) sentence 3
   (G) sentence 4
   (H) sentence 5

(1) The Kenya Colony was a part of the British Empire for about 40 years when the territories of East Africa were annexed by Britain. (2) Due to preferential treatment of British citizens, animosity grew between the natives and the British. (3) Land was distributed unfairly favoring British businesses. (4) That practice came to an end on December 1963, when the Kenya Colony gained independence. (5) Exactly one year later, Kenya became a republic under the name "Republic of Kenya." (6) Many countries need independence as well.

7. Which sentence is irrelevant to the argument presented in the passage and should be deleted?

   (A) sentence 3
   (B) sentence 4
   (C) sentence 5
   (D) sentence 6

(1) The *Energiende* is a planned transition by Germany that seeks to use environmentally friendly alternative energy sources. (2) Industrial pollution is one of the largest problems facing modern nations today. (3) To that end, Germany passed a bill that mandates a reduction in greenhouse gases but an increase in the use of alternative energy. (4) Thus far, Germany has achieved an impressive 27 percent reduction in carbon emissions. (5) However, its groundbreaking achievement is the production of over a third of its energy supply from renewable sources.

8. Which sentence is irrelevant to the argument presented in the passage and should be deleted?

   (E) sentence 1
   (F) sentence 2
   (G) sentence 3
   (H) sentence 5

(Answers are on page 72.)

SUPPORTING DETAILS

By now, you know how to rank items in terms of their precision and specificity. You also know when items are completely unnecessary. In the following type of questions, called **supporting details** questions, you are asked to support the ideas of a given paragraph. Usually there will be an overarching idea, which is a called a **topic**. If you can narrow it down to one word to describe that topic, you're on the right track. From there, you need to select an answer choice, a more specific detail to support that idea.

Here's an example:

1. Most people believe that the best way to improve their performance is to train one skill at a time.
2. They believe that repeating the same action helps them remember the skill.
3. This is true to a certain extent, but studies have shown that there are better ways to train.

The sentence that follows sentence 3 should provide a supporting or relevant detail that helps the reader gain more information about the practices involved in *better ways to train*. To answer these questions, try eliminating answer choices that are MOST irrelevant before you select the relevant supporting detail.

Supporting Details Exercise 1

1. Before there were wild, adventurous eating shows, there was Charles Darwin. Charles Darwin was the president of his school's "Glutton Club," which endeavored to eat the strangest types of meat known to man. <u>During his time, Charles Darwin ate many meats.</u>

   Which sentence should be added to follow and support the underlined sentence?

   (A) Many cultures confine themselves to three or four principal meats, but Darwin was not satisfied with such limitations.
   (B) Some of the most popular meats in the Western world are beef, pork, and poultry.
   (C) Some of these included an armadillo, an unnamed rodent of unusual size, and a rare bird.
   (D) Animals, however, have the right to life like all of us.

2. Cockroaches are champion survivors. They can endure extreme temperatures, go on for days without food or drink, and survive a nuclear holocaust. However, Tardigrades can put them to shame. <u>In fact, the Tardigrade is the toughest organism known to mankind.</u>

   Which sentence should be added to follow and support the underlined sentence?

   (E) Cockroaches do not come close.
   (F) It can lay up to 30 eggs at a time.
   (G) It moves comfortably in either –300 degrees or 300 degrees Fahrenheit.
   (H) Many mysteries surround this amazing creature.

3. A magnet is an object that attracts other magnetic objects through a magnetic field. <u>Because of its "attractive" properties, it is used in a variety of applications.</u>

   Which sentence should be added to follow and support the underlined sentence?

   (A) Magnets, however, can be harmful if used incorrectly.
   (B) Magnets can be found in natural environments.
   (C) Magnets can be found in televisions, computers, and even food.
   (D) Magnets can lose their strength over time.

4. Chickens are bred for either meat or eggs. Those that are bred for meat rarely lay eggs, while those bred for eggs lay eggs almost daily. A pet chicken, however, may be bred for love, as well as eggs, but probably not meat. <u>Most people think raising chickens may take a lot of work, but they're wrong.</u>

   Which sentence should be added to follow and support the underlined sentence?

   (E) Many people have mistaken ideas about animals.
   (F) Unlike your dog, chickens don't need to be walked.
   (G) Chickens typically lay eggs four to five months after they're hatched.
   (H) Worms are the most common forms of naturally occurring protein.

5. Some people have a negative response to seeing orange flecks of carrots on their dishes. However, they weren't always orange. In fact, they were originally purple. During the 1500s, some yellow and white varieties appearing in the wild were selected by a Dutch farmer. <u>Soon, carrots' chemical composition changed as a result of the domestication.</u>

   Which sentence should be added to follow and support the underlined sentence?

   (A) Carrots can be used in soups, baked goods, or even drinks.
   (B) Samuel Johnson once praised the virtues of the newly domesticated wonder.
   (C) Carrots can be associated with animals such as bunnies.
   (D) The carrot stopped producing anthocyanin, which gave the carrot a purple color, and began producing carotene, which gives the carrot its orange color.

6. Everyone knows that paper comes from trees, but just how much paper actually comes from trees? <u>Well, that of course depends on the size of the tree, but we can make an estimate based not on the size of the tree, but on the size of the wood.</u>

   Which sentence should be added to follow and support the underlined sentence?

   (E) The famous redwoods of California are by far the largest of the trees.
   (F) A 4 × 4 block of wood can produce about 100,000 sheets of copy paper.
   (G) Recycled paper can be reused several times, limiting the trees we cut down.
   (H) Some people, however, believe our reliance on paper is coming to an end.

7. It is commonly said that you are what you eat, but the more you eat, the greater your chances of death. This seems counterintuitive. After all, we are living beings, so we need food to survive. <u>However, research shows that too much food cuts your life shorter at the cellular level.</u>

   Which sentence should be added to follow and support the underlined sentence?

   (A) The average American eats about 23 pounds of pizza a year.
   (B) Different people from different cultures consume different quantities of food.
   (C) Eating too much inhibits an enzyme, which weakens the membranes of the energy-producing organ of the cell.
   (D) Doctors recommend a balanced diet that's high in fiber and low in fat.

8. The hippo may look like a gentle monster, but it is in fact a fearsome beast with jaws that can snap a table in half as if it were a biscuit. In the wild, they secrete a reddish fluid that many people mistake for blood. However, this secretion serves a number of useful functions. It can function as an antibiotic, neutralizing harmful bacteria. It can also serve as a moisturizer that can preserve the hippo's youthful looks.

Which sentence should be added to follow and support the underlined sentence?

(E) In conclusion, maintaining the skin's moisture is the most important function of the secretion.

(F) Finally, the hippo can show off its giant teeth to ward off challengers.

(G) Lastly, the secretion can protect the hippo from harmful ultraviolet rays.

(H) Most importantly, the hippo must protect its territory through fear and intimidation.

9. Why is the ocean so salty? The scientific reason is that the rocks on land dissolve into the ocean. However, there are several amusing folklore stories to explain this phenomenon.

Which sentence should be added to follow and support the underlined sentence?

(A) The Moldus, for example, believe that the ocean is salty because it is filled with the sad tears of the Earth.

(B) Fortunately, science has put these crazy ideas to rest.

(C) Folklore is often used to explain the unknown.

(D) Once rainwater breaks down rocks, the rocks produce negatively charged particles called ions.

(Answers are on page 72.)

Supporting Details Exercise 2

(1) For centuries, sleep was often so steeped in mystery that it required an explanation. (2) Some cultures believed that sleep was a gateway into the spirit world, while other cultures believed that it released the soul to travel the world. (3) Psychoanalysts believe it is the window to one's inner psyche, while other scientists believe that it is simply an evolutionary holdover from our primate ancestor. (4) The most recent research from neuroscientists suggests a less fantastical explanation.

1. Which sentence should be added to follow and support sentence 4?

(A) Sleep is something that most people need to ensure a productive day.

(B) It usually takes about 10 to 15 minutes for a person to fall asleep.

(C) Sleep functions as a cleaning mechanism that removes toxins that are associated with dementia.

(D) The problem with sleep research is that it is extremely difficult to establish an objective measure of sleepiness.

(1) The urgent care industry is one of the fastest growing health-care industries in the country today. (2) Each year, over 150 million people go to urgent care centers, resulting in about two urgent care centers opening every day. (3) The reason for this explosion can be attributed to several factors. (4) One of the most important factors is customer demand.

2. Which sentence should be added to follow and support sentence 4?

(E) In order to better evaluate what people need, the term *customer demand* is better defined as a customer "want."

(F) Urgent care centers provide shorter wait times, comparatively lower prices, and more attentive physicians that make their services an attractive alternative to the emergency room.

(G) Customer demand means something different in the health-care industry than it does in other industries.

(H) The most successful business industries are the ones that have their ear on the floor, listening for the demands of their customers.

(1) Nitrogen is a vital element that plants need to produce chlorophyll, the compound by which sunlight is converted into useable energy. (2) Soil rich in nitrogen can drastically improve the agricultural yield of any given plant. (3) However, although nitrogen is one of the most abundant elements on Earth, it is inaccessible to living organisms in its atmospheric form. (4) Thanks to the ingenious research of chemist Fritz Haber, today we can create fertilizer literally from thin air.

3. Which sentence should be added to follow and support sentence 4?

(A) The Haber-Bosch process combines nitrogen from the air with hydrogen under extreme pressures and temperatures.

(B) Hydrogen is also an important element, but not nearly as important as nitrogen.

(C) Creating fertilizer from the thin air can cause numerous problems in the environment.

(D) Soil rich in nitrogen can also enhance the flavor and nutrition of a crop.

(1) The octopus, lacking the physical apparatus that most land animals use to perceive color, appears to be colorblind. (2) However, its tendency to change color during courtship rituals has made scientists reluctant to claim that it is, in fact, colorblind. (3) Nature, it would seem, need not conform to human expectations. (4) Rather than using pigments in the eye, the octopus possesses a pair of strangely shaped pupils, which act like a prism breaking up light in its cephalopod head.

4. Which sentence should be added to follow and support sentence 4?

(E) A prism is a triangular glass that is commonly used to break up light.

(F) The giant squid, like the octopus, may also have the ability to break up light in its gigantic head.

(G) Once light is divided into separate wavelengths, the octopus then processes each wave, allowing for color discrimination.

(H) Many animals have strangely shaped body parts that make for a unique and interesting world.

(Answers are on page 74.)

MAIN IDEAS

Let's go back to the supermarket metaphor. Supermarkets exist to sell you products. To help you find what you're looking for, the supermarket is divided into different aisles. Each aisle contains related items to help you find what you need. The **topic** of a passage is similar to a supermarket aisle. The topic of a passage deals with an overarching idea, thing, or event.

The **main idea**, however, is slightly different. It consists of a topic and additional information about that topic. For instance, a movie is not just about a person, but is instead about a specific person who was down and out on her luck, only to find out that she possessed a superpower that could save the world. When you try to examine the main idea of a passage, you need to link both the topic and what the author wants to say about that topic to come up with the main idea.

To recap:

1. Identify the topic of the paragraph. Usually, you can find the topic from a repeated word or idea.
2. Ask yourself, what does the author want to say about the topic?

Then we have the simple formula: Topic + Author's idea about the topic = Main Idea.

Main Idea Exercise 1

(1)The first is that they all require the use of a ball. (2) The second is that they all originate from one man: Dr. James Naismith. (3) Dr. Naismith, an educator and physician, was tasked with the responsibility of creating a way for young men to channel their restless energy. (4) He knew that he would have to create an activity that required teamwork, physical prowess, and a degree of physical contact.

1. Which introductory sentence added at the beginning of the paragraph would clearly introduce the topic of the passage?

   (A) Basketball, volleyball, and racquetball—what do they all have in common?
   (B) American sports, due to the collaboration and technical skills involved, are often considered more challenging than European sports.
   (C) The history of American sports, from wrestling to baseball, can be traced back to Native Americans.
   (D) Many sports programs in American colleges focus too much on winning and not on helping individuals develop their fullest potential.

(1) Separate papers from plastic. (2) Make sure your plastics are clean. (3) Place aluminum foil in one receptacle and juice cartons in another. (4) It took our society years to train people to recycle properly, and we justify these practices by assuming that recycling helps the environment. (5) However, there are several factors to consider before we can speak intelligently about the virtues and benefits of recycling.

2. Which concluding sentence should be added to the end of the paragraph to best introduce the main claim of the passage?

    (E) Considering the importance of our impact on the environment today, there is a very good incentive to explore deeper.

    (F) Most people believe there are many benefits, while others believe that it is a waste of time.

    (G) Mother Nature is more than just a personification. She is a living, breathing creature who needs our assistance.

    (H) Another important environmentally safe practice is the use of paper bags rather than plastic ones.

(1) The average American does not want to know how their food winds up at their table. (2) All he needs to see is a happy cow staring back at him from a sunny meadow illustrated on the cover of a milk carton. (3) The cartoon cow in its colorful world conveniently covers the exacting and brutal life of the American farmer. (4) Such marketing tactics create a romanticized view of the American farm so that it becomes all the easier to forget where our food comes from.

3. Which concluding sentence should be added to the end of the paragraph to best introduce the main claim of the passage?

    (A) The average American farmer, however, produces food more efficiently than any other farmer in the world.

    (B) Therefore, Americans should all start farming their own food to ensure a steady food supply.

    (C) American farmers are, in fact, the top food exporters in the world.

    (D) However, to understand how food shapes our lives, it is important to recognize the reality behind the advertising.

(1) Video games are blamed for many things. (2) Over the years, they have been blamed for obesity, gun violence, and downright stupidity. (3) What many pundits overlook are the statistics that show the opposite. (4) In highly connected cities with the highest concentrations of video gamers, obesity is less of a problem. (5) Gun violence and video games lack clear links, when one considers that most mass shooters have never been gamers. (6) Finally, IQ scores have been rising over the years, so there goes that "stupid" correlation. (7) However, the content and the realism of video games today make it difficult to ignore the fact that video games have evolved.

4. Which concluding sentence should be added to the end of the paragraph to best introduce the main claim of the passage?

    (E) Parents have a right be concerned when their children are exposed to brutally graphic and realistic violence that serves only to heighten the disconnect between human beings.

    (F) More importantly, the cost of game consoles only serves to reveal the differences between the rich and the poor.

    (G) For centuries, poetry was considered a force that destroyed the character of the youth.

    (H) Television and the Internet make it easier for young children to access inappropriate material.

(1) Spiders routinely devour their mates after courtship. (2) Hamsters eat their babies when they have been touched by humans. (3) Certain species of crabs produce eggs in excess so that the babies can eat their siblings. (4) Fish, like walleye, eat each other. (5) Even certain human societies have practiced cannibalism as a religious ritual.

5. Which introductory sentence added at the beginning of the paragraph would best introduce the topic of the passage?

   (A) From the beginning of time, organisms have relied on hunting to sustain themselves.
   (B) Cannibalism occurs far more frequently than is commonly perceived.
   (C) In a world of declining energy sources, the only way to survive is through sacrifice.
   (D) Animals that work together have a much higher chance of survival than animals that tend to work alone.

(1) The variety of fighters using various techniques revealed that fighting techniques can be distilled into two basic categories: grappling and striking. (2) Grappling refers to close contact moves, which are designed to maneuver the opponent into a painful position. (3) Striking refers to a combination of punches or kicks, designed to knock the opponent into unconsciousness. (4) Those who possess both skills are fearsome fighters in a class of their own.

6. Which introductory sentence added at the beginning of the paragraph would best introduce the topic of the passage?

   (E) From the beginning of time, man has always fought against itself.
   (F) There are several problems with martial arts.
   (G) People believe that martial arts, when practiced correctly, have the potential to enhance one's character.
   (H) When the first Ultimate Fighting Championship aired, fighters of all different techniques rose to the occasion.

(1) The problem was in the existence of words with multiple meanings. (2) Without context, there is no way to tell how words should be used. (3) For instance, the sentence "The toilet button is behind you" can be translated into "The toilet is on your back." (4) "Watch your hand" might be translated into "Burn your careful hands." (5) Although such nuances are hard for computers to comprehend, linguists and programmers are confident that massive troves of data processed through the ever-increasingly powerful computers can eventually overcome this barrier.

7. Which introductory sentence added at the beginning of the paragraph would best introduce the topic of the passage?

   (A) For years, computer translations have been limited by one obstacle.
   (B) Computer prices have declined significantly over the years.
   (C) Learning a language can be extremely difficult for adults.
   (D) Computers have grown in capabilities over the years.

(Answers are on page 76.)

Main Idea Exercise 2

(1) For some students, nothing causes more panic than the due date for an essay quickly approaching the deadline. (2) On the night before the due date, students frantically cobble together a mishmash of words, hoping that it somehow makes sense. (3) However, writing doesn't always have to be associated with stress. (4) Writing can also cause sadness and depression.

(5) On the contrary, writing can reduce stress. (6) Researchers at Humboldt University devised an experiment where an experimental group wrote for 15 minutes about their day for a period of six weeks. (7) They found that the subjects who wrote for 15 minutes a day reported better organization of their thoughts and a clearer idea of their future. (8) The subjects' level of cortisol, a hormone triggered by stress, was significantly lower than that of the control subjects. (9) Desco University reported similar results, where people who kept diaries reported a higher satisfaction in life.

1. Which sentence should replace sentence 4 to more clearly introduce the topic of the passage?

   (A) Writing provides a wide variety of benefits, and it might be wise to rethink one's attitude toward writing.

   (B) People should abandon writing essays because doing so can reduce stress.

   (C) If people try hard enough, they can become excellent essay writers.

   (D) Writing can help a person reach professional success, so people should consider majoring in English.

(1) The great events in history are those where a man or a people have made a stand against tyranny and have preserved or advanced freedom for the people. (2) Sometimes tyranny has taken the form of the oppression of the many by the few in the same nation, and sometimes it has been the oppression of a weak nation by a stronger one. (3) Tyranny is a scourge that needs to be eradicated to preserve the future of democracy.

   (4) At that time, nearly all of Europe was inhabited by rude, barbarous tribes. (5) In all that broad land, the arts and sciences had made their appearance only in the small and apparently insignificant peninsula of Greece, lying on the extreme southeast border adjoining Asia. (6) The numerous harbors and bays which subdivide Greece invited a maritime life, and at a very early time, the descendants of the original shepherds became skillful navigators and courageous adventurers.

2. Which sentence should replace sentence 3 to more clearly introduce the topic of the passage?

   (E) Barbarians were one of the first forms of social organization that gave rise to the civilizations in Europe.

   (F) One of the earliest and most notable of these conflicts took place in Greece 2,400 years ago.

   (G) Regardless of the oppression, people have always emerged as the losers in these conflicts.

   (H) As populations increase to unmanageable levels, oppression becomes an inescapable facet of life throughout the history of civilization.

(1) Way, way off in the distance, far beyond the yellow sands of the desert, you will see something green and shimmering. (2) It is a valley situated between two rivers. (3) It is the Paradise of the Old Testament. (4) It is a land that many people can easily recognize if they had paid attention in history class.

(5) The names of the two rivers are the Euphrates and the Tigris. (6) They begin their course amidst the snows of the mountains of Armenia where Noah's Ark found a resting place and slowly flow through the southern plain until they reach the muddy banks of the Persian Gulf. (7) They perform a very useful service, turning the arid regions of western Asia into a fertile garden.

3. Which sentence should replace sentence 4 to more clearly introduce the topic of the passage?

   (A) It is a place that is mentioned in classrooms all over the world.
   (B) It is the land of mystery and wonder that the Greeks called Mesopotamia—the "land between the rivers."
   (C) It is a land that exists in the dreams of explorers who wish to unlock the mysteries of the Bible.
   (D) It is the land where agriculture and civilization were born.

(1) The birth of democracy can be traced back to Greece. (2) However, the Greeks were not a monolithic block that was made up of a homogenous group. (3) Take the Athenians and the Spartans for example. (4) They were the true founders of democracy. (5) Athens rose high from the plain. It was a city exposed to the fresh breezes from the sea, willing to look at the world with the eyes of a happy child. (6) Sparta, on the other hand, was built at the bottom of a deep valley, and used the surrounding mountains as a barrier against foreign thought. (7) Athens was a city of busy trade, whereas Sparta was an armed camp where people were soldiers for the sake of being soldiers. (8) The people of Athens loved to sit in the sun and discuss poetry or listen to the wise words of a philosopher. (9) The Spartans, on the other hand, never wrote a single line that was considered literature, but they knew how to fight, they liked to fight, and they sacrificed all human emotions to their ideal of military preparedness.

4. Which sentence should replace sentence 4 to more clearly introduce the topic of the passage?

   (E) Their geographical differences led to sharp differences in manners.
   (F) Political aspirations clearly aggravated the conflict between the two powerful states.
   (G) We should all aspire to celebrate their diversity.
   (H) They might have spoken a common language but were different in every other respect.

(1) Madagascar is the home to over 10,000 different species of unique plants. (2) Such diversity, however, is in danger because of the growing needs of the people who live there. (3) Agriculture is the primary form of subsistence, and farmers, clearing the land for agriculture, are destroying the rich variety of vegetation. (4) Moreover, climate change is distorting seasonal rainfall patterns, making it very difficult for plants to adapt. (5) The diversity is very important.

5. Which concluding sentence should replace sentence 5 to better support the information presented in the passage?

   (A) Madagascar's primary export is coffee, and this is also another problem that conservationists have to deal with.
   (B) People must learn more about conservation so that they can make a difference in the world.
   (C) Madagascar's economy is growing at an alarming speed, which may help spur modernization.
   (D) Scientists are concerned about the consequences of such losses because once these species are gone, they can never be studied again.

(1) Over 200 years ago, Thomas Malthus predicted that the world's population would be unsustainable. (2) The rate of population growth would overtake the rate of food production, and millions would inevitably suffer from hunger and famine. (3) Malthus, however, didn't count on the ingenuity of mankind. (4) Agricultural innovations, technological advancements, and industrial food production have helped the population grow by more than sevenfold. (5) Today, people waste about 3.5 million pounds of food each day.

6. Which concluding sentence should replace sentence 5 to better support the information presented in the passage?

   (E) The new problems now are pollution and overproduction.
   (F) The biggest problem today is whether we can feed all of them.
   (G) People should encourage, not criticize, new forms of technology.
   (H) It would seem, then, that Malthus's claims about humans, and not human claims to existence, are unsustainable.

(1) Once upon a less-technologically connected time, talking to yourself was considered a sign of madness. (2) However, times have certainly changed. (3) Today, people casually gesture to no one in particular, as they walk down the aisle of a shopping mall. (4) Drivers can be seen irately arguing with their poor innocent windshields that have no other choice but to listen. (5) Others seem to laugh and giggle as they stare down at their cell phone, completely oblivious to a pole or a hole that awaits their unsuspecting faces and bodies. (6) Who knows what technology will bring in the future?

7. Which concluding sentence should replace sentence 6 to better support the information presented in the passage?

   (A) Obviously, people need their cell phones more than ever before.
   (B) Despite such changes in behavior, the desire to remain connected to other people, regardless of how silly one may appear to an outsider, is unmistakably something that makes us human.
   (C) The telecommunications industry, however, seems interested in only producing profits and cell phone zombies.
   (D) The health risks of cell phone use are well documented in numerous research studies.

(1) Gardens are more than just places to pluck the ingredients for a quick snack. (2) They are a living and natural pharmacy. (3) The roots, leaves, and fruits of various plants can treat a number of conditions. (4) Garlic, for example, has often been used as an antibiotic to ward off infections, while cayenne peppers can be used to treat the flu and bronchitis. (5) People continue to acknowledge the benefits of these natural medicines.

8. Which concluding sentence should replace sentence 5 to better support the argument presented in the passage?

   (E) The cost-effectiveness of growing these natural medicines can harm the biotechnology industry.
   (F) Starting a garden in your backyard today might help you fill up your belly with nutritious dinners and your immune system with natural remedies.
   (G) Educating the public about the benefits of a garden can be difficult for people living in cities.
   (H) Finally, chamomile tea can also help people who suffer from anxiety or insomnia.

(Answers are on page 77.)

Answers for Precision Exercise 1 (pages 53–54)

1. A, D, B, C
2. F, G, H, E
3. C, B, D, A
4. G, E, H, F
5. A, B, D, C
6. E, F, G, H
7. B, C, D, A
8. E, F, G, H
9. B, C, A, D
10. E, F, G, H
11. C, D, A, B
12. F, G, E, H

Answers for Precision Exercise 2 (pages 56–57)

1. **(C)**

Least Precise (cross out)	Most Precise
engage, participate, do	volunteer
community activity that was interesting something that's interesting	interesting community activity

2. **(G)**

Least Precise (cross out)	Most Precise
study all day, make sure, do our best	review the chapter
the test coming up, the upcoming test, the future test	the chapter for the upcoming test

3. **(B)**

Least Precise (cross out)	Most Precise
told people, shared their thoughts, brought up their ideas	cautioned against sharing glasses

4. **(E)**

Least Precise (cross out)	Most Precise
is, makes	differentiates
types of life	animals

5. **(D)**

Least Precise (cross out)	Most Precise
people interested in arts and crafts, people who are interested in arts and crafts	arts and crafts enthusiasts
obtain, get	purchase
resources	fabrics and wood

6. **(H)**

Least Precise (cross out)	Most Precise
physical activities	cardio exercises
eating right, dieting	limiting their caloric intake

Answers for Irrelevant Sentences Exercise (pages 58–60)

1. **(D)** Sentence 4 interrupts the connection between *an efficient and convenient can opener* and the pronoun and keyword *This useful machine.*

2. **(G)** Sentence 3 interrupts the flow of ideas connected by the keyword *transform* in sentence 2 and *the transformation* in sentence 4.

3. **(B)** Sentence 2 interrupts the transition relationship between sentences 1 and 3. The transition word *however* introduces the idea that there is a problem with the name of the great horned owl.

4. **(H)** Sentence 4 introduces the preferences of gardeners, which is not relevant to the topic of plant leaves.

5. **(C)** Sentence 4 contains the pronoun phrase *his work,* which needs to connect to the phrase *published articles.* Sentence 3 breaks up the pairing and inserts an irrelevant fact about microscopes.

6. **(E)** The paragraph narrates a series of events. Each sentence contains a sequence transition (*originally, gradually, soon*) to develop a sequential narrative. Sentence 2 contains an observation that has little to do with the sequence of events.

7. **(D)** The paragraph narrates a series of events related to Kenya. Sentence 6 concludes with an observation about the world in general.

8. **(F)** Sentence 3 contains the pronoun *that,* which connects to *planned transition.* If sentence 2 is not removed, then the pronoun *that* would connect to *industrial pollution,* which would then distort the idea in the paragraph.

Answers to Supporting Details Exercise 1 (pages 61–63)

1. **(C)** The word *meats* in the underlined section connects with the pronoun *these* that introduces the types of meat Darwin ate.

   Before there were wild adventurous eating shows, there was Charles Darwin. Charles Darwin was the president of his school's "Glutton Club," which endeavored to eat the strangest types of meat known to man. <u>During his time, Charles Darwin ate many</u> *meats.* Some of *these* included an armadillo, an unnamed rodent of unusual size, and a rare bird.

2. **(G)**

Cockroaches are champion survivors. They can endure extreme temperatures, go on for days without food or drink, and survive a nuclear holocaust. However, Tardigrades can put them to shame. In fact, the Tardigrade is the toughest organism known to mankind.

(E) Cockroaches do not come close.
This answer choice only repeats the idea without providing a specific example.

(F) It can lay up to 30 eggs at a time.
This has nothing to do with being tough.

(G) It moves comfortably in either –300 degrees or 300 degrees Fahrenheit.
This provides a relevant example that supports the description of the Tardigrade as *the toughest organism*.

(H) Many mysteries surround this amazing creature.
This sentence goes off topic.

3. **(C)** This choice provides relevant examples that support the idea that magnets are *used in a variety of applications*.

A magnet is an object that attracts other magnetic objects through a magnetic field. Because of its "attractive" properties, it is *used in a variety of applications*. Magnets can be found *in televisions, computers, and even food*.

4. **(F)**

Chickens are bred for either meat or eggs. Those that are bred for meat rarely lay eggs, while those bred for eggs lay eggs almost daily. A pet chicken, however, may be bred for love, as well as eggs, but probably not meat. Most people think raising chickens may take a lot of work, but they're wrong.

(E) Many people have mistaken ideas about animals.
This sentence only repeats the idea in the underlined sentence.

(F) Unlike your dog, chickens don't need to be walked.
This sentence provides a clear example to support the idea that raising chickens is not a lot of work.

(G) Chickens typically lay eggs four to five months after they're hatched.
This sentence is about a chicken's reproductive cycle.

(H) Worms are the most common forms of naturally occurring protein.

This sentence is about worms, not chickens. You can only connect this to the paragraph if the sentence suggests that the natural form of protein makes raising chickens easier. It's definitely suggested, but not stated.

5. **(D)** This choice provides a supporting detail that illustrates which chemical composition changed.

Some people have a negative response to seeing orange flecks of carrots on their dishes. However, they weren't always orange. In fact, they were originally purple. During the 1500s, some yellow and white varieties appearing in the wild were selected by a Dutch farmer. Soon, *carrots' chemical composition changed* as a result of the domestication. The carrot *stopped producing anthocyanin*, which gave the carrot a purple color, and began *producing carotene*, which gives the carrot its orange color.

6. **(F)** This choice provides support for the size of the wood and the estimate of amount of paper produced.

Everyone knows that paper comes from trees, but just how much paper actually comes from trees? Well, that of course depends on the size of the tree, but we can make an *estimate* based not on the size of the tree, but on the *size of the wood*.

(F) A *4 × 4 block* of wood can produce *about 100,000 sheets* of copy paper.

7. **(C)** This choice explains what happens *at the cellular level*.

It is commonly said that you are what you eat, but the more you eat, the greater your chances of death. This seems counterintuitive. After all, we are living beings, so we need food to survive. However, research shows that too much food cuts your life shorter at *the cellular level*. Eating too much inhibits an enzyme, which *weakens the membranes of the energy-producing organ of the cell*.

8. **(G)** This choice provides an additional function of the red secretion. In this question, you're providing an additional example that resembles the underlined example.

The hippo may look like a gentle monster, but it is in fact a fearsome beast with jaws that can snap a table in half as if it were a biscuit. In the wild, they secrete a reddish fluid that many people mistake for blood. However, this secretion serves a *number of useful functions*. It can function as an antibiotic, neutralizing harmful bacteria. It can also serve as a moisturizer that can preserve the hippo's youthful looks. Lastly, the secretions can protect the hippo from harmful ultraviolet rays.

9. **(A)** This choice provides an example of an amusing folklore story that explains the saltiness of the oceans.

Why is the ocean so salty? The scientific reason is that the rocks on land dissolve into the ocean. However, there are several amusing *folklore stories to explain* this phenomenon.

(A) The Moldus, for example, *believe that the ocean is salty because* it is filled with the sad tears of the Earth.

Answers for Supporting Details Exercise 2 (pages 63–64)

1. **(C)** Sentence 4 introduces the explanation from the most recent findings. Choice C provides an explanation that best resembles a scientific explanation.

(A) Sleep is something that most people need to ensure a productive day.
This answer choice is out of scope and irrelevant.

(B) It usually takes about 10 to 15 minutes for a person to fall asleep.
This answer choice elaborates on the way people fall asleep and not on the explanation.

(C) Sleep functions as a cleaning mechanism that removes toxins that are associated with dementia.
This is the best answer.

(D) The problem with sleep research is that it is extremely difficult to establish an objective measure of sleepiness.
This touches upon scientific studies of sleep, but it describes a drawback that is not discussed in the previous sentence.

2. **(F)** Choice F provides several reasons that help provide more information about the customer demand that contributes to the rising popularity of urgent cares.

   (E) In order to better evaluate what people need, the term *customer demand* is better defined as a customer "want."
     Although this answer choice links the term *customer demand* it is irrelevant as it looks to redefine a term unnecessarily.

   (F) Urgent cares provide shorter wait times, comparatively lower prices, and more attentive physicians that make their services an attractive alternative to the emergency room.
     This answer choice best illustrates the factors that constitute *customer demand.*

   (G) Customer demand means something different in the health-care industry than it does in other industries.
     The definition of customer demand is irrelevant here.

   (H) The most successful business industries are the ones that have their ear on the floor, listening for the demands of their customers.
     This sentence introduces what may be important for business industries.

3. **(A)** Choice A links *Fritz Haber* with *The Haber-Bosch process* and provides more details on how the fertilizer is created.

   (A) The Haber-Bosch process combines nitrogen from the air with hydrogen under extreme pressures and temperatures.
     This answer choice best supports sentence 4 by explaining how fertilizer is created from air.

   (B) Hydrogen is also an important element, but not nearly as important as nitrogen.
     This answer choice deals with important elements, which is irrelevant.

   (C) Creating fertilizer from the thin air can cause numerous problems in the environment.
     This answer choice brings up environmental problems, which is not discussed in the passage.

   (D) Soil rich in nitrogen can also enhance the flavor and nutrition of a crop.
     This answer choice brings up the impact of nitrogen on food, which is not discussed in the passage.

4. **(G)** Choice G further explains what happens after light breaks up in a cephalopod's head.

   (E) A prism is a triangular glass that is commonly used to break up light.
     An explanation of the use of a prism is unnecessary in this paragraph.

   (F) The giant squid, like the octopus, may also have the ability to break up light in its gigantic head.
     There is no indication that the passage needs to discuss squids.

   (G) Once light is divided into separate wavelengths, the octopus then processes each wave, allowing for color discrimination.
     This is the best answer.

   (H) Many animals have strangely shaped body parts that make for a unique and interesting world.
     The passage discusses cephalopods, not other animals or their traits.

Answers for Main Idea Exercise 1 (pages 65–67)

1. **(A)** The topic is sports, and the author wants to discuss the origin of these sports. Sentence A introduces the origin of all three sports. Also, it connects the pronoun *they* with the proper antecedents.

   (A) *Basketball, volleyball, and racquetball—what do they all have in common?*

   (1) The first is that *they* all require the use of a ball.

2. **(E)** The topic is recycling, and sentence 5 suggests that we need to consider several factors. Sentence E best connects to that idea with the phrase *incentive to explore deeper*.

   (5) However, there are *several factors to consider* before we can speak intelligently about the virtues and benefits of recycling.

   (E) Considering the importance of our impact on the environment today, there is a very *good incentive to explore deeper.*

3. **(D)** The topic is food, and the author wants to discuss how marketing shapes our ideas about the sources of our food.

   (4) Such marketing tactics create a romanticized view of the American farm so that it becomes all the *easier to forget where our food comes from*.

   (D) However, to understand how food shapes our lives, it is *important to recognize the reality behind the advertising.*

4. **(E)** The topic is video games, and the author wants to discuss the impact of video games on children.

   (E) Parents have a right be concerned when their children are exposed to brutally graphic and realistic violence that serves only to heighten the disconnect between human beings.

5. **(B)** The topic is cannibalism, and sentence B introduces the variety of evidence for the existence of cannibalism in the world.

   (1) Spiders routinely devour their mates after courtship. (2) Hamsters eat their babies when they have been touched by humans. (3) Certain species of crabs produce eggs in excess so that the babies can eat their siblings. (4) Fish, like walleye, eat each other. (5) Even human societies have had societies that practiced cannibalism as a religious ritual.

   (B) Cannibalism *occurs far more frequently* than is commonly perceived.

6. **(H)** The topic is fighting techniques, and sentence H best introduces the event that revealed the two main fighting techniques. It also connects with the phrase *The variety of fighters using various techniques* in sentence 1.

   (H) When the first Ultimate Fighting Championship aired, *fighters of all different techniques* rose to the occasion.

   (1) *The variety of fighters using various techniques* revealed that fighting techniques can be distilled into two basic categories: grappling and striking.

7. **(A)** The topic is computer translations, and the author wants to discuss the existing limitation. Sentence A links the idea of *one obstacle* with the phrase *the problem*.

   (A) For years, computer translations have been limited by *one obstacle*.

   (1) *The problem* was in the existence of words with multiple meanings.

Answers to Main Idea Exercise 2 (pages 68–70)

1. **(A)**

   (A) Writing provides a wide variety of benefits, and it might be wise to rethink one's attitude toward writing.
   This sentence introduces the benefit of reduced stress in the following paragraph.

   (B) People should abandon writing essays because doing so can reduce stress.
   This sentence introduces the idea of abandoning the writing of essays, which is not discussed in the following paragraph.

   (C) If people try hard enough, people can become excellent essay writers.
   This sentence claims that working hard leads to better skills in essay writing, which is not discussed in the following paragraph.

   (D) Writing can help a person reach professional success, so people should consider majoring in English.
   This sentence attempts to persuade the reader to major in English, which is not discussed in the following paragraph.

2. **(F)**

   (E) Barbarians were one of the first forms of social organization that gave rise to the civilizations in Europe.
   This sentence introduces barbarians and early forms of social organization, and the following paragraph mentions barbarians in the first sentence. However, the following paragraph primarily discusses the geographical environment of the Greeks. The mentioning of the *barbarous tribes* is a detail used to contextualize the Greek environment.

   (F) One of the earliest and most notable of these conflicts took place in 2,400 years ago.
   This sentence is the best introduction because the pronoun *these conflicts* links with *oppression* in sentence 2. Also, the phrase *2,400 years ago* in the answer choice connects with the phrase *at that time* in sentence 4.

   (G) Regardless of the oppression, people have always emerged as the losers in these conflicts.
   This sentence introduces the consequence of conflicts for *people* in the general sense.

   (H) As populations increase to unmanageable levels, oppression becomes an inescapable facet of life throughout the history of civilization.
   This sentence introduces the impact of oppression in the history of civilization, not for the Greeks.

3. **(B)**

   (A) It is a place that is mentioned in classrooms all over the world.
   This is a tempting answer, since it uses a similar structure with *it is*. However, the phrase *two rivers* in sentence 5 needs an introduction, which choice A does not provide.

   (B) It is the land of mystery and wonder that the Greeks called Mesopotamia—the "land between the rivers."
   This is the best answer, as the phrase *the rivers* in the answer choice introduces the *two rivers* mentioned in sentence 5.

   (C) It is a land that exists in the dreams of explorers who wish to unlock the mysteries of the Bible.

Although a biblical reference is made in sentence 6, it is a minor detail. The other sentences discuss geography associated with the two rivers, not the Bible.

(D) It is the land where agriculture and civilization were born.
This sentence introduces *the land*, so it is not an appropriate introduction.

4. **(H)**

(E) Their geographical differences led to sharp differences in manners.
This is a very tempting answer choice but fails to introduce the main idea. While sentences 5 through 7 make references to geography, sentences 8 and 9 discuss preferences and values rather than manners.

(F) Political aspirations clearly aggravated the conflict between the two powerful states.The following paragraph does not discuss the conflict between Athens and Sparta.

(G) We should all aspire to celebrate their diversity.
The following paragraph does not discuss diversity at all.

(H) They might have spoken a common language but were different in every other respect.
This is the best answer because the paragraph that follows outlines several ways in which the Athenians and Spartans were different.

5. **(D)**

(A) Madagascar's primary export is coffee, and this is also another problem that conservationists have to deal with.
Discussion of the economy is outside the scope of the paragraph's discussion on the loss of diversity.

(B) People must learn more about conservation so that they can make a difference in the world.
This answer choice unnecessarily advocates a course of action. The course of action may be implied, but the paragraph is primarily intended to describe the loss of diversity and its impact.

(C) Madagascar's economy is growing at an alarming speed, which may help spur modernization.
Discussion of the economy is outside the scope of the paragraph's discussion on the loss of diversity.

(D) Scientists are concerned about the consequences of such losses because once these species are gone, they can never be studied again.
This sentence further elaborates on the main claim of the topic, which is the loss of diversity.

6. **(H)**

(E) The new problems now are pollution and overproduction.
The paragraph does not discuss problems but human responses to a prediction.

(F) The biggest problem today is whether we can feed all of them.
This sentence would seem to contradict the main idea of the passage.

(G) People should encourage, not criticize, new forms of technology.
This sentence advocates a course of action, which is not the intended purpose of the passage.

(H) It would seem, then, that Malthus's claims about humans, and not human claims to existence, are unsustainable.

This sentence is the best concluding sentence since it combines expectations and reality of population and resources.

7. **(B)**

(A) Obviously, people need their cell phones more than ever before.

The paragraph illustrates people's preoccupation with cell phones, but the phrase *than ever before* suggests that the passage was discussing the importance of cell phones today.

(B) Despite such changes in behavior, the desire to remain connected to other people, regardless of how silly one may appear to an outsider, is unmistakably something that makes us human.

The phrase *such changes in behavior* connects the previous description to a claim about how the practices are normal and acceptable human behavior to support the idea that *times have . . . changed.*

(C) The telecommunications industry, however, seems interested in only producing profits and cell phone zombies.

This sentence focuses on the interests of the telecommunications industry, which were not discussed at all in the passage.

(D) The health risks of cell phone use are well documented in numerous research studies.

Although there may be risks associated with using cell phones, the main idea in the passage is not to emphasize the dangers of using a cell phone.

8. **(B)**

(A) The cost-effectiveness of growing these natural medicines can harm the biotechnology industry.

While growing your own plants in a garden might be cost-effective, the biotechnology industry is never discussed in the passage, so it is an inappropriate concluding sentence.

(B) Starting a garden in your backyard today might help you fill up your belly with nutritious dinners and your immune system with natural remedies.

This sentence is the best answer choice because it captures the idea that gardens can be used for both food and medicine.

(C) Educating the public about the benefits of a garden can be difficult for people living in cities.

This sentence is a judgment on the difficulties of educating people. The purpose of this passage is not to outline the difficulties.

(D) Finally, chamomile tea can also help people who suffer from anxiety or insomnia.

This is an additional detail, which does not serve to capture the main idea.

Revising/Editing: Exercises 6

PRACTICE SET 1

Revising/Editing Part A

> **Directions:** Read and answer each of the following questions. You will be asked to recognize and correct errors in sentences or short paragraphs. Mark the best answer for each question.

1. Read this paragraph.

> (1) Aquaculture, also known as fish farming or shellfish farming, refers to the breeding of plants and animals in a water environment. (2) Researchers of this exciting field are "farming" all different kinds of aquatic species. (3) The work by thousands of scientists and engineers has made remarkable progress throughout the years. (4) Continued advances in this technology is expanding aquaculture's role in both conservation, and commercial efforts.

How should this paragraph be revised?

(A) Sentence 1: Change *refers* to *referred*, AND delete comma after *farming*.

(B) Sentence 2: Change *are* to *is*, AND insert comma after *kinds*.

(C) Sentence 3: Change *has* to *have*, AND add comma after *progress*.

(D) Sentence 4: Change *is* to *are*, AND delete comma after *conservation*.

2. Read this sentence.

> The Civil War of the 19th century was one of the most brutal deadly wars that claimed more American lives than the two world wars combined.

Which edit should be made to correct this sentence?

(E) Insert a comma after *War*.

(F) Insert a comma after *century*.

(G) Insert a comma after *brutal*.

(H) Insert a comma after *lives*.

3. Read this paragraph.

> (1) The combination of hydraulic fracking and horizontal drilling is mostly responsible for the recent increase in U.S. oil production. (2) However the drilling methods by the fracking industry had come under heavy scrutiny. (3) Some critics looking at the environmental impact point to exploding faucets and the increasing frequency of sinkholes. (4) Others examining the economy suggest that these methods make minimal contributions to overall growth.

How should this paragraph be revised?

(A) Sentence 1: Insert comma after *fracking*, AND change *is* to *are*.
(B) Sentence 2: Insert comma after *However*, AND change *had* to *has*.
(C) Sentence 3: Insert comma after *faucets*, AND change *point* to *points*.
(D) Sentence 4: Insert comma after *suggest*, AND change *suggest* to *suggested*.

4. Read these sentences.

> (1) The SHSAT is offered to all New York City students.
> (2) Students in eighth and ninth grade take the exam.
> (3) Students from all the boroughs are encouraged to take the exam.

What is the best way to combine these sentences?

(E) The SHSAT is offered to all New York City students, who are in the eighth and ninth grade to take the exam, although students from all the boroughs are encouraged to take the exam.
(F) When the SHSAT is offered to all New York City students in the eighth and ninth grade, they are all encouraged to take the exam.
(G) While the SHSAT is offered to all eighth and ninth grade students in New York City, students from all boroughs are encourage to take the exam.
(H) Eighth and ninth grade students from all boroughs of New York City are encouraged to take the SHSAT.

Revising/Editing Part B

Directions: Read the passage below and answer the questions following it. You will be asked to improve the writing quality of the passage and to correct errors so that the passage follows the conventions of standard written English. You may reread the passage if you need to. Mark the best answer for each question.

Tombs of the Egyptian Dynasty

(1) For many years, various European collections of Egyptian antiquities have contained a certain series of objects, which gave certain people great difficulty. (2) There were vases of a peculiar form and color, greenish plates of slate, many of them in curious animal forms, and other similar things. (3) It was known, positively, that these objects had been found in Egypt, but it was impossible to assign them a place in the known periods of Egyptian art.

(4) Egyptian art has long served an important role in museums all over the world. (5) The first light was thrown on this question in two places on the west bank of the Nile. (6) A lucky man found many important objects. (7) Many findings that help us understand the basic foundation of life can be found in the Nile. (8) Containing pottery and the slate tablets that did not seem to be Egyptian, the newly found necropolis and the puzzling objects were assumed to represent the art of a foreign people who had temporarily resided in Egypt in the time between the old and the middle kingdoms. (9) British archaeologists gave this unknown people the name "New Race."

(10) The bold assertion of this appellation made headlines in academia. (11) This theory met with little approval, least of all from German Egyptologists. (12) In spite of much discussion, the question could not then be decided.

5. Which revision of sentence 1 uses the most precise language?

   (A) For many years, various European collections of Egyptian antiquities have contained a certain series of objects, which gave certain people great difficulty.
   (B) For many years, various collections of Egyptian antiquities have contained a certain series of objects, which gave scientists great difficulty.
   (C) For over 100 years, various collections of Egyptian antiquities have contained a certain series of objects, which gave archaeologists great difficulty.
   (D) For over 100 years, various European collections of Egyptian antiquities have contained a certain series of objects, which gave archaeologists great difficulty.

6. Which sentence should replace sentence 4 to more clearly introduce the topic of this passage?

   (E) Learning more about art enhances not only one's understanding of the world, but the very essence of what it means to be human.
   (F) The strange style of the objects, as well as the difficulty in situating their composition, led many investigators to question their origins.
   (G) Egypt has always been a source of mystery and wonder for both the adventurer and the homebody.
   (H) It might produce unusual emotions to know that the few human bones found in the tomb once belonged to the oldest Egyptian king.

7. Which revision of sentence 6 uses the most precise language?

(A) A lucky investigator found an important discovery that contained numerous objects.
(B) An English investigator found an important discovery that contained numerous graves.
(C) A lucky English investigator discovered a very large necropolis containing about three thousand graves.
(D) A lucky English person came across an important discovery of about three thousand graves.

8. Which transition word or phrase should be added to the beginning of sentence 9?

(E) In addition,
(F) However,
(G) Nonetheless,
(H) Therefore,

9. Which sentence is irrelevant to the argument presented in the passage and should be deleted?

(A) sentence 2
(B) sentence 5
(C) sentence 7
(D) sentence 11

Practice Set 1: Answer Explanations

1. **(D)** Examine the underlined subject-noun and predicate-verb pairings for each sentence. The incorrect pairing is *italicized*.

   (1) <u>Aquaculture</u>, also known as fish farming or shellfish farming, <u>refers</u> to the breeding of plants and animals in a water environment. (2) <u>Researchers</u> ~~of this exciting field~~ <u>are</u> "farming" all different kinds of aquatic species. (3) The <u>work</u> ~~by thousands of scientists and engineers~~ <u>has</u> made remarkable progress throughout the years. (4) Continued *advances* ~~in this technology~~ *is* expanding aquaculture's role in both conservation and commercial efforts.

2. **(G)** The words *brutal deadly* are coordinate adjectives. You can use them interchangeably with the word *and* to modify *wars*. *The most deadly and brutal wars* would make sense. "The Civil War of the 19th century was one of the most brutal, deadly wars that claimed more American lives than the two world wars combined."

   Choice E is wrong because a comma between a word and its preposition is unnecessary. Choice F is wrong because a comma between a subject and its predicate verb is unnecessary. Choice H is wrong because a comma between two correlative conjunctions (more *x* than *y*) is unnecessary.

3. **(B)** Examine all the predicate verbs underlined below.

   (1) The combination of hydraulic fracking and horizontal drilling <u>is</u> mostly responsible for the recent increase in U.S. oil production. (2) However, the drilling methods by the fracking industry <u>had</u> come under heavy scrutiny. (3) Some critics looking at the environmental impact <u>point</u> to exploding faucets and the increasing frequency of sinkholes. (4) Others examining the economy <u>suggest</u> that these methods <u>make</u> minimal contributions to overall growth.

   The paragraph is written in the present tense and the predicate verb that doesn't agree is the past tense verb *had*.

4. **(H)**

   (E) The SHSAT is offered to all New York City students, who are in the eighth and ninth grade to take the exam, although students from all the boroughs are encouraged to take the exam.
   This sentence contains an independent clause and two dependent clauses. In addition, it unnecessarily sets up a contrast with the word *although*.

   (F) When the SHSAT is offered to all New York City students in the eighth and ninth grade, they are all encouraged to take the exam.
   This sentence creates an illogical relationship between the two clauses.

   (G) While the SHSAT is offered to all eighth and ninth grade students in New York City, students from all boroughs are encourage to take the exam.
   This sentence creates an illogical relationship between the two clauses.

   (H) Eighth and ninth grade students from all boroughs of New York City are encouraged to take the SHSAT.
   This sentence contains only one clause. It combines information from all three sentences without changing the meaning.

5. **(D)**

Least Precise (cross out)	Most Precise
many years	about 100 years
collections	European collections
certain people, scientists	archaeologists

6. **(F)** Sentence 5 contains the phrase *this question*. This phrase connects best with the phrase *to question* in choice F.

7. **(C)** *A lucky English investigator* provides the most detailed information about the person who made the discovery. The phrase *a very large necropolis containing about three thousand graves* provides the most detailed information about the discovery itself.

8. **(H)** The assumption in sentence 8 led the archaeologists to give the people a new name. Therefore, the most logical relationship is cause and effect. The transition word *Therefore* best connects the two sentences.

9. **(C)** Sentence 7 provides a general statement about the importance of art. It has no relevance to the topic about the question of the object's origins. Sentence 2 is necessary because it provides details on the *difficulty* that archaeologists encountered. Sentence 5 is necessary because it introduces how the mystery of the objects was explored. Sentence 11 is necessary because it concludes the main idea of the paragraph.

PRACTICE SET 2

Revising/Editing Part A

> **Directions:** Read and answer each of the following questions. You will be asked to recognize and correct errors in sentences or short paragraphs. Mark the best answer for each question.

1. Read this paragraph.

> (1) If you've ever driven past Jones Beach, you might have noticed the signs for Robert Moses State Park. (2) Who exactly is this man, whose park sits majestically at the end of Jones Beach? (3) Known as the "master-builder," Robert Moses's plans helped develop the streets and highways of New York City. (4) While his public works project was undoubtedly influential, the impact of his policies remain controversial today.

Which sentence contains an error in construction and should be revised?

(A) sentence 1
(B) sentence 2
(C) sentence 3
(D) sentence 4

2. Read this sentence.

> Although most people are indifferent to the drab, gray New York pigeon paleontologists are fascinated by its ancestor, one of the fiercest predators of its time.

Which edit should be made to correct this sentence?

(E) Delete the comma after **drab**.
(F) Insert a comma after **pigeon**.
(G) Delete the comma after **ancestor**.
(H) Insert a comma after **predators**.

3. Read this paragraph.

> (1) Before the invention of the <u>Internet, people</u> in New York City used to do a lot of different things to keep themselves entertained. (2) One of them was playing <u>sports, games</u> like stickball or handball were summer favorites. (3) If physical activity wasn't your <u>thing, you</u> could go to an underground arcade, where kids would insert quarters into a giant machine to play video games. (4) Whatever you <u>did, you</u> could be sure that you would be with real human beings.

Which revision of the underlined sections corrects the error in sentence structure in the paragraph?

(A) Internet, so the people
(B) sports, and games
(C) thing, therefore you
(D) did, that is you

4. Read this paragraph.

> (1) The British Empire was known for its powerful influence all over the globe. (2) This power was maintained by a formidable navy, which kept a rule to maintain a number of ships that were equal to the combined ships of their two largest rivals. (3) This rule became untenable once the United States matured because its industrial capacity outpaced that of Britain. (4) Nonetheless, the British Empire continued to thrive due largely to its successful economic strength.

How should the paragraph be revised?

(E) Sentence 1: Change *was* to *were* AND *its* to *their*.

(F) Sentence 2: Change *is* to *was* AND *their* to *it*.

(G) Sentence 3: Change *outpaced* to *outpaces* AND *its* to *their*.

(H) Sentence 4: Change *continued* to *continues* AND *its* to *this*.

5. Read this paragraph.

> (1) Several members of the committee believe that the school made a mistake. (2) In a recent meeting, parents of sixth, seventh, and eighth graders plan to speak about the problem. (3) Some of the biggest issues is nutrition, homework, and the graduation venue. (4) Parents believe that addressing all these issues is critical to running a successful year.

How should the paragraph be revised?

(A) Sentence 1: Change *believe* to *believes*.

(B) Sentence 2: Change *plan* to *plans*.

(C) Sentence 3: Change *is* to *are*.

(D) Sentence 4: Change *is* to *are*.

6. Read this paragraph.

> (1) Coffee beans are not really beans in the truest sense. (2) They are, in fact, seeds from the fruit of a coffee tree, which may produce for as long as 50 to 60 years. (3) The oldest and most popular method of processing coffee beans is called the "dry process." (4) In this process, the drying operation is the most important stage that affected the final quality of the coffee.

Which sentence contains an error in construction and should be revised?

(E) sentence 1

(F) sentence 2

(G) sentence 3

(H) sentence 4

Revising/Editing Part B

> **Directions:** Read the passage below and answer the questions following it. You will be asked to improve the writing quality of the passage and to correct errors so that the passage follows the conventions of standard written English. You may reread the passage if you need to. Mark the best answer for each question.

Errors in Our Food Economy

(1) Scientific research need not confine itself to the laboratory, especially when we need to diagnose a problem in our relationship to food. (2) By interpreting the observations of practical life, science has found that several errors are common in the use of food. (3) We must work hard to eliminate food waste so that we can make the world a better place.

(4) Firstly, many people purchase needlessly expensive kinds of food. (5) Mutton costs $12 per pound, whereas chicken costs only $2. (6) Unfortunately, those who spend the most are often the ones who can least afford it, but they do so under a mistaken assumption.

(7) Secondly, the food that we eat does not always contain the proper proportions of the different kinds of nutritive ingredients. (8) We consume relatively too much of the fuel ingredients of food. (9) These ingredients consist primarily of the fats from meat, butter, and starch (which makes up the large part of flour). (10) These proteins help make muscle and sinew, serving as the basis of blood, bone, and brain. (11) Conversely, we consume relatively too little of the protein-rich substances, such as lean meat, fish, and beans.

(12) Thirdly, many people, not only the well-to-do, but also those in moderate circumstances, waste tons of food. (13) Part of the excess is simply thrown away as waste from the table and kitchen; therefore, the injury to health, great as it may be, is doubtless much less than if all were eaten. (14) Those who suffer most from this evil are well-to-do people with sedentary occupations—those who do mental work as opposed to manual laborers.

(15) We are guilty of serious errors in our cooking. (16) We waste a great deal of fuel in the preparation of our food, and a great deal of the food is very badly cooked. (17) Can we afford to spend such a large part of our budget on food? (18) A reform in these methods of cooking is one of the economic demands of our time.

7. Which sentence should replace sentence 3 to best introduce the main claim of the passage?

   (A) These errors include changing our shopping habits, the kinds of foods we eat, and how we cook our food.
   (B) Science can help mankind become a better, more responsible steward of the world it has received.
   (C) Food waste must be discouraged as the population trend reveals no indication of slowing down.
   (D) Mankind has tried to control the sources of all of the major food groups.

8. Which sentence can best follow and support sentence 6?

(E) Much of the food they purchase can easily be bought at a butcher rather than a supermarket.

(F) They do this under the impression that there is a benefit in the costlier materials, when there really isn't.

(G) A vegetarian diet, for example, doesn't necessarily mean that one eats only plants.

(H) The most nutritious foods often do not have the labelling to differentiate them from others.

9. Which transition word or phrase should be added to the beginning of sentence 8?

(A) Therefore,

(B) Nonetheless,

(C) In fact,

(D) Nevertheless,

10. Where should sentence 11 be moved to improve the organization of the third paragraph (sentences 7–11)?

(E) to the beginning of the paragraph

(F) between sentences 7 and 8

(G) between sentences 8 and 9

(H) between sentences 9 and 10

11. Which revision of sentence 12 best maintains the formal style of the passage?

(A) Thirdly, many people, not only the well-to-do, but also those in moderate circumstances, waste tons of food.

(B) Thirdly, many people, not only the well-to-do, but also those in moderate circumstances, blow all their dough on food.

(C) Thirdly, many people, not only the well-to-do, but also those in moderate circumstances, use needless quantities of food.

(D) Thirdly, many people, not only the well-to-do, but also those in moderate circumstances, eat like savages.

12. Which sentence is irrelevant and should be removed?

(E) sentence 8

(F) sentence 13

(G) sentence 16

(H) sentence 17

13. Which concluding sentence should be added after sentence 18 to support the main claim presented in the passage?

(A) Another economic demand is pollution resulting from corporate agriculture.

(B) With the aid of science, we simply cannot fail to rise up and meet that demand.

(C) In the end, we must find a way to encourage the conservation of resources or suffer the consequences.

(D) After all, the American public is notorious for waste and cannot be expected to change its behavior.

Practice Set 2: Answer Explanations

1. **(D)** Examine the pairings of <u>modifiers</u> and *modified objects* below.

   Incorrect: <u>Known as the "master-builder,"</u> *Robert Moses's plans* helped develop the streets and highways of New York City.

   Correct: <u>Known as the "master-builder,"</u> *Robert Moses* created plans that helped develop the streets and highways of New York City.

   Notice the difference between *Robert Moses's plans* and *Robert Moses*. A master builder is a person, not the person's plans.

2. **(F)** Rule number 4. *Although most people are indifferent to the drab, gray New York pigeon* is a subordinate clause. Therefore, a comma is necessary to separate it from the following independent clause.

3. **(B)**

   Sentence 1 contains a modifier and an independent clause. This is not a run-on.

Before the invention of the Internet,	people in New York City used to do a lot of different things to keep themselves entertained.
Modifier	Independent Clause

   Sentence 2 contains two independent clauses. This is a run-on.

One of them was playing sports,	games like stickball or handball were summer favorites.
Independent Clause	Independent Clause

   Correction: One of them was playing sports, **and** games like stickball or handball were summer favorites.

   Sentence 3 contains a dependent clause, an independent clause, and a dependent clause.

If physical activity wasn't your thing,	you could go to an underground arcade,	where kids would insert quarters into a giant machine to play video games.
Dependent Clause	Independent Clause	Dependent Clause

   Sentence 4 contains a dependent clause, an independent clause, and an dependent clause.

Whatever you did,	you could be sure	that you would be with real human beings.
Dependent Clause	Independent Clause	Dependent Clause

4. **(F)** Examine the pairings of <u>antecedents</u> and **pronouns** below.

(1) <u>The British Empire</u> was known for **its** powerful influence all over the globe. (2) This power was maintained by a formidable <u>navy</u>, which kept a rule to maintain a number of ships that were equal to the combined ships of **their** two largest naval rivals. (3) This rule became untenable once the <u>United States</u> matured because **its** industrial capacity outpaced that of Britain. (4) Nonetheless, <u>the British Empire</u> continued to thrive due largely in part to **its** successful economic strength.

Sentence 1: The correct antecedent to the singular pronoun **its** is <u>The British Empire</u>.

Sentence 2: The plural pronoun **their** is an inappropriate replacement for the singular antecedent <u>navy</u>. **Their** should be revised to **its**.

Sentence 3: The correct antecedent to the singular pronoun **its** is <u>United States</u>.

Sentence 4: The correct antecedent to the singular pronoun **its** is <u>The British Empire</u>.

5. **(C)** Examine the subject-noun and predicate-verb pairings for each sentence. The incorrect pairing is *italicized*. Sentence 4 contains two subject-noun/predicate verb pairings that are separated by the word *that*.

(1) Several <u>members</u> ~~of the committee~~ <u>believe</u> that the school made a mistake. (2) In a recent meeting, <u>parents</u> ~~of sixth, seventh, and eighth graders~~ <u>plan</u> to speak about the problem. (3) *Some* ~~of the biggest issues~~ *is* nutrition, homework, and the graduation venue. (4) <u>Parents</u> <u>believe</u> that <u>addressing</u> all these issues <u>is</u> critical to running a successful year.

6. **(H)** Examine all the predicate verbs underlined below.

(1) Coffee beans <u>are</u> not really beans in the truest sense. (2) They <u>are</u>, in fact, seeds from the fruit of a coffee tree, which <u>may</u> produce for as long as 50 to 60 years. (3) The oldest and most popular method of processing coffee beans <u>is</u> called the "dry process." (4) In this process, the drying operation <u>is</u> the most important stage that <u>affected</u> the final quality of the coffee.

The paragraph is written in the present tense, and the predicate verb that doesn't agree is the past tense verb *affected*.

7. **(A)** The purpose of this essay is to inform the audience of the errors we make with food. The phrase *these errors* in choice A connects to the phrase *several errors* in sentence 1 and introduces the three errors in food economy that science has identified.

Choice B introduces the idea that mankind can become a more responsible steward, which is not supported by the passage.

Choice C is implied, but it is not the main claim.

Choice D deals with food, but man's powers over food sources are not discussed anywhere in the passage.

8. **(F)** Choice F explains why people purchase expensive food needlessly, and it connects with the phrase *a mistaken assumption* in sentence 6.

Choice E discusses access to food, not price.

Choice G is an example of a particular diet. Sentence 6 does not introduce any particular type of diet.

Choice H focuses on the labelling of foods and makes no connection to the previous sentences.

9. **(C)** Sentence 8 adds more information to the claim in sentence 7.

10. **(H)** Sentence 8 discusses the tendency to consume too much of a food. Sentence 9 has examples of the food mentioned in sentence 8. Therefore, sentence 11 would best fit after sentence 9 to show contrast. The phrase *These proteins* in sentence 10 connects with the phrase *lean meat, fish, and beans* in sentence 11.

11. **(C)** The phrase *use needless quantities of food* aligns with the style and vocabulary. The other answer choices are too informal.

12. **(H)** Sentence 17 introduces the problem of a person's overall budget.

13. **(B)** Overall, this choice addresses the main claim, which is that science can help fix errors in food economy. The phrase *that demand* best connects with the phrase *economic demands* in sentence 18.

    Choice A introduces another problem rather than concluding the main idea.

    Choice C is too general as it advocates the conservation of resources rather than food.

    Choice D proposes a skeptical attitude about American behavior, which is not discussed at all in the passage.

PRACTICE SET 3

Revising/Editing Part A

> **Directions:** Read and answer each of the following questions. You will be asked to recognize and correct errors in sentences or short paragraphs. Mark the best answer for each question.

1. Read this paragraph.

> (1) The public, enamored with the rising popularity of intellectuals, often views scientists as logical and infallible beings. (2) While logic and precision are important a strong intuition, as well as perseverance, are just as important. (3) A scientist's work, either in the lab or out in the field, requires more than just brains. (4) There are many other things that contribute to a successful intellectual.

How should the paragraph be revised?

(A) Sentence 1: Delete comma after **public**, AND change **views** to **view**.
(B) Sentence 2: Insert comma after **important**, AND change **are** to **is**.
(C) Sentence 3: Delete comma after **field**, AND change **requires** to **required**.
(D) Sentence 4: Insert comma after **successful**, AND change **contribute** to **contributed**.

2. Read this sentence.

> Streaking across the sky the Bobo meteor is one of the most amazing cosmic objects to grace the majestic night sky.

Which edit should be made to correct this sentence?

(E) Add a comma after **across**.
(F) Add a comma after **sky**.
(G) Add a comma after **amazing**.
(H) Add a comma after **majestic**.

3. Read this sentence.

> In the 17th and 18th century, Americans encouraged a relatively, lax immigration policy into the "land of the free," but the economic decline of the 1880s soon led to the introduction of the first law, the Chinese Exclusion Act, that limited free immigration.

Which edit should be made to correct this sentence?

(A) Delete the comma after **relatively**.
(B) Delete the comma after **free**.
(C) Delete the comma after **law**.
(D) Delete the comma after **Act**.

4. Read this paragraph.

> (1) Prior to the rise of the cell phone, people kept in touch through a gadget called the beeper. (2) Invariably rectangular in shape, black in color, and plastic in cover, the beeper would beep and vibrate, as a phone number blinked on a tiny grey screen illuminated by a green light. (3) Soon enough, cell phones gain popularity and the prices drop so that people began to abandon beepers for phones. (4) One of the leading manufacturers of beepers decided to ride the wave of the cell phone and reshaped itself as a cell phone manufacturer.

Which sentence contains an error in construction and should be revised?

(E) sentence 1

(F) sentence 2

(G) sentence 3

(H) sentence 4

5. Read this paragraph.

> (1) It is difficult to attribute one defining factor that contributed to China's rise for analysts. (2) However, China's entrance into the WTO (World Trade Organization) in 2000 coincided with an exponential increase in the country's economic output. (3) Each year, China's economy grew by more than 10 percent. (4) Today, the growth has subsided to 6 percent, but that number is still higher than America's, which currently stands at about 2 percent.

Which sentence contains an error in construction and should be revised?

(A) sentence 1

(B) sentence 2

(C) sentence 3

(D) sentence 4

6. Read these sentences.

> (1) The colonization of Mars is a daunting task that presents numerous challenges.
> (2) Many people are enthused by the idea of a one-way trip.

What is the best way to combine these sentences to clarify the relationship between the ideas?

(E) The colonization of Mars is a daunting task that presents numerous challenges for many people, enthused by the idea of a one-way trip.

(F) The colonization of Mars is a daunting task that presents numerous challenges because many people are enthused by the idea of a one-way trip.

(G) When many people are enthused by the idea of a one-way trip, the colonization of Mars is a daunting task that presents numerous challenges.

(H) Although the colonization of Mars is a daunting task that presents numerous challenges, many people are enthused by the idea of a one-way trip.

Revising/Editing Part B

> **Directions:** Read the passage below and answer the questions following it. You will be asked to improve the writing quality of the passage and to correct errors so that the passage follows the conventions of standard written English. You may reread the passage if you need to. Mark the best answer for each question.

The Harmful Effects of Acid Rain

(1) An ecosystem is a society of plants, animals, and other organisms, along with the environment. (2) Everything in an ecosystem is connected.

(3) The profound effects of acid rain are most clearly seen in aquatic environs, such as lakes, streams, and marshes, where it can be detrimental to wildlife. (4) As it flows through the soil, acidic rainwater can be harmful to the environment. (5) The more acid that is introduced to the wild, the more aluminum is released.

(6) Some types of flora and fauna are able to withstand acidic waters and moderate amounts of aluminum. (7) Others are highly sensitive and will be lost as the acidity declines. (8) Generally, the young offspring of most organisms are more sensitive to surrounding conditions than adults. (9) For instance, most fish eggs cannot hatch at a pH level of 5, while at lower pH levels, some adult fish die. (10) Even if a fish or animal can endure moderately acidic water, the animals or plants it eats might not. (11) For example, frogs can survive in an environmental pH of 4, but the mayflies they eat may not survive pH below 5.

(12) Decaying trees are a common sight in areas affected by acid pollution. (13) Acid rain leaches aluminum from the soil. (14) That aluminum can be used in the manufacturing process through new techniques that have made the United States a leader in aluminum production. (15) Acid rain also removes important nutrients from the soil. (16) Without the chlorophyll-rich covering, the trees are then less able to absorb sunlight, which makes them weak and less able to withstand freezing temperatures. (17) At high elevations, acidic fog and clouds might strip nutrients from trees' foliage, leaving them with a cover of brown or dead leaves and needles.

(18) For humans, exposure to acid rain, or even swimming in a lake affected by acid rain, is no more dangerous than walking in normal rain or swimming in non-acidic lakes. (19) However, when the acid rain evaporates into the atmosphere, it can be harmful to humans.

7. Which sentence can best follow and support sentence 2?

   (A) If something harms one part of an ecosystem—one species of plant or animal, the soil or the water—it can have an impact on everything else.
   (B) Likewise, humans create connections primarily through technology, such as telephones and the Internet.
   (C) The government currently manages 58 national parks around the country, each with its own unique needs.
   (D) The consequences of overdevelopment and pollution are apparently manageable precisely because of the redundancies built into these interconnections.

8. Which revision of sentence 4 uses the most precise language?

   (E) As it flows through the soil, acidic rainwater can absorb harmful stuff from the soil and then flow into other bodies of water.

   (F) As it flows through the soil, acidic rainwater can absorb harmful elements from the earth and then flow into streams and lakes.

   (G) As it flows through the soil, acidic rainwater can absorb contaminants from soil clay particles and then flow into other bodies of water.

   (H) As it flows through the soil, acidic rainwater can absorb contaminants from soil clay particles and then flow into streams and lakes.

9. Which transition word or phrase should be added to the beginning of sentence 6?

   (A) As a result,
   (B) However,
   (C) Unfortunately,
   (D) In other words,

10. What is the best way to combine sentences 12 and 13 to clarify the relationship between ideas?

    (E) Dead or dying trees are a common sight in areas affected by acid rain, and acid rain leaches aluminum from the soil.

    (F) Dead or dying trees are a common sight in areas affected by acid rain, which leaches aluminum from the soil.

    (G) Although dead or dying trees are a common sight in areas affected by acid rain, it leaches aluminum from the soil.

    (H) Whereas dead or dying trees are a common sight in areas affected by acid rain, acid rain leaches aluminum from the soil.

11. Which sentence is irrelevant to the argument presented in the passage and should be deleted?

    (A) sentence 2
    (B) sentence 6
    (C) sentence 10
    (D) sentence 14

12. Where should sentence 17 be moved to improve the organization of the fourth paragraph (sentences 12–17)?

    (E) to the beginning of the paragraph (before sentence 12)
    (F) between sentences 13 and 14
    (G) between sentences 14 and 15
    (H) between sentences 15 and 16

13. Which sentence could best follow sentence 19 and support the main point of the fourth paragraph?

(A) This affects our enjoyment of national parks, which we visit for the scenic views, such as Shenandoah and the Great Smoky Mountains.

(B) Acid rain also contains nitrogen, and this can have an impact on some ecosystems.

(C) Many scientific studies have shown a relationship between these particles and effects on heart function, such as heart attacks, and effects on lung function, such as breathing difficulties for people with asthma.

(D) In areas such as mountainous parts of the Northeast United States, the soil is thin and lacks the ability to adequately neutralize the acid in the rainwater.

Practice Set 3: Answer Explanations

1. **(B)** Examine the subject-noun and predicate-verb pairings for each sentence. The incorrect pairing is *italicized*.

   (1) The <u>public</u>, ~~enamored with the rising popularity of intellectuals, often~~ <u>views</u> scientists as logical and infallible beings. (2) While <u>logic and precision</u> <u>are</u> important, a strong *intuition*, as well as perseverance, *<u>are</u>* just as important. (3) A scientist's <u>work</u>, either in the lab or out in the field, <u>requires</u> more than just brains. (4) There <u>are</u> many other <u>things</u> that contribute to a successful scientific intellectual.

2. **(F)** *Streaking across the sky* modifies *Bobo meteor*, so a comma is appropriate. Choice E is wrong because it creates an odd subject *the sky the Bobo*. Choices G and H are wrong because the two adjectives modifying the nouns *object* and *sky* are not coordinate adjectives.

3. **(A)** A comma is unnecessary between an adverb (a word that adds information to adjectives or verbs) and an adjective. Choice B is wrong because a comma is necessary in between two clauses. Choice C and D are wrong because *the Chinese Exclusion Act* is a nonrestrictive modifier.

4. **(G)** Examine all the predicate verbs underlined below, with the incorrect tenses set in *italics*.

   (1) Prior to the rise of the cell phone, people <u>kept</u> in touch through a gadget called the beeper. (2) Invariably rectangular in shape, black in color, and plastic in cover, the beeper <u>would</u> beep and vibrate, as a phone number <u>blinked</u> on a tiny grey screen illuminated by a green light. (3) Soon enough, cell phones *<u>gain</u>* popularity and the prices *<u>drop</u>* so that people <u>began</u> to abandon beepers for phones. (4) One of the leading manufacturers of beepers <u>decided</u> to ride the wave of the cell phone and <u>reshaped</u> itself as a cell phone manufacturer.

5. **(A)** Examine the pairings of <u>modifiers</u> and *modified adjectives* below.

   Incorrect: It is *difficult* to attribute one defining factor that contributed to China's rise <u>for analysts</u>.

   Correct: It is *difficult* <u>for analysts</u> to attribute one defining factor that contributed to China's rise.

6. **(H)**

   (E) The colonization of Mars is a daunting task that presents numerous challenges for many people, enthused by the idea of a one-way trip.
   This sentence creates an illogical relationship between *colonization of Mars* and *many people*. The colonization presents numerous challenges in the general sense, but the sentence suggests that it presents challenges for people who are excited about the idea.

   (F) The colonization of Mars is a daunting task that presents numerous challenges because many people are enthused by the idea of a one-way trip.
   This sentence creates an illogical causal relationship between the clauses. The enthusiasm of many people should not cause the colonization to be a daunting task.

   (G) When many people are enthused by the idea of a one-way trip, the colonization of Mars is a daunting task that presents numerous challenges.
   This sentence creates an illogical causal relationship between the clauses. The enthusiasm of many people should not occur when the colonization is a daunting task.

   (H) Although the colonization of Mars is a daunting task that presents numerous challenges, many people are enthused by the idea of a one-way trip.
   This sentence creates a proper contrast through the word *Although*.

7. **(A)** This answer choice more fully explains what it means for an ecosystem to be connected. Choice B brings up humans and technology, which is not addressed anywhere in the passage. Choice C provides irrelevant details. Choice D introduces ideas that are not discussed in the passage.

8. **(H)**

Least Precise (cross out)	Most Precise
harmful stuff	contaminants
soil	soil clay particles
other bodies of water	streams and lakes

9. **(B)** Sentence 5 presents one scenario. Sentence 6 presents a contrasting scenario.

10. **(F)** Choice E is grammatically correct, but choice F is more succinct. Choices G and H use transitions words to create an unnecessary contrast.

11. **(D)** The information about the United States leading the aluminum manufacturing industry is irrelevant.

12. **(H)** The key phrase in sentence 16 is *Without the chlorophyll-rich covering*. This phrase should appear after the phrase *a cover of brown or dead leaves* in sentence 17.

13. **(C)** Choice C provides more information on the ways that acid rain can be harmful for humans.

Reading Comprehension 7

GENERAL READING STRATEGY FOR LITERATURE AND NONFICTION

Remember that this is a timed test. You do not have the luxury to spend as much time as you need to think about, for example, the importance of stripes in zebra thermoregulation. Instead, you need to get an idea of what the passage is about in the shortest amount of time so you can answer the six to ten questions that follow.

Here's a step-by-step strategy to approach the Reading Comprehension section:

1. As you read the first paragraph, ask yourself, "What is the topic of this passage?" The topic should be a word or phrase that best describes the content of the passage.
2. As you continue to read the rest of the passage, ask yourself, "What does the author want to say about the topic?"
3. Underline strange or technical words, names or key ideas, or parts you find difficult to understand. By underlining these words, you create a map so that you can find information quickly when answering questions.
4. If you do not understand one part, don't waste time reading it over and over. You may or may not need it to answer the question. If the question asks you about that part, then use the answer choices to help figure it out.
5. Use the questions as a guide to help you reread the passage.

GENERAL READING STRATEGY FOR POETRY

The biggest difficulty in reading poetry is in the word order and the fact that the poem is broken up into lines. It's a good idea to consider the poem as a paragraph and to read it as if it were a normal sentence. Take a look at the poem on the following page, *I Know My Soul*, by Claude McKay.

I Know My Soul
By Claude McKay

I plucked my soul out of its secret place,

And held it to the mirror of my eye,

To see it like a star against the sky,

A twitching body quivering in space,

A spark of passion shining on my face.

And I explored it to determine why

This awful key to my infinity

Conspires to rob me of sweet joy and grace.

And if the sign may not be fully read,

If I can comprehend but not control,

I need not gloom my days with futile dread,

Because I see a part and not the whole.

Contemplating the strange, I'm comforted

By this narcotic thought: I know my soul.

Trying to make sense of the poem, line by line, is a difficult task. Instead, try reading the poem from the beginning of a sentence to the period, as if it were a regular paragraph. Then you might have a better idea of the poem's main idea. Take a look at the same poem in paragraph form:

I plucked my soul out of its secret place, and held it to the mirror of my eye, to see it like a star against the sky, a twitching body quivering in space, a spark of passion shining on my face. And I explored it to determine why this awful key to my infinity conspires to rob me of sweet joy and grace. And if the sign may not be fully read, if I can comprehend but not control, I need not gloom my days with futile dread, because I see a part and not the whole. Contemplating the strange, I'm comforted by this narcotic thought: I know my soul.

Notice in the first sentence, the speaker tells you that he examined his soul. The second sentence discusses a problem with the soul. The third is a bit more complicated, but it suggests that the speaker's concerns may be unnecessary (*I need not gloom . . .*). Finally, the speaker ends with the claim that he is comforted by the thought that he knows his soul.

Paraphrasing the four sentences in such a manner may help you understand the poem enough to answer the questions.

TYPES OF QUESTIONS

The types of questions in the reading comprehension section can be divided into three categories:

1. **Global Questions:** These questions ask you about the main idea or the primary purpose of a passage. Sometimes your answer isn't necessarily the best choice, but it's the least wrong option.
2. **Evidence-based Questions:** These are questions that ask you about the details in the passage. Your answer will be based off the text. Nothing more and nothing less.
3. **Structure Questions:** These questions ask you about the tone or the structure of the passage. They deal less with the actual information in the passage and more with the effect or the function of a given part of the passage.

Approaches to Questions: Process of Elimination

Eliminating answer choices is an important strategy. Before you look for the right answer, always look to eliminate at least TWO answer choices. Remember, the answers are designed to confuse you, so you need to look for a word or a phrase that misinterprets the passage. Once you've eliminated one or two answer choices, it will be easier to compare the correct answer choice to the appropriate section of the passage.

Global Questions

Global questions ask you about the passage as a whole. They begin with stems like *The primary purpose*, *The central idea*, and *The author would most likely agree*. Unless you know exactly what the entire passage is about, answer these questions last. Once you've wrestled with the details and structure questions, you might have a better understanding of the text. Even if you understand the passage, you might not see your ideas reflected in the answer choices.

For global questions, your best strategy is to use the process of elimination *first*. Read all of the answer choices and eliminate the worst one. You can always eliminate at least one answer choice. Then, look at the remaining three and eliminate one more. Finally, compare the remaining answer choices, and determine the final answer by selecting the choice that best describes the passage.

Evidence-based Questions

In a typical English language arts class, you are asked to explore ideas, come up with possible interpretations, or connect different elements from your personal life, as well as background knowledge, to your reading experience. In this way, reading becomes a rich tapestry that can be both personal and profound.

Well, on the SHSAT, you need to forget all that. The test is designed to be objective with very little room for interpretation or subjectivity. It isn't designed to reward "creative" or "smart" answers, but rather the opposite. The answers are unimaginative and as close as possible to specific line references from the passage.

Sounds simple enough right? Wrong. There is only one correct answer, but the test-makers will come up with one or two incorrect answer choices that look very much like the right answer. These are called *distractors*. They're designed to distract you from the right answer. Test-makers will also replace the line reference from the text with similar words so that it will be difficult to distinguish distractors from correct answer choices.

The faster you realize how these questions are constructed, the faster you will learn how to excel on the SHSAT—and on all reading comprehension passages.

Here's an example of how questions are created. First, the test-maker will select a line from the text:

> Cosmic radiation comes from extremely energetic particles from the sun and stars that enter Earth's atmosphere. Some particles make it to the ground, while others interact with the atmosphere to create different types of radiation. Radiation levels increase as you get closer to the source, so the amount of cosmic radiation generally increases with elevation. **The higher the altitude, the higher the dose. That is why those living in Denver, Colorado, receive a higher annual radiation dose from cosmic radiation than someone living at sea level.**

Second, the test-maker will create a question stem and the correct answer. You'll notice that in the bolded lines, the text states that the higher the altitude the higher the dose of radiation. Therefore, Denver must have higher elevation, since it receives *a higher annual radiation dose*.

> (Question Stem) The higher annual radiation in Denver is caused by
> (Correct Answer) (D) higher altitudes.

Then the test-maker will include three distractors that sound very much like the answer choice but change the meaning of the text.

> The higher annual radiation in Denver is caused by
>
> (A) energetic particles coming from Earth's atmosphere.
> (B) radiation levels that increase as you get closer to sea level.
> (C) particles that are closer to the ground.

You'll notice that all of these answers borrow from some part of the passage. That's what makes the wrong answers confusing. For instance, choice A uses the following lines to confuse you:

> Cosmic radiation comes from extremely **energetic particles from** the sun and stars that enter **Earth's atmosphere**. Some particles make it to the ground, while others interact with the atmosphere to create different types of radiation. Radiation levels increase as you get closer to the source, so the amount of cosmic radiation generally increases with elevation.

If you look closely, the energetic particles do not come from Earth's atmosphere, but from suns and stars.

Let's look at choice B, which borrows the words from the following line:

> **Radiation levels increase as you get closer to the source**, so the amount of cosmic radiation generally increases with elevation.

This is wrong because it replaces *the source* with *sea level*. The source is the higher altitude, not sea level.

Finally, look at choice C:

> Some **particles make it to the ground**, while others interact with the atmosphere to create different types of radiation. Radiation levels increase as you get closer to the source, so the amount of cosmic radiation generally increases with elevation.

Choice C seems right based on the first part of the text, but it is important to note that the end of the second sentence suggests the opposite.

Here's another type of evidence-based question you will encounter:

Life on Earth is protected from the full impact of solar and cosmic radiation by the magnetic fields that surround the Earth and by the Earth's atmosphere. The Earth also has radiation belts caused by its magnetic field. The inner radiation belt, or Van Allen Belt, consists of ionizing radiation in the form of very energetic protons—by-products of collisions between galactic cosmic radiation (GCR) and atoms of Earth's atmosphere. The outer radiation belts contain protons and electrons. As we travel farther from Earth's protective shields, we are exposed to the full radiation spectrum and its damaging effects.

Which sentence best shows that maintaining a strong magnetic field is important to life on Earth?

(A) "Life on Earth is protected from the full impact of solar and cosmic radiation by the magnetic fields that surround the Earth and by the Earth's atmosphere."
(B) "The Earth also has radiation belts caused by its magnetic field."
(C) "The inner radiation belt, or Van Allen Belt, consists of ionizing radiation in the form of very energetic protons—by-products of collisions between galactic cosmic radiation (GCR) and atoms of Earth's atmosphere."
(D) "The outer radiation belts contain protons and electrons."

Again, the approach is the same. The SHSAT will create its answer choice first and throw in close distractors. Remember to eliminate them and to make sure that the selected line closely fits the idea in the question stem. This question is asking you to find the line that says *maintaining a strong magnetic field is important to life on Earth.* The best answer choice is A.

The key to answering reading comprehension questions is to locate the text where the answers are formed and then to eliminate the distractors. Even words like *infer, imply,* or *suggest* may be included to distract you. Stay focused on the text!

Structural Questions

Structural questions are partially about the information in the passage and partially about the function or the effect of a section in the passage. With these questions, it is important to look at the answer choices. If the answer choices contain specific, detailed phrases with direct references to ideas in the passage, then you can use the strategy from evidence-based questions. If, however, the answer choices are not very specific and make very little reference to the passage, you will need to find the function. To find the function, it is important that you identify an answer choice that explains what the given sentence is *doing* and not what it is saying. To figure out what it is *doing,* look for a specific key verb phrase. Here is an example of a structural question.

1. Read the following sentence:

   While some hail genetically modified organisms (GMOs) as a scientific revolution for food production, others see them as potentially harmful for humans and the environment.

   Which statement best describes how the sentence fits into the overall structure of the excerpt?

   (A) It **explains the importance** of GMOs.
   (B) It **emphasizes the problem** of GMOs.
   (C) It **illustrates the various attitudes** toward GMOs.
   (D) It **describes the suffering** caused by GMOs.

In this answer choice set, the question is not specific to the details related to the GMOs. The question here tests your understanding of the arrangement of ideas. In these types of structural questions, it is less about the actual information and more about the arrangement of it. To figure out these structural-function questions, use the following steps:

1. Go back to the passage, and read the sentences that come before and after the sentence in the question.
2. Examine the key verbs in the answer choices that describe the function.
3. Eliminate two wrong choices.
4. Compare the remaining two choices that best describe the function or impact of the text.

Let's try one question.

In the summer of last year, major protests erupted in Haiti as the government announced a sharp increase in fuel price; they were forced to do so by an agreement with the International Monetary Fund that ended costly subsidies for petroleum products. After the suspension of the price hike and the prime minister's reluctant resignation, the country has returned to an uneasy calm, as if everyone was waiting for the next match that lights the fuse. For some Americans, these events have confirmed their view of Haiti as a country engaged in a permanent struggle for survival. However, some have pointed out that every bit of the Haitian struggle is related to the legacy of slavery and capitalism, a legacy in which the United States and its banks are deeply complicit. What happened in Haiti never stayed in Haiti. As this island paradise continues to suffer from foreign exploitation, it is worth confronting the continuing cultural and moral debt we owe to Haiti.

1. Read the following sentence.

   However, some have pointed out that every bit of the Haitian struggle is related to the legacy of slavery and capitalism, a legacy in which the United States and its banks are deeply complicit.

Which statement best describes how the sentence fits into the overall structure of the paragraph?

   (A) It recommends an approach about handling the situation in Haiti.
   (B) It indicates a continuation of beliefs that the author believes is problematic.
   (C) It highlights a shift in the way ideas about Haiti have been changing as a result of the United States.
   (D) It introduces a contrast between one point of view and another point of view.

First, read the preceding sentence and the sentence that follows. You will notice that the preceding sentence describes a particular point of view. The word *However* is a key word that tells you that the sentence stands in contrast to the preceding sentence. The sentence that follows further elaborates that idea.

   Second, identify the verb phrase stems in the answer choices.

   (A) It **recommends an approach** about handling the situation in Haiti.
   (B) It **indicates a continuation** of beliefs that the author believes is problematic.
   (C) It **highlights a shift** in the way ideas about Haiti have been changing as a result of the United States.
   (D) It **introduces a contrast** between one point of view and another point of view.

Here, choice A is incorrect because the author does not recommend an approach. Rather, he presents two different ideas, so eliminate choice A.

Next, examine the second half of the answer choices.

(B) It indicates a continuation of **beliefs that the author believes is problematic**.

(C) It highlights a shift **in the way ideas about Haiti have been changing as a result of the United States**.

(D) It introduces a contrast **between one point of view and another point of view**.

You should be able to eliminate choice B. The author does not make any explicit judgement about the ideas surrounding Haiti.

Finally, compare the two remaining answer choices. Both choices seem to say the same thing. (Remember: One is a close distractor!) However, choice C claims that the United States is changing the views. While this answer choice uses *United States* from the original text, it distorts the idea. Choice D is the best fit because the preceding sentence provides one explanation about the situation in Haiti, while the bolded sentence presents a different or *contrasting* point of view.

Reading Comprehension Exercises

8

Directions: Read each of the following passages, and answer the related questions. You may write in your test booklet as needed to take notes. You should reread relevant parts of each text before marking the best answer for each question. Base your answers only on the content within the text.

Long before the traditions of Valentine's Day sprang forth, spymasters worldwide used the art of love to obtain secrets from their enemies. Spymasters, similar to spies in many movies, ensnarled their adversaries in a game of love, allure, and lies. One of the best-known spies was Mata Hari, a Dutch agent convicted of spying for the Germans during World War I. She was accused of obtaining her intelligence by tricking prominent French politicians and officers.

1. Which of the following best describes the main goal of spymasters?

   (A) to hire Mata Hari
   (B) to trick their government employees
   (C) to adhere to the traditions of Valentine's Day
   (D) to collect information about their enemies

Questions 2–3

The Earth's atmosphere is composed of several layers. The lowest layer, the troposphere, extends from the Earth's surface up to about 6 miles or 10 kilometers (km) in altitude. This region of the atmosphere is closest to the Earth. Virtually all human activities occur in the troposphere. Mt. Everest, the tallest mountain on the planet, is only about 5.6 miles (9 km) high. The next layer right above the troposphere is the stratosphere, which continues from 6 miles (10 km) to about 31 miles (50 km). Most commercial airplanes fly in the lower part of the stratosphere, and the temperature increases at higher altitudes.

2. Which of the following is implied by the statement "Virtually all human activities occur in the troposphere"?

   (E) Understanding the troposphere helps us understand all human activities.
   (F) Human activities are destroying the environment.
   (G) Most human activities do not take place in the stratosphere.
   (H) Pollution contributes to the warming of the ozone layer.

3. What is the primary purpose of this passage?

   (A) to inform the reader of a growing problem in the atmosphere
   (B) to persuade the reader to take action on a continuing problem
   (C) to describe the components of the planet's atmosphere
   (D) to explain the role of humans in the atmosphere

Questions 4–5

Increasing time between meals made male mice healthier overall, and they lived longer compared to mice who ate more frequently. This showed that health and longevity improved with increased fasting time, regardless of what the mice ate or how many calories they consumed. Scientists randomly divided 300 mice into two diet groups. One group received a diet of higher fat and sugars, while the other did not. Then these two groups were divided into three subgroups. The first subgroup of mice always had access to food. A second subgroup of mice was fed 40 percent less calories per day than the first group. The third subgroup was meal fed, getting a single meal that added up to the exact number of calories as the first subgroup. The findings showed that out of all three subgroups, the calorie-restricted group showed the largest improvement in overall health.

4. Which sentence best shows the primary purpose of this paragraph?

   (E) "Scientists randomly divided 300 mice into two diet groups."
   (F) "The first subgroup of mice always had access to food."
   (G) "The second subgroup of mice was fed 40 percent less calories per day than the first group."
   (H) "The findings showed that out of all three subgroups, the calorie-restricted group showed the largest improvement in overall health."

5. Which claim is best supported by the information presented in the paragraph?

   (A) People have a better chance of living longer if they eat like mice.
   (B) A diet of higher fat and sugars can contribute to a healthier life.
   (C) The third subgroup was fed more calories than the second group.
   (D) Too much sugar and calories can lead to weight gain.

Questions 6–7

The Coso Rock Art District, a National Historic Landmark deep in the U.S. Navy's testing station at China Lake, serves as a home to one of America's most important petroglyphic and archeological complexes. The 20,000 images already preserved exceed in number almost all other collections, and the archeological resources remain untouched by human contact. Coso rock art has been acknowledged for its importance because of its stylized representational symbolic arrangements, a system that has interested, as well as confused, both experts and amateurs for some time. Recent research at this site has begun to reveal the ancient history of the people here and the ideas and concepts they recorded into the stone. Its status as a rare source of information of the past also highlights the value of the remains of America's endangered cultural history.

6. The Coso Rock Art District is particularly significant because it

   (E) hosts a U.S. Navy facility.
   (F) contains a number of archeological remains.
   (G) records the history of endangered wildlife.
   (H) has images inscribed in stone.

7. Which conclusion is best supported by the paragraph?

(A) Knowledge of the people from the Coso Rock Art District remains incomplete.
(B) The U.S. Navy's testing station is involved in the preservation of the archaeological resources.
(C) Coso rock art has been disturbed by the U.S. Navy.
(D) The Coso Rock Art District is the most important petroglyphic complex in America.

Questions 8–10

While scientific research on insight has existed for some time, powerful tools of neuroscience have only recently been applied to this phenomenon. Tools such as the electroencephalogram (EEG) and functional magnetic resonance imaging (fMRI) have been used to explore the neural mechanisms that underlie creative insights. Examining how insight emerges in the brain is difficult, but scientists developed a way to study insight in the lab. Volunteers were asked to solve dozens of word puzzles while their brains were scanned with EEG or fMRI. One such puzzle was an anagram. In an anagram, a rearrangement of a given set of letters forms a new word: ENLIST = SILENT is an anagram. When the volunteers became aware of the solution to the puzzle, they reported whether the answer came in a flash of insight or through a more deliberate strategy. For puzzles that were solved with insight, the researchers observed a unique pattern of neural activity.

8. Which sentence from the passage best shows how technology is important to the study of human insight?

(E) "Tools such as the electroencephalogram (EEG) and functional magnetic resonance imaging (fMRI) have been used to explore the neural mechanisms that underlie creative insights."
(F) "Volunteers were asked to solve dozens of word puzzles while their brains were scanned with EEG or fMRI."
(G) "When the volunteers became aware of the solution to the puzzle, they reported whether the answer came in a flash of insight or through a more deliberate strategy."
(H) "For puzzles that were solved with insight, the researchers observed a unique pattern of neural activity."

9. What did the study of anagrams reveal?

(A) The EEG does a better job of recording activities in the brain than the fMRI.
(B) The results revealed an important distinction between insight and strategy.
(C) Only anagrams can detect a unique pattern of neural activity.
(D) They revealed that the science of exploring insight in the brain is difficult.

10. Based on the passage, what is the most likely reason that scientists can now study insight?

(E) Scientists could not define insight.
(F) The appropriate technology did not exist before this time.
(G) Volunteers in their research study did not produce the right kinds of answers to the anagrams.
(H) Scientific results from past studies were deliberately misleading.

Questions 11–14

A tall, well-favored youth, coming from the farther South, boarded the train for Richmond one raw, gusty morning. He carried his left arm stiffly, his face was thin and brown, and his dingy uniform had holes in it, some made by bullets; but his air and manner were happy, as if, escaped from danger and hardships, he rode on his way to pleasure and ease. He sat for a time gazing out of the window at the gray, wintry landscape that fled past, and then, having a youthful zest for new things, looked at those who traveled with him in the car. The company seemed to him, on the whole, to lack novelty and interest, being composed of farmers going to the capital of the Confederacy to sell food; wounded soldiers like himself, bound for the same place in search of cure; and one woman who sat in a corner alone, neither speaking nor spoken to, her whole aspect repelling any rash advance.

11. In the paragraph, how do the words "gusty," "stiffly," and "dingy" contribute to the overall meaning of the excerpt?

   (A) They emphasize the main character's resigned attitude about his position in life.
   (B) They illustrate the difficulties of living in an urban environment.
   (C) They critique the oppressive nature of traveling on public transportation.
   (D) They illustrate the contrast between the physical world and the character's attitude.

12. The phrase "as if, escaped from danger and hardships" in the paragraph shows that the main character

   (E) did not really escape danger and hardships.
   (F) did not really appreciate his good fortune.
   (G) felt that his destination was filled with difficulties.
   (H) enjoyed the fact that he was riding the train.

13. Read this text from the paragraph.

   The company seemed to him, on the whole, to lack novelty and interest, being composed of farmers going to the capital of the Confederacy to sell food; wounded soldiers like himself, bound for the same place in search of cure; and one woman who sat in a corner alone, neither speaking nor spoken to, her whole aspect repelling any rash advance.

   These details convey the central idea of the excerpt by showing that the main character

   (A) is gradually changing to conform to the mood of the people in the train.
   (B) fails to consider the problems that others on the train experience every day.
   (C) possesses key differences from his surroundings.
   (D) poses a dangerous threat to himself and the others around him.

14. Read this sentence from the paragraph.

He sat for a time gazing out of the window at the gray, wintry landscape that fled past, and then, having a youthful zest for new things, looked at those who traveled with him in the car.

Which statement explains how the sentence best fits into the overall structure of the paragraph?

(E) It indicates a change in the main character's behavior toward others.

(F) It highlights a shift in the main character's focus of observation.

(G) It introduces a new argument about the importance of observing others.

(H) It emphasizes the most oppressive aspect of the trip.

Questions 15–16

Father

My father knows the proper way
The nation should be run;
He tells us children every day
Just what should now be done.
Line
(5) He knows the way to fix the trusts,
He has a simple plan;
But if the furnace needs repairs,
We have to hire a man.

My father, in a day or two
(10) Could land big thieves in jail;
There's nothing that he cannot do,
He knows no word like "fail."
"Our confidence" he would restore,
Of that there is no doubt;
(15) But if there is a chair to mend,
We have to send it out.

15. The repetition of the phrase "We have to" in 8 and 16 primarily serves to

(A) emphasize the father's manly competence.

(B) reinforce the importance of meeting obligations.

(C) point out an inconsistency.

(D) illustrate the problems in daily life.

16. Which line from the poem best describes the idea that the children do not believe the father?

(E) "My father knows the proper way" (line 1)

(F) "He knows the way to fix the trusts" (line 5)

(G) "There's nothing that he cannot do" (line 11)

(H) "'Our confidence' he would restore" (line 13)

Bombardment

The town has opened to the sun.
Like a flat red lily with a million petals
She unfolds, she comes undone.
A sharp sky brushes upon

Line
(5) The myriad glittering chimney-tips
As she gently exhales to the sun.

Hurrying creatures run
Down the labyrinth* of the sinister flower.
What is it they shun?**

(10) A dark bird falls from the sun.
It curves in a rush to the heart of the vast
Flower: the day has begun.

*labyrinth: a complex maze
**shun: avoid; keep one's distance from

17. The description in the first stanza (lines 1–3) helps establish the central idea by

(A) suggesting that much work needs to be completed in the town.

(B) comparing the sadness of the lily to the incompleteness of the sun.

(C) proposing a solution to a problem through imagery.

(D) illustrating the setting for the beginning of the day.

18. It can be inferred that the creatures "shun"

(E) "a flat red lily with a million petals" (line 2)

(F) "Hurrying creatures" (line 7)

(G) "A dark bird" (line 10)

(H) "the day" (line 12)

Questions 19–23

The following passage has been adapted from Bernd Brunner's essay *Human Forms in Nature: Ernst Haekel's Trip to South Asia and Its Aftermath*. It appears in *The Public Domain Review*.

1 Ernst Haeckel and his sixteen steamer trunks arrived at the harbor of Colombo "in the glorious light of a cloudless tropical morning" on November 21, 1881, after a four-week journey via Trieste, Suez, Aden, and Bombay. The zoologist had high hopes: during the coming four months in Ceylon—now Sri Lanka—he planned to get to know flora and fauna in "that highest and most marvelous variety of form" which existed on the island. Haeckel's enthusiasm was understandable: he was literally entering the promised land of his naturalist dreams.

2 Admittedly, Ceylon at that time was not defined by dream beaches, a devastating tsunami, or decades of conflict between the country's Sinhalese and the Tamil inhabitants—all topics we commonly associate with Sri Lanka today. In Haeckel's era, the teardrop-shaped island nation off India's southeastern coast embodied the concept of "the tropics." It was a place of

paradisiacal plenty bursting with things that were unfamiliar and often brilliantly colored: animals, plants, fruit, spices, and even gemstones. The realm of riches seemed like a dream world from another time. It was also a land of extremes, where the heat and humidity provided fertile conditions for a host of dangers: little-understood diseases that could quickly turn life-threatening: plagues of insects, predatory animals stalking through the thick vegetation, sharks swimming offshore, and torrential downpours.

3 As he later recalled in his book *A Visit to Ceylon*, Haeckel planned to trade "the restraint of our artificial social life" for an existence "in the midst of the simple children of nature . . . forming some conception of that visionary primeval paradise into which the human race was born." After all, he believed that humanity had originated near Ceylon on the hypothetical continent of "Lemuria" in the Indian Ocean. This conviction certainly influenced his decision to travel to Ceylon—along with the fact that his role models, Alexander von Humboldt and Charles Darwin, never made it to that corner of the world.

4 For Haeckel, at the time forty-seven years old and the most important champion of Darwin's theory of evolution on the European continent, the journey to Ceylon represented the fulfillment of a long-held but initially vague desire that took concrete shape over many years. It's clear that he caught his tropical fever early, and that it intensified over decades. But his journey was also motivated by immediate scientific concerns. In the end, he had a range of reasons for traveling to Ceylon: a longing for adventure he had nourished since childhood, scientific ambition, and artistic ambition as well.

19. Read this sentence from paragraph 1.

The zoologist had high hopes: during the coming four months in Ceylon—now Sri Lanka—he planned to get to know flora and fauna in "that highest and most marvelous variety of form" which existed on the island.

What does the author's comment reveal about Haekel's motivation for his trip?

(A) In light of the grand expectations for the trip, Haekel would ultimately fail to match his expectations.

(B) Due to the variety of life that he planned to encounter, Haekel's expectations would ultimately be challenged.

(C) Haekel eagerly anticipated a trip that promised a wealth of knowledge about life on a land well suited for exploration.

(D) Many zoologists and explorers appreciate the variety of life and will go to extremes to preserve endangered animals.

20. Which sentence best supports the idea that Haekel's Ceylon was markedly different from Ceylon today?

(E) "Haeckel's enthusiasm was understandable: he was literally entering the promised land of his naturalist dreams." (paragraph 1)

(F) "Admittedly, Ceylon at that time was not defined by dream beaches, a devastating tsunami, or decades of conflict between the country's Sinhalese and the Tamil inhabitants . . . " (paragraph 2)

(G) "The realm of riches seemed like a dream world from another time." (paragraph 2)

(H) "It was also a land of extremes, where the heat and humidity provided fertile conditions for a host of dangers . . . " (paragraph 2)

21. Read the following sentence from paragraph 3.

> **After all, he believed that humanity had originated near Ceylon on the hypothetical continent of "Lemuria" in the Indian Ocean.**

How does this sentence fit into the overall structure of the passage?

(A) It proposes a novel theory that influenced others to explore Ceylon.

(B) It presents one of several reasons that factored into Haekel's motivation for the exploration.

(C) It shows Haekel's mistaken belief, which he later revised to more closely conform to the theories of his role models.

(D) It reveals a belief that Haekel used to hypothesize about the original location of the Indian Ocean.

22. In paragraph 4, the phrase "tropical fever" is used to highlight

(E) one of the dangers of traveling to Ceylon.

(F) Haekel's enthusiasm for fulfilling a long-awaited desire.

(G) the recklessness associated with traveling to many different places.

(H) a problem which Haekel hoped to solve through his research.

23. Paragraph 4 contributes to the development of the central idea of the passage by

(A) summarizing the key factors that help explain a motivation.

(B) illustrating the benefits gained from an exploration.

(C) highlighting the character strengths of a remarkable individual.

(D) conveying the importance of role models.

Questions 24–30

The following passage has been adapted from Ned Pennant-Rea's essay *The Dancing Plague of 1518*. It appears in *The Public Domain Review*.

1   On a hastily built stage before the busy horse market of Strasbourg, scores of people dance to pipes, drums, and horns. The July sun beats down upon them as they hop from leg to leg, spin in circles and whoop loudly. From a distance they might be carnival revelers. But closer inspection reveals a more disquieting scene. Their arms are flailing and their bodies are convulsing spasmodically. Ragged clothes and pinched faces are saturated in sweat. Their eyes are glassy, distant. Blood seeps from swollen feet into leather boots and wooden clogs. These are not revelers but "choreomaniacs" entirely possessed by the mania of the dance.

2   In full view of the public, this is the height of the choreomania that tormented Strasbourg for a midsummer month in 1518. Also known as the "dancing plague," it was the most fatal and best documented of the more than ten such contagions which had broken out along the Rhine and Moselle rivers since 1374. Numerous accounts of the bizarre events that unfolded that summer can be found scattered across various contemporary documents and chronicles compiled in the subsequent decades and centuries.

3   The physician and alchemist Paracelsus visited Strasbourg eight years after the plague and became fascinated by its causes. According to his *Opus Paramirum*, and various chronicles agree, it all started with one woman. Frau Troffea had started dancing on July 14th on the

narrow cobbled street outside her half-timbered home. As far as we can tell she had no musical accompaniment but simply "began to dance." Ignoring her husband's pleas to cease, she continued for hours, until the sky turned black and she collapsed in a twitching heap of exhaustion. The next morning she was up again on her swollen feet and dancing before thirst and hunger could register. By the third day, people of a great and growing variety—hawkers, porters, beggars, pilgrims, priests, nuns—were drinking in the ungodly spectacle. The mania possessed Frau Troffea for between four and six days, at which point the frightened authorities intervened by sending her in a wagon thirty miles away to Saverne. But some of those who had witnessed her strange performance had begun to mimic her, and within days more than thirty choreomaniacs were in motion, some so monomaniacally that only death would have the power to intervene.

4   The dancing plague had lasted for over a month, from mid-July to late August or early September. At its height, as many as fifteen people were dying each day. The final toll is unknown but, if such a daily death rate was true, could have been into the hundreds.

24. Read this sentence from paragraph 1.

On a hastily built stage before the busy horse market of Strasbourg, scores of people dance to pipes, drums, and horns. The July sun beats down upon them as they hop from leg to leg, spin in circles and whoop loudly.

The words "hastily," "busy," and "whoop loudly" in the sentence convey a(n)

(E) curious sense of serious religious conviction in a ritual.

(F) foreboding feeling of tension and danger for an unexpected event.

(G) bustling atmosphere of lively activities.

(H) acknowledgement of a possibly violent event.

25. Which excerpt from the passage supports the idea that the dancing plague of 1518 was particularly notable for its effects?

(A) "But closer inspection reveals a more disquieting scene." (paragraph 1)

(B) ". . . it was the most fatal and best documented of the more than ten such contagions . . . " (paragraph 2)

(C) "The mania possessed Frau Troffea for between four and six days, at which point the frightened authorities intervened by sending her in a wagon thirty miles away to Saverne." (paragraph 3)

(D) "The dancing plague had lasted for over a month, from mid-July to late August or early September." (paragraph 4)

26. What is most likely the reason the author mentions the "dancing plague" in paragraph 2?

(E) to suggest that it was the only event of its kind ever documented in history

(F) to contrast this event with the legends surrounding its history

(G) to place it in context with other similar phenomena

(H) to argue for the importance of using history in analyzing unusual events

27. How does paragraph 3 contribute to the passage?

   (A) It presents a number of theories that explain the cause of the event.

   (B) It shows how people of the 1500s participated in social activities.

   (C) It emphasizes the importance of dancing to European cultures.

   (D) It provides a narrative account of the event.

28. The dancing plague was most likely started by

   (E) the busy market.

   (F) the midsummer months of 1518.

   (G) Paracelus.

   (H) Frau Troffea.

29. Which of the following is implied by the phrase "if such a daily death rate was true"? (paragraph 4)

   (A) Less than a hundred people must have died from the plague.

   (B) Daily death rates are usually unreliable.

   (C) The deaths from the dancing plague are in fact untrue.

   (D) The actual number of people affected by the plague remains undetermined.

30. With which statement would the author most likely agree?

   (E) One of the ways to stop dancing was through death.

   (F) Choreomania was the most devastating plague of Europe in the 16th century.

   (G) Paracelsus was an important figure who helped stop the plague.

   (H) Frau Troffea began the dance to aggravate her husband Herr Troffea.

Questions 31–41

Excerpt from "The Cask of Amontillado"

By Edgar Allan Poe

1   He had a weak point—this Fortunato—although in other regards he was a man to be respected and even feared. He prided himself on his connoisseurship in wine. Few Italians have the true virtuoso spirit. For the most part their enthusiasm is adopted to suit the time and opportunity— to practise imposture upon the British and Austrian millionaires. In painting and gemmary, Fortunato, like his countrymen, was a quack—but in the matter of old wines he was sincere. In this respect I did not differ from him materially: I was skillful in the Italian vintages myself, and bought largely whenever I could.

2   It was about dusk, one evening during the supreme madness of the carnival season, that I encountered my friend. He accosted me with excessive warmth, for he had been drinking much. The man wore motley. He had on a tight-fitting parti-striped dress, and his head was surmounted by the conical cap and bells. I was so pleased to see him, that I thought I should never have done wringing his hand.

3   I said to him—"My dear Fortunato, you are luckily met. How remarkably well you are looking to-day! But I have received a pipe of what passes for Amontillado, and I have my doubts."

4   "How?" said he. "Amontillado? A pipe? Impossible! And in the middle of the carnival!"

5   "I have my doubts," I replied; "and I was silly enough to pay the full Amontillado price without consulting you in the matter. You were not to be found, and I was fearful of losing a bargain."

6   "Amontillado!"

7   "I have my doubts."

8   "Amontillado!"

9   "And I must satisfy them."

10   "Amontillado!"

11   "As you are engaged, I am on my way to Luchesi. If any one has a critical turn, it is he. He will tell me—"

12   "Luchesi cannot tell Amontillado from Sherry."

13   "And yet some fools will have it that his taste is a match for your own."

14   "Come, let us go."

15   "Whither?"

16   "To your vaults."

31. What is Fortunato's "weak point" (line 1)?

   (A) fear that he commands over experts
   (B) physical power over his enemies
   (C) pride in his accomplishments
   (D) confidence in his knowledge

32. Which sentence from paragraph 1 best shows that the narrator shares some of Fortunato's qualities?

   (E) "He had a weak point—this Fortunato—although in other regards he was a man to be respected and even feared."
   (F) "For the most part their enthusiasm is adopted to suit the time and opportunity"
   (G) "In painting and gemmary, Fortunato, like his countrymen, was a quack"
   (H) "in the matter of old wines he was sincere."

33. In paragraph 1, the word "skillful" characterizes the narrator as

   (A) clever.
   (B) knowledgeable.
   (C) sneaky.
   (D) agile.

34. Read this sentence from paragraph 2.

   He accosted me with excessive warmth, for he had been drinking much.

   Fortunato's attitude toward the narrator can best be described as

   (E) angry.
   (F) hostile.
   (G) friendly.
   (H) suspicious.

35. Which of the following best describes the "Amontillado"?

   (A) a carnival
   (B) a vault
   (C) a wine
   (D) an enemy

36. In paragraph 4, what does Fortunato's reference to the "carnival" primarily serve to express?

   (E) glee over the narrator's gullibility
   (F) disappointment in the narrator's clothing
   (G) disgust at the narrator's presence
   (H) shock at an unexpected revelation

37. Read this sentence from paragraph 5.

   "I have my doubts," I replied.

   How does this contribute to the development of the plot?

   (A) It is intended to express the narrator's regret over Fortnuato's excessive emotions.
   (B) It is intended to express the narrator's concern over a recent acquisition.
   (C) It is intended to express the narrator's opinions about the carnival.
   (D) It is intended to express the narrator's disgust in Fortunato's choice of clothing.

38. The repetition of the word "Amontillado" serves primarily to

   (E) emphasize Fortunato's surprised disbelief.
   (F) hint at the narrator's embarrassment.
   (G) express the urgency of the issue.
   (H) highlight Fortunato's growing aggravation.

39. In paragraph 12, Fortunato claims that Luchesi

   (A) lacks the ability to help the narrator.
   (B) has little respect for learning.
   (C) appreciates Sherry more than Amontillado.
   (D) is critical of the narrator.

40. In paragraph 13, the narrator claims that the "fools"

   (E) equate Fortunato's abilities with those of Luchesi.
   (F) prefer the taste of Sherry to Amontillado.
   (G) confuse the identity of Fortunato with Luchesi.
   (H) are disgusted with Fortunato.

41. In paragraph 16, the "vaults" belong to

   (A) Fortunato.
   (B) Luchesi.
   (C) the narrator.
   (D) Sherry.

Answer Explanations

1. **(D)** The passage states *spymasters worldwide used the art of love to obtain secrets from their enemies.* This best conforms with answer choice D. Choice B is a close distractor, but the specific detail *government employees* is unsupported.

2. **(G)** If most activities take place in the troposphere, then few activities take place in any other part of the atmosphere. Choice G best states that idea.

3. **(C)** Eliminate choice A because the passage does not describe a growing problem. Eliminate choice B because the author is not trying to persuade you of anything. Eliminate choice D because although humans are mentioned, the paragraph does not explain their activities.

4. **(H)** Choices E, F, and G merely describe different parts of the experiment. Choice H restates the conclusion that calorie restriction improves overall health.

5. **(C)** Be careful here. All of these are true inferences, but none are explicitly stated. Choice A is implied. Obviously, they are testing these mice to see how it can help improve human life, but nowhere is the connection explicitly made. Choice B contradicts the study. Choice D is a widely know truism, but look carefully at the passage. There is nothing that supports that claim. Choice C is the best choice because we know that the second group had 40 percent less calories than the first group AND the third group had the same amount as the first group. Therefore, the third group had more calories (60 percent more) than the second group.

6. **(F)** The key phrase *particularly significant* in the question can be connected to the words *most important* in the passage. The next line indicates that the district has *petroglyphic and archeological complexes*, which matches choice F.

7. **(A)** Eliminate incorrect answer choices B and C. You can also eliminate choice D, as the passage never says that the Coso Rock Art District is the *most important* petroglyphic site. The passage states that researchers have only *begun to reveal the ancient history of the people.* Since they have begun, you can assume that their knowledge is not complete, which matches choice A.

8. **(E)** The other answer choices involve details or results of the study, whereas choice E states how technology is being used to understand human insight.

9. **(B)** The important distinction is found in the passage when it says: *they reported whether the answer came in **a flash of insight** or through **a more deliberate strategy**.*

10. **(F)** The first two sentences suggest that new technology has *only recently* enabled scientists to study the brain and explore *the neural mechanisms.*

11. **(D)** The words describe the setting and the character's clothes in primarily negative terms. In the passage, it says *but his air and manner were happy,* which illustrates contrast.

12. **(H)** Choices E, F, and G all characterize his trip as negative. Choice H restates the idea that he found his trip to be pleasurable.

13. **(C)** Eliminate choice A because there is no indication that his mood is changing. Eliminate choice B. He is observing the passengers, but the text doesn't mention him considering their problems. Eliminate choice D because there is no suggestion of danger. The best answer is choice C because the passage indicates that he had a *youthful zest.* The word *zest*, or passion, contrasts with the somber description of the other passengers.

14. **(F)** Eliminate choice E because there is no description of his behavior, just his thoughts. Eliminate choice G because the purpose is not to persuade anyone about the importance of observation. Eliminate choice H because the words *most oppressive* are extreme and not supported by the passage. The text shows that he shifts his gaze from the window to the passengers, which matches choice F.

15. **(C)** The repetition of the phrase shows a course of action that contrasts with the father's positive opinion of himself. Choice A suggests that the father is competent in all ways, and the poem says the opposite. Choice B is wrong because there is no mention of the family's obligations. Choice D is a close distractor, but it is wrong because the repeated phrase points out certain problems in daily life to highlight the areas in which the father is not competent.

16. **(H)** Choices E, F, and G are all descriptions of the father's positive opinion of himself. Choice H, however, says that *he would restore* their confidence in him. If he has to restore their confidence, then that means the children do not have confidence in him.

17. **(D)** Choice A is designed so that you misunderstand the phrase *come undone*. The phrase only suggests that the sun, like a flower, has opened up. Choice B is wrong because there is no indication that the sun is incomplete. Choice C is wrong because there is no proposal.

18. **(H)** Examine the preceding sentence. There you will see that the sun is rising. The result of the sun rising is the creatures running down into the labyrinth. The implication here is that the creatures are running to avoid, or *shun*, the sun. The sun is part of *the day*, so choice H is correct.

19. **(C)** Choice A is wrong because although the sentence mentions his *high hopes*, it does not discuss his disappointment. Choice B is wrong because nowhere in the passage does it discuss that he would ultimately fail. Choice D is wrong because it makes a claim about zoologists and explorers in the general sense. The statement is a claim about Haekel.

20. **(F)** Choices E and H are wrong because they describe the land during Haekel's time. Choice G is wrong because it compares the land of Haekel's time to a time in the more distant past. In choice F, the author mentions *Ceylon at that time* to draw a contrast between today and Haekel's time.

21. **(B)** Choice A is wrong because there is no indication that it was a *novel* theory. It could have been a borrowed or existing theory. Choice C is wrong because it misinterprets the facts in the last paragraph. Haekel did not try to revise his theories to fit Darwin's. Choice D is wrong because he was looking for the origin of humanity, not the location of the Indian Ocean.

22. **(F)** The previous sentence describes what his *tropical fever* refers to: *the journey to Ceylon represented the fulfillment of a long-held but initially vague desire.* All the other answers hope to mislead by playing with unsupported interpretations of the word *fever*.

23. **(A)** Choice B is wrong because the paragraph does not describe his exploration, just his motivations and reasons for the trip. Choice C is wrong because although the passage might contain an admiring tone, the paragraph does not highlight strengths. Choice D is wrong because it improperly focuses on Darwin. Darwin undoubtedly had an influence, but that detail contributes to explaining Haekel's motivation.

24. **(G)** The sentence following the quoted text highlights what appears to be *carnival revelers*. This phrase suggests that choices E, F, and H are wrong. Carnival revelers are essentially party people, so *serious religious conviction, tension and danger,* and *violent event* do not accurately describe the initial impression of the scene.

25. **(B)** Several of the choices might be considered notable, but choice B is the only option with a phrase, *best documented*, that links with the phrase *particularly notable* from the question stem.

26. **(G)** Choice E is wrong because *best documented* doesn't mean it was *the only event ever documented*. Choice F is wrong because there is no discussion of legends. Choice H is wrong because the author is not arguing for the importance of anything. The phrase *best documented of the more than ten such contagions* suggests that the dancing plague occurred within a series of similar events *along the Rhine and Moselle rivers*. It is placed in context, choice G.

27. **(D)** Choice A is wrong because it only provides one person's (Paracelsus's) theory for the origins. Choice B is wrong because it is too broad in scope. The paragraph only describes the events surrounding the dancing plague and not social activities in general. Choice C is wrong because the importance of dancing is never discussed. Choice D fits best because it provides an account from Paracelsus's perspective, describing how the disease unfolded.

28. **(H)** Paragraph 3 provides a direct answer: *it all started with one woman*, Frau Troffea.

29. **(D)** The phrase *if . . . was true* suggests that the death rate might or might not possibly be true. Therefore, choices A and C are wrong. Choice B suggests that it must be false based on the fact that an account is unreliable. This is too extreme. Choice D is the best fit.

30. **(E)** The last sentence of paragraph 3 supports choice E. Choice F can be eliminated because it is too extreme. It might have been the best documented, but it is not characterized as the *most devastating* disease. Choice G is wrong because Paracelsus only described the events. Choice H is wrong because paragraph 3 only shows her ignoring her husband, but it does not explain why.

31. **(D)** The second sentence of the first paragraph says he *prided himself on his connoisseurship in wine*. The last sentence of the paragraph, *skillful in the Italian vintages*, also clarifies what the term *connoisseurship* might mean. Choice A is wrong because the mention of *fear* doesn't necessarily mean the fear from experts. Choice B is wrong because Fortunato's physical power is never discussed. Choice C is wrong because he is proud of his knowledge, not of his accomplishments.

32. **(H)** Referring to Fortunato, the narrator states, *In this respect I did not differ from him . . . .* Here he is suggesting that they both have a knowledge of wines. Choice E is wrong because the author never mentions that he himself has a weak point nor that he is feared like Fortunato. Choice F is wrong because there is no link between the narrator and Fortunato made in this sentence. Choice G is wrong because it merely states that Fortunato was not very good at painting and gemmary. It is never suggested that the narrator is similarly inadequate.

33. **(B)** The narrator claims in that he is *skillful* regarding wine and that he bought it whenever he could, suggesting that he had a lot of experience, or knowledge, about wine.

34. **(G)** The phrase *excessive warmth* has a double meaning. Fortunato is hot from drinking too much, but at the same, it suggests that he has warm feelings for the narrator. There are no clues in the passage to support choices E, F, or H.

35. **(C)** The first paragraph clearly establishes that wine is important to Fortunato. In paragraph 12, Fortunato mentions that the Amontillado can be confused with Sherry, which is another type of wine.

36. **(H)** In paragraph 4, Fortunato says the word *impossible* to reveal his shock at an unexpected revelation about the Amontillado. Choice E is wrong because the narrator might be in glee over Fortunato's gullibility, not the other way around. Choice F is wrong because we do not know how the narrator is dressed. Choice G is wrong because Fortunato's response does not reveal disgust but rather excitement.

37. **(B)** The narrator continues and states that he *was silly enough to pay the full Amontillado price without consulting you*. This serves to suggest that the narrator is expressing his *concern over a recent acquisition* of the Amontillado.

38. **(E)** The exclamation *impossible* in paragraph 4 shows Fortunato's disbelief, choice E.

39. **(A)** In paragraph 11, the narrator suggests that Luchesi can help him in the matter of the Amontillado. In paragraph 12, Fortunato claims that *Luchesi cannot tell Amontillado from Sherry*, which suggests that Luchesi lacks the ability to tell the difference between the two types of wine.

40. **(E)** The narrator claims that *fools . . . have it that his taste is a match for your own*. In other words, only fools believe that Luchesi and Fortunato are equal. None of the other answer choices can be supported by the text.

41. **(C)** The narrator speaks in paragraph 13, Fortunato speaks in paragraph 14, and the narrator speaks in paragraph 15. Since Fortunato speaks in paragraph 16, the possessive *your* points to the narrator.

PART TWO
Mathematics

Taking a Math Test 9

OVERVIEW

To perform well on a test, there is no substitute for a deep and thorough understanding of the material. To excel on a math test, you need to understand the math. One goal of this book is to help you master the math you will be tested on.

That being said, there are a variety of strategies that can help you maximize your score on a math test. Some strategies—like checking the solution to an equation—are good mathematical practice. Others—like being sure to take a guess even if you don't know the answer—are good test-taking practice. You will find many examples throughout the book, both in the chapters and in the worked solutions. So pay close attention and be on the lookout for them!

Be sure to review the "General Test-taking Strategies" chapter before beginning this section. Here are some key things to remember.

Know the Content

You can't do well on a test if you don't understand the content that you will be tested on. There simply are no shortcuts. The Mathematics section of this book is structured to make sure you can master the mathematical content the SHSAT will test you on.

Know the Format

The math section of the SHSAT consists of 57 questions: 52 multiple-choice questions and 5 grid-in questions. Each multiple-choice question has four answer choices. For the grid-in questions, you write the numeric answer in a grid on your answer sheet.

All the questions are valued the same: Early questions are worth the same as late questions; hard questions are worth the same as easy questions; grid-in questions are worth the same as multiple-choice questions. Keep this in mind and use this to your advantage.

Calculators are not allowed on the SHSAT. This means every calculation and computation must be done by you, either in your head or on paper. Make practice with arithmetic—addition, subtraction, multiplication, division with integers, fractions, and decimals—a part of your regular preparation routine.

Know Yourself

What are your strengths and weaknesses? Are you good at solving equations but need to work more on probability and statistics? Are you prone to careless mistakes? Do certain kinds of problems slow you down? Being able to honestly answer questions like these will help you formulate your best strategy for the test.

MATH TEST-TAKING STRATEGIES

There are several mathematical problem-solving strategies that are also good test-taking strategies. Let's review a few and see some examples.

Guessing and Checking

You will learn many algorithms and procedures for solving math problems in your career. Knowing how these procedures work, and how to apply them, is important in understanding mathematics. But sometimes just getting the answer is enough. And in some cases, guessing and checking in a thoughtful, careful, and appropriate way can get you the answer quickly.

➡ Example 1 _____

Solve the equation $6x = 2x - 12$.

Solving this equation using standard algebraic techniques is not complicated (this will be reviewed in a later section).

$$6x = 2x - 12$$
$$4x = -12$$
$$x = -3$$

But some thoughtful guessing and checking can get you the answer, too. Let's guess $x = 0$, which is usually easy to substitute into an equation.

$$6x = 2x - 12$$
$$6(0) = 2(0) - 12$$
$$0 \neq -12$$

Since this last equation is false, we know $x = 0$ is not a solution. So let's try $x = 1$.

$$6x = 2x - 12$$
$$6(1) = 2(1) - 12$$
$$6 \neq -10$$

This doesn't work either. But notice how the two sides of the equation are farther apart when $x = 1$ (6 and -10) than when $x = 0$ (0 and -12). This tells us our next guess should be in the other direction! Let's try $x = -2$.

$$6x = 2x - 12$$
$$6(-2) = 2(-2) - 12$$
$$-12 \neq -16$$

Still wrong, but we're getting closer. One last guess of $x = -3$ gets us there.

$$6x = 2x - 12$$
$$6(-3) = 2(-3) - 12$$
$$-18 = -18$$

Since $-18 = -18$, that means $x = -3$ is a solution to our equation.

You may think this is more work than the usual algebraic approach, and in some instances it might be. But if you work to develop good number sense and mathematical intuition, guessing and checking can be a very efficient strategy.

Here's a second example.

➥ Example 2 _____

Solve for x: $\dfrac{187 - x}{15} = 12$

Again, the algebraic approach is reasonable here. But let's see what some thoughtful guessing and checking can get us.

Notice that the numerator has to be a multiple of 15, since the denominator is 15 and the right-hand side of the equation is an integer. Now, 150 would be a nice number to have in the numerator, since 150 is obviously divisible by 15. By making $x = 37$, our numerator is 150, and we get:

$$\frac{187 - 37}{15} = 12$$
$$\frac{150}{15} = 12$$
$$10 = 12$$

Since this last equation isn't true, we know $x = 37$ isn't our solution. But we're close. If the numerator were 165, we'd get 11 on the left-hand side, and if the numerator were 180, we'd get 12. Since $x = 7$ makes the numerator 180, we see that:

$$\frac{187 - 7}{15} = 12$$
$$\frac{180}{15} = 12$$
$$12 = 12$$

And $x = 7$ is the solution to our equation.

Guessing and checking can be a powerful problem-solving strategy, but it requires fluency with numbers (especially when a calculator isn't allowed, like on the SHSAT). It shouldn't replace the standard techniques for solving problems except when it makes more sense to guess—in those cases, go for it.

Making a Wish

Making a Wish is a powerful problem-solving strategy that relies on the following fact: If a statement is true for all numbers, it must be true for any specific number. When we "make a wish," we turn a general statement into a specific statement, which may be easier to approach.

Here's an example.

➥ Example 3 _____

The number $3n$ is even. How many even numbers are there between $3n - 1$ and $3n + 5$ inclusive?

One approach to this problem would be to abstractly represent the integers between $3n - 1$ and $3n + 5$, like the following:

$$3n - 1, 3n, 3n + 1, 3n + 2, 3n + 3, 3n + 4, 3n + 5$$

Then determine which of these numbers are even.

There's an opportunity to make a wish here. The problem suggests that the answer will be the same for any value of n. So let's make a wish that the value of n is something specific, like 10.

If $n = 10$, then $3n = 30$, which is even, as required. Now we just write out the integers between $3n - 1 = 29$ and $3n + 5 = 35$:

$$29, 30, 31, 32, 33, 34, 35$$

You can see that three of these numbers are even, so our answer is 3.

The key idea is this: If the answer is always the same for any value of n, then whatever the answer is for $n = 10$ (or some other convenient choice) must *always* be the answer. Try out some other values of n in the above problem and you'll see.

➡ Example 4

If $A = 2B = C + 3 = \dfrac{D}{5} > 0$, which variable has the greatest value?

This is a perfect opportunity to make a wish. Wouldn't this problem be easier to deal with if we knew the numeric values of A, B, C, and D? Let's make a wish and see what happens.

Let's start with D, because D appears in a fraction, and if we're going to make a wish, we might as well wish for fractions to disappear. One value of D that would make the fraction disappear is $D = 5$, so let's wish that $D = 5$.

If $D = 5$, then $\dfrac{D}{5} = \dfrac{5}{5} = 1$. (Notice that $\dfrac{D}{5} > 0$, as required). Since $\dfrac{D}{5} = 1$, we have:

$$A = 2B = C + 3 = 1$$

So if $D = 5$, that makes $A = 1$, $B = \dfrac{1}{2}$, and $C = -2$. Therefore, D has the greatest value.

The problem implies that the relationship between A, B, C, and D will be the same for all values of A, B, C, and D that satisfy the given equations. We just picked one set of values ($A = 1$, $B = \dfrac{1}{2}$, $C = -2$, and $D = 5$) and determined the relationship. That's the power, and the secret, to making a wish.

Making a List

Making a list can very useful in certain contexts. Here's an example of this strategy in action.

➡ Example 5

How many numbers between 20 and 42, inclusive, are divisible by neither 2 nor 3?

There are fancy ways to approach this problem, but the straightforward approach works just fine: Just list all the numbers between 20 and 42 and cross off any that are divisible by 2 or 3:

20, 21, 22, 23, 24, 25, 26, 27, 28, 29, 30, 31, 32, 33, 34, 35, 36, 37, 38, 39, 40, 41, 42

First, cross off all the even numbers as they are multiples of 2:

~~20~~, 21, ~~22~~, 23, ~~24~~, 25, ~~26~~, 27, ~~28~~, 29, ~~30~~, 31, ~~32~~, 33, ~~34~~, 35, ~~36~~, 37, ~~38~~, 39, ~~40~~, 41, ~~42~~

Then cross off any multiples of 3 (notice some are already crossed off as they are also multiples of 2):

~~20~~, ~~21~~, ~~22~~, 23, ~~24~~, 25, ~~26~~, ~~27~~, ~~28~~, 29, ~~30~~, 31, ~~32~~, ~~33~~, ~~34~~, 35, ~~36~~, 37, ~~38~~, ~~39~~, ~~40~~, 41, ~~42~~

What's left on our list are numbers that are divisible by neither 2 nor by 3, exactly the numbers we want. Count them up and get the answer, 7.

Trying All Possibilities

With multiple-choice questions, we often have the option of simply trying out all the answers and seeing which one works. This isn't always efficient, so it probably shouldn't be your first approach, but it's a good strategy to keep in mind.

➥ Example 6 _____

Ning's age is now three times Caesar's age. If Caesar will be 17 in five years, how old was Ning 5 years ago?

    (E) 25

    (F) 31

    (G) 36

    (H) 41

Just try all the possibilities for Ning's age and see what it means for Caesar's age:

- If Ning was 25 five years ago, she is 30 now. This makes Caesar 10 now, and he won't be 17 in five years, so this isn't the correct answer.
- If Ning was 31 five years ago, then she is 36 now. This makes Caesar 12 now, and since he will be 17 in five years, this is the correct answer.
- If Ning was 36 five years ago, then she is 41 now. This makes Caesar $\frac{41}{3} = 13\frac{2}{3}$ now, and he won't be 17 in five years, so this isn't the correct answer.
- If Ning was 41 five years ago, then she is 46 now. This makes Caesar $\frac{46}{3} = 15\frac{1}{3}$ now, and he won't be 17 in five years, so this isn't the correct answer.

Of course, once you've identified the correct answer, it isn't necessary to check the other choices unless you have time and want to be sure. Generally speaking, this may not be the most efficient method to solve a problem, but it works well here.

Here's another example:

➥ Example 7 _____

Johan needs to send out thank-you cards after his graduation party. He could buy a package of thank-you cards for $8.50, or he could buy x individual thank-you cards for $0.15 each. What is the largest value of x that would make buying the individual cards less expensive than buying the package?

    (A) 54

    (B) 55

    (C) 56

    (D) 57

Let's just see how much each number of individual thank-you cards would cost. Notice that once you calculate $54 \times 0.15 = 8.10$, you can compute the other values by simply adding on 0.15 over and over:

- 54 cards will cost $54 \times 0.15 = 8.10$
- 55 cards will cost $55 \times 0.15 = 8.25$
- 56 cards will cost $56 \times 0.15 = 8.40$
- 57 cards will cost $57 \times 0.15 = 8.55$

The largest value of x that would make the cost of x individual cards less than the cost of the package is 56.

It's also worth noting that, since we are looking for the largest number x, it would have been more efficient to check the answers in decreasing numerical order. Once we discovered that 56 cards cost less than the package, we would not have to check 55 or 54, since we are looking for the largest number that did the job.

Estimating

Estimation is a very valuable skill in mathematics. Being able to estimate a value allows you to establish context for an answer, and it provides a built-in check on your work.

For example, suppose you need to multiply 57.3 and 19.2. If you just mindlessly calculate 57.3×19.2, a careless error might give you 109.943. But if you are constantly estimating quantities as you go, you'll recognize that 57.3×19.2 should be close to 60×20, which is easily computed to be 1,200. You'll see that 109.943 doesn't make sense as an answer, so you'll catch the error before it becomes a bigger problem.

Estimating can also help narrow down possibilities on multiple-choice questions, like in this example:

➡ Example 8 _____

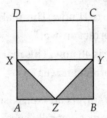

X, Y, and Z are midpoints of the sides of square $ABCD$. The length of a side of the square is 5 cm. What is the sum of the areas of the shaded triangles?

(E) 6.25 sq cm

(F) 7.5 sq cm

(G) 12.5 sq cm

(H) 25 sq cm

Since the square has side length 5 cm, the area of the square is 25 square cm. So half the square has an area of 12.5 sq cm. The shaded region is less than half the square, and this estimate immediately eliminates two answer choices. We're now in good shape to finish solving the problem, but if we have to guess, we now have a 50 percent chance of guessing the correct answer. The correct answer is choice E.

SUMMARY

Your goal is to earn as high a score as possible on the SHSAT. Your best strategy is to work hard, learn the content deeply, and practice consistently. There are no shortcuts.

But there are little things you can do to maximize your performance. Know what to expect on the exam, both in content and in format. Know what to expect on exam day. Have a plan for how you will approach the test, how you will manage your time, and how you will react when you encounter questions you can't answer.

Since the SHSAT is a timed test, being able to solve problems quickly is an advantage. The test-taking techniques described in this chapter—and in subsequent chapters and worked solutions—can often be used to get answers more quickly than the standard approaches. Master the usual ways to solve problems, but look for opportunities to guess and check, or make a wish, or try all the answers. Applying these strategies appropriately can help you solve problems more efficiently and catch errors more easily.

Most importantly, remember that every point counts on the SHSAT. One correct answer could make the difference, so use every minute to find opportunities to earn points and correct errors.

Numbers and Arithmetic 10

OVERVIEW

Numbers are important objects in mathematics, so familiarity and facility with numbers is essential to solving many math problems. All SHSAT math questions will require working with numbers in some way in order to find the answer.

Since calculator use is not permitted on the SHSAT, you must have the skills and confidence to deal with numbers mentally and on paper. To excel on the exam, you must be comfortable adding, subtracting, multiplying, and dividing numbers—including fractions and decimals—all without the aid of a calculator. So let's review some of the basic concepts of numbers and arithmetic and see how they may appear on the exam.

Problem Solving

Here are some of the types of problems you will solve that rely on numbers and arithmetic:

- Simplify expressions involving multiple arithmetic operations, like $3^2 + 4 - (8 - 10)$.
- Simplify fractions and convert to and from decimal representation, like $\dfrac{0.72}{0.64} \times 4$.
- Find the greatest common factor (GCF) and least common multiple (LCM) of sets of integers, for example: Find the GCF of 60, 105, and 180.

Prior Knowledge

Here are some things you need to be comfortable with in order to master working with numbers and arithmetic:

- Doing arithmetic in your head and on paper
- Determining the proper order in which to perform mathematical operations
- Factoring integers
- Simplifying expressions involving fractions and decimals

ARITHMETIC

You have undoubtedly learned to add, subtract, multiply, and divide numbers. But since the use of a calculator is not permitted on the SHSAT, you must be prepared to perform all calculations mentally or with paper and pencil. Every math problem on the SHSAT is likely to involve some kind of computation or calculation, so these skills are fundamental to your preparation.

You must develop confidence and comfort working with numbers, such as adding and multiplying two- and three-digit numbers, dividing and finding remainders, adding and simplifying fractions, converting to and from decimal representation, and so on. Nothing beats practice! You'll see lots of examples in this chapter and throughout this book, but find other ways to sharpen your skills. Make arithmetic practice a part of your regular routine. As you practice, use a calculator just to check your work, not do the work for you.

Here are some basic arithmetic ideas to work on in preparation for the SHSAT.

MULTIPLYING AND DIVIDING

You should be comfortable with the standard algorithms for multiplying and dividing. For instance, you should be able to compute a product like 62×40 in the usual way:

$$
\begin{array}{r}
62 \\
\times\ 40 \\
\hline
00 \\
248 \\
\hline
2480
\end{array}
$$

But it is also useful to think about multiplication as an application of the **distributive property**. The distributive property governs how multiplication and addition work together. The distributive property says that for real numbers a, b, c, x, y, and z, we have:

$$a \times (b + c) = a \times b + a \times c$$
$$(x + y) \times z = x \times z + y \times z$$

When we multiply a sum (like $(b + c)$) by a number a, we think of the a as being distributed over the addition inside the parentheses.

The distributive property can help us multiply 62×40 like this:

$$62 \times 40 = (60 + 2) \times 40 = 60 \times 40 + 2 \times 40 = 2400 + 80 = 2480$$

This may seem like an inefficient way to multiply 62 and 40, but with practice this approach to multiplication can often be quicker than the standard algorithm. And even if you don't use this method all the time, it's always good to have alternate approaches in case you get stuck or want to double-check an answer.

Another benefit of this approach to multiplication is that it can help us to estimate answers. For example, when using the distributive approach to 62×40, we compute 60×40, which is easier to compute than 62×40 and is a reasonable estimate of the actual answer. By using the distributive property, we can see right away that the answer to 62×40 must be around 2,400. If our final answer isn't close to 2,400, we'll know we've done something wrong.

It's also useful to be able to execute the standard algorithms for division, like long division. For example, here's what it looks likes to use long division to compute $\frac{136}{8}$:

$$
\begin{array}{r}
17 \\
8\overline{)136} \\
-8 \\
\hline
56 \\
-56 \\
\hline
0
\end{array}
$$

Since the remainder is 0, we know that 8 divides into 136 evenly.

But it's also useful to keep in mind that division is the inverse operation of multiplication. The question "What is $\frac{136}{8}$?" is the same question as "What do I multiply 8 by to get 136?" If you struggle to answer the first question, the second question may be more approachable. Some good guessing can help you along. For example, $8 \times 10 = 80$ and $8 \times 20 = 160$, so the number we're looking for must be between 10 and 20. Since 136 is closer to 160, we can start counting down by 8: $8 \times 19 = 152$, $8 \times 18 = 144$, $8 \times 17 = 136$. Since $8 \times 17 = 136$, we know $\frac{136}{8} = 17$.

Being able to divide quickly and confidently is crucial in factoring integers and simplifying fractions, as we will see later.

FRACTIONS

Fractions, as well as decimals, appear frequently on the SHSAT, so developing confidence in handling them is important.

Multiplying fractions is straightforward. Recall that the **numerator** of a fraction is the number on top, and the **denominator** of a fraction is the number on the bottom. To multiply two fractions, you just multiply their numerators together and their denominators together. Here are some examples:

$$\frac{3}{7} \times \frac{5}{2} = \frac{3 \times 5}{7 \times 2} = \frac{15}{14} \qquad\qquad \frac{8}{9} \times \frac{3}{5} = \frac{8 \times 3}{9 \times 5} = \frac{24}{45}$$

Notice that in the first multiplication problem, the resulting fraction has a numerator larger than its denominator. This kind of fraction is called an **improper fraction**, and we may choose to write an improper fraction as a **mixed number**, which is a combination of a whole number and a fraction:

$$\frac{15}{14} = 1\frac{1}{14}$$

WARNING!	$3\frac{2}{5}$ means $3 + \frac{2}{5}$, not $3 \times \frac{2}{5}$. This can be a source of confusion, as we often multiply two numbers that are written next to each other.

To divide fractions, it is helpful to think of division as multiplication by the *reciprocal*. For instance, one way to understand $12 \div 3$ (or $\frac{12}{3}$) is as $12 \times \frac{1}{3} = 4$. Here, $\frac{1}{3}$ is the reciprocal of 3.

To divide by a fraction, we multiply by the reciprocal:

$$\frac{5}{4} \div \frac{7}{3} = \frac{5}{4} \times \frac{3}{7} = \frac{15}{28}$$

Two different fractions can represent the same number. For example, even though $\frac{15}{20}$ and $\frac{6}{8}$ are written differently, they represent the same number. They are both equal to $\frac{3}{4}$, or 0.75. The fractions $\frac{15}{20}$, $\frac{6}{8}$, and $\frac{3}{4}$ are all *equivalent*.

It is very important to understand how to work with equivalent fractions. We can see that $\frac{15}{20}$ and $\frac{3}{4}$ are equivalent in the following way:

$$\frac{15}{20} = \frac{5 \times 3}{5 \times 4} = \frac{5}{5} \times \frac{3}{4} = 1 \times \frac{3}{4} = \frac{3}{4}$$

This process is often referred to as **simplifying** a fraction, or reducing it to lowest terms. Notice how we are using fraction multiplication backward, turning $\frac{15}{20}$ into $\frac{5}{5} \times \frac{3}{4}$:

$$\frac{5 \times 3}{5 \times 4} = \frac{5}{5} \times \frac{3}{4}$$

Then we use the fact that $\frac{5}{5} = 1$. This is one approach to simplifying fractions: Write the numerator and the denominator as products and look for common **factors** that can be simplified to 1. For example:

$$\frac{42}{66} = \frac{2 \times 21}{2 \times 33} = \frac{2}{2} \times \frac{21}{33} = 1 \times \frac{21}{33} = \frac{21}{33}$$

And $\frac{21}{33}$ can be further simplified:

$$\frac{21}{33} = \frac{3 \times 7}{3 \times 11} = \frac{3}{3} \times \frac{7}{11} = 1 \times \frac{7}{11} = \frac{7}{11}$$

You could have simplified $\frac{42}{66}$ more efficiently by initially factoring a 6 from both the numerator and denominator:

$$\frac{42}{66} = \frac{6 \times 7}{6 \times 11} = \frac{6}{6} \times \frac{7}{11} = 1 \times \frac{7}{11} = \frac{7}{11}$$

This is the most efficient way to simplify $\frac{42}{66}$, because 6 is the greatest common factor (GCF) of 42 and 66. Being able find GCFs reliably will help you simplify fractions.

Adding fractions is straightforward when the fractions have a **common denominator**. Simply add the numerators and keep the denominator:

$$\frac{4}{15} + \frac{8}{15} = \frac{12}{15}$$

Notice that $\frac{12}{15}$ can be simplified to $\frac{4}{5}$.

When fractions have different denominators, a common denominator must be found in order to add them, like this:

$$\frac{1}{3} + \frac{11}{15} = 1 \times \frac{1}{3} + \frac{11}{15}$$
$$= \frac{5}{5} \times \frac{1}{3} + \frac{11}{15}$$
$$= \frac{5 \times 1}{5 \times 3} + \frac{11}{15}$$
$$= \frac{5}{15} + \frac{11}{15}$$
$$= \frac{16}{15}$$

Here, we write $\frac{1}{3}$ as an equivalent fraction with a denominator of 15, namely $\frac{5}{15}$. Once the fractions have the same denominator, it is easy to add them. Notice that we are using the same techniques used above to simplify fractions, but in reverse. Also note that we could write the improper fraction $\frac{16}{15}$ as a mixed number, $1\frac{1}{15}$.

The most efficient way to find a common denominator is to find the **least common multiple (LCM)** of the denominators, and then rewrite all the fractions using that denominator. Once they have the same denominator, you can just add the numerators and then simplify if necessary.

DECIMALS

Fractions can also be expressed in **decimal form**. A decimal number like 1.5 can be read as "one and five-tenths." This is $1\frac{5}{10}$, which can be simplified to $1\frac{1}{2}$. The number 3.44 is "three and 44 one-hundredths," or $3\frac{44}{100}$, which can be simplified to $3\frac{11}{25}$.

To convert the number $\frac{3}{2}$ to decimal notation is straightforward. Since $\frac{3}{2}$ can be expressed as $1\frac{1}{2}$, or "one and a half," then we know that $\frac{3}{2} = 1.5$. Knowing that $\frac{1}{2}$ is 0.5 in decimal notation makes this an easy conversion.

But what if we wanted to express $\frac{7}{25}$ in decimal form? One way to do this is using long division. We divide 7 by 25.

$$
\begin{array}{r}
0.28 \\
25\overline{)\,7.00} \\
-50 \\
\hline
200 \\
-200 \\
\hline
0
\end{array}
$$

And so $\frac{7}{25} = 0.28$. But another way is to recognize that $\frac{7}{25}$ can easily be expressed as an equivalent fraction with a denominator of 100, namely:

$$\frac{7}{25} = \frac{4}{4} \times \frac{7}{25} = \frac{28}{100}$$

Since $\frac{28}{100}$ is "twenty-eight one-hundredths," we can immediately write the decimal representation as 0.28.

OPERATIONS AND EXPRESSIONS

Expressions are the result of combining numbers using mathematical operations. To evaluate an expression means to perform the indicated operations and simplify the result. In some cases, this may produce a single number, in others just a simpler version of the original expression.

Look at the following example:

$$4 \times \left(3^2 - 2\right) - 10 \times 3 + 5$$

This expression involves familiar numbers and familiar operations, but we have to be careful about which operations we perform first. There is an **order of operations** that must be followed when computing, and this must always be kept in mind when we evaluate expressions.

A good rule of thumb regarding the order of mathematical operations is *work from the inside out*. Look for grouping symbols—parentheses, brackets, division bars—and perform the operations inside those grouping symbols first. The proper use and interpretation of grouping symbols greatly reduces confusion about the order of operations.

When grouping symbols aren't present, we default to the following set of rules. We read expressions left to right (just as we read English), and we perform operations in the following order: exponents before multiplication and division; multiplication and division before addition and subtraction. This is often referred to as **PEMDAS**: Parentheses, Exponents, Multiplication, Division, Addition, Subtraction. PEMDAS gives a rough outline of the order of operations.

Back to our example, we perform the operations inside the parenthesis first:

$$4 \times \left(3^2 - 2\right) - 10 \times 3 + 5 = 4 \times (9 - 2) - 10 \times 3 + 5$$
$$= 4 \times (7) - 10 \times 3 + 5$$

Next, we perform the multiplication:

$$= 4 \times (7) - 10 \times 3 + 5$$
$$= 28 - 30 + 5$$

And lastly, remembering to read left to right, we finish up with the addition and subtraction:

$$28 - 30 + 5 = -2 + 5 = 3$$

WARNING!	A problem with PEMDAS is that it suggests that addition should always come before subtraction, which is not true. When deciding whether to add or subtract first, remember we read left to right.

Our expression involves only numbers, but expressions can also involve variables. For example, we might have an expression like this:

$$4(x + 3) + 2(x - 4) - (x - 3)$$

Even though there isn't anything we can do inside the parentheses, we can still simplify this expression using the distributive property:

$$4(x + 3) + 2(x - 4) - (x - 3) = 4 \times x + 4 \times 3 + 2 \times x - 2 \times 4 - x + 3$$

But you must be very careful with signs when using the distributive law. Notice that:

$$2(x - 4) = 2 \times x - 2 \times 4$$

The second term in the above expression is the result of multiplying 2 and -4 together. Expressions of this form are particularly important to pay attention to:

$$-(x - 3) = -x + 3$$

The negative sign in front of the parentheses is really multiplication by -1. When in doubt, you can rewrite $-(x - 3)$ like this:

$$-(x - 3) = (-1)(x - 3)$$

And then you see that the -1 must be multiplied by everything in the parentheses:

$$-(x - 3) = (-1)(x - 3)$$
$$= (-1)x - (-1)3$$
$$= -x + 3$$

Returning to our expression, we can multiply and combine like terms, and our expression can be dramatically simplified:

$$4(x + 3) + 2(x - 4) - (x - 3) = 4 \times x + 4 \times 3 + 2 \times x + 2 \times (-4) - x + 3$$
$$= 4x + 12 + 2x - 8 - x + 3$$
$$= 5x + 7$$

WARNING!	The most common mistakes when multiplying come from mishandling negative numbers. Pay close attention when you distribute!

ABSOLUTE VALUE

A particular mathematical operation that appears on the SHSAT is **absolute value**, which is denoted using two vertical bars: $|\ |$. Here are some examples of absolute value expressions:

$$|5| \qquad |12.3| \qquad |-3.1| \qquad |-4+2| \qquad |0| \qquad |a|$$

The absolute value of a number is the distance from that number to 0 on the number line. This is a geometric approach to absolute value, but we can also think of absolute value in a procedural way: the absolute value of a non-negative number is the number itself, and the absolute value of a negative number is the negation of that number.

Here are some simple examples:

$$|5| = 5 \qquad |12.3| = 12.3 \qquad |-3.1| = 3.1 \qquad |0| = 0$$

Things can get a little more complicated. For example, what is $|x|$? Well, that depends. If x is a non-negative number, then $|x| = x$. But if x is a negative number, then $|x| = -x$. Absolute values of variable expressions can be challenging to deal with.

And the absolute value of an expression can also be tricky. It's important to recognize that absolute value bars are a grouping symbol like parentheses. That means it is important to simplify the expression inside the absolute value bars before finding the absolute value of what's inside. Take care when evaluating expressions like $|-4+3|$:

$$|-4+3| = |-1| = 1$$

Just like with parenthesis, you must perform the operations inside the absolute value bars first.

WARNING!	A common mistake with absolute value is to "distribute" the absolute value like this: $|-4+3| = |-4|+|3| = 4+3 = 7$, which is incorrect. The correct answer is $|-4+3| = |-1| = 1$. If you find yourself confused, just compare $|0|$ and $|3+-3|$.

NUMBERS

There are many different kinds of numbers: natural numbers, integers, rational numbers, real numbers, and even more. For the SHSAT, you need to be particularly familiar with the following kinds of numbers.

Natural numbers are the numbers 1, 2, 3, 4 ... and so on. **Integers** are the natural numbers and all their negations: ... $-5, -4, -3, -2, -1, 0, 1, 2, 3...$ and so on.

To **factor** an integer means to write it as a product of two or more integers. For example, we could factor 24 in the following ways:

$$24 = 4 \times 6 \qquad 24 = 3 \times 8 \qquad 24 = 2 \times 12 \qquad 24 = 1 \times 24 \qquad 24 = 2 \times 3 \times 4$$

These are all valid **factorizations** of the number 24. When we talk about *the factors* of 24, we mean all the positive numbers that evenly divide 24. Thus, the factors of 24 are:

$$1, 2, 3, 4, 6, 8, 12, 24$$

There are a few simple divisibility rules that allow you to determine if a small number evenly divides a larger number, and is thus a factor. Here are the rules:

- A number is divisible by 2 if and only if its ones digit is 0, 2, 4, 6, or 8.
- A number is divisible by 3 if and only if the sum of its digits is a multiple of 3. For example, 27 is divisible by 3 since $2 + 7 = 9$ is divisible by 3. Also, 837 is divisible by 3 since $8 + 3 + 7 = 18$ and 18 is divisible by 3. But 563 is not divisible by 3, since $5 + 6 + 3 = 14$, and 14 is not divisible by 3.
- A number is divisible by 4 if and only if it divisible by 2 twice: For example, $672 = 2 \times 336$, and since 336 is even and thus divisible by 2, we see that $672 = 4 \times 168$.
- A number is divisible by 5 if and only if its ones digit is either 0 or 5.
- A number is divisible by 6 if and only if it is divisible by both 2 and 3, since $6 = 2 \times 3$.
- A number is divisible by 9 if and only if the sum of its digits is a multiple of 9. For example, 747 is divisible by 9, since $7 + 4 + 7 = 18$, which is divisible by 9. But 926 is not, since $9 + 2 + 6 = 17$, which is not divisible by 9.
- A number is divisible by 10 if and only if its ones digit is 0.

Some problems on the SHSAT ask you to find the **greatest common factor (GCF)** of two or more numbers. This means you want to find the largest number that is a factor of all the given numbers.

For example, the greatest common factor of 24 and 36 is 12, since 12 is a factor of both numbers and no factor of both 24 and 36 is greater than 12. One way to see this is to list the factors of both 24 and 36:

Factors of 24: 1, 2, 3, 4, 6, 8, 12, 24
Factors of 36: 1, 2, 3, 4, 6, 9, 12, 18, 36

Since 12 appears on both lists, it is a common factor of 24 and 36. Since it is the largest number on both lists, it is the greatest common factor of 24 and 36.

A related kind of problem is to find the least common multiple (LCM) of two or more numbers. The least common multiple of two or more numbers is the smallest number that has all the given numbers as factors.

For example, the least common multiple of 24 and 36 is 72. We can see this by listing multiples of both 24 and 36 and finding the smallest number on both lists.

Multiples of 24: 24, 48, 72, 96, 120, 144 …
Multiples of 36: 36, 72, 108, 144, 180 …

Since 72 appears on both lists, it is a common multiple of 24 and 36. Since it is the smallest number on both lists, it is the least common multiple of 24 and 36.

WARNING!	Notice that 144 is also on both lists. 144 is a common multiple of 24 and 36, but it is not the *least* common multiple, since 72 is a smaller common multiple.

Prime numbers are important in the study of division and may appear on the SHSAT. A number is prime if the only way to factor it is as 1 times itself. (By definition, the number 1 is not considered a prime.) For example, the number 17 is prime, since the only way to factor it is:

$$17 = 1 \times 17$$

The first ten prime numbers are 2, 3, 5, 7, 11, 13, 17, 19, 23, and 29. The list of prime numbers goes on forever, but it does not follow a simple pattern.

Lastly, it is important to understand simple properties of **even** and **odd numbers**. A number is even if it is a multiple of 2, and it is odd if it is not a multiple of 2. For example, 6, 24, and 1,244 are all even, since they are all multiples of 2. But 11, 19, and 137 are odd, since they are not multiples of 2.

The first 10 even numbers, starting at 0, are 0, 2, 4, 6, 8, 10, 12, 14, 16, and 18. The first 10 odd numbers, starting at 1, are 1, 3, 5, 7, 9, 11, 13, 15, 17, and 19. Notice that the difference between consecutive even numbers is 2 and the difference between consecutive odd numbers is also 2. This can be useful when dealing with even and odd numbers abstractly. For example, if we know the number x is even, then we know that the next even number is $x + 2$, and the next even number after that is $x + 4$. This is also true if x is odd: $x + 2$ will be the next odd number, and $x + 4$ will the next odd number after that.

WARNING!	A common mistake is to think that numbers of the form x, $x + 2$, $x + 4$, $x + 6 \ldots$ must be even. But if x is odd, then these numbers are all odd!

PROBLEM SOLVING

Now let's work through some problems involving numbers and arithmetic that are similar to those you might face on the SHSAT.

➡ Example 1 _____

1. $100(1 + 0.4)^2 - 100 =$

    (A) 40
    (B) 96
    (C) 140
    (D) 196

Simplifying this expression requires arithmetic and proper application of the order of operations. The first rule of the order of operations is to work from the inside out, so first deal with what is inside the parentheses:

$$100(1 + 0.4)^2 - 100 = 100(1.4)^2 - 100$$

We generally evaluate expressions left to right, but an exponent is involved here (1.4^2), so we must perform that operation first. Remember to be careful when multiplying decimal numbers.

$$
\begin{array}{r}
1.4 \\
\times 1.4 \\
\hline
56 \\
14 \\
\hline
1.96
\end{array}
$$

Or if you know your perfect squares, you know $14^2 = 196$, which means $1.4^2 = 1.96$.

This is a good opportunity to ask, "Does this make sense?" For example, if you multiplied 1.4×1.4 and got 19.6, that wouldn't make sense. Multiplying two numbers less than 2 should yield a result less than 4.

Now that we know $1.4^2 = 1.96$, we can finish evaluating the expression:

$$100(1+0.4)^2 - 100 = 100(1.4)^2 - 100$$
$$= 100(1.96) - 100$$
$$= 196 - 100$$
$$= 96$$

And so our answer is choice B, 96.

➡ Example 2 _____

$$3\frac{4}{5} + 6\frac{7}{10} + 5\frac{2}{5} + 2\frac{1}{2}$$

2. What is the value of the expression shown above?

(E) $16\frac{7}{20}$

(F) $17\frac{7}{20}$

(G) $17\frac{2}{5}$

(H) $18\frac{2}{5}$

We have to find the sum of four fractions with different denominators, so we must find a common denominator. But before we do that, we can make the problem a little easier.

Recall that a mixed number, written like $3\frac{4}{5}$, is really a sum: $3\frac{4}{5} = 3 + \frac{4}{5}$. So before we add any fractions, let's rethink our problem like this:

$$3\frac{4}{5} + 6\frac{7}{10} + 5\frac{2}{5} + 2\frac{1}{2} = 3 + \frac{4}{5} + 6 + \frac{7}{10} + 5 + \frac{2}{5} + 2 + \frac{1}{2}$$

Now, let's rearrange our sum so we can add up all the integer parts first and get them out of the way:

$$3 + \frac{4}{5} + 6 + \frac{7}{10} + 5 + \frac{2}{5} + 2 + \frac{1}{2} = 3 + 6 + 5 + 2 + \frac{4}{5} + \frac{7}{10} + \frac{2}{5} + \frac{1}{2}$$
$$= 16 + \frac{4}{5} + \frac{7}{10} + \frac{2}{5} + \frac{1}{2}$$

Now we just have to add the fractions. All the denominators are factors of 10, so 10 can be our common denominator. Now we rewrite all our fractions with a denominator of 10:

$$\frac{4}{5} + \frac{7}{10} + \frac{2}{5} + \frac{1}{2} = \frac{2}{2} \times \frac{4}{5} + \frac{7}{10} + \frac{2}{2} \times \frac{2}{5} + \frac{5}{5} \times \frac{1}{2}$$
$$= \frac{8}{10} + \frac{7}{10} + \frac{4}{10} + \frac{5}{10}$$

Now that they have the same denominator, we can easily add our fractions.

$$\frac{8}{10} + \frac{7}{10} + \frac{4}{10} + \frac{5}{10} = \frac{24}{10}$$

So:

$$16 + \frac{4}{5} + \frac{7}{10} + \frac{2}{5} + \frac{1}{2} = 16 + \frac{24}{10}$$

After some simplifying, handling mixed numbers and equivalent fractions, we finally get:

$$3\frac{4}{5} + 6\frac{7}{10} + 5\frac{2}{5} + 2\frac{1}{2} = 16 + \frac{4}{5} + \frac{7}{10} + \frac{2}{5} + \frac{1}{2}$$
$$= 16 + \frac{24}{10}$$
$$= 16 + 2\frac{4}{10}$$
$$= 18\frac{2}{5}$$

The answer is choice H, $18\frac{2}{5}$.

Estimation offers a quicker solution to this problem. Since $3 + 6 + 5 + 2 = 16$, $\frac{4}{5} + \frac{2}{5} > 1$, and $\frac{7}{10} + \frac{1}{2} > 1$, we know immediately that $3\frac{4}{5} + 6\frac{7}{10} + 5\frac{2}{5} + 2\frac{1}{2} > 16 + 1 + 1 = 18$. Since only one answer choice is above 18, it must be the correct one.

➥ Example 3 _____

3. Which of the following numbers has factors that include the smallest factor (other than 1) of 119?

   (A) 51
   (B) 52
   (C) 54
   (D) 56

To answer this question, we need to determine the factors of 119. Here's where knowledge of the divisibility tests come in handy. Since 119 is odd, it is not divisible by 2. Since its digital sum (11) is not divisible by 3, then 119 is not divisible by 3. Since 119 doesn't end in 0 or 5, it's not divisible by 5. So let's try 7:

$$
\begin{array}{r}
17 \\
7)\overline{119} \\
-7 \\
\hline
49 \\
-49 \\
\hline
0
\end{array}
$$

When we divided 119 by 7, we get 17 with a remainder of 0. This means that $7 \times 17 = 119$, and so 7 is a factor of 119. (In fact, this is the prime factorization of 119, since both 7 and 17 are prime numbers.)

This means 7 is the smallest positive factor of 119 that is greater than 1. So now the question is which of the following numbers, 51, 52, 54, or 56, has 7 as a factor? Perhaps you recognize $56 = 7 \times 8$ right away, but if not, you can make a quick list of multiples of 7:

$$7, 14, 21, 28, 35, 42, 49, 56$$

This shows that the only answer on the list is choice D, 56.

➡ Example 4 _____

4. The least of 7 consecutive integers is r and the greatest is s. What is the value of $\frac{r+s}{2}$ in terms of r?

(E) $2r$

(F) $3r$

(G) $r+3$

(H) $r+6$

The trick to handling this problem is knowing how to represent consecutive integers. Since consecutive integers differ by 1—for example, 12, 13, 14—we can represent seven consecutive integers starting at r like this:

$$r, r+1, r+2, r+3, r+4, r+5, r+6$$

Notice that the seventh consecutive integer is $r+6$, which can be a source of confusion. Take a moment to count the numbers above to make sure there are really seven integers on that list.

The greatest number on the list is $r+6$, so $s = r+6$. Now we need to evaluate $\frac{r+s}{2}$ in terms of r:

$$\frac{r+s}{2} = \frac{r+r+6}{2} = \frac{2r+6}{2} = \frac{2r}{2} + \frac{6}{2} = r+3$$

And we see the answer is choice G, $r+3$. Notice that we have to be careful simplifying the fractions at the end.

WARNING!	A common mistake in simplifying a fraction like $\frac{a+b}{2}$ is to only divide one of the numbers in the numerator by 2. Remember: $\frac{a+b}{2} = \frac{a}{2} + \frac{b}{2}$.

The "make a wish" strategy offers a potentially faster solution to this question. Let's make a wish that the first integer in our list of seven consecutive integers is 10. So our list of seven consecutive integers looks like this:

$$10, 11, 12, 13, 14, 15, 16$$

Once again, count to make sure there are seven integers on that list.

Now, the largest integer on our list is 16. That means $s = 16$. Since $r = 10$, we can compute $\frac{r+s}{2}$:

$$\frac{r+s}{2} = \frac{10+16}{2} = \frac{26}{2} = 13$$

Notice that $13 = r+3 = 10+3$. Just as importantly, again using $r = 10$, we see that:

$$13 \neq 2r = 20$$
$$13 \neq 3r = 30$$
$$13 \neq r+6 = 16$$

So by making a wish, we can see that the only possible answer is choice G, $r+3$.

5. What is the least common multiple of 12, 30, and 18?

(A) 45
(B) 60
(C) 90
(D) 180

One approach to finding the least common multiple (LCM) of a set of numbers is to make a list of the multiples of each number and then identify the smallest number that is on all the lists. Notice that our lists only need to go up to 180, since that is the largest answer choice.

Number	Multiples
12	12, 24, 36, 48, 60, 72, 84, 96, 108, 120, 132, 144, 156, 168, 180
30	30, 60, 90, 120, 150, 180
18	18, 36, 54, 72, 90, 108, 126, 144, 162, 180

Since 180 is the smallest number that is on all three lists of multiples, 180 is the least common multiple of 12, 30, and 18. The answer is D.

You could also approach this problem by trying all the possible answers, which may lead you to the answer more quickly. One of the answer choices is the LCM of the three numbers, which means it must be divisible by all three numbers. Since 45 is not divisible by 30, you can eliminate A; since 60 is not divisible by 18 you can eliminate B; and since 90 is not divisible by 12, you can eliminate C. As we've already seen, 180 is the only choice divisible by all three numbers, so it is the LCM of 12, 30, and 18.

SUMMARY

Facility with numbers and operations is essential to success on the SHSAT, so relevant practice with arithmetic must be part of your test preparation. Virtually every math question on the SHSAT will involve some kind of calculation, and since calculators are not permitted on the exam, you must be comfortable and confident performing calculations efficiently by hand.

Practice multiplying and dividing two-digit and three-digit numbers; practice factoring integers and simplifying fractions; practice adding and subtracting fractions with different denominators; practice converting decimals to fractions and vice versa. Make up your own questions, and use a calculator to check your work.

Of course you should practice every kind of problem you might face on the SHSAT, but since arithmetic factors into so many of the problems, both directly and indirectly, this is one topic you definitely need to focus on in order to do well.

EXERCISES

Here is some targeted practice with numbers and arithmetic. Remember, no calculators!

1. Evaluate: $10(2 - 0.1)^2 - 5$

2. Simplify: $\dfrac{168}{192}$

3. Compute: $\dfrac{2}{5} + \dfrac{3}{4} - \dfrac{7}{10}$

4. Express $\dfrac{57}{40}$ as a decimal.

5. Compute: $20(1 + 1.1)^2 + \dfrac{14}{5}$

6. Evaluate: $|3 - 7| + |12 + 4| - |-3.5 + 1|$

7. Compute: 123×87

8. Find the value of $3x(x - 2y)$ when $x = 5$ and $y = 4$.

9. Find the greatest common divisor of 126, 234, and 270.

10. Find the greatest common divisor of 125, 175, and 275.

(Answers are on page 203.)

Equations and Inequalities 11

OVERVIEW

Math problems frequently involve equations, and you'll encounter many equations, in many different contexts, on the SHSAT. A firm grasp of working with equations—how to set them up, how to solve them, and how to check them—is essential to your test preparation.

The most important equations and inequalities involve variables. An equation involving a variable essentially asks a question: What value or values of the variable make the equation true? To solve an equation is to find, and check, those values.

Solving equations requires working with numbers, variables, and expressions. This material was covered in the previous chapter, but as you practice working with equations and inequalities, keep looking for opportunities to sharpen your arithmetic skills and number fluency.

Problem Solving

Here are some of the types of problems you will solve that rely on equations and inequalities:

- Find the solution to an equation involving one variable, like $4x - 12 = x + 6$.
- Set up equations that model situations and solve them, for example: "José is twice as old as Keisha is now; in 10 years, Keisha will be three-fourths of José's age. How old is Keisha now?"
- Find solution sets of inequalities, like $-3 \le 2x + 4 \le 10$, and represent them graphically.

Prior Knowledge

Here are some things you need to be comfortable with in order to master working with equations and inequalities:

- Handling numbers and performing arithmetic
- Manipulating expressions and equations
- Translating sentences into mathematical equations
- Understanding how to check solutions to equations and inequalities

EQUATIONS

An equation is a mathematical statement that two expressions are equal. Here are some simple examples of equations:

$$12 = 7 + 5 \qquad \frac{24}{4} = 3 \times 2 \qquad 3 = 4 - 1 \qquad 10 = 2 + 2 \qquad 5x = x + 16$$

Equations can be true or false. For example, the equation $12 = 7 + 5$ is true, and the equation $10 = 2 + 2$ is false. What about $5x = x + 16$? Is this equation true or false?

Since this equation involves a variable, which could represent any number, the answer to this question depends on the value of x. If $x = 4$, the equation is true; but if $x = 5$ (or $x = -3$ or $x = 14.6$, or many other values), the equation will be false.

Generally speaking, an equation involving variables is really asking the question "What value, or values, of the variables make the equation true?" The answer to this question is the *solution to the equation*. A solution to the equation $5x = x + 16$ is $x = 4$, because when we substitute $x = 4$ into the equation, the equation is true.

$$5x = x + 16$$
$$5(4) = 4 + 16$$
$$20 = 20$$

Since $20 = 20$ is true, that means $x = 4$ is a solution to the equation $5x = x + 16$. As it turns out, $x = 4$ is the only solution to this equation. Any other value of x will make this equation false. For example, we could try $x = 5$:

$$5x = x + 16$$
$$5(5) = 5 + 16$$
$$25 = 21$$

Since $25 = 21$ is not true, $x = 5$ is not a solution to the equation $5x = x + 16$. In fact, no value of x other than 4 will work. Try out some other values to convince yourself.

To *solve an equation* is to find the solution, or solutions, to the equation. We use techniques from algebra and arithmetic to solve equations. For equations involving one variable, our guiding strategy is to *isolate the variable*. This means we collect all the terms involving the variable on one side of the equation and combine them, and get everything else on the other side of the equation. Then simplify as much as possible.

We accomplish this by performing various mathematical operations on the equation, which we are allowed to do as long as we perform the same operation on both sides of the equation. Here's how we would solve the equation $5x = x + 16$ by isolating the variable x:

$5x = x + 16$	(Original equation)
$5x - x = x + 16 - x$	(Subtract x from both sides)
$4x = 16$	(Combine like terms)
$\dfrac{4x}{4} = \dfrac{16}{4}$	(Divide both sides of the equation by 4)
$x = 4$	(Simplify)

This is a simple example, and we will see more complex examples shortly. But regardless of how complex the process is, you can always check a solution by substituting it into the original equation and seeing if it is true. As we saw above:

$$5x = x + 16$$
$$5(4) = 4 + 16$$
$$20 = 20$$

And since $20 = 20$ is a true equation, we know $x = 4$ is a solution to $5x = x + 16$.

Let's look at a few more examples.

➡️ Example 1

Solve $6x - 18 = 3x + 48$.

$$6x - 18 = 3x + 48 \qquad \text{(Original equation)}$$
$$6x - 18 + 18 = 3x + 48 + 18 \qquad \text{(Add 18 to both sides)}$$
$$6x = 3x + 66 \qquad \text{(Simplify)}$$
$$6x - 3x = 3x + 66 - 3x \qquad \text{(Subtract } 3x \text{ from both sides)}$$
$$3x = 66 \qquad \text{(Simplify)}$$
$$\frac{3x}{3} = \frac{66}{3} \qquad \text{(Divide both sides by 3)}$$
$$x = 22 \qquad \text{(Simplify)}$$

Above we isolated the variable x by moving all the x terms to the left-hand side and moving all other terms to the right-hand side. We can, and should, check our solution, by substituting $x = 22$ into the original equation:

$$6(22) - 18 = 3(22) + 48$$
$$132 - 18 = 66 + 48$$
$$114 = 114$$

This is true, so $x = 22$ is a solution to the equation.

➡️ Example 2

Solve $7y + 12 = -2y + 9$.

$$7y + 12 = -2y + 9 \qquad \text{(Original equation)}$$
$$9y = -3 \qquad \text{(Add } 2y \text{ to both sides and simplify)}$$
$$y = -\frac{1}{3} \qquad \text{(Divide both sides by 9 and simplify)}$$

It's always good to check, and in this case checking is also a good way to practice working with fractions and negative numbers.

$$7\left(-\frac{1}{3}\right) + 12 = -2\left(-\frac{1}{3}\right) + 9 \qquad \text{(Substitute } y = -\frac{1}{3} \text{ in the original equation)}$$
$$-\frac{7}{3} + 12 = \frac{2}{3} + 9 \qquad \text{(Multiply, carefully!)}$$
$$-\frac{7}{3} + \frac{36}{3} = \frac{2}{3} + \frac{27}{3} \qquad \text{(Find common denominators and rewrite)}$$
$$\frac{29}{3} = \frac{29}{3} \qquad \text{(Simplify)}$$

Since $\frac{29}{3} = \frac{29}{3}$ is true, we know $y = -\frac{1}{3}$ is a solution to $7y + 12 = -2y + 9$. We could also have solved this equation by isolating y on the right-hand side of the equation. Try it out and see what happens!

➥ **Example 3** _____

Solve $\frac{1}{2}z - 7 = \frac{1}{3}z - 5$.

$$\frac{1}{2}z - 7 = \frac{1}{3}z - 5 \qquad \text{(Original equation)}$$

$$\frac{1}{2}z - \frac{1}{3}z = -5 + 7 \qquad \text{(Subtract } \frac{1}{3}z \text{ from both sides, add 7 to both sides)}$$

$$\frac{3}{6}z - \frac{2}{6}z = 2 \qquad \text{(Find a common denominator)}$$

$$\frac{1}{6}z = 2 \qquad \text{(Simplify)}$$

$$z = 12 \qquad \text{(Multiply both sides by 6)}$$

You should check this solution to make sure it works. (You will likely end up with $-1 = -1$, which is true.)

Here's a slightly different approach, using a technique that is common when dealing with equations involving fractions:

$$\frac{1}{2}z - 7 = \frac{1}{3}z - 5 \qquad \text{(Original equation)}$$

$$6\left(\frac{1}{2}z - 7\right) = 6\left(\frac{1}{3}z - 5\right) \qquad \text{(Multiply both sides by 6)}$$

$$6 \times \frac{1}{2}z - 6 \times 7 = 6 \times \frac{1}{3}z - 6 \times 5 \qquad \text{(Apply the distributive property)}$$

$$3z - 42 = 2z - 30 \qquad \text{(Simplify)}$$

$$z = 12 \qquad \text{(Solve as normal)}$$

Here, the first thing we do is multiply both sides of the equation by 6, the common denominator of our two fractions. This has the result of eliminating all the fractions from our equation, which we can then solve in the usual way.

WARNING!	Multiplying both sides of an equation by the common denominator of all fractions can be a useful technique, but make sure to multiply everything!

GUESSING AND CHECKING

Consider the following equation:

$$12x + 21 = 129$$

We can use the techniques demonstrated above to solve for x. But thinking flexibly about numbers and equations can sometimes get us to the solution a little quicker.

Notice that $12 \times 10 = 120$, which isn't far from 129. Let's plug in $x = 10$ and see what happens:

$$12(10) + 21 = 129$$
$$120 + 21 = 129$$
$$141 = 129$$

We know $x = 10$ isn't a solution to our equation, because 141 does not equal 129. But notice that plugging in $x = 10$ gave us something that was a bit too big on the left-hand side. So let's try $x = 9$ next:

$$12(9) + 21 = 129$$
$$108 + 21 = 129$$
$$129 = 129$$

Bingo! Since $129 = 129$, we know $x = 9$ is a solution to our equation. Here, we used the strategy of *guessing and checking*. A few thoughtful guesses got us to the solution, which has now already been checked.

Thoughtful guessing and checking is a very useful problem-solving strategy, and it's one of the reasons fluency with numbers and arithmetic is so important. Don't be afraid to guess and check! But don't rely on it too much. For example, it's unlikely that you will guess that $x = 2.17$ is the solution to this equation:

$$10x + 0.3 = 25x - 32\frac{1}{4}$$

WARNING!	Guessing and checking, done properly, can find solutions. But some equations have multiple solutions. Just because you find one doesn't mean you've found them all.

INEQUALITIES

An inequality is a mathematical statement that one expression is greater than or less than another. Here are some examples:

$$3 < 9 \qquad 4 \geq 1 \qquad \frac{7}{9} > \frac{13}{18} \qquad 0 > 5 \qquad x \leq 10$$

Like equations, inequalities can be true or false. The inequality $3 < 9$ ("three is less than nine") is true, as is the inequality $4 \geq 1$ ("four is greater than or equal to one"). However, the inequality $0 > 5$ ("zero is greater than five") is false, since 0 is less than 5.

And like equations, we usually interpret an inequality involving variables as a question: What value of the variables will make the inequality true? So, what values of x make $x \leq 10$ true?

There are many. Infinitely many! The values $x = 3$, $x = 8$, and $x = 9$ all make the inequality true, since all these numbers are less than or equal to 10. And there are others like $x = \frac{15}{2}$, $x = 5.1782$, $x = -3$, and even $x = 10$, since it is true that $10 \leq 10$ ("ten is less than *or equal to* ten"). The set of all solutions to an inequality is often referred to as the *solution set* of the inequality.

WARNING!	When thinking about values for variables, we often think only about positive integers. Train yourself to think about negative numbers, fractions, and decimals, too.

One way to represent all the solutions to this inequality is on a number line. For example, here is the graphical representation of the inequality $x \leq 10$.

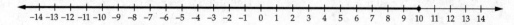

We shade all the numbers that are solutions to the inequality. Here, that is everything to the left of, and including, 10. Notice how we use arrows to indicate that the solution set continues on with the number line.

We put a closed dot on 10 because 10 is included in the solution set: 10 is less than or equal to 10. If we were graphing the inequality $x < 10$, we would use an open dot like this:

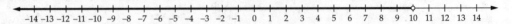

This shows that 10 is not included in the solution set, since it is not true that $10 < 10$.

To solve more complicated inequalities, we use the same principle we used to solve equations. We isolate the variable by performing the same mathematical operations on both sides of the inequality. And, as with equations, we can check our solutions by testing some values to make sure they make the inequality true.

Here are some examples:

➥ Example 1

Solve $4x > x + 6$.

$$4x > x + 6 \qquad \text{(Original equation)}$$
$$4x - x > x + 6 - x \qquad \text{(Subtract } x \text{ from both sides)}$$
$$3x > 6 \qquad \text{(Combine like terms)}$$
$$\frac{3x}{3} > \frac{6}{3} \qquad \text{(Divide both sides by 3)}$$
$$x > 2 \qquad \text{(Simplify)}$$

We can graph the solution set of the inequality on the number line like this:

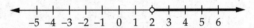

Notice we use on open dot because 2 is not a solution (2 is not greater than 2), and shade to the right of 2, because we want the numbers larger than 2.

It's always a good idea to test a value in our solution set. Let's test $x = 10$, which is bigger than 2:

$$4x > x + 6$$
$$4(10) > (10) + 6$$
$$40 > 16$$

Since this is true, $x = 10$ is in our solution set.

➥ Example 2

Solve $2x + 1 \geq 3x + 1.5$.

$$2x + 1 \geq 3x + 1.5 \qquad \text{(Original inequality)}$$
$$2x + 1 - 2x \geq 3x + 1.5 - 2x \qquad \text{(Subtract } 2x \text{ from both sides)}$$
$$1 \geq x + 1.5 \qquad \text{(Simplify)}$$
$$1 - 1.5 \geq x + 1.5 - 1.5 \qquad \text{(Add 1.5 to both sides)}$$
$$-0.5 \geq x \qquad \text{(Simplify)}$$

When we graph the solution set of the inequality on the number line, we use a closed dot on -0.5 because -0.5 is a solution (-0.5 is less than or equal to -0.5) and shade to the left of -0.5, because we want the numbers less than -0.5.

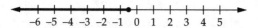

Let's test $x = -10$, which is less than -0.5:

$$2x + 1 \geq 3x - 1.5$$
$$2(-10) + 1 \geq 3(-10) - 1.5$$
$$-20 + 1 \geq -30 - 1.5$$
$$-21 \geq -31.5$$

This is true, so $x = -10$ is in our solution set.

WARNING!	It's always useful to test solutions to an inequality, but you can't test them all. There are infinitely many! With inequalities, checking values is good practice, but it's no guarantee.

There is one situation to beware of when you are solving inequalities. Consider the following true inequality:

$$5 > 2$$

Watch what happens when you multiply both sides of the inequality by -1:

$$5 > 2$$
$$(-1)5 > (-1)2$$
$$-5 > -2$$

This new inequality is false: -5 is less than -2! When we multiply or divide both sides of an inequality by a negative number, we must reverse the direction of the inequality. For example:

$$5 > 2$$
$$(-1)5 < (-1)2$$
$$-5 < -2$$

This is true, since -5 is less than -2. Here's another example:

➥ Example 3

Solve $3x \leq 5x - 22$.

$3x \leq 5x - 22$	(Original inequality)
$3x - 5x \leq 5x - 22 - 5x$	(Subtract $5x$ from both sides)
$-2x \leq -22$	(Combine like terms)
$\dfrac{-2x}{-2} \geq \dfrac{-22}{-2}$	(Divide both sides by -2 and *reverse the inequality*)
$x \geq 11$	(Simplify)

This may seem strange at first, but you can always test solutions to make sure you've done the work correctly. For example, $x = 100$ should be a solution to our inequality since $100 \geq 11$. Let's check it out:

$$3x \leq 5x - 22$$
$$3(100) \leq 5(100) - 22$$
$$300 \leq 500 - 22$$
$$300 \leq 478$$

This is true, so $x = 100$ is a solution to our inequality. If we had made the common mistake of not reversing the inequality, we would have ended up with $x \leq 11$ as our solution set. If we tested out $x = 0$ as a solution (since $0 < 11$), we would get:

$$3x \leq 5x - 22$$
$$3(0) \leq 5(0) - 22$$
$$0 \leq 0 - 22$$
$$0 \leq -22$$

This is false, since 0 is greater than -22. In this case, checking a solution alerts us to the fact that we probably did something wrong. And if you know you did something wrong when solving an inequality, look to see if you multiplied or divided by a negative number and forgot to the reverse the inequality.

One way to avoid this potential problem is to anticipate multiplying or dividing by negative numbers and avoid it. For example, refer to the following:

$$3x \leq 5x - 22$$

When solving this inequality, you could isolate x on the right-hand side instead of the left-hand side:

$3x \leq 5x - 22$	(Original inequality)
$3x - 3x \leq 5x - 22 - 3x$	(Subtract $3x$ from both sides)
$0 \leq 2x - 22$	(Combine like terms)
$22 \leq 2x$	(Add 22 to both sides)
$11 \leq x$	(Divide both sides by 2)

By anticipating the $-2x$ on the left-hand side when subtracting $5x$ from both sides of the inequality, we chose instead to isolate x on the right-hand side. This prevents us from having to divide both sides of the inequality by a negative number.

WARNING!	When dividing both sides of an inequality by a negative number, remember to switch the direction of the inequality sign.

COMPOUND INEQUALITIES

Compound inequalities are combinations of two (or more) inequalities that are usually joined with the words *and* or *or*, The words *and* and *or* are the keys to understanding how the two inequalities relate to one another.

If two inequalities are joined by the word *and*, a solution to the compound inequality must satisfy both inequalities simultaneously. For example, refer to the following:

$$x < 10 \text{ and } x > 1$$

Solutions to this compound inequality are the numbers that are both less than 10 and bigger than 1, numbers like 3, 5.7, 9.99, and so on. We can represent these numbers graphically like this:

The solution sets of *and* compound inequalities often look like line segments, with closed or open dots on either end.

We can write this particular compound inequality as a string of inequalities:

$$1 < x < 10$$

This is a common way to represent compound inequalities that are joined by the word *and*.

Inequalities joined by the word *or*, like $x \geq 4$ or $x \leq -2$, have solutions that satisfy *at least one* of the inequalities. For example, $x = 9$ is a solution to the above compound inequality because $9 \geq 4$. It doesn't matter that 9 is not less than -2. In an *or* compound inequality, a solution only needs to satisfy one of the inequalities.

The graphs of *or* compound inequalities usually look like this:

Notice that we shade every number that is either less than -2 or greater than 4.

Here is an example of solving a compound inequality:

➧ Example 4 _____

Solve $-5 \leq 3x - 2 < 10$.

First, we split the string of inequalities into two inequalities joined by the word *and*:

$$-5 \leq 3x - 2 \text{ and } 3x - 2 < 10$$

We can solve each inequality separately:

$$
\begin{array}{ccc}
-5 \leq 3x - 2 & & 3x - 2 < 10 \\
-3 \leq 3x & \text{and} & 3x < 12 \\
-1 \leq x & & x < 4
\end{array}
$$

We can then put the two inequalities back together:

$$-1 \leq x \text{ and } x < 4$$

And if you wish, you can rewrite as a string of inequalities:

$$-1 \leq x < 4$$

Either way, the graph of the solution set looks like this:

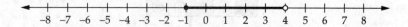

A convenient value to test in the solution set is $x = 0$.

$$-5 \leq 3x - 2 < 10$$
$$-5 \leq 3(0) - 2 < 10$$
$$-5 \leq -2 < 10$$

This produces a true statement, providing evidence that we have found the correct solution set.

PROBLEM SOLVING

Now let's work through some problems involving equations and inequalities that are similar to those you might face on the SHSAT.

➥ Example 1 _____

Sample Grid-In Question

1. For what value of z does $6z + 25 = 3z - 8$?

Our approach here is the same as in the above examples. We will isolate the variable z by performing the same operations on both sides of the equation.

$6z + 25 = 3z - 8$	(Original equation)
$6z + 25 - 3z = 3z - 8 - 3z$	(Subtract $3z$ from both sides)
$3z + 25 = -8$	(Combine like terms)
$3z + 25 - 25 = -8 - 25$	(Subtract 25 from both sides)
$3z = -33$	(Simplify)
$\dfrac{3z}{3} = \dfrac{-33}{3}$	(Divide both sides by 3)
$z = -11$	(Simplify)

We can check our solution by substituting $z = -11$ into the original equation:

$$6z + 25 = 3z - 8$$
$$6(-11) + 25 = 3(-11) - 8$$
$$-66 + 25 = -33 - 8$$
$$-41 = -41$$

Since the final equation is true, we know $z = -11$ is the solution to the equation. Remember to always check your solutions. It's a simple way to build confidence and catch errors.

2. The set of possible values of m is $\{4, 6, 8\}$. What is the set of possible values of k if $2k = 3m - 2$?

   (E) $\{8, 12, 16\}$

   (F) $\{5, 8, 11\}$

   (G) $\{10, 16, 22\}$

   (H) $\{12, 18, 24\}$

For each of the three possible values of m, there is a corresponding value for k. The task is to find those k values.

A chart is a useful way to organize work for this problem. You can start the chart like this:

m	$3m - 2$
4	$3(4) - 2 = 10$
6	$3(6) - 2 = 16$
8	$3(8) - 2 = 22$

Then, since $2k = 3m - 2$, you can continue the chart like this:

m	$3m - 2$	$2k$
4	10	10
6	16	16
8	22	22

Lastly, you can add a final column:

m	$3m - 2$	$2k$	k
4	10	10	5
6	16	16	8
8	22	22	11

So the set of all possible values of k is $\{5, 8, 11\}$, which is choice F.

Notice that choice G corresponds to the values of $2k$. Remember that incorrect answer choices are often chosen deliberately to mislead the test-taker. If you aren't paying close attention, you may see the numbers $\{10, 16, 22\}$ come up during your work and jump to the conclusion that this must be the answer. Always make sure you are answering the question that was asked.

You can also approach this problem by manipulating the equation $2k = 3m - 2$ and solving for k:

$$k = \frac{3m - 2}{2}$$

Now plug in each of the values for m to get the corresponding values for k. You can solve for m and test out the answer choices to see which set of k values yields $\{4, 6, 8\}$ as the set of m values.

$$m = \frac{2k + 2}{3}$$

➡ Example 3 _____

3. Alina bought 8 bottles of water for $0.90 each and 12 pounds of fish. She paid a total of $61.20 for these items, not including tax. What was the price per pound of the fish?

(A) $4.50
(B) $5.40
(C) $7.20
(D) $54.00

Some problems on the SHSAT involve setting up and applying an equation. Informally, this is what our equation looks like:

(price per water bottle) × *(# of water bottles)* + *(price per pound of fish)*
× *(pounds of fish)* = *total spent*

There are five quantities in the above equation and we know four of them. We don't know the price per pound of fish, so we declare a variable to represent it. Let's declare f to be the price per pound of fish. Now we can write an equation that relates to what we know and what we don't know:

$$0.90 \times 8 + f \times 12 = 61.20$$

This is now a simple equation, which we can solve in the usual way:

$$0.90 \times 8 + f \times 12 = 61.20$$
$$7.20 + 12f = 61.20$$
$$12f = 54.00$$
$$f = 4.50$$

So the price per pound of fish is $4.50, which is choice A. A quick check shows us we have the correct answer:

$$0.90 \times 8 + 4.5 \times 12 = 61.20$$
$$7.20 + 54 = 61.20$$

You can also solve this problem without formally setting up an equation. Compute the amount spent on water ($7.20) and subtract it from the total ($61.20) to get the amount spent on fish ($54.00). Now you can find the price per pound of fish by dividing the price of the fish by the number of pounds, to get the following:

$$\frac{\$54.00}{12 \text{ pounds}} = \$4.50 \text{ per pound}$$

This involves the same basic work as setting up and solving an equation, but it is done in a more intuitive way. It's good to have multiple methods to solve problems, but make sure you master the fundamental skills of declaring variables and setting up equations. You'll need those skills to solve more complex problems.

Also, this a problem you could solve by working backwards and trying all the possible answer choices. Multiply each of the answer choices by 12 to get the total cost of the fish, then add the cost of the water ($7.20) and see which answer leads to $61.20.

Answer	Price per Pound of Fish (f)	Total Cost of Fish ($12 \times f$)	Total Cost ($12 \times f + 7.20$)
A	4.50	54.00	61.20
B	5.40	64.80	72.00
C	7.20	86.40	93.60
D	54.00	648.00	655.20

In fact, trying all the answer choices works very quickly here. Only choice A yields a total cost for the fish below the total amount paid, which means it must be the answer.

➡ Example 4 _____

4. Describe the values of x that satisfy the inequality $-5 < -2x + 1 < 7$.

    (E) $3 < x$ or $x < -3$
    (F) $-3 < x < 3$
    (G) $2 < x$ or $x < -4$
    (H) $-4 < x < 2$

First, we split the string of inequalities into a pair of inequalities joined with *and*:

$$-5 < -2x + 1 \quad \text{and} \quad -2x + 1 < 7$$

Then solve each inequality individually.

$-5 < -2x + 1$	(Original inequality)
$-5 - 1 < -2x + 1 - 1$	(Subtract 1 from both sides)
$-6 < -2x$	(Simplify)
$\dfrac{-6}{-2} > \dfrac{-2x}{-2}$	(Divide both sides by -2 and reverse the inequality!)
$3 > x$	(Simplify)

Remember, when multiplying or dividing both sides of an inequality by a negative number, you must reverse the order of the inequality.

We solve the other inequality similarly and get the following:

$$-2x + 1 < 7$$
$$-2x < 6$$
$$x > -3$$

Again, remember to reverse the direction of the inequality because of the division by -2. Now our two inequalities have become:

$$3 > x \quad \text{and} \quad x > -3$$

This can also be rewritten as a string of inequalities:

$$-3 < x < 3$$

This is choice F. Notice that choice H is what you would get if you added 1 to both inequalities, instead of subtracting 1.

The solution set can be graphed on the number line using open circles because the endpoints are not included.

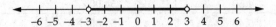

It's always wise to test a value, so let's see if $x = 0$, which is in our solution set, satisfies our original inequality.

$$-5 < -2x + 1 < 7$$
$$-5 < -2(0) + 1 < 7$$
$$-5 < 1 < 7$$

Since the last compound inequality is true, $x = 0$ is indeed a solution.

Remember, if you are worried about forgetting to reverse the inequality when you multiply or divide by a negative number, you can try to avoid it by looking ahead. For example, when solving $-5 < -2x + 1$, simply work to isolate x on the left-hand side of the equation.

$-5 < -2x + 1$	(Original inequality)
$-5 + 2x < -2x + 1 + 2x$	(Add $2x$ to both sides)
$-5 + 2x < 1$	(Simplify)
$2x < 6$	(Add 5 to both sides)
$x < 3$	(Divide by 2)

This approach avoids dividing both sides of the inequality by a negative number, and so we need not worry about reversing the direction of the inequality.

➡ Example 5 _____

5. The sum of three consecutive integers is -21. If 1 is subtracted from each integer, what is the product of the three resulting integers?

   (A) -504
   (B) -336
   (C) 336
   (D) 504

Here is another example of a problem where you might set up and solve an equation. Since we don't know the three integers in question, we should declare variables to represent them. But because the integers are consecutive, we only need to declare one variable, since if x is the smallest integer, we can write our three consecutive integers like this:

$$x, \ x+1, \ x+2$$

We know the sum of these integers is -21, so we can write the equation and solve for x.

$$x + x + 1 + x + 2 = -21$$
$$3x + 3 = -21$$
$$3x = -24$$
$$x = -8$$

So our three consecutive integers x, $x+1$, $x+2$, are:

$$x = -8$$
$$x+1 = -8+1 = -7$$
$$x+2 = -8+2 = -6$$

If we subtract 1 from each of the three integers, we get:

$$-8-1 = -9$$
$$-7-1 = -8$$
$$-6-1 = -7$$

The product of these three new numbers is:

$$(-9)(-8)(-7) = -9 \times 8 \times 7 = -72 \times 7 = -504$$

So choice A, -504, is our answer.

Being able to set up and solve the equation is important, but guessing and checking can get you to the answer faster. For example, it's not hard to guess the three consecutive integers that add up to -21. They are probably negative, and since their average is $\frac{-21}{3} = -7$, they are probably all around -7. That means you can likely find $(-8) + (-7) + (-6) = -21$ without solving an equation, and then complete the problem from there. Notice that 504 is one of the answer choices, which is what you would get if you forgot about the negative signs. But a little forethought allows you to immediately eliminate both positive answer choices. If three consecutive integers add up to -21, each of them must be a negative number, and the product of three negative numbers is negative. Thus, with little work, you know the answer must be choice A or B.

SUMMARY

Equations arise frequently in mathematics, so being able to solve them confidently and correctly is essential to being a good problem solver. Along with solving equations on the SHSAT, you'll probably have to set some up as well. Practice manipulating equations by performing the same operation on both sides, isolating variables, and checking your solutions. Guessing and checking can be an invaluable strategy in finding solutions to equations, but remember not to rely on it exclusively.

Dealing with inequalities is a lot like dealing with equations, but there are differences. Inequalities usually have a solution set—infinitely many solutions that we represent on the number line. And you have to be careful performing operations on both sides of an inequality. If you multiply or divide by a negative number, you must reverse the direction of the inequality.

The key to equations and inequalities is that a solution is a value of the variable that makes the equation, or inequality, true. Find this value using algebra, arithmetic, or even guessing; but however you find it, make sure you check it. Doing so will help you build confidence, catch errors, and earn more points on the SHSAT.

EXERCISES

Here is some targeted practice with equations and inequalities.

1. Solve for x: $10x - 14 = 6x + 50$

2. Solve for x: $4x + 2 \geq -10$

3. Solve for y: $5y + 12 = 8y + 20$

4. Solve for a: $5 - 2a \geq 12$

5. Solve for x in terms of y: $y = \frac{2}{3}x - 8$

6. Solve for z: $-4 \leq \frac{z}{2} + 3 < 15$

7. The sum of two consecutive integers is -11. If each integer is decreased by 2, what is the product of the two new integers?

8. Solve for x: $10 < -2x - 4 < 24$

9. Solve for x: $\frac{2}{3}x - \frac{5}{6} = \frac{4}{5}x - \frac{31}{30}$

10. Four loaves of bread are bought for $2.75 each, and nine pounds of meat are bought. A total of $57.35 is spent. What is the price per pound of the meat?

(Answers are on page 203.)

Ratios and Proportions

12

OVERVIEW

Ratios are used to describe the relative sizes of related quantities, like flour to sugar in a recipe or Yankees fans to Mets fans at a subway series game. Ratios are usually expressed as fractions, like $\frac{3}{4}$, or using colon-notation, like 3 : 4. Ratios are used to describe how some quantities, like money, are distributed. Ratios can also describe rates, like miles per hour.

Proportions are equations involving ratios. By solving proportions, we can use ratios, which typically describe relative size, to answer questions about absolute size. We can also find percentages, which are a kind of proportion useful in understanding relative size and share.

Problem Solving

Here are some of the types of problems you will solve using ratios and proportions:

- Use a small sample to understand a larger population: If 12 of every 20 students in school bring their own lunch, how many of the school's 310 students bring their own lunch?
- Compute and apply percentages: If the value of a $500 investment grows by 8% per year, how much is it worth after two years?
- Deal with scale drawings: If 1 inch on a diagram represents 25 feet, how many feet would 3.5 inches represent?

Prior Knowledge

Here are some things you need to be comfortable with in order to master working with ratios and proportions:

- Simplifying fractions and recognizing equivalent fractions
- Solving simple equations using multiplication and division
- Interpreting data from charts and tables
- Reading and decoding word problems

RATIOS

A **ratio** expresses the relationship between the relative sizes of two quantities. Ratios are often represented as fractions. For example, in a class of 40 students where 18 are boys, we would say the ratio of boys to total students is:

$$\frac{18}{40}$$

This number $\frac{18}{40}$ is the *ratio of boys to total students in class*. There are a number of ways to read and interpret this number. We can say, "The ratio of boys to total students is $\frac{18}{40}$," "The ratio of boys to total students is 18 to 40," and "For every 40 students in class, 18 are boys." This last interpretation will be particularly helpful in certain kinds of problem solving.

The ratio expresses the relationship between a part (the number of boys) and the whole (the total number of students in the class). This is a common use of ratios.

Another common use of ratios is to express relationships between parts. For example, if in our class of 40 students, 18 are boys and 22 are girls, we could write the ratio of boys to girls as the following:

$$\frac{18}{22}$$

We can interpret this ratio as "For every 22 girls in class, there are 18 boys in class." We could also interpret this as "For every 18 boys in class, there are 22 girls in class."

WARNING!	A common mistake in dealing with ratios is to compare part to part when part to whole is required, or vice versa. Pay close attention to the kind of ratio you are using.

Another way to express ratios is using colon notation. In colon notation, the ratio $\frac{18}{40}$ is expressed as 18 : 40, and the ratio $\frac{18}{22}$ is expressed as 18 : 22. The meaning of the ratio is the same.

One virtue of the colon notation is that you can express a ratio involving more than two quantities. For example, suppose a bag of candies contained 12 red candies, 15 blue candies, and 24 green candies. We can express the relationship between the different quantities of candies as the following ratio:

$$12 : 15 : 24$$

We read this as "The ratio of red candies to blue candies to green candies is 12 to 15 to 24." One way to interpret this is that for every 12 red candies, there are 15 blues candies and 24 green candies. The colon notation is helpful here since it would be difficult to use fractions to express a ratio involving three quantities.

In working with ratios, the ability to simplify fractions and recognize equivalent forms of different fractions is essential. Notice that:

$$\frac{18}{40} = \frac{9 \times 2}{20 \times 2} = \frac{9}{20}$$

This allows us to say that the ratio of boys to total students in our class is 9 to 20. Although the individual numbers in the ratios are different, the ratios are the same because $\frac{18}{40}$ and $\frac{9}{20}$ represent the same number. Just as we can simplify a fraction, we can simplify a ratio.

We can also use grouping to see that these ratios are the same. If the ratio of boys to total students is $\frac{9}{20}$, this means that out of every 20 students, 9 are boys. Since 40 is two groups of 20, and each group of 20 students has 9 boys, we see that there will be 18 boys among the 40 students. This grouping strategy is a useful technique in solving problems involving ratios.

Our other example ratios can be simplified as well. Since $\frac{18}{22} = \frac{9}{11}$, we can say that the ratio of boys to girls in class is $\frac{9}{11}$, or 9 to 11. And the three-part ratio can also be simplified. Since each of the numbers 12, 15, and 24 is divisible by 3, we can divide out the 3 from the ratio 12 : 15 : 24 and get 4 : 5 : 8. The ratio of red candies to blue candies to green candies is 4 to 5 to 8.

Another common use of ratios is to express how one quantity is distributed among another. For example, if you bought 8 movie tickets for $60, the total amount spent divided by the number of tickets purchased is:

$$\frac{\$60}{8 \text{ tickets}}$$

This ratio can be simplified:

$$\frac{60}{8} = \frac{30}{4} = \frac{15}{2} = \frac{7.5}{1}$$

The simplified ratio, $\frac{\$7.50}{1 \text{ ticket}}$, gives the cost of a single ticket.

Being able to determine the amount of one quantity per unit of another quantity can be useful in problem solving. A particular example of this involves rates. For example, if you are travelling by car and cover 180 miles in four hours, we can compute the ratio of total distance to total time.

$$\frac{180 \text{ miles}}{4 \text{ hour}}$$

This is speed, since speed $= \dfrac{\text{distance}}{\text{time}}$.

By simplifying $\dfrac{180}{4} = 45 \dfrac{\text{miles}}{\text{hour}}$, we can compute the distance travelled *per hour*, namely 45 miles per hour. Notice that the units used in this ratio (miles/hour, or miles per hour) also indicates that this ratio is a rate.

PROPORTIONS

A **proportion** is an equation in which two ratios are equal. Often in a proportion, one or more of the components of the ratios are unknown, so we must solve equations to find them.

In our previous example, the ratio of boys to total students in class was 18 to 40. Suppose that the ratio of boys to total students in the entire school was the same as in this one class, namely 18 to 40. If we knew the total number of students in the school, we could use a proportion to find the total number of boys in the school.

Let's say there are 320 total students in the school, and the ratio of boys to total students is 18 to 40. Let B be the number of boys in the school. We can set up the following proportion:

$$\frac{B}{320} = \frac{18}{40}$$

This proportion says that the ratio of boys in school to total students in school $\left(\dfrac{B}{320}\right)$ is the same as the ratio of boys in our class to total students in our class $\left(\dfrac{18}{40}\right)$.

By solving this equation for B, we can determine the total number of boys in the school. First, we multiply both sides of the equation by 320 to isolate B, and then we simplify the right-hand side:

$$320 \times \frac{B}{320} = 320 \times \frac{18}{40}$$
$$B = 320 \times \frac{18}{40}$$
$$B = \frac{320}{40} \times 18$$
$$B = 8 \times 18$$
$$B = 144$$

Thus, in the school of 320 students, there are 144 boys. To check, we should verify that:

$$\frac{144}{320} = \frac{18}{40}$$

The ability to simplify fractions and recognize equivalent fractions will be of great help here. Notice that:

$$\frac{144}{320} = \frac{8 \times 18}{8 \times 40} = \frac{18}{40}$$

In fact, simplifying fractions in the initial proportion would have made the process easier. Since $\frac{18}{40} = \frac{9}{20}$, we know that the ratio of 18 to 40 is the same as the ratio of 9 to 20, so we could have started with the following:

$$\frac{B}{320} = \frac{9}{20}$$

With smaller numbers to multiply, the arithmetic is easier.

A common technique in solving proportions is **cross-multiplying**. For instance, suppose we knew that there were 144 boys in the school and we wanted to determine the number of girls in the school. We could use the ratio of 18 boys to 22 girls to set up another proportion:

$$\frac{18}{22} = \frac{144}{G}$$

Here G is the total number of girls in the school. First, let's replace $\frac{18}{22}$ with $\frac{9}{11}$, an equivalent, but simpler, ratio.

$$\frac{9}{11} = \frac{144}{G}$$

Now we can cross-multiply. Cross-multiplying, also known as the **means-extremes principle**, allows us to replace the equation $\frac{a}{b} = \frac{c}{d}$ with the equation $ad = bc$. This is nothing more than multiplying both sides of the equation by bd, but it is used often enough to be thought of as its own technique.

In our case, we can replace $\frac{9}{11} = \frac{144}{G}$ with $9G = 11 \times 144$, and then solve for G.

$$9G = 11 \times 144$$
$$G = \frac{11 \times 144}{9}$$
$$G = \frac{11 \times 9 \times 16}{9}$$
$$G = 11 \times 16$$
$$G = 176$$

So there are 176 girls in the school.

When problem solving, it's always a good idea to constantly ask yourself, "Does my answer make sense?" We know that the number of boys is 144. Does it make sense that the number of girls is 176? Think back to the original ratio of 18 boys to 22 girls. There are more girls than boys, but it is pretty close to being evenly divided. So 176 girls and 144 boys seems reasonable.

We found the number of girls in school using a proportion, but if we knew the 320 students were all boys and girls, and we knew that 144 of the students were boys, we could find G in another way: The number of boys plus the number of girls should equal 320.

$$B + G = 320$$
$$144 + G = 320$$
$$G = 320 - 144$$
$$G = 176$$

This is what we found using our method of proportions. It's good to practice with proportions, but it is always helpful to be thinking of alternate ways to find and check your answers.

PERCENTAGES

Percentage is one of the most familiar applications of ratios and proportions. *Per cent* means "out of 100," which suggests a ratio. To say 43% of Americans like baseball is to say that 43 out of every 100 Americans like baseball, and 43 out of 100, or $\frac{43}{100}$, is a ratio. Generally speaking, percentage is a ratio that compares a part to the whole.

Computing percentages involves solving proportions. Returning to our original example, suppose we know 18 out of 40 students are boys. To find the percentage of students that are boys, we solve the proportion, where x is the percentage, or the part out of 100.

$$\frac{18}{40} = \frac{x}{100}$$

Therefore:

$$x = 100 \times \frac{18}{40} = \frac{100}{40} \times 18 = \frac{5}{2} \times 18 = 5 \times \frac{18}{2} = 5 \times 9 = 45$$

And so 45% of the students are boys. Notice that this agrees with our earlier observation that boys made up a little less than half (which is 50%) of the students.

Another typical application of percentage is computing the change in some given quantity. Suppose an investment of $250 increases in value by 4% in one year. How much is the investment worth now?

Let Z be the amount of increase in value of the investment. To find 4% of 250, we can set up the following proportion:

$$\frac{Z}{250} = \frac{4}{100}$$

Solving for Z gives us:

$$Z = 250 \times \frac{4}{100} = 250 \times \frac{1}{25} = 10$$

Since investment increased in value by $10, which is 4% of 250, the investment is now worth $250 + $10 = $260. You could also solve this problem by finding 4% of $250 directly:

$$0.04 \times \$250 = \$10$$

Since $0.04 = \frac{4}{100}$, this is essentially the same technique as above.

It's also possible to directly compute the amount after a year of increase. Notice that our answer is found by adding $250 + $10 to get $260, where $10 represents the increase, namely, 4% of the original $250. The $250 represents the original investment, or 100% of the original $250. We can think of the equation this way:

$$260 = 250 + 10$$
$$260 = 1.00 \times 250 + 0.04 \times 250$$
$$260 = (1.00 + 0.04) \times 250$$
$$260 = 1.04 \times 250$$

That is, to find how much the $250 investment is worth after one year of 4% growth, we can simply compute $1.04 \times 250 = 260$.

When solving problems with percentages, 10% is a particularly nice percentage to work with, as 10% is $\frac{10}{100} = \frac{1}{10} = 0.1$. Computing 10% of a quantity is easy—just divide by 10. For example, 10% of 250 is 25. This creates an opportunity to estimate and check your work. If 10% of 250 is 25, then 5% of 250 is 12.5, and so it seems reasonable that 4% of 250 is 10.

WARNING!	The percent sign means "out of one hundred." For example, **8% means** "8 out of 100." Thus, when performing a calculation involving **8%, you need** to use the number $\frac{8}{100}$, or 0.08.

PROBLEM SOLVING

Now let's work through some problems involving ratios and proportions that are similar to those you might face on the SHSAT.

➡ Example 1 _____

Sample Grid-in Question

1. A baker makes chocolate cupcakes and vanilla cupcakes in a ratio of 7 : 5. If 228 cupcakes are baked, how many are vanilla?

   One approach is to determine the ratio of vanilla cupcakes to total cupcakes. Out of every 12 cupcakes, 7 are chocolate and 5 are vanilla. So the ratio of vanilla cupcakes to total cupcakes is 5 to 12. Now we can set up and solve a proportion. Let V be the total number of vanilla cupcakes.

$$\frac{5}{12} = \frac{V}{228}$$

   Therefore, $V = 228 \times \frac{5}{12} = \frac{228}{12} \times 5 = 19 \times 5 = 95$.

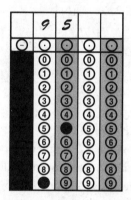

   Another approach is to think in terms of groups of 12 cupcakes. In every group of 12 cupcakes, 5 are vanilla. The 228 total cupcakes can be thought of as $\frac{228}{12} = 19$ groups of 12. In each of those 19 groups, 5 are vanilla, so there are $19 \times 5 = 95$ total vanilla cupcakes. This grouping approach is particularly useful for three-part ratios.

WARNING!	Common incorrect answers to this question include 19 (the number of groups of 12 cupcakes) and 133 (the number of chocolate cupcakes).

   Remember to develop the habit of asking, "Does my answer make sense?" An answer of 19 doesn't make sense, because, given the ratio, that's definitely not enough vanilla cupcakes out of 288. And 133 doesn't make sense because the ratio tells us fewer than half of the cupcakes should be vanilla, and half of 228 is 114.

   Scale diagrams are commonly used in questions involving ratios and proportions.

➥ Example 2 _____

2. In a scale drawing, 0.2 inches represents 100 miles. How many inches represent 1 mile?

(E)   0.002

(F)   0.02

(G) 200

(H) 500

This begins as a proportion problem. Let x be the number of inches representing 1 mile. Our scale relationship, given in inches to miles, yields the following proportion:

$$\frac{0.2 \text{ inches}}{100 \text{ miles}} = \frac{x \text{ inches}}{1 \text{ miles}}$$

Now this is an arithmetic problem. We solve for x:

$$x = 1 \times \frac{0.2}{100}$$
$$= \frac{0.2}{100}$$
$$= \frac{\frac{2}{10}}{100}$$
$$= \frac{2}{10} \times \frac{1}{100}$$
$$= \frac{2}{1000}$$
$$= 0.002$$

The answer is 0.002 inches, which is choice E.

Does our answer make sense? One mile is 100 times shorter than 100 miles, so the number of inches should be 100 times smaller than 0.2. This reasoning allows you to eliminate answer choices G and H immediately. Choice H is the answer to the question, "How many miles are represented by 1 inch?"

Notice how being able to write the ratio $\frac{0.2}{100}$ as $\frac{2}{1000}$ made finding the decimal representation of our answer (0.002, or *two thousandths*) easier. As has been mentioned many times, fluency with arithmetic is essential to success on the SHSAT exam.

➥ Example 3 _____

3. A country has five kinds of coins: *algos*, *broots*, *cloops*, *drings*, and *ergs*.

$$1 \text{ algo} = 3 \text{ broots}$$
$$2 \text{ cloops} = 7 \text{ drings}$$
$$4 \text{ algos} = 9 \text{ ergs}$$
$$1 \text{ cloop} = 4 \text{ ergs}$$

The relationship between the coins is shown above. Which coin is most valuable?

(A) algo

(B) broot

(C) cloop

(D) dring

Notice that the relative values of all the coins are expressed as ratios. First, since 1 algo is worth 3 broots, algos are more valuable than broots. We can eliminate choice B. A cloop is more valuable than a dring, since 2 cloops is worth the same as 7 drings, so we can eliminate choice D.

So the most valuable coin is either an algo or a cloop, which can be compared in terms of ergs: 4 algos is worth 9 ergs, so 1 algo is worth $\frac{9}{4} = 2\frac{1}{4}$ ergs. A cloop is worth 4 ergs, so since a cloop is worth more ergs than an algo, it is more valuable. Thus, the answer is choice C.

Another approach is to make all the given ratios directly comparable, which we can do by changing each of the ratios so they all have four coins on the left. This can be accomplished by multiplying each ratio by the appropriate amount.

$$4 \text{ algos} = 12 \text{ broots}$$
$$4 \text{ cloops} = 14 \text{ drings}$$
$$4 \text{ algos} = 9 \text{ ergs}$$
$$4 \text{ cloops} = 16 \text{ ergs}$$

By making all the ratios have 4 coins on the left, the algos and cloops are now directly comparable. We see that 4 algos are worth 9 ergs and 4 cloops are worth 16 ergs. If 4 cloops are worth more ergs than 4 algos, then 1 cloop is more valuable than 1 algo. And since algos are more valuable than broots, we now know that the cloop is the most valuable coin.

Here is a typical algebra problem involving ratios.

➡ **Example 4** _____

4. The sum of the numbers x, y, and z is 60. The ratio of x to y is $2 : 5$, and the ratio of y to z is $5 : 8$. What is the value of x?

(E) 2

(F) 8

(G) 16

(H) 20

One way to solve this is to set up a system of equations. We are given that $x + y + z = 60$. We also have our proportions:

$$\frac{x}{y} = \frac{2}{5} \text{ and } \frac{y}{z} = \frac{5}{8}$$

A general strategy in dealing with an equation like $x + y + z = 60$ is to try to rewrite the equation so that it uses only a single variable. Since y appears in both proportions, we can solve for x and z in terms of y:

$$x = \frac{2}{5}y \text{ and } z = \frac{8}{5}y$$

When we substitute into $x + y + z = 60$, our equation will have a single variable, and we can solve for it:

$$x + y + z = 60$$

$$\frac{2}{5}y + y + \frac{8}{5}y = 60$$

$$\frac{2}{5}y + \frac{5}{5}y + \frac{8}{5}y = 60$$

$$\frac{15}{5}y = 60$$

$$3y = 60$$

$$y = 20$$

Since $y = 20$, we can find x by substitution: $x = \frac{2}{5}y = \frac{2}{5}(20) = 8$.

A potentially faster approach is to notice that the given ratios can be combined into a single three-part ratio. If the ratio of x to y is 2 to 5, and the ratio of y to z is 5 to 8, then the ratio of x to z is 2 to 8. Thus, we can express the ratio of $x : y : z$ as $2 : 5 : 8$.

Notice that $2 + 5 + 8 = 15$. Our goal is to split 60 up among x, y, and z according to this ratio, but now it is convenient to think in groups of 15. If we were splitting up 15 among x, y, and z, x would get 2, y would get 5, and z would get 8. Since there are four groups of 15 in 60, if x gets 2 in each of the four groups, x gets $2 \times 4 = 8$ altogether.

The first approach requires more effort, but it is a more general approach that works in any situation. The second approach is more efficient, but it relies on our ability to create a three-part ratio. While it might not always be easy to create a three-part ratio, these are the sorts of time-saving opportunities frequently available on the SHSAT. Train yourself to look for, and take advantage of, these opportunities.

You could also try all the possibilities here. For example, if $x = 2$, that would make $y = 5$ and $z = 8$. Since these don't sum to 60, choice E cannot be the correct answer. If $x = 16$, then $y = 40$, and $z = 64$, and since these don't sum to 60, G cannot be the correct answer. This may be the fastest way to the answer. Look for these opportunities throughout the test.

Lastly, here's an example of using a ratio as a rate.

➡ Example 5

5. Christina must solve 130 math problems over the holiday break. It took her 42 minutes to solve the first 30 problems. How much more time will it take her to complete her assignment?

(A)   84 minutes
(B)   130 minutes
(C)   140 minutes
(D)   182 minutes

One approach to this problem is to set up a proportion, and there are several to choose from. For example, you could set up a part-to-whole proportion, where T is the total amount of time necessary to complete all 130 problems.

$$\frac{42 \text{ minutes}}{30 \text{ problems}} = \frac{T \text{ minutes}}{130 \text{ problems}}$$

We can then solve for T:

$$T = 130 \times \frac{42}{30}$$

$$= \frac{130}{30} \times 42$$

$$= \frac{13}{3} \times 42$$

$$= 13 \times \frac{42}{3}$$

$$= 13 \times 14$$

$$= 182$$

But choice D is not the correct answer. Since T is the total time required to solve *all the problems*, we must subtract off the time Christina already spent solving the first 30 problems to find the amount of time required to finish the remaining problems. Thus, the answer is $182 - 42 = 140$ minutes, or choice C. Remember to always pay attention to what your variables represent.

WARNING!	Remember to always answer the question that was asked, not a different question you mistakenly believe was asked.

Another approach is to set up a part-to-part proportion. Let R equal the time needed to complete the remaining 100 math problems.

$$\frac{42 \text{ minutes}}{30 \text{ problems}} = \frac{R \text{ minutes}}{100 \text{ problems}}$$

Solving for R gives us the following:

$$R = 100 \times \frac{42}{30} = \frac{100}{30} \times 42 = \frac{10}{3} \times 42 = 10 \times \frac{42}{3} = 10 \times 14 = 140$$

This approach gives us the correct answer without having to worry about subtracting off the time already spent on the task.

An alternate and efficient approach is to simply ask, "How long does it take complete a single problem?" The answer is $\frac{42}{30} = 1.4$ minutes/problem. Here we again see a ratio as a rate, and this allows us to determine that it would take $100 \times 1.4 = 140$ minutes to complete the remaining 100 problems.

SUMMARY

When setting up a ratio, pay attention to whether you are creating a part-to-part ratio or a part-to-whole ratio. When setting up a proportion, make sure you are equating comparable ratios, and when using variables, make sure you know what they represent. Problems involving ratios and proportions require fluency in handling fractions and decimals, as well as solving equations.

As in all problem solving, it is helpful to frequently ask yourself whether the question makes sense and use estimates and units to help answer that question. And in end, always remember to ask yourself, "Am I answering the question that was asked?"

EXERCISES

Here is some targeted practice with ratios and proportions.

1. Solve for x: $\dfrac{24}{x} = \dfrac{84}{21}$

2. If $x + y = 270$ and $x : y = 7 : 11$, what is x?

3. What is 12% of 360?

4. 18 movie tickets cost \$130.50. How much would 7 movie tickets cost?

5. On a map, one inch represents 150 miles. Two cities are 345 miles apart. How far apart are they on the map?

6. How many seconds are there in 0.1 days?

7. Solve for y: $\dfrac{y+2}{9} = \dfrac{y}{5}$

8. Five out of every 18 candies are blue. The rest are red. In a bag of 468 candies, how many are red?

9. A teacher has to grade 99 papers. It takes him 36 minutes to grade the first 22 papers. How long will it take to finish grading?

10. If $x + y + z = 170$, $x : y = 2 : 3$, and $y : z = 6 : 7$, what is z?

(Answers are on page 203.)

Counting, Probability, and Statistics

13

OVERVIEW

Counting is one of the most basic mathematical skills, important in its own right as well as for its role in other kinds of math problems. On the SHSAT, you'll be asked to count possible outcomes that result from choosing repeatedly in the same way, or choosing multiple times in different ways. And you'll have to count frequencies by reading and interpreting charts, tables, and graphs.

You will also use counting and related principles to compute basic probabilities, like choosing a certain kind of cookie from a jar, or selecting a certain kind of student from a class. Probability is a measure of likelihood, and the way we compute probability requires you to count both favorable outcomes and total possible outcomes.

Lastly, in this section we will discuss some elementary statistical ideas like mean and median, and we will look at examples of interpreting data in charts, tables, and graphs, and using that information to solve counting and probability problems.

Problem Solving

Here are some of the types of problems you will solve that rely on counting, probability, and statistics:

- Count the number of ways something can occur, like the number of ways you can make a pizza by choosing 2 of 6 different toppings
- Compute the probability of an event occurring, like drawing a blue marble from a bag with 6 blue marbles and 9 red marbles
- Find the mean of a set of numbers, like the average student test score in a class
- Interpret charts, tables, and graphs and use them to solve problems

Prior Knowledge

Here are some things you need to be comfortable with in order to master working with counting, probability, and statistics:

- Doing arithmetic in your head and on paper
- Multiplying and simplifying fractions
- Reading and interpreting charts, tables, and graphs

COUNTING OUTCOMES

The Fundamental Counting Principle

When we face decisions, we have options. In analyzing our decisions, we often want to know how many options we have. We want to count the number of possible **outcomes**.

Counting outcomes is simple when there is only one choice to make. If there are eight crayons in a box, then choosing a crayon from the box has eight possible outcomes. If there are two options for lunch—sandwich or pizza—then there are two possible outcomes for lunch.

But things get a little more complicated when we make multiple choices. Luckily, we have the **Fundamental Counting Principle (FCP)** to guide us. The Fundamental Counting Principle says that if you are making two choices, your total number of options is equal to the product of the number of options you have for each choice.

For example, suppose you are choosing your outfit for the day, and you have three shirts (red, blue, and green) and two pairs of pants (brown and black) to choose from. How many different possible outfits could you wear?

The Fundamental Counting Principle tells us you have $2 \times 3 = 6$ different outfits. One way to think of this is that for each shirt you could wear, there are two possible outfits you could make: one with the brown pants and one with the black pants. Three shirts and two outfits per shirt means $3 \times 2 = 6$ total outfits. You could also consider it from the pants' perspective. For each pair of pants, you could choose one of three shirts. Thus, there are $2 \times 3 = 6$ total outfits. A useful way to visualize this is to imagine you have two spots to fill:

_____   _____

The first spot must be filled with a choice of shirt and the second with a choice of pants:

Red shirt   Brown pants
_____   _____

Since you have three options for the first choice and two for the second, you can put these numbers in the spots and multiply them:

$$\underline{\quad 3 \quad} \times \underline{\quad 2 \quad} = 6$$

You could also simply write out the entire **sample space**, or the list of all possible outfits. Using **ordered pairs** of the form (shirt, pants), we can represent every possible outfit like this:

(red, brown)   (blue, brown)   (green, brown)

(red, black)   (blue, black)   (green, black)

We can just count and find that there are six total options.

In our outfit example, the choices we make for shirt and pants are **independent**, which means that one choice doesn't affect the other. But sometimes making one choice may impact later choices. This affects how we count, and so it's important to be on the lookout for this situation.

For example, suppose you are choosing a two-digit ID number where each digit has to come from the set {0, 1, 2, 3, 4, 5, 6, 7, 8, 9}. How many possible ID numbers are there?

If you think of building an ID number by choosing the first digit and then the second, the FCP tells you there are $10 \times 10 = 100$ possible ID numbers, since you have 10 options for each digit.

But what if the two digits in your ID had to be different? For example, what if numbers like 99 and 22 weren't allowed? How would this change the calculation?

Again, imagine you are building your ID number one digit at a time. You still have 10 options for the first digit, but once you make that choice, you can't use that number again. That means you only have 9 options for the second. Your second choice depends on the first. The FCP still allows us to compute the total possible ID numbers: 10 options for the first and 9 options for the second means $10 \times 9 = 90$ possible ID numbers.

In the language of counting and probability, this is called choosing **without replacement**. After you make your first choice, that number is not *replaced* in the set. That option is no longer available to choose again. This impacts how we use the FCP.

When repeated digits were allowed, we were choosing **with replacement**. If we chose a 5 for our first digit, the 5 is *replaced* in the set before we choose the second digit, so we are free to select it again.

There is another nice path to the answer in this problem. There are 100 possible ways to make a two-digit number. How many of them have duplicate digits? We can just list them out—00, 11, 22, 33, 44, 55, 66, 77, 88, and 99—and see that there are 10 of them. So the number of ID numbers without repeating digits is $100 - 10 = 90$. This is called **counting the complement**, and it is a very useful principle. Sometimes it is easier to count the things you don't want than the things you do.

A Special Case: Counting Pairs

Suppose there are 5 distinct candies in a jar: red, blue, green, orange, and yellow. How many different ways could you pick a pair of the candies?

Using the Fundamental Counting Principle gets us halfway to the correct answer. Let's imagine you pick the candies one at a time. There are five options for the first candy, and then four options for the second candy. This means there should be $5 \times 4 = 20$ possible ways to choose the two candies.

But not quite! Suppose you chose the red candy first, and then the yellow candy. How would that be different from choosing the yellow candy first and then the red? If you only care about which *pair* of candies you ended up with, there's no difference at all. But our technique above sees the pair (red, yellow) as different from (yellow, red), so we have to adjust it. Luckily, the fix is simple.

When using the FCP as above, every pair is counted exactly twice: for example, (red, yellow) and (yellow, red); or (green, blue) and (blue, green). This means that if we just divide our answer by 2, we'll take care of the double-counting problem. This gives us $\frac{20}{2} = 10$ pairs. You can verify this by simply listing all 10 possible pairs of candies.

This is a special counting situation that comes up often enough to be on the lookout for it. If you have n different things to choose from, and you want to choose a pair of them, there are $\frac{n(n-1)}{2}$ possible pairs you could end up with.

Inclusion-Exclusion and Venn Diagrams

Let's say you are interested in what kinds of movies people like, so you ask a group of your friends. You find that 13 of them like action movies and 8 of them like comedies. How many friends did you ask? It's tempting to say 21, but that isn't necessarily the right answer. Do you see why? Some of your friends might like action movies *and* comedies.

Suppose you knew that 3 of your friends like both action movies and comedies. Now you can figure out exactly how many friends you asked.

Since 13 friends like action movies and 3 like both action movies and comedies, you can see that 10 friends *only like* action movies. Similarly, $8 - 3 = 5$ friends like *only* comedies. So your friends are now divided up into these three groups:

Only Like Action Movies	Like Both	Only Like Comedies
10	3	5

The key characteristic of these three groups is that they don't overlap: every person is in one, and only one, of these groups. So now we can see that you asked $10 + 5 + 3 = 18$ friends altogether.

The reason $13 + 8 = 21$ is the wrong answer is because the two categories—friends who like action movies and friends who like comedies—overlap. The friends who like both get counted twice when you add 13 and 8. One way to avoid this issue is to separate your friends into groups that don't overlap, as we did above.

This approach is formalized in the principle of **inclusion-exclusion**. Suppose that in a group of objects, some have property A and some have property B. Let $\#\,(\;)$ denote the "number of" something. The following formula can be used to find the total number of objects:

$\#\,(\text{total objects}) = \#\,(\text{have property } A) + \#\,(\text{have property } B) - \#\,(\text{have both properties } A \text{ and } B)$

In our above example, property A is "likes action movies" and property B is "likes comedies," so we can compute the total number of friends as:

$$\#\,(\text{friends asked}) = \#\,(\text{like action movies}) + \#\,(\text{like comedies}) - \#\,(\text{like both})$$
$$\#\,(\text{friends asked}) = 13 + 8 - 3 = 18$$

To avoid double-counting those in both groups, we subtract off the number in both, which means we end up counting them only once. This is what we want. This idea can be represented visually in a **Venn diagram**.

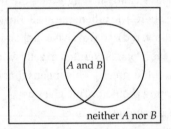

Here, the rectangle represents all the objects you could consider. The circle on the left represents all the things that have property A. The circle on the right represents all the objects that have property B. The overlap of the two circles, or their **intersection**, represents the objects that have both properties A and B. Finally, everything that is inside the rectangle but outside the two circles represents the objects that have neither of the properties A or B.

The question of how many total friends were asked is similar to the question "What is the total area of the two overlapping circles?" If we just add the areas of the two circles, we will double-count the area of their overlap. Our options are to either subtract the area of the overlap off (like in the inclusion-exclusion formula) or to break the area up into pieces that don't overlap.

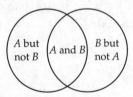

This is what we did when we divided the friends up in the table:

Only Like Action Movies	Like Both	Only Like Comedies
10	3	5

SIMPLE PROBABILITY

The Basic Probability Formula

Probability is a mathematical measure of how likely something is to happen. For example, if you roll a six-sided die once, there is a $\frac{1}{6}$, or 16.6%, chance you will roll a 3, and there is a $\frac{1}{2}$, or 50%, chance you will roll an even number.

Here is the basic formula for computing probability:

$$\text{Probability} = \frac{\text{number of favorable outcomes}}{\text{total number of outcomes}}$$

Here, "favorable outcomes" and "total outcomes" depend on the context of the problem. Different problems will have different twists and turns, but computing probability usually comes down to this formula. Notice that probability will always be a number between 0 and 1, since the number of favorable outcomes can't be less than zero and can't be more than the number of total outcomes. This means the ability to work fluently with fractions will be important.

A six-sided die has the numbers 1, 2, 3, 4, 5, and 6 on its faces. What is the probability of rolling a 3? Well, a "favorable outcome" is rolling a 3, and there is only one way to do that. The total number of outcomes is 6 because there are 6 different numbers on the faces of the die.

$$\frac{\text{number of favorable outcomes}}{\text{total number of outcomes}} = \frac{1}{6}$$

Therefore, the probability of rolling a 3 is $\frac{1}{6}$.

What about rolling an even number? There are three even numbers on the die: 2, 4, and 6. These are the three favorable outcomes. There are still 6 total outcomes. So the probability of rolling an even number is the following:

$$\frac{\text{number of favorable outcomes}}{\text{total number of outcomes}} = \frac{3}{6} = \frac{1}{2}$$

What is the probability of not rolling a 3? As usual, one way to approach this problem is to count favorable and total outcomes. Here, a favorable outcome is anything other than a 3: a 1, 2, 4, 5, or 6. So there are 5 favorable outcomes, and still 6 total outcomes, so the probability of rolling something other than a 3 is $\frac{5}{6}$.

Another way to approach this is by thinking about the complement. If rolling a 3 is a favorable outcome, what is an "unfavorable" outcome? The answer is *every other outcome* is unfavorable. This means:

$$\text{\# (unfavorable outcomes)} = \text{\# (total outcomes)} - \text{\# (favorable outcomes)}$$

If we divide both sides of this equation by the number of total outcomes, we get:

$$\frac{\#(\text{unfavorable outcomes})}{\#(\text{total outcomes})} = \frac{\#(\text{total outcomes})}{\#(\text{total outcomes})} - \frac{\#(\text{favorable outcomes})}{\#(\text{total outcomes})}$$

$$\frac{\#(\text{unfavorable outcomes})}{\#(\text{total outcomes})} = 1 - \frac{\#(\text{favorable outcomes})}{\#(\text{total outcomes})}$$

But these are probabilities! Essentially this formula says that:

(probability that something doesn't happen) = 1 − (probability that it does happen)

So, since the probability of rolling a 3 is $\frac{1}{6}$, this makes the probability of not rolling a 3 equal to $1 - \frac{1}{6} = \frac{5}{6}$. Just as it is sometimes easier to count the things that don't happen, sometimes it's easier to compute the probability that something doesn't happen.

Now suppose you roll the die twice. What is the probability that you first roll a 3 and then roll an even number? You could start using the FCP. There is one way to roll a 3 and three ways to roll an even number, so there are $1 \times 3 = 3$ ways we could roll a 3 and then an even number. (We can just list them: (3, 2), (3, 4), and (3, 6)). There are $6 \times 6 = 36$ possible outcomes when rolling a six-sided die twice: (1, 1), (1, 2), (1, 3), and so on, up to (6, 5), (6, 6). So the probability you roll a 3 first and then an even number is:

$$\frac{\text{number of favorable outcomes}}{\text{total number of outcomes}} = \frac{1 \times 3}{6 \times 6} = \frac{3}{36} = \frac{1}{12}$$

However, there is a more efficient way. When you want to know the probability of two events both happening, usually you multiply the probabilities. This means that the probability you roll a 3 first and then an even number is the following:

$$(\text{probability of rolling a 3}) \times (\text{probability of rolling an even number}) = \frac{1}{6} \times \frac{1}{2} = \frac{1}{12}$$

This is a very useful shortcut in computing probabilities involving multiple events. Let's look at a few examples of how multiplying probabilities can come up on the SHSAT.

➡ Example 1 _____

Suppose there are 10 marbles in a jar: 6 red and 4 blue. If you choose a marble at random from the jar, what is the probability that the marble is red?

This is a straightforward probability calculation. There are 6 favorable outcomes (6 red marbles) and 10 total outcomes (10 total marbles), so the probability is $\frac{6}{10} = \frac{3}{5}$.

Now let's change the problem a bit.

➡ Example 2 _____

Suppose there are 10 marbles in a jar: 6 red and 4 blue. If you choose a marble at random from the jar, put it back, then choose another, what is the probability that the first marble was red and the second marble was blue?

Here, we will multiply probabilities. The probability of the first marble being red is $\frac{6}{10}$, which we can simplify to $\frac{3}{5}$, and the probability of the second marble being blue is $\frac{4}{10} = \frac{2}{5}$, so the probability of both is $\frac{3}{5} \times \frac{2}{5} = \frac{6}{25}$.

Notice how important it is that we put the red marble back after we chose it. We computed the probability of choosing a blue marble second to be $\frac{4}{10}$ because there are 4 blue marbles and 10 total marbles. If we had not put the red marble back, there would be only 9 total marbles to choose from.

This is the difference between choosing **with replacement** and **without replacement**. In our example, we are choosing **with replacement**. After we choose the red marble, we replace it in the jar.

Choosing **without replacement** would lead to a different answer. Let's see how:

Suppose there are 10 marbles in a jar: 6 red and 4 blue. If you choose a marble at random from the jar without replacement, then choose another, what is the probability that the first marble was red and the second marble was blue?

Here, the probability of choosing the red marble first doesn't change; it's $\frac{6}{10} = \frac{3}{5}$. But since we don't replace the red marble, the probability of choosing a blue marble second does change. There are still four favorable outcomes (4 blue marbles), but now there are only 9 total outcomes (9 total marbles). Thus, the probability of choosing a blue marble second is $\frac{4}{9}$, and the probability of both is $\frac{3}{5} \times \frac{4}{9} = \frac{12}{45} = \frac{4}{15}$.

When solving probability problems involving selections, make sure you know whether the selections are being made with or without replacement. It makes a big difference in your answer.

WARNING!	In multiple-choice probability questions, it is typical to include the answers that correspond to both selections with replacement and without replacement. Make sure you know which one applies!

SIMPLE STATISTICS

Statistics is the study of data, or sets of numbers. Here are some basic statistical concepts that appear on the SHSAT.

Given a set of numbers, the **range** is the difference between the largest number and the smallest number. For example, suppose there are 7 people in a room and their ages are 15, 3, 61, 6, 12, 10, and 33. Since 61 is the largest number in the set and 3 is the smallest, the range of this set of numbers is $61 - 3 = 58$.

The **mean**, or **average**, of a set of numbers is the sum of all the numbers in the set divided by the number of numbers in the set. Using the example above, the mean, or average, age of the people in the room is computed as follows:

$$\frac{15 + 3 + 61 + 6 + 12 + 10 + 33}{7} = \frac{140}{7} = 20$$

Thus, the average age is 20.

A useful fact about the average of a set of numbers is that the sum of all the numbers is equal to the average times the numbers of numbers. For example, above we found that the average of the seven numbers is 20, and $7 \times 20 = 140$, which is the sum of the seven numbers.

The **median** of a set of numbers is the number in the middle when the numbers are listed in order. For example, our ages are:

15, 3, 61, 6, 12, 10, 33

To find the median, we first put the numbers in order:

3, 6, 10, 12, 15, 33, 61

The number in the middle, which is 12, is the median. If our list has an even number of numbers in it, there will be no middle number. In that case, the median is the average of the two numbers on either side of the middle. For example, the median of 4, 7, 11, 17, 29, 64 is the average of 11 and 17, which is $\frac{11+17}{2} = \frac{28}{2} = 14$.

The median has the property that half the numbers in the data set are below the median and half are above it.

WARNING!	The median is only the "middle number" after the numbers have been put in order!

Tables, Histograms, and Charts

An important aspect of working with data is how it is represented. There are many ways data can be presented to a reader. It is important to understand how to interpret and use the different representations.

A common representation of data is a **frequency table**. Here is an example:

Chemistry Exam Scores

Test Score	Number of Students
90	3
80	5
70	2

In the table above, the frequency of each test score is given: 3 students earned a 90, 5 students earned an 80, and 2 students earned a 70.

What is the average test score? If you aren't paying attention to the frequency, you might say the average test score is the following:

$$\frac{90+80+70}{3} = \frac{240}{3} = 80$$

This computation of average suggests there are three numbers in our data set: 90, 80, and 70. But there are really ten numbers in our data set: there are three 90s, five 80s, and two 70s. When we compute the average, we need to take the frequency into account.

$$\frac{90+90+90+80+80+80+80+80+70+70}{10} = \frac{810}{10} = 81$$

So the actual average of all ten test scores is 81.

Notice we don't have to write out all three 90s, and five 80s, and both 70s. We can simply use the frequencies as multipliers:

$$\frac{3 \times 90 + 5 \times 80 + 2 \times 70}{10} = \frac{810}{10} = 81$$

Frequency tables also can appear as part of probability questions. For example, suppose a student is selected at random from the ten students in this chemistry class. What is the probability that student scored above a 70 on the test? Since eight out of ten students scored above 70, the probability is $\frac{8}{10}$, or 80%, that the randomly selected student scored above 70.

WARNING!	When using tables to solve problems, be sure to pay attention to the frequency of the data.

In addition to frequency tables, you will see pie charts and bar graphs in the example problems and practice exams. A pie chart shows how a population is divided among a set of options, for example, which kind of ice cream cone is preferred among a group of people.

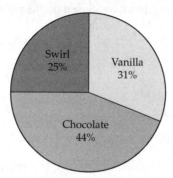

Preferred Soft Serve Cone

Notice that by counting everything represented in the pie chart, you should get the entire population, or 100%.

A bar graph can be used to visually represent a table or chart, such as a survey of favorite classes among students.

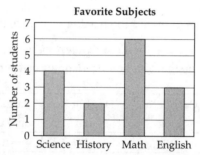

Here the height of each bar indicates the number of times each subject was chosen. Notice that you can determine the total number of students surveyed by adding up the heights of each bar.

Interpreting the data from charts and graphs correctly is crucial, so make sure you know what you are looking at!

PROBLEM SOLVING

Now let's work through some problems involving counting, probability, and statistics that are similar to those you might face on the SHSAT.

➡ Example 1

Sample Grid-in Question

1. A survey asked students what pets they have. Based on the results, the following statements are all true:

- 24 students have cats
- 18 students have dogs
- 5 students have both dogs and cats
- 7 students have no dogs or cats

How many students were surveyed?

It is tempting to say that since 24 students have cats, 18 have dogs, and 7 have neither cats nor dogs, a total of $24 + 18 + 7 = 49$ students were surveyed. But this is incorrect. As discussed earlier in this chapter, this approach doesn't take into consideration the fact that some students have both cats and dogs.

When we add the 24 cat owners and the 18 dog owners to get 42, we have counted every student who owns both a cat and a dog twice. To make sure we count them only once, we subtract off the number of students who own both:

(total students) = # (own a cat) + # (own a dog) − # (own both) + # (own neither)

This gives us a total of $24 + 18 - 5 + 7 = 44$ students. Another way to think about problems like this is to divide all the students up into four non-overlapping categories:

Pet(s) Owned	Cat but No Dog	Dog but No Cat	Both Cat and Dog	Neither Cat nor Dog
# of Students	19	13	5	7

Since none of these categories overlap, there won't be any double-counting when we add the numbers together: $19 + 13 + 5 + 7 = 44$ total students. Visually, we can picture this situation in a Venn diagram:

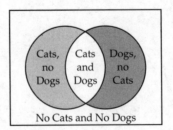

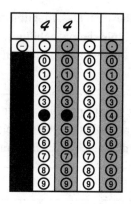

| | WARNING! | When counting objects with multiple properties, be sure to beware of double counting! Drawing a Venn diagram can help. |

➡ Example 2 _____

2. In a sample of 10 cards, 4 are blue and 6 are green. If 2 cards are selected at random from the sample, one at a time without replacement, what is the probability that both cards are not green?

(E) $\dfrac{3}{25}$

(F) $\dfrac{2}{15}$

(G) $\dfrac{4}{25}$

(H) $\dfrac{1}{3}$

Let's approach this problem by thinking about drawing the two cards one at a time. What is the probability that the first card we draw is not green? Since there are six green cards out of ten total cards, the probability of drawing a green card would be $\dfrac{6}{10} = \dfrac{3}{5}$. Using the strategy of considering the complement, this means the probability of drawing a card that is not green is $1 - \dfrac{3}{5} = \dfrac{2}{5}$. Note: Using the fact that "not green" in this problem means "blue," and there are four blue cards, we can more quickly find the desired probability to be $\dfrac{4}{10} = \dfrac{2}{5}$.

So the probability that the first card is not green is $\dfrac{2}{5}$. What about the second card? Here, we need to be careful about whether or not we are drawing **with replacement**. After we draw the first card, are we putting it back in the pile to potentially draw again? Or are we keeping it out? The answer to this question will make a big difference in our probability calculation.

In this problem, we are sampling **without replacement**, which means we don't put the card back. So after we draw a not-green card first, there will be 3 not-green cards left out of a total of 9 cards. This means the probability of drawing a not-green card the second time is $\dfrac{3}{9} = \dfrac{1}{3}$.

To find the probability of both of these events—first drawing a not-green card and then drawing another not-green card—we multiply the probabilities. This gives us $\frac{2}{5} \times \frac{1}{3} = \frac{2}{15}$, which is choice F. Notice that choice G is the answer you would get if you considered drawing cards *with replacement*: $\frac{2}{5} \times \frac{2}{5} = \frac{4}{25}$.

WARNING!	When approaching probability problems that involve making selections, always be aware of whether you are selecting with or without replacement. It makes a big difference in the final answer!

➡ Example 3

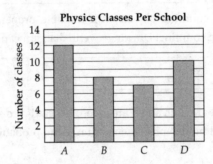

3. The graph above shows the number of physics classes in four schools, labeled *A, B, C,* and *D.* In school *A*, each physics class has 14 students; in school *B*, each physics class has 22 students; in school *C*, each physics class has 25 students; in school *D*, each physics class has 15 students. Which school has the most students taking physics?

(A) *A*

(B) *B*

(C) *C*

(D) *D*

To answer this question you must be able to read and interpret the bar chart and then use the rest of the information in the question. The bar chart shows that school *A* has the most physics classes, with 12. But we need to find which school has the highest total number of students taking physics, not which school has the highest number of physics classes.

To find out how many students at each school take physics, we must multiply the number of classes with the number of students per class:

- School *A*: (12 classes) × (14 students per class) = 168 students
- School *B*: (8 classes) × (22 students per class) = 176 students
- School *C*: (7 classes) × (25 students per class) = 175 students
- School *D*: (10 classes) × (15 students per class) = 150 students

We see that School *B* has the highest number of students taking a physics class, so the answer is choice B.

➤ Example 4

4. In a certain school, course grades range from 0 to 100. Alexandra took 5 courses and her average course grade was 90. Ronaldo took 6 courses. If both students have the same sum of course grades, what was Ronaldo's average?

(E) 72
(F) 75
(G) 80
(H) 90

Let's imagine that Alexandra's individual course grades are represented by the variables x, y, z, w, and v. Since we know Alexandra's average is 90, we can use the formula for finding the mean of five numbers:

$$\frac{x+y+z+w+v}{5} = 90$$

Notice that by multiplying both sides of the equation by 5, we can find the sum we are looking for:

$$\frac{x+y+z+w+v}{5} = 90$$
$$5 \times \frac{x+y+z+w+v}{5} = 5 \times 90$$
$$x+y+z+w+v = 450$$

So the sum of Alexandra's course grades is 450. This is also the sum of Ronaldo's six course grades. Since the average course grade is equal to the sum of the course grades divided by the number of courses, this makes Ronaldo's average course grade $\frac{450}{6} = 75$, which is choice F.

Notice that it makes sense that Ronaldo's average is lower than Alexandra's, since they had the same sum of course grades but he took more courses. In fact, this reasoning allows you to eliminate answer choices G and H immediately.

Another approach to finding the sum of Alexandra's grades is to use the "make a wish" strategy. If Alexandra had a 90 for every course grade, then her average course grade would be 90. This means the sum of her course grades would be $90 + 90 + 90 + 90 + 90 = 5 \times 90 = 450$.

➤ Example 5

5. The below table shows the number of siblings per student at a school with 400 students. How many of the students in this school have at least two siblings?

Number of Siblings per Student

Number of Siblings	Percent of Students
0	18
1	41
2	22
3	12
4 or more	7

(A) 41
(B) 76
(C) 88
(D) 164

The keys to answering this question correctly are recognizing the phrase *at least two* and then pulling the proper information from the table. *At least two siblings* means 2, 3, or 4 or more siblings. To find the appropriate percentage, you must add the percentages from the table. This means that the percentage of students with at least 2 siblings is 22% + 12% + 7% = 41%. However, 41 (choice A) is not correct, because the question asks for the total *number* of students with 2 or more siblings, not the percentage of students with 2 or more siblings.

To find the total *number* of students with at least two siblings, you must find 41% of 400. This can be done by multiplying $0.41 \times 400 = \frac{41}{100} \times 400 = 41 \times 4 = 164$. Alternately, note that 1% of 400 is 4, so 41% of 400 is $41 \times 4 = 164$. The correct answer is choice D.

WARNING!	Be on the lookout for phrases like "at least" and "at most" when reading math problems. Be sure you know how to handle them!

SUMMARY

Counting is an important mathematical skill, and on the SHSAT you will be expected to solve counting problems that involve making selections and also categorizing items by their properties. Be sure you review the basic strategies and know the common mistakes to avoid.

Counting outcomes also is the basis for probability. When computing probabilities, make sure you correctly count the favorable outcomes and the total outcomes, and be sure to know if you are selecting with or without replacement.

Lastly, when working with visual representations of data, like charts, tables, and graphs, make sure you interpret the data correctly. And as with all questions on the SHSAT, read the question carefully—make sure you know what is being asked, and be on the lookout for important phrases that can affect the answer.

EXERCISES

Here is some targeted practice with counting, probability, and statistics.

1. A jar has 10 red marbles and 15 blue marbles. If a marble is chosen randomly from the jar, what is the probability it is red?
2. What is the mean of the numbers in the set $\{4, 9, -1, 22, 6\}$?
3. A lock combination consists of three digits. How many different lock combinations are there?
4. In a classroom of students, 28 like pizza and 24 like hamburgers. If 17 like both, how many students are there in the class?
5. A jar has 10 red marbles and 15 blue marbles. If a marble is chosen twice from the jar with replacement, what is the probability that the marble was red both times?
6. There are 8 different pencils in a pencil jar. How many different pairs of pencils could you take from the jar?
7. How many two-digit even numbers are there? (The first digit of a two-digit number cannot be zero.)
8. A jar has 6 chocolate cookies and 4 strawberry cookies. If 2 cookies are chosen without replacement, what is the probability they are both chocolate?
9. The average of a, b, c, and d is 22. The average of a, b, c, d, and x is 20. What is the value of x?
10. In a survey, 72% of people said they liked watching TV and 64% said they liked reading books. What is the smallest possible percentage of people who like both?

(Answers are on page 203.)

Geometry

14

OVERVIEW

Geometry is a broad subject worthy of serious study, but in this section, we will narrowly focus our attention on a few specific topics from geometry that appear on the SHSAT.

One of the fundamental geometric ideas is measurement. We measure distance, angles, areas, and volumes. We will review basic strategies for the measurement of geometric objects and see how properties of shapes and configurations create relationships among those measurements. It is particularly important to know how angles formed by intersecting lines, parallel lines, triangles, and parallelograms are related to one another.

It is also important to be able to quickly and efficiently compute areas and volumes. Since no formulas are given on the SHSAT, you must commit the basic formulas to memory. These include areas and perimeters of triangles, squares, rectangles, and circles, and the volumes of cubes and rectangular prisms. We will see how to apply these formulas and how to use the properties of those shapes to our advantage.

Problem Solving

Here are some of the types of problems you will solve that rely on geometry:

- Determine the position of points on a number line, like the midpoint of A and B
- Find angle measures, like in triangles and parallelograms
- Compute areas of circles, squares, and triangles, and compute volume of rectangular prisms

Prior Knowledge

Here are some things you need to be comfortable with in order to master working with geometry:

- Addition and subtraction of negative numbers and fractions
- Solving simple equations
- Basic properties of the number line
- Characteristics of basic shapes, like squares, rectangular, and circles

THE NUMBER LINE

The **number line** is a geometric representation of all the real numbers. Each point on the line is associated with a real number, with the positive numbers extending to the right and the negative numbers extending to the left.

Here is a standard representation of the number line:

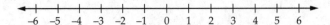

Notice that only some numbers are labeled on this number line. The number line extends infinitely in both directions (as indicated by the arrows at either end). Also, all of the points in between the labeled numbers represent real numbers, such as $\frac{1}{2}$, -5.712, and $\sqrt{2}$. We just haven't written their labels in.

Suppose the points A, B, C, D, and E are arranged on the number line as shown below:

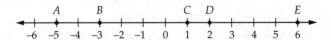

The number associated with each point is its **coordinate**. For example, the coordinate of E is 6, and the coordinate of A is -5. One nice feature of the number line is that you can find the distance between two points by finding the difference in their coordinates.

For example, you can see on the number line that the distance from point C to point D, which we denote CD, is one unit. But you can also compute this distance by subtracting 1 from 2: $CD = 2 - 1 = 1$. (Another way to say that the distance from C to D is 1 is to say that the length of the line segment CD, which we can also write as $\overline{CD}$, is 1.) When finding distance or length, we subtract the smaller coordinate from the larger coordinate, which ensures that the distance or length we compute won't be negative.

We can compute the distances from D to E and from C to E the same way: $DE = 6 - 2 = 4$ and $CE = 6 - 1 = 5$. This illustrates another important geometric property of the number line. Since D is between points C and E, the following relationship must be true:

$$CD + DE = CE$$

This just says that, as long as D is between C and E, the distance from C to E is equal to the distance from C to D plus the distance from D to E. We have broken the line segment CE into the two parts: line segments CD and DE. This is known as **partitioning** a line segment.

Subtraction also works in finding the distance to, and between, points on the negative side of the number line. For example, the distance from A to B is $AB = -3 - (-5) = -3 + 5 = 2$, and the distance from C to B is $CB = 1 - (-3) = 1 + 3 = 4$. And since B is between A and C, we can conclude that $AC = AB + BC = 2 + 4 = 6$, which we can verify by subtracting the coordinates: $AC = 1 - (-5) = 1 + 5 = 6$.

WARNING!	When finding distances on the number line, be careful when subtracting negative numbers!

The **midpoint** of a line segment is the point halfway between the two endpoints of the line segment. For example, you can see on the number line that the midpoint of DE is the point whose coordinate is 4. Let's call that point M:

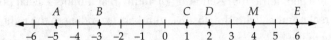

An important feature of the midpoint of a line segment is that it is **equidistant** to both ends of the line segment. That means the distance from midpoint to either endpoint is equal. We can see above that $DM = ME = 2$.

To find the midpoint of two points on the number line, you find the average of the two coordinates. For example, since D has coordinate 2 and E has coordinate 6, the midpoint of DE has coordinate $\frac{2+6}{2} = \frac{8}{2} = 4$. Similarly, you can find that the midpoint of BC is $\frac{-3+1}{2} = \frac{-2}{2} = -1$, and the midpoint of AE is $\frac{-5+6}{2} = \frac{1}{2}$.

| WARNING! | Remember, even if only the integer points are labeled, all the numbers— including fractions and decimals—are present on the number line. |

ANGLES

Angles are formed when lines, line segments, or rays intersect. When we **measure** an angle, we assign a number to it. There are different ways to measure angles, but we will measure angles in **degrees**.

Turning in a full circle around a point corresponds to an angle measure of 360°.

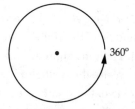

Half of a full turn is thus 180°, which corresponds to a straight line.

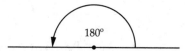

Another important angle is one-quarter of a full turn, which is 90°. This is called a **right angle,** and lines that make right angles are called **perpendicular**. We indicate a right angle in a diagram like this:

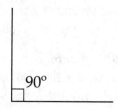

Angles whose measures are between 0° and 90° are called **acute**, and angles whose measures are between 90° and 180° are called **obtuse**.

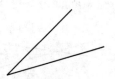

Acute angle

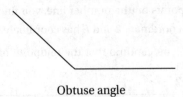

Obtuse angle

We name angles using the points on the lines that form them. For example, consider the following angle:

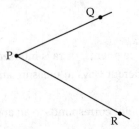

This angle could be called either $\angle QPR$ or $\angle RPQ$. The **vertex** of the angle—the point where the two lines meet—must appear in the middle of the angle's name. In some situations, we might also simply refer to this angle as $\angle P$, but this naming approach can sometimes be ambiguous.

To denote the measure of an angle, we use the symbols $m\angle$. Thus, $m\angle QPR$ refers to the measure of $\angle QPR$. When we split an angle into two, the sum of the measures of the two smaller angles is equal to the measure of the larger angle. This is similar to the partitioning of line segments described above. For example, see the diagram below:

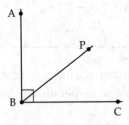

We know that $m\angle ABP + m\angle PBC = m\angle ABC$. So if we know that $m\angle PBC = 28°$, we could use the fact that $\angle ABC$ is a right angle and thus $m\angle ABC = 90°$ to compute $m\angle ABP$:

$$m\angle ABP + m\angle PBC = m\angle ABC$$
$$m\angle ABP + 28° = 90°$$
$$m\angle ABP = 90° - 28°$$
$$m\angle ABP = 62°$$

When two lines intersect, they form two pairs of **vertical angles**. Vertical angles are the angles that lie on opposite sides of the vertex of the angle.

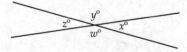

In the above diagram, there are a pair of acute vertical angles and a pair of obtuse vertical angles. Notice the alternate method of labeling angles. Here, we are identifying angles by labeling them with their measures: $x°, y°, z°,$ and $w°$.

An important property of vertical angles is that they are **congruent**, or equal in measure. Thus, in the diagram, we have that $x = z$ and $y = w$. And if we knew that, say $x = 42$, we would not only know that $z = 42$, but also that $y = w = 138$. This is because the angles with measure $x°$ and $y°$ form a straight line, and so their measures add up to $180°$. Therefore:

$$x + y = 180$$
$$42 + y = 180$$
$$y = 180 - 42$$
$$y = 138$$

Parallel lines are lines that never intersect. We indicate parallel lines in a diagram by drawing arrows on them, like this:

Here, we say line m and line n are parallel, and we write $m \parallel n$. When parallel lines are crossed by a **transversal**, a third line intersecting both, many pairs of congruent angles are formed:

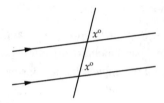

The two congruent angles above are called **corresponding angles**, and they are congruent. The angles below are called **alternate interior angles**, and they are also congruent:

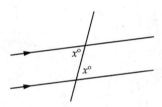

Notice that there is a vertical angle relationship between the alternate interior angle and the corresponding angle:

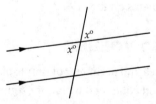

The two angles below are called **same-side interior angles**:

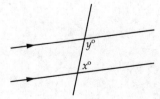

These angles are not necessarily congruent, but they are **supplementary**. That means their measure must add up to 180°. This can be shown by using the alternate interior angle property.

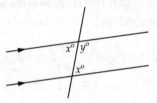

Since the angles with measures $x°$ and $y°$ form a straight line, we have that $x + y = 180$.

These properties of angles formed by parallel lines are particularly helpful in solving problems involving parallelograms, which are quadrilaterals with two pairs of opposite, parallel sides:

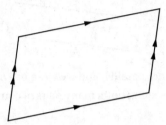

Because of the above properties, we know that opposite angles in a parallelogram are always congruent, and same-side angles in a parallelogram are always supplementary. We can see this by extending the sides and examining all the angle relationships present in the parallelogram.

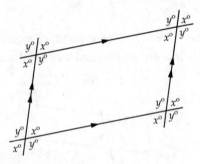

In the above diagram, we have $x + y = 180$.

Finally, another important property of angles is that the sum of the measures of the interior angles of a triangle is equal to 180°. You will use this fact in conjunction with the other angle properties to solve many geometry problems on the SHSAT.

PERIMETER, AREA, AND VOLUME

You must be able to compute the area and perimeter of simple plane figures on the SHSAT. The area of a figure is a measure of the region contained within the figure. The perimeter of a figure is the sum of the lengths of the sides of the figure.

Here are some important formulas to remember:

	Square	Rectangle	Triangle	Circle
Diagram				
Area	$A = s^2$	$A = lw$	$A = \dfrac{1}{2}bh$	$A = \pi r^2$
Perimeter	$P = 4s$	$P = 2l + 2w$	$P = a + b + c$	$C = 2\pi r$

WARNING!	No formulas will be given on the SHSAT, so make sure you know these basic area formulas and how to use them.

A **quadrilateral** is a polygon with four sides. A **square** is a quadrilateral with four congruent sides and four right angles. The area of a square is equal to its side length squared: $A = s^2$. The perimeter is equal to $4s$, since all four sides are the same length: $P = s + s + s + s = 4s$.

A **rectangle** is a quadrilateral with two pairs of opposite congruent sides and four right angles. The area of a rectangle is its length times its width: $A = lw$. The perimeter of a rectangle is $P = l + w + l + w = 2l + 2w$. Notice that if $l = w$, the rectangle is a square and the formulas for the rectangle become the formulas for the square.

A **triangle** is a polygon with three sides. The perimeter of a triangle is just the sum of its side lengths: $P = a + b + c$. The area of a triangle is half the product of the base and height: $A = \dfrac{1}{2}bh$. The base could be any side of the triangle and the height is the length of the perpendicular line segment from that base to the opposite vertex of the triangle.

A **right triangle** is a triangle with a right angle. In right triangles, the two **legs** are perpendicular.

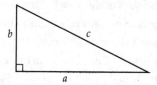

When computing the area of a right triangle, we can think of either leg as the base and the other the height. This makes the area of a right triangle equal to half the product of the legs. The area of the above right triangle is $A = \dfrac{1}{2}ab$.

Notice how the area of this triangle is exactly half the area of the rectangle with side lengths a and b. This makes sense when you think about making another copy of the triangle and rotating it to produce the following rectangle:

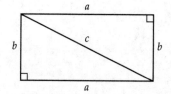

The area of a **circle** is given by the formula $A = \pi r^2$, where π is the irrational number $3.141592\ldots$, whose decimal expansion never repeats or ends, and r is the radius of the circle. The radius is the distance from the center to the circle itself, and all radii in a given circle are the same length. In problems involving π, sometimes it is better to compute final answers in terms of π than to use a decimal approximation for π such as 3.14. And when estimating answers, it can be useful to approximate π with 3.

Since circles aren't polygons and don't have sides, we use the word **circumference** instead of perimeter. The formula for the circumference of a circle is $C = 2\pi r$.

The **volume** of a three-dimensional object is a measure of the region within the figure. On the SHSAT, you may need to apply the formulas for the volume of some simple figures.

	Cube	Rectangular Prism	Cylinder
Diagram			
Volume	$V = s^3$	$V = lwh$	$V = \pi r^2 h$
Surface Area	$SA = 6s^2$	$SA = 2lh + 2lw + 2wh$	$SA = 2\pi r^2 + 2\pi rh$

The volume of a cube with side length s is given by $V = s^3$. The volume of a rectangular prism, or box, is given by $V = lwh$, where l, w, and h are the length, width, and height of the prism. The volume of a cylinder is $V = \pi r^2 h$, where r is the radius of the circular base, h is the height of the cylinder, and π is the irrational number mentioned above.

The **surface area** of a figure is the sum of the areas of the faces of the figure. Since the cube has six square faces, each with side length s, the surface area of a cube is given by the formula $SA = 6s^2$. A rectangular prism has six rectangular faces: two have dimensions l and h, two have dimensions l and w, and two have dimensions w and h. This makes the formula for the surface area of a rectangular prism $SA = 2lh + 2lw + 2wh$. Notice that if $l = w = h$, the rectangular prism is a cube. The surface area of a cylinder is given by the formula $SA = 2\pi r^2 + 2\pi rh$, where the $2\pi r^2$ comes from the areas of the two circles on top and bottom, and $2\pi rh$ is the **lateral** surface area, which is the area of the side piece.

PROBLEM SOLVING

Now let's work through some problems involving geometry that are similar to those you might face on the SHSAT.

➡ Example 1 _____

Sample Grid-in Question

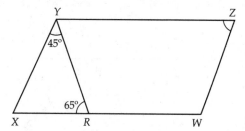

1. In the figure above, *XYZW* is a parallelogram. The measure of ∠*XRY* is 65°, and the measure of ∠*XYR* is 45°. What is the measure of ∠*XWZ*?

Here, we will use properties of angles in triangles and parallelograms to find the measure of the desired angle.

Since *XYR* is a triangle, the sum of the measures of its interior angles is 180°.

$$m\angle XRY + m\angle XYR + m\angle YXR = 180°$$

Substituting the known values for *m*∠*XRY* and *m*∠*XYR* gives us 65° + 45° + ∠*YXR* = 180°. Simplifying gives us 110° + ∠*YXR* = 180°, and so ∠*YXR* = 70°.

Since *XYZW* is a parallelogram, we know that adjacent angles are supplementary. This is because $\overline{XY} \parallel \overline{WZ}$ and the adjacent angles, say ∠*YXR* and ∠*XWZ*, are same-side interior angles. Thus, *m*∠*YXR* + *m*∠*XWZ* = 180°, and since ∠*YXR* = 70°, we have *m*∠*XWZ* = 180° − 70° = 110°.

Another approach uses alternate interior angles. Since $\overline{XW} \parallel \overline{YZ}$ and $\overline{YR}$ is a transversal, we see that ∠*XRY* and ∠*RYZ* are alternate interior angles, and are thus congruent. This means that *m*∠*RYZ* = *m*∠*XRY* = 65°. This allows us to find *m*∠*XYZ*.

$$m\angle XYZ = m\angle XYR + m\angle RYZ = 45° + 65° = 110°$$

Finally, since *XYZW* is a parallelogram, we know opposite angles are congruent, which means *m*∠*XWZ* = *m*∠*XYZ* = 110°.

➡ Example 2 _____

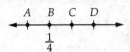

2. On the number line above, $AB = 2$, $AD = 10$, and $CD = 3\frac{1}{8}$. What is the position of point C?

(E) $3\frac{3}{8}$

(F) $4\frac{1}{8}$

(G) $4\frac{3}{8}$

(H) $5\frac{1}{8}$

Here, we must find the position, or coordinate, of the point C. To do that, we will find the distance from C to B and use the known position of B.

By the partition property of line segments, we know that $AB + BD = AD$. We can solve this equation for BD and get $BD = AD - AB$. Since $AD = 10$ and $AB = 2$, we substitute and see that $BD = 10 - 2 = 8$. Similarly, using the fact that $BD = BC + CD$, we can compute BC. So $BC = BD - CD = 8 - 3\frac{1}{8} = 4\frac{7}{8}$. Finally, the position of C is the position of B plus the distance from B to C, which is BC. This makes the coordinate of C:

$$\frac{1}{4} + 4\frac{7}{8} = \frac{2}{8} + 4\frac{7}{8}$$
$$= 4\frac{9}{8}$$
$$= 5\frac{1}{8}$$

That is choice H.

WARNING!	When solving problems on the number line, remember that some numbers represent positions and some numbers represent distances.

➡ Example 3 _____

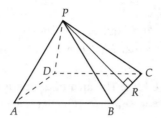

3. In the pyramid above, each triangular face has the same area, and the base *ABCD* is a square that measures 6 centimeters on each side. If the length of $\overline{PR}$ is 10 centimeters, what is the surface area of the pyramid excluding the base?

(A) 30 square cm

(B) 60 square cm

(C) 120 square cm

(D) 240 square cm

This pyramid may seem intimidating at first, but this is just a problem about finding the area of triangles.

We want to find the surface area of the pyramid *excluding the base*. This means we ignore the square base and just focus on the triangular faces. But we are told that each face has the same area, which means we only need to find the area of one of the triangular faces and multiply that by 4.

The area of a triangle is one-half the product of the base and the height. The base of each triangular face is a side of the square, whose length is known to be 6 cm. The height of the triangle is given by the length of $\overline{PR}$, which is 10 centimeters. Thus, the area of each triangular face is $\frac{1}{2} \times 6 \times 10 = \frac{1}{2} \times 60 = 30$ square centimeters. Therefore, the area of all four triangular faces is $4 \times 30 = 120$ square centimeters, which is choice C. Notice that choice A is the area of one triangle, and choice D is what you would get if you forgot the one-half in the formula for the area of a triangle.

➡ Example 4 _____

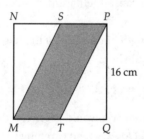

16 cm

4. *T* and *S* are midpoints of the sides of square *MNPQ*, as shown above. What is the area of the shaded region?

(E) 64 square cm

(F) 128 square cm

(G) 256 square cm

(H) 512 square cm

To find the area of the shaded region, we will take a complementary approach. We will find the area that *isn't* in the shaded region and subtract that from the total area of the square. Let's first focus on the triangles *TPQ* and *SMN*.

Since *T* and *S* are midpoints, we know that $SN = 8$ and $TQ = 8$. Since *MNPQ* is a square, all its angles are right angles, which means that $\triangle TPQ$ and $\triangle SMN$ are both right triangles with legs of length 8 and 16. In a right triangle, the area is half the product of the legs, which means that the area of each triangle is $\frac{1}{2} \times 8 \times 16 = 8 \times 8 = 64$. The area of a square is its side-length squared, which means the area of *MNPQ* is $16^2 = 256$. The shaded region is what remains of the square when the two unshaded triangles are removed, so the area of the shaded region is equal to the area of the square minus the area of the two triangles. This is $256 - 2 \times 64 = 256 - 128 = 128$ square cm, which is choice F.

A quicker way to see the answer is to imagine $\triangle TPQ$ sliding over to the left so that it would fit perfectly together with $\triangle SMN$, where they would occupy half the square. This means the shaded region occupies the other half of the square, which is $\frac{1}{2} \times 256 = 128$ square cm.

Notice that estimating quickly eliminates two of the answer choices. Since the area of the square is $16^2 = 256$ and the shaded area lies within the square, its area must be less than 256 square cm. Thus, the answer must be either choice E or F.

➡ Example 5

5. A wooden box has a square base of area 36 square centimeters. The height of the box is 2 times the length of one side of the base. What is the volume of the box?

   (A) 72 cubic cm
   (B) 144 cubic cm
   (C) 216 cubic cm
   (D) 432 cubic cm

To find the volume of the box, we need to find the length, width, and height of the box and multiply them together. Begin by sketching the box to help visualize the problem and to record relevant information.

Since the base of the box is a square, we know the width and length are equal. We also know the area of the base is 36 square cm. Because the base is a square and $6^2 = 36$, this means the side length of the square base is 6 cm.

Since the height is 2 times the length of one side of the base, the height is $2 \times 6 = 12$ cm. This allows us to compute the volume of the box:

$$V = lwh = 6 \times 6 \times 12 = 6 \times 72 = 432 \text{ cubic cm}$$

Notice that answer choice A is what you would get if you thought the height of the box was 2, instead of *twice the length of the base*. Always read carefully!

SUMMARY

In this section, we have seen some of the ways geometric ideas and procedures will appear on the SHSAT. You must be comfortable locating points on the number line and using properties of length and distance to compute coordinates. You must know how to work with angles in different situations, like intersecting lines, triangles, and parallelograms. And you must be able to compute areas and volumes and apply those techniques in a variety of different settings.

And remember, no formulas will be given on the SHSAT. This means you must commit the basic formulas to memory and have them at the ready when needed.

EXERCISES

Here is some targeted practice with geometry.

1. Point M is located at $-1\frac{3}{4}$ on the number line. Point N is located to the right of M, and $MN = 5\frac{3}{8}$. What is the coordinate of point M?

2. Two interior angles of a triangle measure $37°$ and $98°$. What is the measure of the third interior angle?

3. A square has area 64 cm^2. What is the perimeter of the square?

4. On the number line, point A has coordinate 7 and point B has coordinate $2\frac{1}{2}$. What is the coordinate of the midpoint of $\overline{AB}$?

5. A cube-shaped box has volume 27 cm^3. The side length of the cube is doubled. What is the volume of the new cube?

6. A circle has area 81π. What is the circumference of the circle?

7. The perimeter of a rectangle is 180 cm. The ratio of the length to the width of the rectangle is $2:1$. What are the dimensions of the rectangle?

8. In a parallelogram, the measure of an angle is one-third the measure of the adjacent angle. What is the measure of the smallest angle in the parallelogram?

9. A cube-shaped box has surface area 384 cm^2. What is the volume of the box?

10. A circle of radius 5 is removed from the interior of a circle of radius 6. What is the area of the remaining region?

(Answers are on page 203.)

Answers for Chapters 10-14

15

Numbers and Arithmetic Exercises Answers (page 146)

1. **31.1**
2. $\dfrac{7}{8}$
3. $\dfrac{9}{20}$
4. **1.425**
5. **91**
6. **17.5**
7. **10,701**
8. **−45**
9. **18**
10. **25**

Equations and Inequalities Answers (page 162)

1. $x = 16$
2. $x \geq -3$
3. $y = -\dfrac{8}{3}$
4. $a \leq -3.5$
5. $x = \dfrac{3}{2}y + 12$
6. $-14 \leq z < 24$
7. **56**
8. $-14 < x < -7$
9. $x = \dfrac{3}{2}$
10. **$5.15**

Ratios and Proportions Answers (page 174)

1. $x = 6$
2. $x = 105$
3. **43.2**
4. **$50.75**
5. **2.3 inches**
6. **8,640**
7. $y = 2.5$
8. **338**
9. **126 minutes**
10. $z = 70$

Counting, Probability, and Statistics Answers (page 188)

1. $\dfrac{2}{5}$
2. **8**
3. **1,000**
4. **35**
5. $\dfrac{4}{25}$
6. **28**
7. **45**
8. $\dfrac{1}{3}$
9. **12**
10. **36%**

Geometry Answers (page 201)

1. $3\dfrac{5}{8}$
2. **45°**
3. **32 cm**
4. $4\dfrac{3}{4}$
5. **216 cm³**
6. **18π**
7. **30 cm by 60 cm**
8. **45°**
9. **512 cm³**
10. **11π**

Ninth-Grade Mathematics Supplement

16

Here are some sample questions and solutions representative of what might appear on the Mathematics section of the ninth-grade version of the SHSAT.

PRACTICE GRID-IN QUESTIONS

1. Assume $S(x)$ is the sum of all the positive odd integers less than or equal to x. What is the value of $S(11)$?

2. Simplify $\sqrt{24} \times \sqrt{150}$.

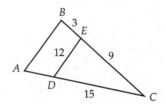

3. In the diagram above, $\triangle CDE$ is similar to $\triangle CAB$. What is the perimeter of $\triangle CAB$?

4. To determine the price for fixing a damaged sink, a plumber charges a fixed fee plus an hourly rate for each hour she works. If her price for 6 hours of work is $330, and her price for 11 hours of work is $530, what is the fixed fee the plumber charges?

(E) $40

(F) $60

(G) $90

(H) $200

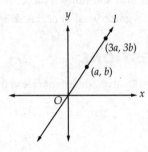

5. Straight line l passes through the origin, as shown in the figure above. What is the slope of line l in terms of a and b?

(A) $\dfrac{b}{a}$

(B) $\dfrac{a}{b}$

(C) $\dfrac{3a}{b}$

(D) $\dfrac{3b}{a}$

6. Simplify $\dfrac{w^8 w^{-4}}{w^2}$.

(E) w^2

(F) w^4

(G) w^6

(H) w^{10}

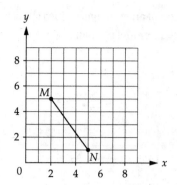

7. If point M is reflected over the line $x = 5$ to produce M', what is the area of triangle $MM'N$?

(A) 4 square units

(B) 8 square units

(C) 12 square units

(D) 24 square units

$$\frac{24.2 \times 10^{-6}}{2.2 \times 10^{3}}$$

8. What is the quotient of the expression above, expressed in scientific notation?

(E) 1.1×10^{-8}

(F) 1.1×10^{-9}

(G) 1.1×10^{-10}

(H) 1.1×10^{9}

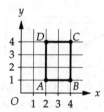

9. Rectangle $ABCD$ is rotated $180°$ counter-clockwise about the origin to form rectangle $A'B'C'D'$. What are the coordinates of D'?

(A) $(4, 2)$

(B) $(-4, -2)$

(C) $(-4, -4)$

(D) $(-2, -4)$

10. Which of the following expressions is negative in value?

(E) $2\pi - 6$

(F) $18 - 5\pi$

(G) $21 - 7\pi$

(H) $12\pi - 36$

11. The graph shows the population of an endangered bird species in a nature preserve since 2000. A student drew a line of best fit to model the data.

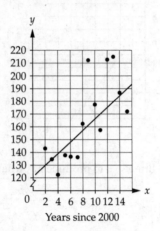

Years since 2000

Which statement best describes the line of best fit that the student drew?

(A) The line of best fit is not a strong model for the data, because the points are not close to the line.

(B) The line of best fit is not a strong model for the data, because it does not pass through any of the data points.

(C) The line of best fit is a strong model for the data, because both the line and the data show a positive trend.

(D) The line of best fit is a strong model for the data, because about half the data points are on each side of the line.

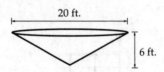

12. Water is pumped into a tank that is shaped like the right inverted cone shown above. The cone has a base diameter of 20 feet and a height of 6 feet. What is the volume, in cubic feet, of the water in the tank when the height of the water is 3 feet?

(E) 25π cu ft.

(F) 75π cu ft.

(G) 100π cu ft.

(H) 200π cu ft.

13. The symbol $[a, b, c]$ means $c^2 - \dfrac{ab + bc}{2}$. What is the value of $[1, 6, 4]$?

(A) −9

(B) 1

(C) 7

(D) 31

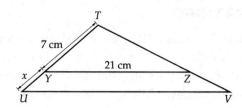

14. In the figure above, $\triangle TUV$ is similar to $\triangle TYZ$. If the length of YZ is 21 cm, what is the length of UV in terms of x?

(E) $3x$

(F) $3x + 21$

(G) $x + 7$

(H) $\frac{1}{3}x + 7$

15. Simplify $\dfrac{4x^4\sqrt{135}}{x^{-3}\sqrt{60}}$.

(A) $9x$

(B) $9x^7$

(C) $6x$

(D) $6x^7$

ANSWER EXPLANATIONS

1. **(36)** Compute this directly by listing all the positive odd integers less than or equal to 11 and finding their sum, which is $1 + 3 + 5 + 7 + 9 + 11 = 36$. There is also an intriguing property of sums of consecutive odd numbers: the sum of the first n consecutive odd integers is n^2. Here, we are adding the first six consecutive odd integers, and the sum is $6^2 = 36$. **Note:** The word *odd* and the phrase *less than* are very important here. If you don't read carefully, you may compute the wrong sum!

2. **(60)** Start with the fact that $\sqrt{24} \times \sqrt{150} = \sqrt{24 \times 150}$. Multiply 24 and 150 to get 3,600, so $\sqrt{24 \times 150} = \sqrt{3600}$. Since $60^2 = 3,600$, we have $\sqrt{3600} = 60$. Another approach is to simplify each radical expression before multiplying them: $\sqrt{24} = \sqrt{4 \times 6} = \sqrt{4} \times \sqrt{6} = 2\sqrt{6}$ and $\sqrt{150} = \sqrt{25 \times 6} = \sqrt{25} \times \sqrt{6} = 5\sqrt{6}$. So:

$$\sqrt{24} \times \sqrt{150} = 2\sqrt{6} \times 5\sqrt{6}$$
$$= 10 \times \sqrt{6} \times \sqrt{6}$$
$$= 10 \times 6 = 60$$

3. **(48)** Since $\triangle CDE$ is similar to $\triangle CAB$, we know that the corresponding side-lengths of the triangles are in proportion, thus $\dfrac{CE}{CB} = \dfrac{CD}{CA} = \dfrac{DE}{AB}$. Substitute known values to get $\dfrac{9}{12} = \dfrac{15}{CA} = \dfrac{12}{AB}$, and solve the two proportions $\dfrac{9}{12} = \dfrac{15}{CA}$ and $\dfrac{9}{12} = \dfrac{12}{AB}$ to find that $AB = 16$ and $CA = 20$. This makes the perimeter of $\triangle CAB$ equal to $CB + CA + AB = 12 + 20 + 16 = 48$. Or, note that the perimeter of $\triangle CDE$ is 36, and the scale factor from $\triangle CDE$ to $\triangle CAB$ is $\dfrac{4}{3}$, making the perimeter of $\triangle CAB$ equal to $36 \times \dfrac{4}{3} = 48$. **Note:** Always be careful when setting up proportions in similar triangles. For example, BE is not a side of either triangle, so don't use it if you are comparing sides.

4. **(G)** Let $F =$ the fixed fee and $H =$ hourly rate, and write two equations:

$$F + 6H = 330 \text{ and } F + 11H = 530$$

We can solve this system of equations by isolating F in the first equation ($F = 330 - 6H$) and substituting it into the second equation, which becomes $(330 - 6H) + 11H = 530$. Simplifying gives us $330 + 5H = 530$, and solving for H yields $5H = 200$, and so $H = 40$. This is the hourly rate, and we can find the flat fee by substituting $H = 40$ back into the equation:

$$F = 330 - 6H = 330 - (6 \times 40) = 330 - 240 = 90$$

Alternately, notice that $530 - 330 = 200$ must be the price of 5 hours at the hourly rate, which you can then use to find the fixed fee. **Note:** The hourly rate, 40, is an answer choice. Be careful!

5. **(A)** The slope of the line passing through two points is the change in the y-coordinate divided by the change in the x-coordinate, which is often denoted $\dfrac{\Delta y}{\Delta x}$ (the small triangle here is the Greek letter delta, and in mathematics it often means *change in*). Slope is sometimes referred to as "rise over run," which means how much the line "rises" (vertical change) over how much it "runs" (horizontal change). For the given line, we use the two labeled points to find the required changes. The change in the y-coordinate, or Δy, is $3b - b = 2b$; the change in the x-coordinate, or Δx, is $3a - a = 2a$. Thus, the slope is $\dfrac{\Delta y}{\Delta x} = \dfrac{2b}{2a} = \dfrac{b}{a}$. **Note:** A common error is to mistakenly write the slope as $\dfrac{\Delta x}{\Delta y}$; this incorrect answer is one of the choices.

6. **(E)** Use laws of exponents to simplify the expression. Since $w^8 w^{-4} = w^{8+-4} = w^4$, we have $\frac{w^8 w^{-4}}{w^2} = \frac{w^4}{w^2} = w^{4-2} = w^2$. Alternately, since $w^{-4} = \frac{1}{w^4}$, we have:

$$\frac{w^8 w^{-4}}{w^2} = \frac{w^8}{w^2 w^4} = \frac{w^8}{w^6} = w^{8-6} = w^2$$

7. **(C)** Since point M is three units to the left of the line $x = 5$, its reflection over the line $x = 5$, M', is three units to the right of the line $x = 5$. Thus, the coordinates of M' are $(8, 5)$. The formula for the area of a triangle is $A = \frac{1}{2}b \times h$. Here, we take the base of the triangle to be MM', which has length 6, and the height is the distance from N to MM', which is 4. This makes the area of the triangle $\frac{1}{2}6 \times 4 = 12$. Or, notice that triangle $MM'N$ is formed by reflecting the triangle with vertices M, N, and $(5, 5)$ over the line $x = 5$. This triangle has area $\frac{1}{2}3 \times 4 = 6$, so triangle $MM'N$ has twice that area.

8. **(E)** It is useful here to split this fraction up into two parts. Use the fact that $\frac{24.2 \times 10^{-6}}{2.2 \times 10^3} = \frac{24.2}{2.2} \times \frac{10^{-6}}{10^3}$. Now handle each fraction separately: $\frac{24.2}{2.2} = \frac{242}{22} = 11$, and $\frac{10^{-6}}{10^3} = 10^{-6-3} = 10^{-9}$. So $\frac{24.2 \times 10^{-6}}{2.2 \times 10^3} = 11 \times 10^{-9}$. We need to write this number with a 1.1 as the **significand** (the part in front of the 10^n in scientific notation). To do that, notice that $1.1 = \frac{11}{10}$. So:

$$11 \times 10^{-9} = 11 \times \frac{1}{10^9}$$
$$= \frac{11}{10} \times \frac{1}{10^8}$$
$$= 1.1 \times 10^{-8}$$

9. **(D)** When a point is rotated $180°$ about the origin, the coordinates of its image are the negations of the original coordinates. That is, when the point (x, y) is rotated about the origin $180°$, its image is the point $(-x, -y)$. Since the coordinates of D are $(2, 4)$, the coordinates of D' are $(-2, -4)$.

10. **(G)** Use the fact that π, which is approximately 3.141592, is a number between 3 and 4. Since $\pi > 3$, we know that $2\pi > 6$, and so $2\pi - 6 > 0$, which means choice E is not correct. Since $\pi < 3.2$, we know that $5\pi < 5 \times 3.2 = 16$, and so $18 - 5\pi > 18 - 16 = 2$, and choice F is not the answer. Again, since $\pi > 3$, we know $7\pi > 21$, and so $21 - 7\pi < 0$, so choice G is the answer. For completeness, notice that $12\pi > 12 \times 3 = 36$, so $12\pi - 36 > 0$.

11. **(C)** Lines of best fit are usually close to some points but can be far from others, so choice A is a bad criterion for judging a line of best fit (and in fact, many of the points are close to the line). Lines of best fit often pass through none of the points in a data set, so choice B cannot be the answer. And lines of best fit do not necessarily divide the data set into two equal parts above and below the line, so choice D is not the answer. But both the line and the data increase as we read the graph from left to right, indicating a positive trend in both. Thus choice C is the answer.

12. **(E)** The volume of a cone is given by $V = \frac{1}{3}\pi r^2 h$, where r is the radius of the base and h is the height of the cone. The trick here is to determine the radius of the base of the cone of water, which has a height of 3 ft. Consider the cross-section of the cone shown below:

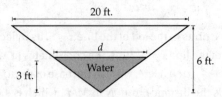

The triangular cross-section of the water is similar to the triangular cross-section of the larger cone. This means we can write the proportion $\frac{3\,\text{ft.}}{6\,\text{ft.}} = \frac{d}{20\,\text{ft.}}$, which makes $d = 10$ feet. This is the diameter of the cone of water, so the radius of the cone of water is 5 ft. Thus, the volume of the cone of water is $V = \frac{1}{3}\pi r^2 h = \frac{1}{3}\pi \times 5^2 \times 3 = 25\pi$ cu ft. **Note:** The volume of the overall cone, 200π, is one of the answer choices, as is half that volume, which you might naively believe to be the answer since the height of the water is half the height of the cone.

13. **(B)** We have:

$$[\![1,6,4]\!] = 4^2 - \frac{1\times 6 + 6 \times 4}{2}$$
$$= 16 - \frac{6+24}{2}$$
$$= 16 - \frac{30}{2}$$
$$= 16 - 15$$
$$= 1$$

14. **(F)** Since $\triangle TUV$ is similar to $\triangle TYZ$, we can set up the following proportion: $\frac{7}{7+x} = \frac{21}{UV}$. Now we solve for UV: $7 \times UV = (7+x)\times 21$, and so $UV = \frac{(7+x)\times 21}{7} = (7+x)\times 3 = 21 + 3x$.

Note: Don't make the common mistake of writing $\frac{7}{x} = \frac{21}{UV}$. The proportion we want compares the side-lengths of the similar triangles $\triangle TYZ$ and $\triangle TUV$, and x is not a side-length of $\triangle TUV$!

15. **(D)** First, focus on the x terms. Using laws of exponents, we see that $\frac{x^4}{x^{-3}} = x^{4-(-3)} = x^7$. (Notice this immediately eliminates two of the answer choices.) Now focus on the radical expressions: $\frac{\sqrt{135}}{\sqrt{60}} = \frac{\sqrt{9\times 15}}{\sqrt{4\times 15}} = \frac{\sqrt{9}\times\sqrt{15}}{\sqrt{4}\times\sqrt{15}} = \frac{3}{2}$. Thus, $\frac{4x^4\sqrt{135}}{x^{-3}\sqrt{60}} = 4\times x^7 \times \frac{3}{2} = 6x^7$.

Practice Tests

ANSWER SHEET
Practice Test 1

Part I: English Language Arts

1. Ⓐ Ⓑ Ⓒ Ⓓ	16. Ⓔ Ⓕ Ⓖ Ⓗ	31. Ⓐ Ⓑ Ⓒ Ⓓ	46. Ⓔ Ⓕ Ⓖ Ⓗ
2. Ⓔ Ⓕ Ⓖ Ⓗ	17. Ⓐ Ⓑ Ⓒ Ⓓ	32. Ⓔ Ⓕ Ⓖ Ⓗ	47. Ⓐ Ⓑ Ⓒ Ⓓ
3. Ⓐ Ⓑ Ⓒ Ⓓ	18. Ⓔ Ⓕ Ⓖ Ⓗ	33. Ⓐ Ⓑ Ⓒ Ⓓ	48. Ⓔ Ⓕ Ⓖ Ⓗ
4. Ⓔ Ⓕ Ⓖ Ⓗ	19. Ⓐ Ⓑ Ⓒ Ⓓ	34. Ⓔ Ⓕ Ⓖ Ⓗ	49. Ⓐ Ⓑ Ⓒ Ⓓ
5. Ⓐ Ⓑ Ⓒ Ⓓ	20. Ⓔ Ⓕ Ⓖ Ⓗ	35. Ⓐ Ⓑ Ⓒ Ⓓ	50. Ⓔ Ⓕ Ⓖ Ⓗ
6. Ⓔ Ⓕ Ⓖ Ⓗ	21. Ⓐ Ⓑ Ⓒ Ⓓ	36. Ⓔ Ⓕ Ⓖ Ⓗ	51. Ⓐ Ⓑ Ⓒ Ⓓ
7. Ⓐ Ⓑ Ⓒ Ⓓ	22. Ⓔ Ⓕ Ⓖ Ⓗ	37. Ⓐ Ⓑ Ⓒ Ⓓ	52. Ⓔ Ⓕ Ⓖ Ⓗ
8. Ⓔ Ⓕ Ⓖ Ⓗ	23. Ⓐ Ⓑ Ⓒ Ⓓ	38. Ⓔ Ⓕ Ⓖ Ⓗ	53. Ⓐ Ⓑ Ⓒ Ⓓ
9. Ⓐ Ⓑ Ⓒ Ⓓ	24. Ⓔ Ⓕ Ⓖ Ⓗ	39. Ⓐ Ⓑ Ⓒ Ⓓ	54. Ⓔ Ⓕ Ⓖ Ⓗ
10. Ⓔ Ⓕ Ⓖ Ⓗ	25. Ⓐ Ⓑ Ⓒ Ⓓ	40. Ⓔ Ⓕ Ⓖ Ⓗ	55. Ⓐ Ⓑ Ⓒ Ⓓ
11. Ⓐ Ⓑ Ⓒ Ⓓ	26. Ⓔ Ⓕ Ⓖ Ⓗ	41. Ⓐ Ⓑ Ⓒ Ⓓ	56. Ⓔ Ⓕ Ⓖ Ⓗ
12. Ⓔ Ⓕ Ⓖ Ⓗ	27. Ⓐ Ⓑ Ⓒ Ⓓ	42. Ⓔ Ⓕ Ⓖ Ⓗ	57. Ⓐ Ⓑ Ⓒ Ⓓ
13. Ⓐ Ⓑ Ⓒ Ⓓ	28. Ⓔ Ⓕ Ⓖ Ⓗ	43. Ⓐ Ⓑ Ⓒ Ⓓ	
14. Ⓔ Ⓕ Ⓖ Ⓗ	29. Ⓐ Ⓑ Ⓒ Ⓓ	44. Ⓔ Ⓕ Ⓖ Ⓗ	
15. Ⓐ Ⓑ Ⓒ Ⓓ	30. Ⓔ Ⓕ Ⓖ Ⓗ	45. Ⓐ Ⓑ Ⓒ Ⓓ	

Part II: Mathematics

58.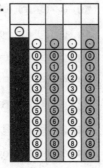

59.

60.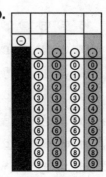

61.

62.

63. Ⓐ Ⓑ Ⓒ Ⓓ	76. Ⓔ Ⓕ Ⓖ Ⓗ	89. Ⓐ Ⓑ Ⓒ Ⓓ	102. Ⓔ Ⓕ Ⓖ Ⓗ
64. Ⓔ Ⓕ Ⓖ Ⓗ	77. Ⓐ Ⓑ Ⓒ Ⓓ	90. Ⓔ Ⓕ Ⓖ Ⓗ	103. Ⓐ Ⓑ Ⓒ Ⓓ
65. Ⓐ Ⓑ Ⓒ Ⓓ	78. Ⓔ Ⓕ Ⓖ Ⓗ	91. Ⓐ Ⓑ Ⓒ Ⓓ	104. Ⓔ Ⓕ Ⓖ Ⓗ
66. Ⓔ Ⓕ Ⓖ Ⓗ	79. Ⓐ Ⓑ Ⓒ Ⓓ	92. Ⓔ Ⓕ Ⓖ Ⓗ	105. Ⓐ Ⓑ Ⓒ Ⓓ
67. Ⓐ Ⓑ Ⓒ Ⓓ	80. Ⓔ Ⓕ Ⓖ Ⓗ	93. Ⓐ Ⓑ Ⓒ Ⓓ	106. Ⓔ Ⓕ Ⓖ Ⓗ
68. Ⓔ Ⓕ Ⓖ Ⓗ	81. Ⓐ Ⓑ Ⓒ Ⓓ	94. Ⓔ Ⓕ Ⓖ Ⓗ	107. Ⓐ Ⓑ Ⓒ Ⓓ
69. Ⓐ Ⓑ Ⓒ Ⓓ	82. Ⓔ Ⓕ Ⓖ Ⓗ	95. Ⓐ Ⓑ Ⓒ Ⓓ	108. Ⓔ Ⓕ Ⓖ Ⓗ
70. Ⓔ Ⓕ Ⓖ Ⓗ	83. Ⓐ Ⓑ Ⓒ Ⓓ	96. Ⓔ Ⓕ Ⓖ Ⓗ	109. Ⓐ Ⓑ Ⓒ Ⓓ
71. Ⓐ Ⓑ Ⓒ Ⓓ	84. Ⓔ Ⓕ Ⓖ Ⓗ	97. Ⓐ Ⓑ Ⓒ Ⓓ	110. Ⓔ Ⓕ Ⓖ Ⓗ
72. Ⓔ Ⓕ Ⓖ Ⓗ	85. Ⓐ Ⓑ Ⓒ Ⓓ	98. Ⓔ Ⓕ Ⓖ Ⓗ	111. Ⓐ Ⓑ Ⓒ Ⓓ
73. Ⓐ Ⓑ Ⓒ Ⓓ	86. Ⓔ Ⓕ Ⓖ Ⓗ	99. Ⓐ Ⓑ Ⓒ Ⓓ	112. Ⓔ Ⓕ Ⓖ Ⓗ
74. Ⓔ Ⓕ Ⓖ Ⓗ	87. Ⓐ Ⓑ Ⓒ Ⓓ	100. Ⓔ Ⓕ Ⓖ Ⓗ	113. Ⓐ Ⓑ Ⓒ Ⓓ
75. Ⓐ Ⓑ Ⓒ Ⓓ	88. Ⓔ Ⓕ Ⓖ Ⓗ	101. Ⓐ Ⓑ Ⓒ Ⓓ	114. Ⓔ Ⓕ Ⓖ Ⓗ

Practice Test 1

PART 1—ENGLISH LANGUAGE ARTS

SUGGESTED TIME: 90 MINUTES, 57 QUESTIONS

Revising/Editing

QUESTIONS 1–10

IMPORTANT NOTE: The Revising/Editing section (Questions 1–10) is in two parts: Part A and Part B.

REVISING/EDITING PART A

Directions: Read and answer each of the following questions. You will be asked to recognize and correct errors in sentences or short paragraphs. Mark the best answer for each question.

1. Read this paragraph.

> (1) People often associate monosodium glutamate better known as MSG, with headaches and nausea, but there was no evidence to substantiate that link. (2) In fact, the compounds associated with MSG are commonly found in beef, pork, or chicken. (3) Scientists believe the sicknesses might be the result of a "nocebo effect." (4) The nocebo effect, like the placebo effect, isn't caused by an actual substance but merely by suggestion.

How should this paragraph be revised?

(A) Sentence 1: Change *was* to *is*, AND insert a comma after *glutamate*.
(B) Sentence 2: Change *associated* to *associating*, AND delete comma after *pork*.
(C) Sentence 3: Change *believe* to *believed*, AND insert a comma after *believe*.
(D) Sentence 4: Change *caused* to *cause*, AND delete comma after *effect*.

GO ON TO THE NEXT PAGE

2. Read this sentence.

> Typically occurring in the spring, a nor'easter, a gigantic cyclone, gets its name from the direction of the winds, that tend to blow northeast to southwest.

Which edit should be made to correct this sentence?

(E) Delete the comma after **spring**.

(F) Delete the comma after **nor'easter**.

(G) Delete the comma after **cyclone**.

(H) Delete comma after **winds**.

3. Read this paragraph.

> (1) Molasses syrup, a product made from sugar and beets, are primarily used for sweetening foods. (2) Molasses syrup is rich with glucose and fructose, compounds rich in energy. (3) Because of its taste, sugar molasses syrup is used for human consumption, while beet molasses syrup is used for animal consumption. (4) Because of its adhesive properties, molasses syrup is also used as an additive component in mortar for brickwork.

Which sentence should be revised to correct a subject-verb agreement?

(A) sentence 1

(B) sentence 2

(C) sentence 3

(D) sentence 4

4. Read these sentences.

> (1) In ancient Greece, there were two major philosophical schools.
> (2) Stoicism advocated a quiet contemplation.
> (3) Epicureanism pursued worldly pleasures.

What is the best way to combine these sentences?

(E) In ancient Greece, there were two major philosophical schools, and one was Stoicism, which advocated a quiet contemplation, and the other was Epicureanism, which pursued worldly pleasures.

(F) In the two major philosophical schools of ancient Greece, Stoicism advocated a quiet contemplation, while Epicureanism pursued worldly pleasures.

(G) While Stoicism advocated a quiet contemplation, Epicureanism pursued worldly pleasure, and these were the two major philosophical schools of ancient Greece.

(H) The two major philosophical schools, one being Stoicism that advocated quiet contemplation and the other being Epicureanism that pursued worldly pleasures, were in ancient Greece.

GO ON TO THE NEXT PAGE

> **Directions:** Read the passage below and answer the questions following it. You will be asked to improve the writing quality of the passage and to correct errors so that the passage follows the conventions of standard written English. You may reread the passage if you need to. Mark the best answer for each question.

The Importance of Sleep

(1) People will often reduce their sleep for careers, family schedules, or even a movie. (2) If insufficient sleep is a routine in your life, you may be at an increased risk for diabetes, obesity, heart disease, poor mental health, and even death. (3) Even one night of insufficient sleep can have a strong impact on you the next day.

(4) How much sleep you need fluctuates as you get older. (5) Scientists recommend that you get a certain amount of sleep as you age. (6) To prevent dementia in old age, some scientists recommend keeping your brain active by playing games.

(7) There are some important practices that can help your sleep health. (8) Be consistent: head to bed at the same time every night and wake up at the same time in the morning, including on the weekends. (9) Make sure your bedroom is silent, dim, calming, and at a comfortable temperature. (10) Avoid large meals, coffee, and alcoholic drinks before bedtime.

(11) Better sleep habits can improve the quality of your sleep. (12) Getting sufficient sleep is important, but good sleep quality is also necessary. (13) Good sleep is difficult to define, but indicators of bad sleep are unmistakable. (14) These include feeling sleepy or tired even after getting enough sleep, constantly waking up during the night, and having symptoms of sleep disorders (such as snoring or gasping for air). (15) It's important to identify these indicators because they can lead to better habits.

5. Which transition word or phrase should be added to the beginning of sentence 2?

   (A) As a result,
   (B) However,
   (C) Therefore,
   (D) Regardless,

6. Which sentence could best follow sentence 3 and support the main point of the fourth paragraph?

   (E) A third of U.S. adults report that they usually get less than the recommended amount of sleep.
   (F) Sleeping aids, such as melatonin and CPAP machines, can help solve for the lack of sleep.
   (G) You're more likely to feel sleepy, be in a bad mood, be less productive at work, and be involved in a motor vehicle crash.
   (H) It is unlikely that most people will do something about this neglected issue.

GO ON TO THE NEXT PAGE

7. Which revision of sentence 5 uses the most precise language?

(A) Scientists recommend that a person get more sleep as they grow older.

(B) The American Academy of Sleep Medicine and the Sleep Research Society recommend more sleep as people age.

(C) The American Academy of Sleep Medicine and the Sleep Research Society recommend 9 to 12 hours for school-aged children, 8 to 10 for teens, and 7 or more for adults.

(D) The American Academy of Sleep Medicine and the Sleep Research Society recommend more sleep for more people of different ages, shapes, and sizes.

8. Which sentence best follows the structure and style of the sentences in paragraph 3 (sentences 7–10)?

(E) Get some exercise because being physically active during the day can help you fall asleep more easily at night.

(F) If you get some exercise, then being physically active during the day can help you fall asleep more easily at night.

(G) Physical activity during the day can help you fall asleep with exercise.

(H) Being physically active by getting some exercise can help you fall asleep more easily at night.

9. Where should sentence 11 be moved to improve the organization of the fourth paragraph (sentences 11–15)?

(A) between sentence 12 and 13

(B) between sentence 13 and 14

(C) between sentence 14 and 15

(D) after sentence 15

10. Which sentence is irrelevant in the passage and should be deleted?

(E) sentence 1

(F) sentence 6

(G) sentence 9

(H) sentence 12

GO ON TO THE NEXT PAGE

Reading Comprehension

> **Directions:** Read each of the following six texts, and answer the related questions. You may write in your test booklet as needed to take notes. You should reread relevant parts of each text before marking the best answer for each question. Base your answers only on the content within the text.

Bringing the Ocean Home

The following passage has been adapted from Bernd Brunner's essay *Bringing the Ocean Home*. It appears in *The Public Domain Review*.

1   The popularization of observing the interaction between marine animals and aquatic plants in glass tanks can be attributed to the Englishman Philip Henry Gosse, who was the first person to resolutely use the word "aquarium" for such objects. In his 1853 book *A Naturalist's Rambles on the Devonshire Coast*, the Latin term "vivarium" was used interchangeably with "marine aquarium," but one year later the die was cast for the latter in his book *The Aquarium: An Unveiling of the Wonders of the Deep Sea*.

2   Gosse was born in 1810 in Poole in the south of England, the son of an impoverished travelling miniature painter. As a young man Gosse made his way across the Atlantic to Newfoundland, where he dealt with seal and cod fleets in the Carbonear harbour. In his early twenties he devoted himself wholeheartedly to collecting insects. For two years he documented every insect he could get hold of. Along with some of his friends, he decided to move to mainland Canada in hopes of establishing a rural commune and opening a museum of stuffed birds. After both ventures failed, Gosse returned to England, where he found work as a teacher in Hackney until he received an invitation from the Society for the Promotion of Christian Knowledge to write several books, which led to unexpected success. Gosse's newfound notoriety led to an invitation to Jamaica later that year, and his time in the Caribbean gave birth to three further books, all successes, and the author established himself as an important voice among the publishing naturalists of the period.

3   Of all Gosse's works, the most successful was *The Aquarium*, in which he described his observations of coastal life and—a year after establishing the first public aquarium at the London Zoo—gave his readers instructions on how to build a miniature ocean of their very own. A saltwater aquarium, he asserted, was the perfect way to get acquainted with the peculiar creatures of the ocean without having to descend into the depths using complicated diving equipment. He was amused by a French zoologist, Henri Milne-Edwards, who stalked around at the bottom of the Mediterranean wearing a "water-tight dress, suitable spectacles, and a breathing tube" in order to take a closer look at the submarine world. All this was so much easier to achieve, Gosse proclaimed, in the safe environment of one's own four walls.

GO ON TO THE NEXT PAGE

4 *The Aquarium* was more than a cultural sensation: it was also a financial success. A year later, a smaller *Handbook to the Marine Aquarium* was published for those who had not been able to afford the first book. From the collecting of ferns, the Victorian citizen now turned their attention toward the exploitation of the coastal regions. The rapidly expanding middle class found this new fad a topic suitable for conversation as well as education. As Henry D. Butler retrospectively wrote about the British aquarium mania in his book *The Family Aquarium*—"The aquarium was on everybody's lip. The aquarium rang in every body's ear. Morning, noon, and night, it was nothing but the aquarium."

11. Which statement best describes the central idea of the passage?

   (A) Philip Henry Gosse's innovative work did not receive the recognition it deserved until much later, after its financial success.
   (B) Philip Henry Gosse overcame remarkable challenges and difficulties to produce an aquarium, which would change the way we understood the world underwater.
   (C) Philip Henry Gosse's invention was initially acknowledged as a powerful way to understand the ways organisms live under the sea, but many people eventually lost interest as it grew in popularity.
   (D) Philip Henry Gosse's dedication to his work eventually led to the creation of the aquarium, which provided a number of benefits to researchers and the public alike.

12. Gosse believed that his invention could be beneficial by

   (E) making the marine diving techniques simpler and easier to accomplish.
   (F) providing a wealth of knowledge about environmental pollution.
   (G) helping ordinary citizens explore a world that is normally inaccessible.
   (H) collecting flora and fauna from a wide variety of environments.

13. What is most likely the reason the author uses the clause "the die was cast" in paragraph 1?

   (A) to suggest that an outcome was set
   (B) to create an element of despair
   (C) to highlight the importance of a hardworking mindset
   (D) to foreshadow the impact of luck in any kind of success

14. Which sentence best shows that Gosse's dedication contributed to his success?

   (E) "The popularization of observing the interaction between marine animals and aquatic plants in glass tanks can be attributed to the Englishman Philip Henry Gosse, who was the first person to resolutely use the word 'aquarium' for such objects." (paragraph 1)
   (F) "In his early twenties he devoted himself wholeheartedly to collecting insects." (paragraph 2)
   (G) "After both ventures failed, Gosse returned to England, where he found work as a teacher in Hackney until he received an invitation from the Society for the Promotion of Christian Knowledge to write several books, which led to unexpected success." (paragraph 2)
   (H) "All this was so much easier to achieve, Gosse proclaimed, in the safe environment of one's own four walls." (paragraph 3)

GO ON TO THE NEXT PAGE

15. Which claim is best supported by the information in paragraph 2?

    (A) Gosse's success can be attributed primarily to luck.

    (B) Gosse might not have gained his dedication and devotion to work if he had not been born into an impoverished family.

    (C) Gosse did not always experience success in his work.

    (D) Gosse became the most important naturalist in the 19th century.

16. Which impact did Gosse's invention have on the people of his time?

    (E) It popularized the usage of Latin in naming inventions.

    (F) It reduced the price of exploring the submarine environments.

    (G) It led to the exploitation of precious coastal resources.

    (H) It contributed to the increased emphasis on the importance of the environment.

GO ON TO THE NEXT PAGE

John Honeyman and the Battle of Trenton

1   Intelligence played a significant role in the Revolutionary War. General George Washington's victory over Hessian forces—or German regiments hired by the British—at the Battle of Trenton on December 26, 1776, ranks as an occasion where intelligence properly gathered and utilized secured a major Patriot victory. The Battle of Trenton and the war might have turned out completely different without the help of a willing double agent: John Honeyman.

2   The Battle of Trenton, New Jersey, marked the first major American victory in the Revolutionary War. Prior to this time, Patriot forces had endured nearly constant defeat as the British pushed them from New York and into Pennsylvania. The Continental Congress pleaded for a victory to save the cause.

3   In response, Washington decided to attack the exposed Hessian garrison at Trenton, comprised of roughly 1,400 men in three regiments under the command of Col. Johann Rall. Washington's plan depended on surprise and on intelligence provided by John Honeyman.

4   Born in Ireland, Honeyman was the son of a poor farmer. Although he had little formal education, he learned several trades and taught himself to read and write. At age 29, he enlisted in the British Army and served with distinction in the French and Indian War. Honeyman moved to Philadelphia in 1775 and met George Washington while he was there to attend meetings of the Continental Congress. Although he had served the British, Honeyman was sympathetic to the Americans and offered his services to Washington.

5   Posing as a Loyalist, Honeyman moved to Griggstown, New Jersey, where he practiced his trades as a butcher and weaver. A recognized wartime hero, he moved freely within the town and gathered intelligence about British and Hessian forces. Honeyman then arranged his capture by Continental forces and met with Washington, providing details on the strength, location, morale, and security arrangements of the Hessian troops. With Washington's help, Honeyman escaped and returned to Trenton where he told Colonel Rall of his feigned capture and escape, reporting that the Continental Army was in such a low state of morale that it could not attack.

6   On Christmas night, Washington crossed the swollen Delaware River with 2,400 soldiers and made the long, cold march over muddy roads to Trenton. When Continental forces attacked after dawn, 300 surprised Hessians surrendered immediately, as the remainder struggled to mount a defense. When the brief battle had ended, the Americans counted a handful of casualties, while the Hessians lost more than 1,000 men, including 918 prisoners. All four Hessian colonels, including Rall, were killed. By noon, Continental forces had moved safely back across the Delaware, giving the Continental Congress and the Patriot cause a wonderful Christmas gift: new confidence and hope.

GO ON TO THE NEXT PAGE

17. Read this sentence from paragraph 1.

> **General George Washington's victory over Hessian forces—or German regiments hired by the British—at the Battle of Trenton on December 26, 1776, ranks as an occasion where intelligence properly gathered and utilized secured a major Patriot victory.**

What does the author's comment reveal about the nature of the victory?

(A) The victory required more than superior arms and manpower.

(B) Most Americans did not believe that they would be victorious.

(C) The Battle of Trenton was one of the most important battles to contribute to American victory.

(D) The German regiments lost to the George Washington's forces because they were not intelligent.

18. Which statement is best supported by paragraph 2?

(E) The Battle of Trenton was more important than any other victory during the American Revolution.

(F) The Patriot forces suffered only defeat prior to the victory at Trenton.

(G) Pennsylvania was easier to defend than New York.

(H) Support for the war would have been difficult without the victory at Trenton.

19. How does paragraph 3 contribute to the development of ideas in the passage?

(A) It highlights Washington's ability to identify a key weakness of the Hessian forces.

(B) It explains the importance of intelligence in military victories.

(C) It provides the context to introduce John Honeyman's role in the victory.

(D) It creates an important setting that the author will use to describe the Hessian victory.

20. Which sentence is the best summary of how John Honeyman became involved in the American Revolution?

(E) John Honeyman was commissioned by the Continental Congress, which later assigned him to serve under George Washington's command.

(F) George Washington learned of John Honeyman's impressive record at the French and Indian War and drafted him into his service.

(G) John Honeyman met George Washington and decided to serve under Washington because of his feelings about Americans.

(H) John Honeyman taught himself to read and write, which led to his gradual understanding that the British needed to be repelled from America.

21. Honeyman helped Washington's forces primarily by

(A) leading a raid against Hessian forces.

(B) spreading misinformation about the Hessian forces while working as a butcher and a weaver.

(C) confusing the Hessian forces about the location of the Continental Army.

(D) misrepresenting the condition of the Continental Army.

GO ON TO THE NEXT PAGE

22. Which sentence best exemplifies Honeyman's contribution to the American cause?

    (E) "Intelligence played a significant role in the Revolutionary War." (paragraph 1)

    (F) "The Continental Congress pleaded for a victory to save the cause." (paragraph 2)

    (G) "With Washington's help, Honeyman escaped and returned to Trenton where he told Colonel Rall of his feigned capture and escape, reporting that the Continental Army was in such a low state of morale that it could not attack." (paragraph 5)

    (H) "By noon, Continental forces had moved safely back across the Delaware, giving the Continental Congress and the Patriot cause a wonderful Christmas gift: new confidence and hope." (paragraph 6)

23. In paragraph 6, the word "handful" is used to highlight

    (A) the difficulty the Continental Army had to overcome in order to achieve victory.

    (B) the extent of the success achieved by the Continental Army.

    (C) the resourceful efforts of Honeyman that contributed to Washington's victory.

    (D) the weakness of the Hessian army prior to Washington's attack.

24. What is implied by the phrase "a wonderful Christmas gift" (paragraph 6)?

    (E) The Hessians were overly generous in their behavior toward Americans.

    (F) People can find a way to celebrate the spirit of Christmas even during war.

    (G) The victory renewed American faith in the revolution.

    (H) The celebration of Christmas is a time-honored tradition that can be traced back to the American Revolution.

GO ON TO THE NEXT PAGE

Excerpt from *The Scarlet Letter*

By Nathaniel Hawthorne

1   One peculiarity of the child's deportment remains yet to be told. The very first thing which she had noticed in her life, was—what?—not the mother's smile, responding to it, as other babies do, by that faint, embryo smile of the little mouth, remembered so doubtfully afterwards, and with such fond discussion whether it were indeed a smile. By no means! But that first object of which Pearl seemed to become aware was—shall we say it?—the scarlet letter on Hester's bosom! One day, as her mother stooped over the cradle, the infant's eyes had been caught by the glimmering of the gold embroidery about the letter; and putting up her little hand she grasped at it, smiling, not doubtfully, but with a decided gleam, that gave her face the look of a much older child. Then, gasping for breath, did Hester Prynne clutch the fatal token, instinctively endeavouring to tear it away, so infinite was the torture inflicted by the intelligent touch of Pearl's baby-hand. Again, as if her mother's agonised gesture were meant only to make sport for her, did little Pearl look into her eyes, and smile. From that epoch, except when the child was asleep, Hester had never felt a moment's safety: not a moment's calm enjoyment of her. Weeks, it is true, would sometimes elapse, during which Pearl's gaze might never once be fixed upon the scarlet letter; but then, again, it would come at unawares, like the stroke of sudden death, and always with that peculiar smile and odd expression of the eyes.

2   Once this freakish, elvish cast came into the child's eyes while Hester was looking at her own image in them, as mothers are fond of doing; and suddenly for women in solitude, and with troubled hearts, are pestered with unaccountable delusions she fancied that she beheld, not her own miniature portrait, but another face in the small black mirror of Pearl's eye. It was a face, fiend-like, full of smiling malice, yet bearing the semblance of features that she had known full well, though seldom with a smile, and never with malice in them. It was as if an evil spirit possessed the child, and had just then peeped forth in mockery. Many a time afterwards had Hester been tortured, though less vividly, by the same illusion.

3   In the afternoon of a certain summer's day, after Pearl grew big enough to run about, she amused herself with gathering handfuls of wild flowers, and flinging them, one by one, at her mother's bosom; dancing up and down like a little elf whenever she hit the scarlet letter. Hester's first motion had been to cover her bosom with her clasped hands. But whether from pride or resignation, or a feeling that her penance might best be wrought out by this unutterable pain, she resisted the impulse, and sat erect, pale as death, looking sadly into little Pearl's wild eyes. Still came the battery of flowers, almost invariably hitting the mark, and covering the mother's breast with hurts for which she could find no balm in this world, nor knew how to seek it in another. At last, her shot being all expended, the child stood still and gazed at Hester, with that little laughing image of a fiend peeping out—or, whether it peeped or no, her mother so imagined it—from the unsearchable abyss of her black eyes.

4   "Child, what art thou?" cried the mother.

5   "Oh, I am your little Pearl!" answered the child.

6   But while she said it, Pearl laughed, and began to dance up and down with the humoursome gesticulation of a little imp, whose next freak might be to fly up the chimney.

GO ON TO THE NEXT PAGE

7　"Art thou my child, in very truth?" asked Hester.

8　Nor did she put the question altogether idly, but, for the moment, with a portion of genuine earnestness; for, such was Pearl's wonderful intelligence, that her mother half doubted whether she were not acquainted with the secret spell of her existence, and might not now reveal herself.

9　"Yes; I am little Pearl!" repeated the child, continuing her antics.

10　"Thou art not my child! Thou art no Pearl of mine!" said the mother half playfully; for it was often the case that a sportive impulse came over her in the midst of her deepest suffering. "Tell me, then, what thou art, and who sent thee hither?"

11　"Tell me, mother!" said the child, seriously, coming up to Hester, and pressing herself close to her knees. "Do thou tell me!"

12　"Thy Heavenly Father sent thee!" answered Hester Prynne.

13　But she said it with a hesitation that did not escape the acuteness of the child. Whether moved only by her ordinary freakishness, or because an evil spirit prompted her, she put up her small forefinger and touched the scarlet letter.

14　"He did not send me!" cried she, positively. "I have no Heavenly Father!"

15　"Hush, Pearl, hush! Thou must not talk so!" answered the mother, suppressing a groan. "He sent us all into the world. He sent even me, thy mother. Then, much more thee! Or, if not, thou strange and elfish child, whence didst thou come?"

16　"Tell me! Tell me!" repeated Pearl, no longer seriously, but laughing and capering about the floor. "It is thou that must tell me!"

17　But Hester could not resolve the query, being herself in a dismal labyrinth of doubt. She remembered—betwixt a smile and a shudder—the talk of the neighbouring townspeople, who, seeking vainly elsewhere for the child's paternity, and observing some of her odd attributes, had given out that poor little Pearl was a demon offspring: such as, ever since old Catholic times, had occasionally been seen on earth, through the agency of their mother's sin, and to promote some foul and wicked purpose. Luther, according to the scandal of his monkish enemies, was a brat of that hellish breed; nor was Pearl the only child to whom this inauspicious origin was assigned among the New England Puritans.

GO ON TO THE NEXT PAGE

25. Over the course of the passage, the primary focus shifts from

(A) a character's inner thoughts to observations made by other characters.

(B) an exchange between two strangers to casual disagreement.

(C) a description of a relationship between two characters to a particular moment involving the two characters.

(D) the physical setting of a scene to the different aspects of a character's personality traits.

26. In paragraph 1, how do the words "caught by the glimmer gold embroidery" contribute to the meaning of the paragraph?

(E) It highlights the excitement of a pending revelation.

(F) It suggests a captivating aspect of a physical object.

(G) It emphasizes the oppressive relationship between the two characters.

(H) It exaggerates the wealth one character is intent on keeping hidden.

27. The line "that gave her face the look" in paragraph 1 evokes Pearl's

(A) hatred toward the other character.

(B) appearance that belies her age.

(C) desire to act mature.

(D) concern about what others will think of her.

28. Which of the following best reflects Hester's belief that the child is both disturbing yet familiar?

(E) "Once this freakish, elvish cast came into the child's eyes while Hester was looking at her own image in them, as mothers are fond of doing." (paragraph 2)

(F) "It was as if an evil spirit possessed the child, and had just then peeped forth in mockery." (paragraph 2)

(G) "In the afternoon of a certain summer's day, after Pearl grew big enough to run about, she amused herself with gathering handfuls of wild flowers, and flinging them, one by one, at her mother's bosom" (paragraph 3)

(H) "But whether from pride or resignation, or a feeling that her penance might best be wrought out by this unutterable pain, she resisted the impulse, and sat erect, pale as death, looking sadly into little Pearl's wild eyes." (paragraph 3)

GO ON TO THE NEXT PAGE

29. Read this text from paragraphs 4 to 10.

> **"Child, what art thou?" cried the mother.**
>
> **"Oh, I am your little Pearl!" answered the child.**
>
> **But while she said it, Pearl laughed, and began to dance up and down with the humoursome gesticulation of a little imp, whose next freak might be to fly up the chimney.**
>
> **"Art thou my child, in very truth?" asked Hester.**
>
> **Nor did she put the question altogether idly, but, for the moment, with a portion of genuine earnestness; for, such was Pearl's wonderful intelligence, that her mother half doubted whether she were not acquainted with the secret spell of her existence, and might not now reveal herself.**
>
> **"Yes; I am little Pearl!" repeated the child, continuing her antics.**
>
> **"Thou art not my child! Thou art no Pearl of mine!" said the mother half playfully; for it was often the case that a sportive impulse came over her in the midst of her deepest suffering. "Tell me, then, what thou art, and who sent thee hither?"**

This dialogue suggests that Hester's attitude toward the child can best be described as

(A) pure joy.
(B) careless indifference.
(C) complete despair.
(D) anxious concern.

30. Which of the following best suggests that Pearl is not unique in her circumstance?

(E) "Then, gasping for breath, did Hester Prynne clutch the fatal token, instinctively endeav- ouring to tear it away, so infinite was the torture inflicted by the intelligent touch of Pearl's baby-hand." (paragraph 1)

(F) "she fancied that she beheld, not her own miniature portrait, but another face in the small black mirror of Pearl's eye" (paragraph 2)

(G) "'He did not send me!' cried she, positively. 'I have no Heavenly Father!'" (paragraph 3)

(H) "Luther, according to the scandal of his monkish enemies, was a brat of that hellish breed; nor was Pearl the only child to whom this inauspicious origin was assigned among the New England Puritans." (paragraph 17)

GO ON TO THE NEXT PAGE

31. In paragraph 17, the "townspeople" are characterized primarily as

   (A) arrogant.
   (B) boastful.
   (C) egotistical.
   (D) judgmental.

32. Which of the following best reveals Pearl's perceptive nature?

   (E) "But she said it with a hesitation that did not escape the acuteness of the child."
       (paragraph 13)
   (F) "Whether moved only by her ordinary freakishness, or because an evil spirit prompted
       her, she put up her small forefinger and touched the scarlet letter." (paragraph 13)
   (G) "She remembered—betwixt a smile and a shudder—the talk of the neighbouring towns-
       people, who, seeking vainly elsewhere for the child's paternity, and observing some of
       her odd attributes, had given out that poor little Pearl was a demon offspring."
       (paragraph 17)
   (H) "nor was Pearl the only child to whom this inauspicious origin was assigned among the
       New England Puritans." (paragraph 17)

GO ON TO THE NEXT PAGE

Divining the Witch of York

The following passage has been adapted from Ed Simon's essay *Divining the Witch of York*. It appears in *The Public Domain Review*.

1　Most sources claimed that Ursula Soothtell died during the rule of Elizabeth I in 1561, but with eight decades separating her supposed death and the first appearance of her name in print, it's fair to assume a degree of invention in her biography. Despite her legendary ugliness (Ursula's seventeenth-century biographer described her as "a thing so strange in an infant, that no age can parallel"), at the age of twenty-four she married a carpenter named Toby Shipton, and it is to posterity that she would come to be known as "Mother Shipton." A less appropriate surname, because as "Smith" and "Taylor" indicate profession, so too did "Soothtell."

2　Mother Shipton would become the most famed of soothe tellers in English history, renowned for her prophecies and used as a symbolic familiar in the art of divination for generations, the very constructed personage of the seer, a work of poetry unto herself. Mother Shipton, England's Nostradamus, the sixteenth-century Sibyl, the Yorkshire prophetess, the Knaresborough witch whose crooked face has stared out from prints hanging on occultist's walls and in the names of country pubs since the initial printing of her predictions in 1641, should serve as a potent point of reflection for what exactly we talk about when we talk about prophecies.

3　Some scholars have argued that she is a complete fiction. There are those, however, that argue she was in some way an actual person, embellished through local tradition into a folk legend. There is at least one clue earlier than the seventeenth century which indicates that the prophetess may be based in more than pure invention. In 1537, as Catholic rebels in Yorkshire rebelled against Henry VIII and his dissolution of the monasteries, the assailed king wrote a letter to the Duke of Norfolk in which he disdainfully refers to a "witch of York." It is perhaps the earliest reference to what may be the real Mother Shipton. As the anonymous author in an 1868 edition of *Notes and Queries* concluded, "Although the fact of the existence of Mother Shipton rests wholly upon Yorkshire tradition, she can scarcely be regarded as a myth."

4　One particular title was crucial to the embellishment of her myth, her biography as written by the Irish novelist Richard Head in 1667. Head's *The Life and Death of Mother Shipton* was responsible for the majority of invented biographical details, building upon the bare narrative scaffolding of dozens of popular pamphlets. From Head's imagination came details such as Agatha's demonic wedding feast with Satan, accounts of magical feats performed by Ursula in front of worthies such as Cardinal Wolsey, and, most enduringly, the graphic and purple description of Mother Shipton's physical appearance, which occupies hundreds of words, describing her as "very morose and big-boned," with "very great goggling, but sharp and firey eyes; her nose of an incredible and unproportionable length."

5　Head then goes on for several sentences describing said nose in magnificently baroque prose, its "many crooks and turnings," and its adornment with "many strange pimples of divers colours, as red and blue mixed, which, like vapours of brimstone, gave such a lustre to the affrighted spectators in the dead time of the night, that one of them confessed several times, that her nurse needed

GO ON TO THE NEXT PAGE

no other light" to assist her in the birth of the prophetess. Head offers similarly purple descriptions of Mother Shipton's cheeks, her teeth, her mouth, her neck, her shoulders, her legs, and her toes, telling us that it was as if "her body had been screwed together piece after piece, and not rightly placed." In short, Head rather cruelly makes clear what Mother Shipton looked like—a witch.

33. Which statement best describes the central idea of the passage?

   (A) Mother Shipton is a fictional character that does not look like the actual person she was modeled after.
   (B) Ursula Soothtell was a tragic character who suffered unnecessary abuse from the people around her.
   (C) Mother Shipton may be modeled after an actual person with unusual characteristics that resemble those commonly associated with a witch.
   (D) The history of Ursula Soothtell was a mystery until historians uncovered a recent finding that confirms her existence.

34. In paragraph 2, how does the following phrase "England's Nostradamus, the sixteenth-century Sibyl, the Yorkshire prophetess, the Knaresborough witch" contribute to the development of the paragraph?

   (E) It identifies the key roles Mother Shipton played in the course of her career as a witch.
   (F) It lists the most important witches of Mother Shipton's time.
   (G) It emphasizes the extent of the influence that Mother Shipton developed over time.
   (H) It describes the most influential individuals in the occultist's history.

35. Which sentence from the passage best supports the idea that some believe that Mother Shipton is not a work of fiction?

   (A) "Mother Shipton would become the most famed of soothe tellers in English history, renowned for her prophecies and used as a symbolic familiar in the art of divination for generations." (paragraph 2)
   (B) "Mother Shipton, England's Nostradamus, the sixteenth-century Sibyl, the Yorkshire prophetess, the Knaresborough witch whose crooked face has stared out from prints hanging on occultist's walls and in the names of country pubs." (paragraph 3)
   (C) "There is at least one clue earlier than the seventeenth century which indicates that the prophetess may be based in more than pure invention." (paragraph 3)
   (D) "In short, Head rather cruelly makes clear what Mother Shipton looked like—a witch." (paragraph 5)

36. Which statement best describes Richard Head's impact on Mother Shipton?

   (E) He described only the most famous physical characteristics that Mother Shipton was known for.
   (F) He created most of the characteristics that may or may not have been true.
   (G) He was the most famous biographer to write about Mother Shipton.
   (H) He based his accounts of Mother Shipton on his observation of Agatha's demonic wedding feast.

GO ON TO THE NEXT PAGE

37. Which sentence from the passage is most similar to the narrator's judgment of Richard Head's biography?

(A) "Most sources claimed that Ursula Soothtell died during the rule of Elizabeth I in 1561." (paragraph 1)

(B) "Mother Shipton would become the most famed of soothe tellers in English history, renowned for her prophecies and used as a symbolic familiar in the art of divination for generations." (paragraph 2)

(C) "Some scholars have argued that she is a complete fiction." (paragraph 3)

(D) "There is at least one clue earlier than the seventeenth century which indicates that the prophetess may be based in more than pure invention." (paragraph 3)

38. In Richard Head's biography, it can be inferred that Cardinal Wolsey most likely

(E) had not seen Mother Shipton's performances.

(F) enjoyed a wonderful time at Agatha's wedding party.

(G) did not particularly appreciate the evils of witchcraft.

(H) made negative comments about Mother Shipton's appearance.

39. How do the words "baroque" and "adornment" contribute to the ideas in paragraph 5?

(A) They indicate that the descriptions were not intended to be objective descriptions.

(B) They highlight the positive ways in which Head attempted to describe Mother Shipton.

(C) They suggest that Head's descriptions are shallow and superficial, lacking true creativity.

(D) They suggest a threatening and dark tone that captures the essence of a witch.

40. According to Head, the source of the "light" in paragraph 5 came from

(E) Mother Shipton's magical spell.

(F) the nurse.

(G) Mother Shipton's nose.

(H) the vapors of brimstone.

41. Which statement about Mother Shipton is best supported by the passage?

(A) Historians will never know the truth about Mother Shipton.

(B) Mother Shipton was the most famous witch in history.

(C) Mother Shipton would not approve of the way she was described by Head.

(D) Henry VIII may have met Ursula Soothtell.

42. The excerpts suggests that Mother Shipton's name most probably comes from

(E) fictional stories.

(F) her marriage.

(G) Richard Head.

(H) Henry VIII.

GO ON TO THE NEXT PAGE

The Road Not Taken

By Robert Frost

Two roads diverged in a yellow wood,

And sorry I could not travel both

And be one traveler, long I stood

Line And looked down one as far as I could

(5) To where it bent in the undergrowth;

Then took the other, as just as fair,

And having perhaps the better claim,

Because it was grassy and wanted wear;

Though as for that the passing there

(10) Had worn them really about the same,

And both that morning equally lay

In leaves no step had trodden black.

Oh, I kept the first for another day!

Yet knowing how way leads on to way,

(15) I doubted if I should ever come back.

I shall be telling this with a sigh

Somewhere ages and ages hence:

Two roads diverged in a wood, and I—

I took the one less traveled by,

(20) And that has made all the difference.

43. The description in the first stanza (lines 1–5) helps establish the central idea of the poem by

   (A) describing the beauty of nature to introduce the journey of the traveler.
   (B) personifying the wood to demonstrate the power of nature.
   (C) listing the speaker's thoughts to reflect a sense of uncertainty.
   (D) highlighting a series of problems to reveal what most travelers experience.

GO ON TO THE NEXT PAGE

44. How does "the undergrowth" in line 5 contribute to the meaning of the poem?

    (E) It reveals why the speaker regrets walking in the woods.

    (F) It explains why the speaker's view is limited.

    (G) It suggests that the world is twisted deep inside.

    (H) It foreshadows the problems that the traveler will encounter on his walk.

45. What impact do the phrases "just as fair" in line 6 and "about the same" in line 10 have on the meaning of the poem?

    (A) They establish the idea that there is always a better way.

    (B) They highlight the importance of noticing the beautiful things in life.

    (C) They emphasize the fact that both roads are fundamentally similar.

    (D) They suggest that people always want to improve some aspects of the world.

46. Read line 13.

    "Oh, I kept the first for another day!"

    How does the line contribute to the development of ideas in the stanza?

    (E) The line supports the stanza's claim that precious moments in life should be remembered for the future.

    (F) The line introduces the idea that the speaker has some reservations about his choices.

    (G) The line expresses the idea that humans neglect the importance of time.

    (H) The line urges the reader to consider how precious each moment is.

47. The repetition of the line "Two roads diverged in a wood" in line 18 serves primarily to

    (A) bring the poem to a conclusion.

    (B) introduce a new topic.

    (C) support the previous statement.

    (D) indicate a problem.

48. The dash in the phrase "and I—" on line 18 serves to convey the speaker's

    (E) excitement.

    (F) confusion.

    (G) hesitation.

    (H) despair.

49. How does the poet develop the idea of the two roads?

    (A) by using similes to describe the environment

    (B) by providing a series of thoughts and reflections

    (C) by explaining the debate over the benefits of one option over the other

    (D) by using abstract language to express a powerful demonstration of emotions

GO ON TO THE NEXT PAGE

Darwin's Polar Bear

The following passage has been adapted from Michael Engelhard's essay *Darwin's Polar Bear*. It appears in *The Public Domain Review*.

1 As any good high school student should know, the beaks of Galápagos "finches" (in fact the islands' mockingbirds) helped Darwin to develop his ideas about evolution. But few people realize that the polar bear, too, informed his grand theory.

2 Letting his fancy run wild in *On the Origin of Species*, the man accustomed to thinking in eons hypothesized "a race of bears being rendered, by natural selection, more and more aquatic in their structure and habits, with larger and larger mouths, till a creature was produced as monstrous as a whale." Darwin based this speculation on a black bear the fur trader-explorer Samuel Hearne had observed swimming for hours, its mouth wide open, catching insects in the water. If the supply of insects were constant, Darwin thought, and no better-adapted competitors present, such a species could well take shape over time.

3 The oldest polar bear fossils found are from Svalbard and northern Norway and have been dated at 115,000–130,000 years old, before the beginning of the last Ice Age. However, some biologists think that polar bears and brown bears diverged from their common ancestor as early as 600,000 years ago. According to current research, polar bears evolved from brown bears that ventured onto the frozen ocean to stalk marine mammals, possibly after climate separated them from the main population. This was not a single, clean-cut departure, and repeated pairings between both species have turned the family tree into a thicket. Shrinking sea ice could force polar bears to mingle with their southern cousins again, particularly as the latter now travel farther north. In coastal Arctic Alaska, grizzlies have been observed feasting in the company of polar bears on bowhead whale carcasses, and interbreeding has been documented.

4 After he had been ridiculed for his musings on a future insect-eating cetacean bear, Darwin altered that passage in the second edition of *Origin* and removed it from subsequent ones. In a letter to the Irish algae specialist William Henry Harvey, Darwin complained how "The Bear case has been well laughed at, and disingenuously distorted by some into my saying that a bear could be converted into a whale." Still, Darwin insisted that "there is no especial difficulty in a Bear's mouth being enlarged to any degree useful to its changing habits—no more difficulty than man has found in increasing the crop of the pigeon, by continued selection, until it is literally as big as whole rest of body." Lamont's observations and theories as well as later findings about polar bear evolution vindicated the eminent naturalist and his ursine thought experiment.

GO ON TO THE NEXT PAGE

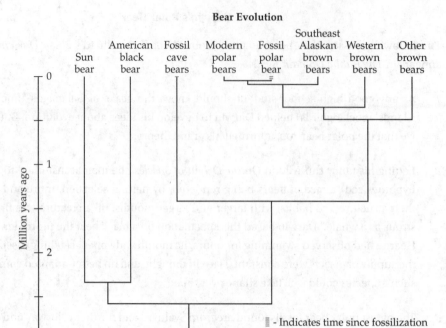

Bear Evolution

Sun bear | American black bear | Fossil cave bears | Modern polar bears | Fossil polar bear | Southeast Alaskan brown bears | Western brown bears | Other brown bears

Million years ago

≡ - Indicates time since fossilization

50. Which statement best describes the central idea of the passage?

(E) Darwin's observations of polar bear evolution contributed to his theories.

(F) Polar bears and grizzlies may have evolved together.

(G) Many of Darwin's theories were criticized by other scientists.

(H) Darwin could not have developed his theories without the help from Samuel Hearne.

51. What was the main way Samuel Hearne influenced Darwin's ideas?

(A) He proposed a modification to Darwin's existing theory on natural selection.

(B) He provided an observation that Darwin used to develop an idea.

(C) He suggested a theory that Darwin would oppose.

(D) He discovered an unknown species that would change the way Darwin thinks about natural selection.

52. In paragraph 3, the word "thicket" best contributes to the development of the paragraph by

(E) illustrating the environment in which polar bears thrive.

(F) suggesting that polar bears remain mysterious.

(G) revealing the locations in which most polar bears can be found.

(H) emphasizing the complexities of polar bear evolution.

GO ON TO THE NEXT PAGE

53. Which sentence from paragraph 3 best shows that environment played a key role in polar bear evolution?

   (A) "The oldest polar bear fossils found are from Svalbard and northern Norway and have been dated at 115,000–130,000 years old, before the beginning of the last Ice Age."
   (B) "However, some biologists think that polar bears and brown bears diverged from their common ancestor as early as 600,000 years ago."
   (C) "According to current research, polar bears evolved from brown bears that ventured onto the frozen ocean to stalk marine mammals, possibly after climate separated them from the main population."
   (D) "This was not a single, clean-cut departure, and repeated pairings between both species have turned the family tree into a thicket."

54. Which statement best describes the impact of warming temperatures in the Arctic?

   (E) There will be greater interaction between different types of bears.
   (F) There will be a rise in sea levels, leading to higher temperatures.
   (G) Polar bears will not be able to live in their environments.
   (H) Grizzly bear populations will overtake the polar bear populations.

55. What role does paragraph 4 play in the structure of the passage?

   (A) It provides detailed examples that support the previous paragraph.
   (B) It summarizes the central idea found in the rest of the passage.
   (C) It relates an anecdote that continues the narrative in an earlier part of the passage.
   (D) It challenges existing theories.

56. How does the chart support the ideas in the passage?

   (E) It shows the numerous types of bear populations throughout the world.
   (F) It reveals the impact of the climate on the divergence between the polar bear and the brown bear.
   (G) It supports the idea that the line of polar bears and brown bears split about 600,000 years ago.
   (H) It challenges the belief that polar bears and brown bears are related.

57. What was most likely the reason for Darwin's letter to William Henry Harvey?

   (A) He did not like the responses to his theory.
   (B) He felt that the public too easily confused brown bears with polar bears.
   (C) He believed that bears were being attacked unfairly by people who did not understand them.
   (D) He felt that William Henry Harvey's magazine misrepresented his ideas.

GO ON TO THE NEXT PAGE

PART 2—MATHEMATICS

57 QUESTIONS, SUGGESTED TIME: 90 MINUTES

IMPORTANT NOTES: (1) Formulas are not provided. (2) Figures other than graphs are not necessarily drawn to scale. (3) Diagrams are in one plane unless stated otherwise. (4) Graphs are drawn to scale. Unless stated otherwise, all relationships on graphs are according to appearance. (5) Simplify all fractions.

Grid-In Questions

QUESTIONS 58–62

DIRECTIONS: Solve each problem. On the answer sheet, write your answer in the boxes at the top of the grid. Start on the left side of each grid. Print only one number or symbol in each box. Under each box, fill in the circle that matches the number or symbol you wrote above. **DO NOT FILL IN A CIRCLE UNDER AN UNUSED BOX. DO NOT LEAVE A BOX BLANK IN THE MIDDLE OF AN ANSWER.**

58. For what value of w is $6w + 36 = 2w - 16$?

59. A car dealership has SUVs and sedans in a ratio of $5 : 9$. How many sedans does the car dealership have if there are 140 SUVs?

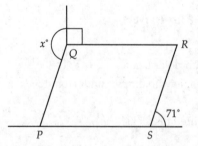

60. In the figure above, *PQRS* is a parallelogram. What is the value of x?

61. The sum of three consecutive integers is -15. If 1 is added to each integer, what is the product of the three resulting integers?

62. A survey asked students about their color preferences. Based on the results, the following statements are all true:

- 78 students like green.
- 84 students like yellow.
- 29 students like both green and yellow.
- 34 students like neither green nor yellow.

How many students were surveyed?

GO ON TO THE NEXT PAGE

> **DIRECTIONS:** Solve each question. Select the best answer from the choices given. Mark the letter of your choice on the answer sheet.

63. Ms. Bradley went to the store and bought six bottles of water for $0.75 each and 8 pounds of meat. Her total was $46.10 for these items, not including tax. What was the price per pound of the meat?

    (A) $5.20
    (B) $5.75
    (C) $33.60
    (D) $41.60

64. Which of the following numbers has an odd number of positive factors?

    (E) 12
    (F) 24
    (G) 36
    (H) 48

65. A metal plate used in a mechanical device must have a thickness of 0.02 inch, with an allowable error of 1%. What is the least allowable thickness of the metal square?

    (A) 0.0002 in.
    (B) 0.0198 in.
    (C) 0.0202 in.
    (D) 0.01 in.

66. On a car, the radius of each tire is 1 foot. If the car travels at 2,200 feet per minute, how many revolutions does one tire make in 2 minutes? (Use the approximation $\frac{22}{7}$ for π.)

    (E) 700
    (F) 1,925
    (G) 13,828
    (H) 15,400

67. $100 (2 + 0.2)^2 - 100 =$

    (A) 102
    (B) 120
    (C) 340
    (D) 384

68. The following chart shows scores on math test:

Score	Number of Students
85	3
75	5
65	2

    What is the mean score of the 10 students in the table above?

    (E) 22.5
    (F) 69
    (G) 75
    (H) 76

69. Greg and Cleo are playing a game and they each have a certain numbers of chips. Greg starts with twice as many chips as Cleo. After he gives her 8 chips, he still has 9 more than Cleo. How many chips did Greg have before he gave the 8 chips to Cleo?

    (A) 18
    (B) 34
    (C) 48
    (D) 50

GO ON TO THE NEXT PAGE

70. The perimeter of a rectangle is 350 centimeters. The ratio of the length to the width is 4 : 3. What are the dimensions of this rectangle?

(E) 40 cm by 30 cm

(F) 100 cm by 75 cm

(G) 125 cm by 50 cm

(H) 200 cm by 150 cm

71. Which number line below shows the solution to the inequality $2 < \frac{x}{2} < 4$?

(A)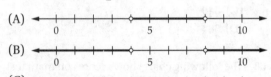

(B)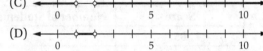

(C)

(D)

72.
$$1 \text{ dollar} = 9 \text{ fleegs}$$
$$1 \text{ dollar} = 0.5 \text{ grat}$$

Karen has 36 fleegs and 100 grats. If she exchanges the fleegs and grats for dollars according to the rates above, how many dollars will she receive?

(E) $54

(F) $204

(G) $374

(H) $524

73. A box of colored pencils contains exactly 8 red pencils. The probability of choosing a red pencil from the box is $\frac{2}{7}$. How many of the pencils in the box are not red?

(A) 5

(B) 17

(C) 20

(D) 28

74. In a scale diagram, 1 inch represents 250 feet. How many inches represent 100 feet?

(E) 0.1 in.

(F) 0.4 in.

(G) 0.5 in.

(H) 2.5 in.

75.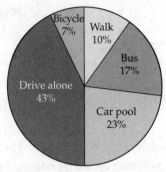

How People Get to Work in Westville

The chart above shows how people in Westville get to work. If there are 15,000 total people in Westville, how many more people ride the bus than walk to work?

(A) 1,050

(B) 1,500

(C) 1,920

(D) 2,550

76. In Smallville, 48% of the population is female, and 65% of the population commutes to work daily. Also, 10% of the population is male and does not commute to work daily. What percentage of the total Smallville population is female and does commute to work daily?

(E) 17%

(F) 23%

(G) 38%

(H) 65%

77. The set of possible values of m is $\{2, 4, 6\}$. What is the set of possible values of k if $2k = m + 4$?

(A) $\{3, 4, 5\}$

(B) $\{6, 8, 10\}$

(C) $\{3, 5, 7\}$

(D) $\{12, 16, 20\}$

GO ON TO THE NEXT PAGE

78. In a sample of 10 cards, 4 are red and 6 are blue. If 2 cards are selected at random from the sample, one at a time without replacement, what is the probability that both cards are not red?

(E) $\frac{3}{10}$

(F) $\frac{1}{3}$

(G) $\frac{9}{25}$

(H) $\frac{3}{5}$

79.

1 dreck = 3 klemps

3 fligs = 2 zorks

2 zorks = 5 drecks

4 groms = 1 flig

A nation has five types of coins: drecks, fligs, groms, klemps, and zorks. The relationship between the coins is shown above. Which coin is most valuable?

(A) dreck

(B) flig

(C) klemp

(D) zork

80.

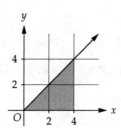

What is the area of the shaded region in the graph above?

(E) 0.5 square units

(F) 4 square units

(G) 8 square units

(H) 16 square units

81.

Number of People in Vehicle	Percent of Vehicles
1	38%
2	32%
3	22%
4	6%
5 or more	2%

As vehicles passed through a checkpoint, a researcher recorded the number of people in each vehicle. The table above shows the percent distribution for the 450 vehicles that passed through the checkpoint yesterday morning. How many of the vehicles contained at least 3 people?

(A) 30

(B) 99

(C) 135

(D) 315

82. Today, Jin's age is $\frac{1}{3}$ of Mary's age. In four years, Jin's age will be $\frac{1}{2}$ of Mary's age. How old is Mary today?

(E) 6 years old

(F) 9 years old

(G) 12 years old

(H) 16 years old

83. In a scale drawing of a triangular banner, one side measures 16 centimeters and the other two sides each measure 18 centimeters. On the actual banner, these two sides each measure 36 feet. What is the length of the remaining side of the banner?

(A) 16 ft.

(B) 32 ft.

(C) 34 ft.

(D) 48 ft.

GO ON TO THE NEXT PAGE

84. There are 154 teachers on the faculty of Central University, and there are 604 first-year students. The student-to-faculty ratio for the entire university is 12 to 1. What is the total number of second-, third-, and fourth-year students?

(E) 1,244

(F) 1,318

(G) 1,836

(H) 1,848

85.
$$2\frac{3}{5} + 4\frac{1}{10} + 5\frac{1}{5} + 3\frac{1}{2}$$

What is the value of the expression shown above?

(A) $14\frac{7}{20}$

(B) $14\frac{2}{5}$

(C) $15\frac{7}{20}$

(D) $15\frac{2}{5}$

86. A car is travelling at 70 kilometers per hour, and 1 kilometer = 1,000 meters. Which of the following calculations would give the car's speed in meters per minute?

(E) $\dfrac{70 \cdot 1,000}{1}$

(F) $\dfrac{70 \cdot 3,600}{1,000}$

(G) $\dfrac{70 \cdot 1,000}{3,600}$

(H) $\dfrac{70 \cdot 1,000}{60}$

87. Which of the following numbers has factors that include the smallest factor (other than 1) of 143?

(A) 30

(B) 39

(C) 44

(D) 49

88. $9 + (2n + 4) - (4n + 8) =$

(E) $5 - 2n$

(F) $5 + 2n$

(G) $21 - 2n$

(H) $21 + 2n$

89. The least of 3 consecutive integers is k. What is the sum of the three consecutive integers in terms of k?

(A) $k + 2$

(B) $k + 3$

(C) $3k$

(D) $3k + 3$

90. Julia leased a car for three years. She paid a one-time fee of $1,200 and an additional $250 per month for the full three years. At the end of the three years, what is the total amount Julia paid for leasing this car?

(E) $1,950

(F) $4,200

(G) $10,200

(H) $11,200

91. There are 10 different cookies on a plate. Amin will choose 2 of these cookies to pack in his lunch. How many different pairs of 2 cookies can he choose from the 10?

(A) 20

(B) 45

(C) 90

(D) 100

92. Suppose $P = \dfrac{w}{x}$ and $Q = \dfrac{x}{y}$, and w, x, and y, do not equal 0. What is $\dfrac{Q}{P}$ in terms of w, x, and y?

(E) $\dfrac{w}{y}$

(F) $\dfrac{y}{w}$

(G) $\dfrac{wy}{x^2}$

(H) $\dfrac{x^2}{wy}$

GO ON TO THE NEXT PAGE

93.

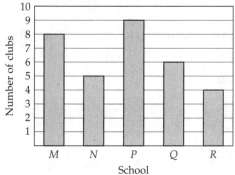

Number of Clubs in Five Schools

The graph above shows the number of clubs per school for five small schools. Clubs at schools M and N each have 25 students per club. Clubs at School P have 20 students per club. Clubs at schools Q and R each have 40 students per club. Which of the five schools has the greatest number of students participating in clubs?

(A) School M

(B) School P

(C) School Q

(D) School R

94. An unmarked straight stick will be laid end over end to measure a distance of exactly 70 feet. The same stick will be used in the same way to measure a distance of exactly 56 feet. What is the length of the longest stick that can be used for both measurements?

(E) 2 feet

(F) 7 feet

(G) 14 feet

(H) 28 feet

95. Robyn must read 180 pages for school this weekend. It took her 20 minutes to read the first 30 pages. At this rate, how much additional time will it take her to finish the reading?

(A) $1\frac{2}{3}$ hr.

(B) $1\frac{5}{9}$ hr.

(C) 2 hr.

(D) $5\frac{1}{3}$ hr.

96. For a presentation, Darla can create 3 slides in 18 minutes working at a constant rate. Kaito can create 7 slides in 12 minutes working at his own constant rate. What is the total number of slides the two of them can create in one hour?

(E) 16

(F) 35

(G) 45

(H) 50

97. In the set of integers from 18 to 44, inclusive, there are five integers that are multiples of both 2 and 3. How many integers in this set are multiples of neither 2 nor 3?

(A) 9

(B) 10

(C) 14

(D) 22

98.

On the number line shown above, $LN = \frac{1}{10}$. Point M (not shown) is located between point L and point N. Which value below is a possible value for M?

(E) 3.41

(F) 3.48

(G) 3.54

(H) 3.61

99. A box contains 4 apple candies, 3 blueberry candies, and 3 watermelon candies. If Brandon selects 2 candies at random from this box, without replacement, what is the probability that both candies are not blueberry?

(A) $\frac{9}{100}$

(B) $\frac{1}{15}$

(C) $\frac{7}{15}$

(D) $\frac{49}{100}$

GO ON TO THE NEXT PAGE

100. If $3n$ is a positive even number, how many odd numbers are in the range from $3n$ up to and including $3n + 7$?

(E) 3
(F) 4
(G) 5
(H) 6

101.

On the number line above, points W, X, Y, and Z are integers, and $WX : XY : YZ = 3 : 3 : 2$. What is the length of WY?

(A) 3
(B) 6
(C) 12
(D) 18

102. At Northwood middle school, course grades range from 0 to 100. Alejandro took four courses and his average course grade was 85. Rene took five courses. If both students have the same sum of course grades, what was Rene's average?

(E) 62
(F) 68
(G) 76
(H) 85

103.
$$\frac{5}{13} = 0.\overline{384615}$$

In the infinitely repeating decimal above, 3 is the first digit in the repeating pattern. What is the 323rd digit?

(A) 1
(B) 3
(C) 5
(D) 6

104.
$$\frac{q}{r} = s$$

In the equation above, q, r, s, and t are all positive numbers. Which of these is equal to $\frac{1}{q}$?

(E) $\frac{1}{rs}$

(F) $\frac{1}{s}$

(G) $\frac{s}{r}$

(H) $\frac{r}{s}$

105.

Scores on Biology Test		
Section	Lowest Score	Range
I	71	23
II	62	34
III	66	31

The same test was given to each of the three sections of Ms. Chen's biology class. The table above shows both the lowest score and the range of scores on this test for each section. What is the overall range of all scores in all three sections?

(A) 28
(B) 31
(C) 34
(D) 35

106. The sum of the numbers x, y, and z is 50. The ratio of x to y is $2 : 3$, and the ratio of y to z is $3 : 5$. What is the value of y?

(E) 3
(F) 10
(G) 15
(H) 25

GO ON TO THE NEXT PAGE

107.

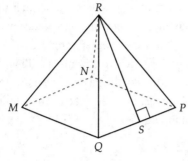

In the pyramid above, each triangular face has the same area, and the base *MNPQ* is a square that measures 6 centimeters on each side. If the length of $RS = 10$ centimeters, what is the surface area of the pyramid excluding the base?

(A) 60 sq cm

(B) 120 sq cm

(C) 144 sq cm

(D) 156 sq cm

108. A sports store has a container of handballs: 7 blue, 5 red, 9 yellow, 11 white, and 14 green. If 1 ball is picked from the container at random, what is the probability that it will be green?

(E) $\dfrac{1}{46}$

(F) $\dfrac{1}{14}$

(G) $\dfrac{7}{23}$

(H) $\dfrac{7}{17}$

109. Using the approximation 2.54 centimeters = 1 inch, how many centimeters are in 5 feet 1 inch?

(A) 24.02

(B) 114.30

(C) 129.54

(D) 154.94

110. Each week, Leandra has fixed expenses of $1,300 at her furniture shop. It costs her $150 to make a chair in her shop, and she sells each chair for $275. What is Leandra's profit if she makes and sells 35 chairs in 1 week?

(E) $3,075

(F) $3,950

(G) $4,375

(H) $5,250

111.

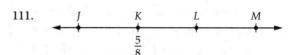

On the number line above, $JK = 2\dfrac{1}{2}$, $JM = 10\dfrac{3}{4}$, and $LM = 2\dfrac{1}{8}$. What is the position of point *L*?

(A) $5\dfrac{1}{4}$

(B) $6\dfrac{3}{8}$

(C) $6\dfrac{3}{4}$

(D) $7\dfrac{3}{4}$

112. If $3x - 4y = 12$, what is *x* in terms of *y*?

(E) $x = -\dfrac{4}{3}y + 4$

(F) $x = -\dfrac{4}{3}y + 12$

(G) $x = \dfrac{4}{3}y + 4$

(H) $x = -\dfrac{4}{3}y + 12$

GO ON TO THE NEXT PAGE

113.

Number of Servings of Fruits and Vegetables	Number of Students
0	3
1	6
2	3
3	4
4	3
5	1

There are 20 students in a class. The frequency table above shows the number of students in this class who ate 0, 1, 2, 3, 4, or 5 servings of fruits and vegetables yesterday. What is the mean number of servings of fruits and vegetables eaten yesterday per student in this class?

(A) 1

(B) 2

(C) $2\frac{1}{20}$

(D) $2\frac{1}{2}$

114. A paste used to cover a billboard is made by mixing the following ingredients by weight: 5 parts powder, 3 parts water, 1 part resin, and 1 part hardener. To cover one billboard requires 25 pounds of the paste. How many total pounds of the resin are required to cover four billboards?

(E) 2.5

(F) 5

(G) 10

(H) 20

English Language Arts

1. **A**	16. **H**	31. **D**	46. **F**
2. **H**	17. **A**	32. **E**	47. **C**
3. **A**	18. **H**	33. **C**	48. **G**
4. **F**	19. **C**	34. **G**	49. **B**
5. **B**	20. **G**	35. **C**	50. **E**
6. **G**	21. **D**	36. **F**	51. **B**
7. **C**	22. **G**	37. **C**	52. **H**
8. **E**	23. **B**	38. **E**	53. **C**
9. **D**	24. **G**	39. **A**	54. **E**
10. **F**	25. **C**	40. **G**	55. **C**
11. **D**	26. **F**	41. **D**	56. **G**
12. **G**	27. **B**	42. **F**	57. **A**
13. **A**	28. **E**	43. **C**	
14. **G**	29. **D**	44. **F**	
15. **C**	30. **H**	45. **C**	

Mathematics

58. **−13**	73. **C**	88. **E**	103. **A**
59. **252**	74. **F**	89. **D**	104. **E**
60. **161**	75. **A**	90. **G**	105. **D**
61. **−60**	76. **F**	91. **B**	106. **G**
62. **167**	77. **A**	92. **H**	107. **B**
63. **A**	78. **F**	93. **C**	108. **G**
64. **G**	79. **D**	94. **G**	109. **D**
65. **B**	80. **G**	95. **A**	110. **E**
66. **E**	81. **C**	96. **G**	111. **C**
67. **D**	82. **G**	97. **A**	112. **G**
68. **H**	83. **B**	98. **H**	113. **C**
69. **D**	84. **E**	99. **C**	114. **G**
70. **F**	85. **D**	100. **F**	
71. **A**	86. **H**	101. **D**	
72. **F**	87. **C**	102. **F**	

ANSWER EXPLANATIONS

English Language Arts

1. **(A)** Examine all the predicate verbs bolded below.

   (1) People often **associate** monosodium glutamate, better known as MSG, with headaches and nausea, but there **was** no evidence to substantiate that link. (2) In fact, the compounds associated with MSG **are** commonly found in beef, pork, or chicken. (3) Scientists **believe** the sicknesses might be the result of a "nocebo effect." (4) The nocebo effect, like the placebo effect, **isn't** caused by an actual substance but merely by suggestion.

2. **(H)** Commas should not be placed before the relative pronoun *that*. Choice E is wrong because the comma separates the modifier *Typically occurring in the spring* and the modified object *a nor'easter*. Choices F and G are wrong because *a gigantic cyclone* is another modifier that needs the commas.

3. **(A)** In sentence 1, the subject noun is the singular *syrup* and the connecting predicate noun is the plural *are*.

   (1) Molasses ~~*syrup, a product made from sugar and beets, are*~~ primarily used for sweetening foods. (2) Molasses syrup is rich with glucose and fructose, compounds rich in energy. (3) Because of its taste, sugar molasses syrup is used for human consumption, while beet molasses syrup is used for animal consumption. (4) Because of its adhesive properties, molasses syrup is also used as an additive component in mortar for brickwork.

4. **(F)** The best answer is choice F. It expresses the idea with the fewest number of clauses.

5. **(B)** Sentence 1 discusses a situation in which people cut back on sleep for perceived benefits. Sentence 2 provides a contrasting image in which cutting back on sleep produces harmful impacts.

6. **(G)** The best answer is choice G. Choice G provides more information in the phrase *affect you next day* of sentence 1. Choice E is related to sleep, but the statistic is irrelevant. Choice F provides a solution, but a discussion of the solution is not discussed until later in the paragraph. Choice H introduces a new idea, which is irrelevant.

7. **(C)** The best answer is choice C.

Least Precise	Most Precise
more sleep	9 to 12 hours for school-aged children, 8 to 10 for teens, and 7 or more for adults.
people age	
people of ages, shapes, and sizes	

8. **(E)** The best answer is choice E. The previous sentences begin with a verb (*Be, Make, Avoid*). Choice E follows that style.

9. **(D)** The best answer is choice D. The phrase *Better sleep habits* connects best with the ending phrase *better habits* in sentence 15.

   Choice A is wrong because it interrupts the discussion of good sleep and definition of good sleep. Choice B is wrong because it would interrupt the link between the antecedent *signs* and its pronoun *These*. Choice C is wrong because it interrupts the link between the symptoms of poor sleep and the phrase *these indicators*.

10. **(F)** Although choice F discusses the importance of sleep, it unnecessarily emphasizes dementia, which is irrelevant in that paragraph.

11. **(D)** Choice D can best be supported by paragraphs 2 (*dedication*) and 3 (*creation and benefits of the aquarium*). Choice A is wrong because paragraphs 2 and 3 note his success. Choice B is wrong because there is no discussion of his *remarkable challenges*. Choice C is wrong because the passage never mentions people losing interest.

12. **(G)** The sentence *A saltwater aquarium . . . without having to descend into the depths* best supports this choice. Choice E is wrong because paragraph 3 suggests that the aquarium allowed the public to get to know the ocean without *complicated diving equipment*. Choice F is wrong because there is no mention of pollution in this passage. Choice H is wrong because there is no mention of collecting plants or animals in this passage.

13. **(A)** The first part of the sentence suggests that the two terms *vivarium* and *marine aquarium* were used interchangeably. The phrase can be replaced with the words *the outcome was set* to preserve the meaning and ideas of the sentence.

14. **(G)** This choice reveals how Gosse returned to work after his failure, which *led to unexpected success*. Choice E makes no mention of dedication or success. Choice F shows dedication, but not success. Choice H refers to the ease of observing wildlife, not success.

15. **(C)** Paragraph 2 mentions that *both ventures failed*. Choice A is wrong because luck is never explicitly or implicitly mentioned. Choice B is wrong because it links his impoverished past as the cause for his success. He came from an impoverished background, but the author never cites that as the cause. Choice D is wrong because it is too extreme. Nowhere does it claim he was *the most important naturalist*.

16. **(H)** The passage mentions that people *turned their attention toward the exploitation of the coastal regions*. Choice E is wrong because this passage does not deal with naming conventions. Choice F is wrong because the passage does not say that Gosse's invention led to a decreased price on exploration. Choice G is wrong because the passage suggests that the aquarium led to awareness, not to exploitation.

17. **(A)** The first sentence of the paragraph suggests that intelligence, not just arms and manpower, played a significant part in the victory. Choice B is wrong because there is no mention of American opinions on the war. Choice C is wrong because of the words *the most important*. Choice D is a close distractor, but it distorts the definition of the word *intelligence*. As used in the passage, the word refers not to a person's reasoning abilities but a form of information.

18. **(H)** The last sentence of the paragraph suggests that *the cause* was dependent on a victory. Choice E is wrong because although it was important, there is no indication that it was comparatively more important than others. Choice F is wrong because the word *only* is too extreme. The first sentence of the paragraph says it was the *first major victory*, meaning that there could have been minor victories prior to the Battle of Trenton. Choice G is wrong because the paragraph makes no mention of which was easier to defend.

19. **(C)** John Honeyman is first introduced, and the paragraph suggests that he played a crucial role. Choice A is wrong because the paragraph says the plan depended *on surprise*, not Washington's ability to identify a weakness. Choice B is wrong because it says that intelligence is important, but it does not explain why it is. Choice D is wrong because the Hessians did not win.

20. **(G)** Paragraph 4 suggests that Honeyman met Washington and was *sympathetic* to the American cause. Choice E is wrong because Honeyman was never *commissioned*. Choice F is wrong because Honeyman was never *drafted*. Choice H is wrong because although he taught himself to read and write, this skill was not mentioned as the factor that led him to help.

21. **(D)** The last sentence of the paragraph shows that Honeyman gave Colonel Rall inaccurate information, which helped Washington plan an attack. Choice A is wrong because Honeyman never led a raid. Choice B is wrong because Honeyman spread misinformation about American forces not Hessian forces. Choice C is wrong because he provided misinformation about the condition of the American forces, not their location.

22. **(G)** This sentence provides a concrete example of Honeyman's actions that led to the victory. Answer choice E is wrong because it is a general claim about the importance of intelligence. Answer choice F is wrong because it deals with the Continental Congress, not Honeyman. Answer choice H is wrong because it is a generalized description of the impact of the victory, not an exemplification.

23. **(B)** The word *handful* contrasts with the *more than 1,000* men that the Hessians lost. The contrast serves to heighten the success of the victory.

24. **(G)** The last phrase *new confidence and hope* supports *renewed the American faith*. Choice E is wrong because the Hessians did not lose because of their generosity. Choice F and H are wrong because they take Christmas out of the context of the war.

25. **(C)** Paragraphs 1 and 2 describe the mother's ideas and feelings about the child. Paragraph 3 introduces a particular moment on *the afternoon of a certain summer's day*. Choice A is wrong because although we are introduced to the mother's thoughts in paragraphs 1 through 3, it leads into a dialogue between the two characters, not observations made by other characters. Choice B is wrong because the two characters are not strangers. Choice D is wrong because there is little to no emphasis on the physical setting.

26. **(F)** The phrase serves to show that the child was fascinated by the physical letter. Choice E is wrong because the emotion that follows is better characterized as anxiety than excitement. Choices G and H are wrong because neither oppression nor wealth is discussed in the paragraph.

27. **(B)** The words that follow the quoted text are *of a much older child*, which matches the answer choice *appearance that belies her age*. Choice A is wrong because there is no discussion of *hatred*. Choices C and D make unnecessary inferences that are not supported by the text.

28. **(E)** The word *disturbing* is supported by *freakish, elvish*. The word *familiar* is supported by *looking at her own image*.

29. **(D)** The line *and might not now reveal herself* suggests that Hester, the mother, is concerned about revealing something that she does not want Pearl to know.

30. **(H)** The line *nor was Pearl the only child* suggests that there are others in Pearl's circumstances.

31. **(D)** The line *had given out that poor little Pearl was a demon offspring* reflects the judgment the people had made about Pearl because they could not find the information they were looking for.

32. **(E)** The line *did not escape the acuteness* links with the question stem *perceptive*.

33. **(C)** Paragraph 3 suggests that she *may* be an actual person, and the last sentence of the excerpt supports the idea that Shipton possessed the characteristics associated with a witch. Choice A is wrong because the excerpt suggests that she could be modeled after an actual person. Choice B is wrong because there is little emphasis on the tragic aspect of Shipton. Choice D is wrong because the excerpt alludes to various sources and not a *recent finding*.

34. **(G)** The topic sentence introduces Mother Shipton's growing fame. The phrase supports that idea. Choice E is wrong because the list shows titles, not different roles. Choices F and H are wrong because the names all refer to Mother Shipton, and not other witches.

35. **(C)** The phrase *based in more than pure invention* means that Mother Shipton may not be an invented creation.

36. **(F)** The second sentence of paragraph 4 clearly suggests that his work *was responsible for the majority of invented . . . details*. Choices E and G are wrong because of the word *most*. Choice H is wrong because paragraph 4 says that the account came from *Head's imagination*.

37. **(C)** The author claims in paragraph 4 that Head's work was *an embellishment of her myth* and *from Head's imagination*. The sentence that best suggests that the account was comprised of mythical embellishments of the imagination is choice C.

38. **(E)** Again, the phrase *from Head's imagination* best supports the claim in choice E as the performances were not real.

39. **(A)** Even if you do not know the word *baroque* (which means highly decorated and eye-catching), the last sentence of the paragraph makes it clear that the descriptions were cruel. This supports the claim that the descriptions were not meant to be objective.

40. **(G)** The topic sentence of paragraph 5 introduces the nose, which is then discussed at length.

41. **(D)** Paragraph 3 shows that *the assailed king wrote a letter to the Duke of Norfolk in which he disdainfully refers to a "witch of York."* This line suggests that the king might have been acquainted with Mother Shipton.

42. **(F)** The first paragraph traces the name Mother Shipton to the marriage to Toby Shipton.

43. **(C)** The repetition of *And* accompanies a series of thoughts that lead up to the undergrowth where he could no longer see. This reflects the *uncertainty*. Choice A is wrong because no words suggest beauty. Choice B is wrong because the reference to the wood is not a personification. Choice D is wrong because the stanza makes no general claim about travelers.

44. **(F)** Line 4 suggests that he looked as far as he could and that his view stops at the undergrowth. Choice E is wrong because he regrets the fact that *he could not travel both* roads, but he doesn't regret walking in the woods. Choice G is wrong because it misapplies the word *bent*. The word *bent* describes where the road is going. Choice H is wrong because the problem is not the undergrowth or the inability to see farther, but it is not knowing which road to take.

45. **(C)** The answer is in line 11. The line says that *both . . . equally lay*, meaning that they were essentially the same.

46. **(F)** The answer is in line 15. The exclamation suggests a regret about his choice.

47. **(C)** Choice B is wrong because the poem is still on the same topic. Choice C is wrong because the previous statement suggests that he will be telling this story later in his life. Line 18 doesn't serve to support it. Choice D is wrong because the line is about what he would say, not to suggest that there is a problem.

48. **(G)** The dash serves as a pause. We do not know why he is making the pause, but we do know that he is hesitating. Choice E is wrong because line 16 says that he tells this with a *sigh*. Sighs are not indicative of excitement. Choice F is wrong because line 20 suggests clarity. Choice H is wrong because *despair* is too extreme.

49. **(B)** Each stanza reflects on the process and the implications of the speaker's decisions. Choice A is wrong because there are no similes. The road might be symbolic, but the poem does not employ any comparisons. Choice C is wrong because the author never mentions the benefits. Choice D is wrong because the author uses concrete imagery as a basis for his thoughts.

50. **(E)** Paragraph 1 explicitly links bears to his theories. Choices F, G, and H are all true and implied throughout the passage, but they are details that help support the central idea.

51. **(B)** The second sentence in paragraph 2 supports this response. *Darwin based this speculation* . . . Choice A is wrong because he only provided an observation. Choice C is wrong because Hearne never proposed a theory. Choice D is wrong because there is no indication that the bear was an unknown species.

52. **(H)** The answer is in the line that precedes the word *thicket*. *This was not a single, clean-cut departure* serves to highlight the complexities. Choices E and G are wrong because they deal with physical locations, which the word *thicket* does not imply. Choice F is an overstatement. The word *thicket* relates to tracing the lineage, not the idea of bears in the general sense.

53. **(C)** The keyword *environment* from the question appears in choice C, which shows that *climate* played a large role in the evolution of the bears.

54. **(E)** In paragraph 3, the phrase *Shrinking sea ice* links warming in the Arctic to greater mingling between the bears.

55. **(C)** Paragraph 4 picks up on paragraph 2's story about how Hearne's observation influenced Darwin's theories. Choice A is wrong because the paragraph does not provide an example of the ideas in the previous paragraph about polar bear evolution. Choice B is wrong because it is not a summary, but a continuation of a narrative. Choice D is wrong because it shows that Darwin omitted a controversial part of his theory; it doesn't challenge the theories in the world today.

56. **(G)** The split on the right side of the illustration occurs at around 500,000 years ago. This conforms with the statement in paragraph 3.

57. **(A)** The first sentence of paragraph 4 clearly shows that he was *ridiculed for his musings* and that he subsequently *removed it* in the second edition. This shows that the ridicule influenced his decision.

Mathematics

58. **(−13)** Isolate w in the equation. Subtract $2w$ from both sides of $6w + 36 = 2w - 16$ to get:

$$4w + 36 = -16$$

Then subtract 36 from both sides to get:

$$4w = -52$$

Divide both sides by 4 to get:

$$w = \frac{-52}{4} = -13$$

This is also a good question to use thoughtful guessing and checking.

59. **(252)** Let s be the total number of SUVs. Set up the proportion:

$$\frac{5}{9} = \frac{140}{s}$$

Then solve for s. Cross-multiply to get $5s = 9 \times 140$. Next, divide by 5 and simplify:

$$s = \frac{9 \times 140}{5}$$
$$= 9 \times \frac{140}{5}$$
$$= 9 \times 28$$
$$= 252$$

Note: Since there are 9 SUVS for every 5 cars, the total number of SUVs should be less than twice the total number of cars. This checks out, since 252 is less than $2 \times 140 = 280$.

60. **(161)** Since $\angle PSR$ is supplementary to the 71°-degree angle, $m \angle PSR = 180 - 71 = 109$. In a parallelogram, opposite angles are congruent, so $m \angle Q = m \angle PSR$, and $m \angle Q = 109$. Since the measure of a right angle is 90° and the sum of the measures of all the angles around a point is 360°, we have $m \angle Q + x + 90 = 360$. Substitution gives us $109 + x + 90 = 360$, and simplifying yields $x = 161$.

61. **(−60)** To find the three consecutive integers, set up and solve the equation $x + (x + 1) + (x + 2) = -15$. Or you can just guess and check to determine that the consecutive integers -4, -5, and -6 sum to -15. Adding one to each integer gives us -3, -4, and -5, and their product is $(-3)(-4)(-5) = -3 \times -4 \times -5 = -60$.

62. **(167)** A Venn diagram is helpful in these kinds of problems.

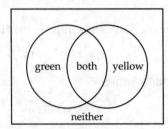

The total number of students surveyed is equal to the number of students who like green or yellow plus the number of students who like neither. When counting the number of students who like green or yellow, be careful not to double-count those who like both. A common mistake is to compute the number of students who like green or yellow as (number who like green) + (number who like yellow). But this counts those who like both colors twice. To compensate, we must subtract from this the number who like both. Thus, the number of students who like green or yellow is: (number who like green) + (number who like yellow) − (number who like both). Adding to this the number who like neither gives us a final answer of $78 + 84 − 29 + 24 = 167$.

63. **(A)** Let $m =$ the price per pound of meat. Then $0.75 \times 6 + m \times 8 = 46.10$. Solving for m gives us $m = 5.2$, so the answer is $5.20. Alternately, the total price of the meat is the total price minus the price of the water ($0.75 \times 6 = 4.50$):

$$\$46.10 − \$0.75 \times 6$$

$$= \$46.10 − \$4.50$$

$$= \$41.60$$

Divide by 8 pounds to get the price per pound. Notice that answer choice D is the total price of the meat, not the price per pound. Always read carefully and answer the question that was asked.

64. **(G)** List the factors of each number and count:

Factors of 12: 1, 2, 3, 4, 6, 12 (6 factors)

Factors of 24: 1, 2, 3, 4, 6, 8, 12, 24 (8 factors)

Factors of 36: 1, 2, 3, 4, 6, 9, 12, 18, 36 (9 factors)

Factors of 48: 1, 2, 3, 4, 6, 8, 12, 16, 24, 48 (10 factors)

The only number with an odd number of factors is 36. **Note:** Only perfect squares have an odd number of positive factors. Explore a bit and see if you can figure out why!

65. **(B)** Since 1% is $\frac{1}{100} = 0.01$, 1% of 0.02 is $0.01 \times 0.02 = 0.0002$. This is the allowable error, so the thickness of the device must be between $0.02 − 0.0002 = 0.0198$ and $0.02 + 0.0002 = 0.0202$. The least allowable thickness is therefore 0.0198. **Note:** 1% is a small error, so the least allowable thickness should be close to the desired thickness of 0.02 inches. This reasoning eliminates two of the answer choices.

66. **(E)** The circumference of a circle of radius r is $C = 2\pi r$, which makes the circumference of our wheel $C = 2\pi(1 \text{ foot}) = 2\pi$ feet. With each revolution of the wheel, the car travels a distance equal to the circumference of the wheel. Thus, the total number of revolutions of the wheel is equal to the total distance divided by the circumference of the wheel. In two minutes the car travels 4,400 feet, and since we are told to use $\frac{22}{7}$ as an approximation for π, we can compute the total number of revolutions of the wheel as follows:

$$\text{Number of Revolutions} = \frac{4,400 \text{ feet}}{\frac{44}{7} \text{ feet}}$$
$$= \frac{4,400}{1} \times \frac{7}{44}$$
$$= \frac{4,400}{44} \times \frac{7}{1}$$
$$= 100 \times 7$$
$$= 700$$

67. **(D)** Simplify using the order of operations:

$$100(2 + 0.2)^2 - 100 =$$
$$100(2.2)^2 - 100 =$$
$$100(4.84) - 100 =$$
$$484 - 100 = 384$$

68. **(H)** The mean of a set of numbers is the sum of the numbers divided by the number of numbers. Notice that the frequency of each number is important. You must count three 85s, five 75s, and two 65s. Thus the mean is the following:

$$\frac{85 + 85 + 85 + 75 + 75 + 75 + 75 + 75 + 65 + 65}{10} =$$
$$\frac{3 \times 85 + 5 \times 75 + 2 \times 65}{10} =$$
$$\frac{255 + 375 + 130}{10} =$$
$$\frac{760}{10} = 76$$

Alternately, notice that the average of 85 and 65 is 75. Given this fact, and the five 75s, the average of all 10 numbers should be around 75. Since there are more 85s than 65s, the average should be closer to 85 than to 65. The only reasonable answer is 76.

69. **(D)** Testing all the answers is a good strategy here.

If Greg starts with 18 chips, Cleo starts with 9. If Greg gives Cleo 8 chips, he'll have 10 and she'll have 17, so Greg won't have 9 more than Cleo. Choice A is not the answer.

If Greg starts with 34 chips, Cleo starts with 17. After the transfer, Greg will have 26 and Cleo will have 25. Choice B is not the answer.

If Greg starts with 48 chips, Cleo starts with 24. After the transfer, Greg will have 40 and Cleo will have 32. Greg does not have 9 more chips that Cleo. Choice C is not the answer.

If Greg starts with 50 chips, Cleo starts with 25. After the transfer, Greg will have 42 and Cleo will have 33. Greg has 9 more chips than Cleo. Choice D is the answer.

You can also solve this problem by letting x be the number of chips Cleo starts with. Greg then starts with $2x$. After the transfer, Greg has $2x - 8$ and Cleo has $x + 8$. Solving the equation $2x - 8 = x + 8 + 9$ for x gives $x = 25$, and Greg started with $2x = 2(25) = 50$ chips.

70. **(F)** A good approach is to let the length be $4x$ and the width be $3x$, which makes the ratio of length to width $\frac{4x}{3x} = \frac{4}{3}$ as required. Since the perimeter of a rectangle is equal to two times the length plus two times the width, we can set up the equation $2(4x) + 2(3x) = 350$. Solving, we get $14x = 350$, and so $x = \frac{350}{14} = \frac{7 \times 50}{7 \times 2} = 25$. So our length is $4(25) = 100$ and our width is $3(25) = 75$.

Alternately, notice that only two of the answer choices (F and G) define a rectangle whose perimeter is 350, and only one has side lengths in a ratio of 4 to 3.

Note: Remember that perimeter counts the length and width twice!

71. **(A)** You can multiply through by 2 to turn the compound inequality $2 < \frac{x}{2} < 4$ into $4 < x < 8$. The graph of this solution set is choice A. Also, since this is an "and" inequality, the graph of the solution set is most likely either choice A or D. Testing $x = 1.5$, which is in the solution set graphed in choice D, and seeing that the inequality is false (it is not the case that $2 < \frac{1.5}{2} < 4$) shows that the answer is choice A.

72. **(F)** At 9 fleegs per dollar, 36 fleegs is $4. At 0.5 grat per dollar, one grat is $2, so 100 grat is $200. Thus, the total value is $204. A common mistake here is to convert 100 grats into $50, which gives choice E, but the conversion rate shows that a grat is more valuable than a dollar, so 100 grats should be more than $100.

73. **(C)** The probability of drawing a red pencil is equal to $\frac{\text{\# of red pencils}}{\text{\# of total pencils}}$, which is $\frac{2}{7}$. Let p be the total number of pencils. Then $\frac{2}{7} = \frac{8}{p}$. Solving, we get $2p = 56$, and so $p = 28$. Since p is the total number of pencils, the number of non-red pencils is $28 - 8 = 20$. **Note:** 28 is an answer choice. Always be sure you are answering the question that was asked.

74. **(F)** Let x be the number of inches representing 100 feet. We can set up a proportion and solve for x:

$$\frac{1 \text{ inch}}{250 \text{ feet}} = \frac{x \text{ inches}}{100 \text{ feet}}$$

$$x = \frac{100}{250} = \frac{10}{25} = \frac{2}{5} = 0.4$$

Also, if 1 inch is 250, then half an inch is 125 feet. This estimation eliminates two of the answer choices and tells us that the correct answer is near 0.5 inches.

75. **(A)** Since $17 \times 15 = 225$, 17% of 15,000 is $0.17 \times 15,000 = 2,550$ (as a quick check, note that 10% of 15,000 is 1,500, so 17% should be less than twice 1,500, which is 3,000). Since 10% of 15,000 is 1,500, we know that 2,550 people ride the bus and 1,500 walk. Thus, 1,050 more people ride the bus than walk.

76. **(F)** We can use a Venn diagram to represent our situation.

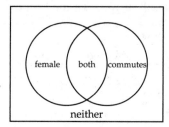

Notice that "neither" here means "a person who is not a female and who doesn't commute," which we take to mean "males who don't commute." Let x be the number of women who commute. We have the equation $0.48 + 0.65 - x + 0.10 = 1.00$, with the 1.00 on the right representing 100% of the population. Solving gives us $x = 0.23$, or 23%. Trying each answer choice in the standard inclusion-exclusion formula would also be a good approach.

77. **(A)** We compute the value of k for each value of m:

When $m = 2$, $2k = 2 + 4 = 6$, so $k = 3$.

When $m = 4$, $2k = 4 + 4 = 8$, so $k = 4$.

When $m = 6$, $2k = 6 + 4 = 10$, so $k = 5$.

Thus, the values of k are $\{3, 4, 5\}$. Notice that, because of the answer choices, once we determine k could be 4, we know the answer is choice A, as no other choice included 4.

78. **(F)** The probability that the first card drawn is not red is $\frac{6}{10}$. Since the card is not replaced, the probability that the second card drawn is not red is $\frac{5}{9}$ (there is one less non-red card and one less card overall). To find the probability of both of these events, we multiply their probabilities.

$$\frac{6}{10} \times \frac{5}{9} = \frac{30}{90} = \frac{1}{3}$$

79. **(D)** Since 1 dreck is equal to 3 klemps, a dreck is more valuable than a klemp. We denote this $d > k$. Similarly, the other conversions tells us that $z > f$, $z > d$, and $f > g$. Since $z > f$ and $f > g$, we can conclude that $z > g$. Similarly, $z > d$ and $d > k$ gives us $z > k$. This establishes that z is greater in value than all of the other coins.

80. **(G)** The area of a triangle is equal to $\frac{1}{2}$ the product of its base and height. In the diagram, the shaded triangle has a base of four units and a height of four units. Its area is therefore $\frac{1}{2} \times 4 \times 4 = 8$. Alternately, note that the shaded region is half of a square of area 16.

81. **(C)** The total percentage of vehicles containing at least 3 people is 22% + 6% + 2% = 30%, and 30% of 450 is 0.30 × 450 = 135. Notice that using the fact that 10% of 450 is 45 can be useful in computing 30% of 450, and it can also be helpful in estimating the answer. **Note:** The number of vehicles that contained exactly 3 people is one of the answer choices. Remember to be on the lookout for phrases like *at least* and *at most*.

82. **(G)** Using a chart and testing all answers is a good approach to this problem.

Today		In 4 Years	
Mary's Age	**Jin's Age**	**Mary's Age**	**Jin's Age**
6	2	10	6
9	3	13	7
12	4	16	8
16	$5.\overline{3}$	20	$9.\overline{3}$

The chart shows us the one situation in which Jin is half Mary's age in 4 years, namely, when Mary is 12 today.

83. **(B)** Since the side lengths of 18 cm in the scale drawing become sides of length 36 feet on the actual banner, the scale factor is $\frac{18\,\text{cm}}{36\,\text{ft}} = \frac{1\,\text{cm}}{2\,\text{ft}}$. Thus, 16 cm in the scale diagram will be 32 feet on the banner. You can also set up and solve the proportion $\frac{18\,\text{cm}}{36\,\text{ft}} = \frac{16\,\text{cm}}{x\,\text{ft}}$, where x is the length of the third side of the banner, and find that $x = 32$ ft.

84. **(E)** With 154 teachers and a 12 to 1 student to teacher ratio, there are 154 × 12 = 1,848 total students. Subtracting off the first year students gives us 1,848 − 604 = 1,244 students. Be careful not to answer 1,848 just because that number appears in your calculations; 1,848 is the number of total students, and the question asked for only the number of 2nd, 3rd, and 4th year students. Always read carefully.

85. **(D)** First, add the whole number parts to get 14, then deal with the fractions. Convert the fractions to the common denominator of 10 and add:

$$\frac{3}{5} + \frac{1}{10} + \frac{1}{5} + \frac{1}{2} = \frac{6}{10} + \frac{1}{10} + \frac{2}{10} + \frac{5}{10}$$
$$= \frac{14}{10}$$
$$= 1\frac{4}{10}$$
$$= 1\frac{2}{5}$$

The final answer is $14 + 1\frac{2}{5} = 15\frac{2}{5}$. Converting each number to decimal representation (2.6 + 4.1 + 5.2 + 3.5) could also be helpful here. **Note:** $14\frac{2}{5}$ is an answer choice. Be careful when adding the fractions to make sure you count the extra 1 from the improper fraction.

86. **(H)** Speed is initially given as $\frac{70\,\text{km}}{1\,\text{hr.}}$. Since 1 km = 1,000 m, we can rewrite the numerator $\frac{70 \times 1,000\,\text{km}}{1\,\text{hr.}}$, and since 1 hour = 60 minutes, we can rewrite the denominator to get our answer, $\frac{70 \times 1,000\,\text{km}}{60\,\text{min}}$, or $\frac{70 \times 1,000}{60}$.

87. **(C)** To solve this problem, you must know the factorization of 143, namely $143 = 11 \times 13$. If you don't see it immediately, try dividing 143 by primes (2, 3, 5, 7, 11, etc.) until something divides it evenly. Once you find that 11 is the smallest factor of 143, the question now is which answer choice has 11 as a factor. The answer is choice C. Notice that answer choice B, 39, shares a factor with 143 (namely 13), but it doesn't share 143's smallest factor.

88. **(E)** Use the distributive property to remove parentheses, being especially careful with distributing negative signs: $9 + (2n + 4) - (4n + 8) = 9 + 2n + 4 - 4n - 8$. Then combine like terms to get $5 - 2n$. Note that the other answer choices follow from common mistakes. For example, if you do not distribute the -1 to the 8, you'll end up with $21 - 2n$, which is choice G. Be careful when you distribute!

89. **(D)** The three consecutive integers can be represented as k, $k + 1$, and $k + 2$. Their sum is $k + k + 1 + k + 2 = 3k + 3$, so the answer is D. This is also a good opportunity to use the "make a wish" strategy: if $k = 10$, then the three integers are 10, 11, and 12. Their sum is 33. Now plug 10 in to the answer choices, and you'll see that only answer choice D gives you 33.

90. **(G)** The monthly payments of $250 add up to $250 \times 12 = \$3,000$ per year, and so $3 \times \$3,000 = \$9,000$ over three years. This plus the $1,200 one-time fee equals $10,200. Notice that answer choice F is what you get when you only consider one year of payments.

91. **(B)** There are 10 choices for the first cookie. Once that cookie is selected, there are 9 choices for the second cookie. The fundamental counting principle tells us to multiply the number of options for each choice, giving us $10 \times 9 = 90$. But this is not the correct answer, because the order in which the cookies are selected makes no difference; choosing cookie A first, then cookie B gives us the same pair of cookies as choosing cookie B first, then A. Thus, our calculation above double counts the number of pairs of cookies, and so the correct answer is $\frac{90}{2} = 45$.

92. **(H)** $\frac{Q}{P}$ is equal to $\dfrac{\frac{x}{y}}{\frac{w}{x}}$. To divide fractions, we multiply by the reciprocal.

$$\frac{\frac{x}{y}}{\frac{w}{x}} = \frac{x}{y} \times \frac{x}{w} = \frac{x^2}{yw}$$

Note that answer choice E is equal to PQ and choice G is equal to $\frac{P}{Q}$.

93. **(C)** The chart gives us the number of clubs at each school, which must be multiplied by the number of students per club to find the total number of students. School M has 8 clubs with 25 students each for a total of 200 students. School N has 5 clubs with 25 students each, for 125 students. School P has 9 clubs with 20 students each for 180 students. School Q has 6 clubs with 40 students each for a total of 240 students. And School R has 4 clubs with 40 students each for a total of 160 students. School Q has the most students.

94. **(G)** This question essentially asks, "What is the greatest common factor of 70 and 56?" The answer is 14, and it can be found by listing the factors of both 70 and 56 and finding the largest number on both lists. Alternatively, you can just try dividing each answer choice into both numbers to find the largest one that works; 70 is not divisible by 28, but both 70 and 56 are divisible by 14, so 14 must be the answer. Notice that sticks of length 2 and 7 would both work, but neither is the longest stick that could work.

95. **(A)** Let x be the total number of minutes required to read 180 pages. Solve this proportion for x:

$$\frac{30 \text{ pages}}{20 \text{ min}} = \frac{180 \text{ pages}}{x \text{ min}}$$

$$x = \frac{2}{3} \times 180$$

$$= 2 \times 60$$

$$= 120$$

Thus, it takes 120 minutes to read all 180 pages. Since Robyn has already read for 20 minutes, she will need $120 - 20 = 100$ minutes more. Convert 100 minutes to hours, $\frac{100}{60} = \frac{10}{6} = \frac{5}{3} = 1\frac{2}{3}$, to get the answer. Alternately, you can count up by 20-minute intervals: 30 pages in 20 minutes, 60 pages in 40 minutes, 90 pages in 60 minutes, and so on. In this case, you will end up with the correct answer, but even if you don't, you will get an estimate for what the correct answer should be. **Note:** 2 hours is an answer choice, which is what you would get if you forgot to subtract the 20 minutes she has already read.

96. **(G)** Since Darla can make 3 slides in 18 minutes, she can make 1 slide in 6 minutes, which means she can make 6 slides in 1 hour. Since $12 \times 5 = 60$, we see that Kaito, who can make 7 slides in 12 minutes, can make $7 \times 5 = 35$ slides in one hour. Thus, the two of them can make $10 + 35 = 45$ slides in one hour.

97. **(A)** A straightforward way to solve this problem is to list out the integers from 18 to 44 and cross out any that are multiples of 2 or 3, like this:

~~18~~, 19, ~~20~~, ~~21~~, ~~22~~, 23, ~~24~~, 25, ~~26~~, ~~27~~, ~~28~~, 29, ~~30~~, 31, ~~32~~, ~~33~~, ~~34~~, 35, ~~36~~, 37, ~~38~~, ~~39~~, ~~40~~, 41, ~~42~~, 43, ~~44~~

And count the numbers left to get 9.

98. **(H)** Since the answer choices are given as decimals, start by converting $3\frac{17}{25}$ into decimal form. Because $\frac{17}{25} = \frac{68}{100}$, that means $3\frac{17}{25} = 3.68$. That makes the location of point L $3\frac{17}{25} - \frac{1}{10} = 3.68 - 0.1 = 3.58$. Only choice H is located between 3.58 and 3.68.

99. **(C)** To start there are 10 candies total and 7 non-blueberry candies. The probability that the first candy is not blueberry is $\frac{7}{10}$. Since the first candy is not put back, there are now 9 total candies and 6 non-blueberry candies, which makes the probability that the second candy selected is not blueberry $\frac{6}{9}$. To find the probability of both candies not being blueberry, we multiply: $\frac{7}{10} \times \frac{6}{9} = \frac{42}{90} = \frac{14}{30} = \frac{7}{15}$. Notice that if you mistakenly consider the problem *with replacement*, you will get answer choice D.

100. **(F)** The numbers in the given range are $3n$, $3n + 1$, $3n + 2$, $3n + 3$, $3n + 4$, $3n + 5$, $3n + 6$, $3n + 7$. If $3n$ is even, then $3n + 1$, $3n + 3$, $3n + 5$, and $3n + 7$ will all be odd, so the answer is 4. This is also a great place to "make a wish": if $n = 10$, then $3n = 30$, a positive even number. The numbers in the given range are thus 30, 31, 32, 33, 34, 35, 36, and 37, and there are four odd numbers here. Notice that if you ignore the word *inclusive* and do not include the last number, you may make an incorrect choice.

101. **(D)** The length of WZ is $9 - (-15) = 24$. If WZ were 8 units long, the ratio $WX : XY : YZ = 3 : 3 : 2$ would give us that $WX = 3$, $XY = 3$, and $YZ = 2$. Since WZ is 3×8 long, each of WX, XY, and YZ are three times as long. Thus, in our diagram, $WX = 9$, $XY = 9$, and $YZ = 6$. (Check that these sum to 24 and are in the $3 : 3 : 2$ ratio.) Thus, $WY = 18$. Notice that the *position* of Y on the number line, namely $-15 + 18 = 3$, is choice A.

102. **(F)** The average of a set of numbers is their sum divided by the number of numbers. Let S be the sum of Alejandro's course grades. If Alejandro had an average of 85 in four courses, then $\frac{S}{4} = 85$, and so $S = 4 \times 85 = 340$. So the sum of Rene's five course grades is 340, and her average is $\frac{340}{5} = 68$.

103. **(A)** The repeating pattern is 6 digits long. We can determine the digit in position k by dividing k by 6 and looking at the remainder. If the remainder is 1, the digit will be the first in the pattern; if the remainder is 2, the digit will be the second in the pattern, and so on up to remainder 0, which corresponds with the 6th digit in the pattern. For example, the 7th digit in the pattern is the same as the 1st, and the remainder when 7 is divided by 6 is 1. Thus, we divide 323 by 6 and get 53 with a remainder of 5. Thus, the 323rd digit is the same as the 5th digit, namely 1.

104. **(E)** Isolate q in the equation $\frac{q}{r} = s$ to get $q = rs$. Now reciprocate both sides to get $\frac{1}{q} = \frac{1}{rs}$. You could also "make a wish" here, say, letting $q = 10$, $r = 2$, and $s = 5$, which makes $\frac{q}{r} = s$. If $q = 10$, then $\frac{1}{q} = \frac{1}{10}$, and only one of the answer choices equals $\frac{1}{10}$ for $r = 2$, and $s = 5$.

105. **(D)** The range of a set of data is the difference between the highest and lowest value. The lowest score among all the sections is 62. The highest scores in sections I, II, and III are $71 + 23 = 94$, $62 + 34 = 96$, and $66 + 31 = 97$, respectively. This makes the highest score in any section 97. Thus, the overall range is $97 - 62 = 35$.

106. **(G)** Organized guessing and checking is a good strategy here. We will guess numbers x, y, z that are in the proper ratios.

x	y	z	$x+y+z$
2	3	5	10
4	6	10	20
6	9	15	30
8	12	20	40
10	15	25	50

When $x + y + z = 50$, $y = 15$. An algebraic approach, starting with $z = \frac{5}{3}y$ and $x = \frac{2}{3}y$ will also work.

107. **(B)** The surface area excluding the base is the area of the four triangles on the sides of the pyramid. The area of a triangle is $\frac{1}{2}$ the base times the height. Each triangle has base 6 and height 10, and thus an area of $\frac{1}{2} \times 6 \times 10 = 30$. The sum of the areas of the four triangles is thus 120. Notice that choice D is the surface area of the pyramid including the base.

108. **(G)** The probability of a green ball being chosen is equal to $\frac{\text{\# of green balls}}{\text{\# of total balls}}$. There are 14 green balls and $7 + 5 + 9 + 11 + 14 = 46$ total balls, so the desired probability is $\frac{14}{46} = \frac{7}{23}$.

109. **(D)** Since there are 12 inches in 1 foot, there are $12 \times 5 = 60$ inches in 5 feet, and thus 61 inches in 5 feet 1 inch. The answer is thus $2.54 \times 61 = 154.94$. A common error is to convert 1 foot into 10 inches. In this problem, that would give you choice C.

110. **(E)** The profit per chair is $\$275 - \$150 = \$125$, so the profit on 35 chairs is $35 \times \$125 = \$4,375$. Subtracting the fixed expenses of $\$1,300$, we find the total profit to be $\$4,375 - \$1,300 = \$3,075$. Notice that answer choice G is what you get if you forget to subtract off the fixed expenses.

111. **(C)** Since $JM = JK + KL + LM$, we can substitute and solve for KL:

$$JM = JK + KL + LM$$

$$10\frac{3}{4} = 2\frac{1}{2} + KL + 2\frac{1}{8}$$

Solving for KL gives us:

$$KL = 10\frac{3}{4} - 2\frac{1}{2} - 2\frac{1}{8}$$

$$= 10\frac{6}{8} - 2\frac{4}{8} - 2\frac{1}{8}$$

$$= 6\frac{1}{8}$$

Point L is KL units to the right of K, which is located at $\frac{5}{8}$, which we can find by adding:

$$\frac{5}{8} + 6\frac{1}{8} = 6\frac{6}{8} = 6\frac{3}{4}$$

112. **(G)** We isolate x as we would in any equation. From $3x - 4y = 12$ we add $4y$ to both sides to get $3x = 4y + 12$, and then divide both sides by 3 to get:

$$x = \frac{4y + 12}{3}$$
$$= \frac{4}{3}y + 4$$

Pay close attention to signs. A common error is to leave the negative sign with y, which yields answer choice E.

113. **(C)** Note that this is a frequency chart. You are not finding the mean, or average, of 0, 1, 2, 3, 4, and 5 (answer choice B). You are finding the average of three 0s, six 1s, three 2s, four 3s, three 4s, and one 5, representing the 20 total students in the class.

$$\text{Mean} = \frac{3 \times 0 + 6 \times 1 + 3 \times 2 + 4 \times 3 + 3 \times 4 + 1 \times 5}{20}$$
$$= \frac{0 + 6 + 6 + 12 + 12 + 5}{20}$$
$$= \frac{41}{20}$$
$$= 2\frac{1}{20}$$

114. **(G)** Notice that 1 part of the 10 parts making up the paste is the resin. That is, the resin constitutes $\frac{1}{10}$ of the paste. Since one billboard requires 25 pounds of paste, one billboard requires $\frac{1}{10}$ of 25 pounds, or 2.5 pounds, of resin. Thus, four billboards would require $4 \times 2.5 = 10$ pounds of resin. Notice that 2.5 is an answer choice, which is the amount of resin required for one billboard.

ANSWER SHEET
Practice Test 2

Part I: English Language Arts

1. Ⓐ Ⓑ Ⓒ Ⓓ
2. Ⓔ Ⓕ Ⓖ Ⓗ
3. Ⓐ Ⓑ Ⓒ Ⓓ
4. Ⓔ Ⓕ Ⓖ Ⓗ
5. Ⓐ Ⓑ Ⓒ Ⓓ
6. Ⓔ Ⓕ Ⓖ Ⓗ
7. Ⓐ Ⓑ Ⓒ Ⓓ
8. Ⓔ Ⓕ Ⓖ Ⓗ
9. Ⓐ Ⓑ Ⓒ Ⓓ
10. Ⓔ Ⓕ Ⓖ Ⓗ
11. Ⓐ Ⓑ Ⓒ Ⓓ
12. Ⓔ Ⓕ Ⓖ Ⓗ
13. Ⓐ Ⓑ Ⓒ Ⓓ
14. Ⓔ Ⓕ Ⓖ Ⓗ
15. Ⓐ Ⓑ Ⓒ Ⓓ

16. Ⓔ Ⓕ Ⓖ Ⓗ
17. Ⓐ Ⓑ Ⓒ Ⓓ
18. Ⓔ Ⓕ Ⓖ Ⓗ
19. Ⓐ Ⓑ Ⓒ Ⓓ
20. Ⓔ Ⓕ Ⓖ Ⓗ
21. Ⓐ Ⓑ Ⓒ Ⓓ
22. Ⓔ Ⓕ Ⓖ Ⓗ
23. Ⓐ Ⓑ Ⓒ Ⓓ
24. Ⓔ Ⓕ Ⓖ Ⓗ
25. Ⓐ Ⓑ Ⓒ Ⓓ
26. Ⓔ Ⓕ Ⓖ Ⓗ
27. Ⓐ Ⓑ Ⓒ Ⓓ
28. Ⓔ Ⓕ Ⓖ Ⓗ
29. Ⓐ Ⓑ Ⓒ Ⓓ
30. Ⓔ Ⓕ Ⓖ Ⓗ

31. Ⓐ Ⓑ Ⓒ Ⓓ
32. Ⓔ Ⓕ Ⓖ Ⓗ
33. Ⓐ Ⓑ Ⓒ Ⓓ
34. Ⓔ Ⓕ Ⓖ Ⓗ
35. Ⓐ Ⓑ Ⓒ Ⓓ
36. Ⓔ Ⓕ Ⓖ Ⓗ
37. Ⓐ Ⓑ Ⓒ Ⓓ
38. Ⓔ Ⓕ Ⓖ Ⓗ
39. Ⓐ Ⓑ Ⓒ Ⓓ
40. Ⓔ Ⓕ Ⓖ Ⓗ
41. Ⓐ Ⓑ Ⓒ Ⓓ
42. Ⓔ Ⓕ Ⓖ Ⓗ
43. Ⓐ Ⓑ Ⓒ Ⓓ
44. Ⓔ Ⓕ Ⓖ Ⓗ
45. Ⓐ Ⓑ Ⓒ Ⓓ

46. Ⓔ Ⓕ Ⓖ Ⓗ
47. Ⓐ Ⓑ Ⓒ Ⓓ
48. Ⓔ Ⓕ Ⓖ Ⓗ
49. Ⓐ Ⓑ Ⓒ Ⓓ
50. Ⓔ Ⓕ Ⓖ Ⓗ
51. Ⓐ Ⓑ Ⓒ Ⓓ
52. Ⓔ Ⓕ Ⓖ Ⓗ
51. Ⓐ Ⓑ Ⓒ Ⓓ
52. Ⓔ Ⓕ Ⓖ Ⓗ
53. Ⓐ Ⓑ Ⓒ Ⓓ
54. Ⓔ Ⓕ Ⓖ Ⓗ
55. Ⓐ Ⓑ Ⓒ Ⓓ
56. Ⓔ Ⓕ Ⓖ Ⓗ
57. Ⓐ Ⓑ Ⓒ Ⓓ

ANSWER SHEET
Practice Test 2

Part II: Mathematics

58.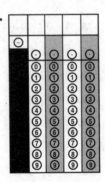

59.

60.

61.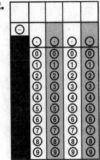

62.

63. Ⓐ Ⓑ Ⓒ Ⓓ	76. Ⓔ Ⓕ Ⓖ Ⓗ	89. Ⓐ Ⓑ Ⓒ Ⓓ	102. Ⓔ Ⓕ Ⓖ Ⓗ
64. Ⓔ Ⓕ Ⓖ Ⓗ	77. Ⓐ Ⓑ Ⓒ Ⓓ	90. Ⓔ Ⓕ Ⓖ Ⓗ	103. Ⓐ Ⓑ Ⓒ Ⓓ
65. Ⓐ Ⓑ Ⓒ Ⓓ	78. Ⓔ Ⓕ Ⓖ Ⓗ	91. Ⓐ Ⓑ Ⓒ Ⓓ	104. Ⓔ Ⓕ Ⓖ Ⓗ
66. Ⓔ Ⓕ Ⓖ Ⓗ	79. Ⓐ Ⓑ Ⓒ Ⓓ	92. Ⓔ Ⓕ Ⓖ Ⓗ	105. Ⓐ Ⓑ Ⓒ Ⓓ
67. Ⓐ Ⓑ Ⓒ Ⓓ	80. Ⓔ Ⓕ Ⓖ Ⓗ	93. Ⓐ Ⓑ Ⓒ Ⓓ	106. Ⓔ Ⓕ Ⓖ Ⓗ
68. Ⓔ Ⓕ Ⓖ Ⓗ	81. Ⓐ Ⓑ Ⓒ Ⓓ	94. Ⓔ Ⓕ Ⓖ Ⓗ	107. Ⓐ Ⓑ Ⓒ Ⓓ
69. Ⓐ Ⓑ Ⓒ Ⓓ	82. Ⓔ Ⓕ Ⓖ Ⓗ	95. Ⓐ Ⓑ Ⓒ Ⓓ	108. Ⓔ Ⓕ Ⓖ Ⓗ
70. Ⓔ Ⓕ Ⓖ Ⓗ	83. Ⓐ Ⓑ Ⓒ Ⓓ	96. Ⓔ Ⓕ Ⓖ Ⓗ	109. Ⓐ Ⓑ Ⓒ Ⓓ
71. Ⓐ Ⓑ Ⓒ Ⓓ	84. Ⓔ Ⓕ Ⓖ Ⓗ	97. Ⓐ Ⓑ Ⓒ Ⓓ	110. Ⓔ Ⓕ Ⓖ Ⓗ
72. Ⓔ Ⓕ Ⓖ Ⓗ	85. Ⓐ Ⓑ Ⓒ Ⓓ	98. Ⓔ Ⓕ Ⓖ Ⓗ	111. Ⓐ Ⓑ Ⓒ Ⓓ
73. Ⓐ Ⓑ Ⓒ Ⓓ	86. Ⓔ Ⓕ Ⓖ Ⓗ	99. Ⓐ Ⓑ Ⓒ Ⓓ	112. Ⓔ Ⓕ Ⓖ Ⓗ
74. Ⓔ Ⓕ Ⓖ Ⓗ	87. Ⓐ Ⓑ Ⓒ Ⓓ	100. Ⓔ Ⓕ Ⓖ Ⓗ	113. Ⓐ Ⓑ Ⓒ Ⓓ
75. Ⓐ Ⓑ Ⓒ Ⓓ	88. Ⓔ Ⓕ Ⓖ Ⓗ	101. Ⓐ Ⓑ Ⓒ Ⓓ	114. Ⓔ Ⓕ Ⓖ Ⓗ

Practice Test 2

PART 1—ENGLISH LANGUAGE ARTS

SUGGESTED TIME: 90 MINUTES, 57 QUESTIONS

Revising/Editing

QUESTIONS 1-10

IMPORTANT NOTE: The Revising/Editing section (Questions 1-10) is in two parts: Part A and Part B.

REVISING/EDITING PART A

Directions: Read and answer each of the following questions. You will be asked to recognize and correct errors in sentences or short paragraphs. Mark the best answer for each question.

1. Read this paragraph.

> (1) Many holidays today can be traced to pagan holidays, which were often celebrated to welcome seasonal changes. (2) Christmas, for example, was celebrated as Saturnalia by the Romans, which feasted on the surplus from their harvests. (3) Valentine's Day replaced Lupercalia, which was celebrated in the spring to welcome the start of a new year. (4) Finally, Halloween took over Lemuria, which took place in the fall.

Which sentence should be revised to correct an inappropriate shift in pronoun?

(A) sentence 1
(B) sentence 2
(C) sentence 3
(D) sentence 4

GO ON TO THE NEXT PAGE

2. Read this paragraph.

> (1) Times Square today isn't what it used to be, in the past, it was a very dark, lawless place. (2) In the 1990s, crime rates dropped drastically, and tourist-friendly establishments sprouted all along the streets. (3) Many credit Mayor Rudy Giuliani, who decided to make the area more friendly by passing harsh laws that criminalized many activities and by increasing the number of police officers patrolling the area. (4) Critics, however, point to an overall decline in crime rates all across the United States and suggest that Giuliani's policies were insignificant.

Which sentence should be revised to correct a run-on?

(E) sentence 1
(F) sentence 2
(G) sentence 3
(H) sentence 4

3. Read this sentence.

> Anyone who is serious about losing weight should consider both physical activities and eating right.

Which of these is the most precise revision for the words *physical activities and eating right*?

(A) physical activities and limiting caloric intake
(B) cardio exercises and eating right
(C) physical activities and dieting
(D) cardio exercises and limiting caloric intake

4. Read these sentences.

> (1) The killer whale feeds on most marine animals.
> (2) Many of these animals are sea birds, cephalopods, turtles, sharks, and fish.
> (3) The killer whale avoids eating dolphins and manatees.

What is the best way to combine these sentences?

(E) The killer whale feeds on most marine animals, and some of these are sea birds, cephalopods, turtles, sharks, and fish, but it avoids dolphins and manatees.
(F) The killer whale feeds on most marine animals, of the types to be included being sea birds, cephalopods, turtles, sharks, and fish, with some avoidance of dolphins and manatees.
(G) The killer whale feeds on most marine animals, such as sea birds, cephalopods, turtles, sharks, and fish, but it avoids dolphins and manatees.
(H) The killer whale feeds on most marine animals, sea birds, cephalopods, turtles, sharks, and fish, it avoids dolphins and manatees.

GO ON TO THE NEXT PAGE

Directions: Read the passage below and answer the questions following it. You will be asked to improve the writing quality of the passage and to correct errors so that the passage follows the conventions of standard written English. You may reread the passage if you need to. Mark the best answer for each question.

Gut Check!

(1) Your digestive system is always at work. (2) When you scarf down a pizza, it takes a twisty trip that starts with being chewed up and ends with you going to the bathroom. (3) Pizza can upset your stomach if you are not too careful with the grease.

(4) The most extensive component of the digestive system is the gastrointestinal (GI) tract. (5) The gastrointestinal tract is a long, muscular tube that runs from your mouth to your rectum. (6) It's over 25 feet long and works with other parts of the digestive system to break that pizza and soda down into smaller particles of nutrients. (7) Blood absorbs these nutrients and carries them throughout the body to be used for energy, growth, and repair.

(8) With such a long GI road, it's common to run into bumps or potholes. (9) About 50 to 70 million Americans are affected by diseases in the digestive tract, like gastroesophageal reflux disease (GERD) or irritable bowel syndrome (IBS). (10) GERD occurs when your stomach acid comes back up into your throat. (11) This causes unpleasant symptoms like heartburn and indigestion. (12) IBS constitutes a variety of symptoms like pain in the abdomen, constipation, diarrhea, and changes in bowel habits. (13) People with IBS often live with shame. (14) Many more people have other digestive problems, like bloating and stomach pain.

(14) There are many factors that can impact gut health. (15) How your body's built, your family and genetic history, how you manage stress, and what you eat can all affect your gut. (16) There are a lot of lifestyle-related GI issues, and there are often no quick fixes for that. (17) In general, people do well when they practice healthy habits.

(18) Research has found that people who have early life stress are more likely to develop IBS. (19) This increased risk for IBS went down when people confided in someone they trust about the stress they experienced.

5. Which sentence should replace sentence 3 to more clearly introduce the topic of this passage?

   (A) Sometimes this can lead to an embarrassing situation, which most people would rather not talk about.
   (B) There are numerous over-the-counter drugs that can relieve an upset stomach or indigestion, but these medicines should be taken with care.
   (C) The digestive system is known to possess a particular type of intelligence, so trusting your gut isn't usually too far off the mark.
   (D) A lot happens in between, and the health of your gut plays a key role in your overall health and well-being.

6. What is the best way to combine sentences 4 and 5 to clarify the relationship between the ideas?

   (E) The most extensive component of the digestive system is the gastrointestinal (GI) tract because the gastrointestinal tract is a long, muscular tube that runs from your mouth to your rectum.

   (F) The most extensive component of the digestive system is the gastrointestinal (GI) tract, a long, muscular tube that runs from your mouth to your rectum.

   (G) Whereas the most extensive component of the digestive system is the gastrointestinal (GI) tract, the gastrointestinal tract is a long, muscular tube that runs from your mouth to your rectum.

   (H) Since the most extensive component of the digestive system is the gastrointestinal (GI) tract, the gastrointestinal tract is a long, muscular tube that runs from your mouth to your rectum.

7. Which sentence is irrelevant to the ideas presented in the third paragraph (sentences 8–14) and should be deleted?

   (A) sentence 9
   (B) sentence 11
   (C) sentence 13
   (D) sentence 14

8. Which transition word or phrase should be added to the beginning of sentence 15?

   (E) In addition,
   (F) For instance,
   (G) As a result,
   (H) Consequently,

9. Which revision of sentence 17 uses the most precise language?

   (A) In general, people do well when they create a more routine schedule, eat a healthy diet and smaller more frequent meals, add in some exercise, and get a good amount of sleep.

   (B) In general, people do well when they decide to create a life that focuses on habits that ensure a good balance of restful and exciting activities.

   (C) In general, people do well when they focus on many habits that will enable them to get both rest and exercise.

   (D) In general, people do well when they decide to live a healthy life.

GO ON TO THE NEXT PAGE

10. Read this sentence.

> Doctors, dieticians, or even a perceptive friend may help you identify some of those issues and address poor habits to improve your GI health.

Where should this sentence be added to best support the ideas in the fourth paragraph (sentences 14–17)?

(E) at the top of the paragraph
(F) between sentences 14 and 15
(G) between sentences 15 and 16
(H) between sentences 16 and 17

11. Which sentence should be added before sentence 18 to most clearly introduce the topic of the paragraph?

(A) Technological advances have made early detection of GI diseases easier, but they are still difficult to identify without the diagnosis of a learned physician.
(B) Exercise and meditation are useful ways to reduce stress.
(C) Strangely, GI diseases affect women more than men.
(D) One of the biggest factors associated with GI disease is stress.

12. Which concluding sentence should follow sentence 19 to best support the topic presented in the passage?

(E) When Americans decide to take care of their GI health, their GI health physicians may lose their jobs.
(F) Finding healthy ways to manage stress is important for GI health, and your health overall.
(G) Another problem that can be helped by managing stress is insomnia.
(H) Without good GI health, other systems cannot function properly and may be at risk.

GO ON TO THE NEXT PAGE

Reading Comprehension

QUESTIONS 13–57

> **Directions:** Read each of the following six texts, and answer the related questions. You may write in your test booklet as needed to take notes. You should reread relevant parts of each text before marking the best answer for each question. Base your answers only on the content within the text.

Putting Cacao to Paper in Early Modern Europe

The following passage has been adapted from Christine Jones's essay *Pods, Pots, and Potions: Putting Cacao to Paper in Early Modern Europe*. It appears in *The Public Domain Review*.

1. Lauded as the "food of the gods" (*Theobroma*) by the Swedish botanist Carl Linnaeus in 1753, the cacao plant (*Theobroma cacao*) has always elicited a certain amount of scientific curiosity and mystical reverence from Europeans. Tucked away under the canopy within the planet's narrow equatorial zone, the only environment in which it grows, and first cultivated in the lands that now constitute Guatemala and Belize, cacao had spent centuries well hidden from Continental eyes.

2. However, after Hernán Cortés and his army took Tenochtitlan, the capital of the Aztec empire, for Spain in 1521, cacao was among the first marvels they wrote home about to describe the new world bounty they'd won for the Castilian crown. Conquistador Bernal Díaz del Castillo wrote down in his record of conquest that frothed chocolate was "the best thing they have to drink." Others hailed it as the key to Moctezuma's famed virility. Cacao, the base ingredient in chocolate, was also used as currency in Mesoamerica. It was not long before colonists took a keen interest in this fortifying drink and the money that grew on trees.

3. Unlike that of a typical fruit, the sweet white flesh of the lumpy autumnal-colored pods that sprout from the cacao tree was considered by locals and European settlers alike to be "of little or no use" and as having a "phlegmatic" texture. Its seeds were the valuable prize. Local women followed ancient recipes to produce from these hard, dry seeds an oily, frothy drink that by all accounts could cure almost anything. That cold cacao beans could become a warming energy drink perplexed early-modern humoral science. Overall, the botanical source of chocolate proved biologically curious, even as the drink became irresistibly compelling. As early Spanish colonists learned, it was not for nothing that the cacao tree had an elevated status in the cosmology and agriculture of Mesoamerica. In the century following conquest, cacao, which had been sacred to the Aztec and to the Maya before them, ranked among crops like tobacco and sugar that proved addictive to the European consumer and crucial to the economic exploitation of the New World.

GO ON TO THE NEXT PAGE

4   Spain imported beans regularly and Madrileño urbanites whipped up a vogue for the chocolate drink, whose popularity then spilled over into France, England, and beyond. Comparatively few Europeans had, however, seen the plant in its native ecosystem. Curious armchair explorers relied for their knowledge of chocolate's raw ingredient on illustrations done by clerics and scientists who had voyaged across the Atlantic and documented the landscape. The history of such illustrations of cacao dates back to the first generation after conquest, and it not only provides us with a bevy of wonderful botanical studies, but also chronicles cacao's European reception from the mid-sixteenth to the mid-eighteenth century.

13. Which statement best describes the central idea of the passage?

(A) The colonization of the Americas led to the cultivation of cacao in Europe.
(B) Europeans failed to recognize the true value of the cacao.
(C) Cacao was an important plant for numerous reasons to various cultures.
(D) The cacao remains a mystery for Europeans who wish to understand its meaning.

14. How does paragraph 2 contribute to the passage?

(E) It presents the most probable reason for the popularity of cacao.
(F) It shows how Americans valued cacao.
(G) It argues that cacao was more important in Mesoamerica than in Europe.
(H) It describes the early European responses to the cacao.

15. Which of the following is implied by the phrase "money that grew on trees."

(A) The Europeans decided to use cacao as a form of currency.
(B) Money was very easy to make because of cacao.
(C) Colonists believed that a strong drink and money could be grown on trees.
(D) Cacao was considered highly valuable.

16. In paragraph 3, the word "curious" serves to highlight

(E) how people were intent on finding the origin of the cacao.
(F) how Spanish colonists wanted badly to find the ancient recipe.
(G) the interest the mysterious characteristics of cacao generated.
(H) that Spanish colonists were being too nosy in their quest to learn about the cacao.

GO ON TO THE NEXT PAGE

17. Which sentence from the passage best supports the idea that commercial interests drove the cultivation of the cacao?

    (A) "the cacao plant (*Theobroma cacao*) has always elicited a certain amount of scientific curiosity and mystical reverence from Europeans." (paragraph 1)

    (B) "Conquistador Bernal Díaz del Castillo wrote down in his record of conquest that frothed chocolate was 'the best thing they have to drink.'" (paragraph 2)

    (C) "In the century following conquest, cacao, which had been sacred to the Aztec and to the Maya before them, ranked among crops like tobacco and sugar that proved addictive to the European consumer and crucial to the economic exploitation of the New World." (paragraph 3)

    (D) "Spain imported beans regularly and Madrileño urbanites whipped up a vogue for the chocolate drink, whose popularity then spilled over into France, England, and beyond." (paragraph 4)

18. Read the following sentence.

> **Curious armchair explorers relied for their knowledge of chocolate's raw ingredient on illustrations done by clerics and scientists who had voyaged across the Atlantic and documented the landscape.**

The sentence contributes to the development of ideas in the excerpt by

    (E) suggesting that clerics and scientists were the primary producers of chocolate.

    (F) showing that information about cacao available to the public was limited to secondary information.

    (G) highlighting the contributions of armchair explorers in the understanding of chocolate.

    (H) revealing the importance of landscape in the production of chocolate.

19. With which statement would the author of this excerpt most likely agree?

    (A) Cacao was the most important crop of 16th-century Europe.

    (B) The addictive chemicals of cacao made it a popular product for Europeans.

    (C) The Spanish colonists did not have an important impact on the popularization of cacao.

    (D) The interest in cacao was not limited to its taste.

GO ON TO THE NEXT PAGE

Inventing the Recording

The following passage has been adapted from Eva Moreda Rodriguez's essay *Inventing the Recording*. It appears in *The Public Domain Review*.

1   Thomas Edison initially believed that the phonograph would be most in demand in offices and companies. Recorded sound, he thought, would make business communication easier by doing away with the ambiguities of written language. However, the Improved Phonograph and Perfected Phonograph, both of which he launched in 1888, took recording technologies in a different direction. Audiences turned out not to be interested in the phonograph because of its practical uses, but because it entertained them; the first phonograph parlor opened in San Francisco in 1889, and was soon followed by thousands of others all over the United States.

2   In Spain—more rural, less industrialized—phonographs were instead paraded around cities and towns and temporarily installed in civic centers, schools, hotels, and churches. For a modest fee, locals from all social classes were able to acquaint themselves with the latest discoveries of science. Some of the names and endeavors of these Spanish phonography pioneers have found their way to us today through advertisements and reports in local newspapers. Many of them were agents of Edison's or funfair impresarios, and we know of a cornet player and entertainer by the name of Lorenzo Colís who in the summer of 1894 toured a phonograph around the Basque Country and La Rioja, and visited the Ortuella area.

3   It was not the thrill of listening to internationally famous performers and speakers that drew audiences to these phonographic sessions. Accounts suggest that phonograph operators were most successful when they recorded local musicians and speakers in front of the audience and then immediately played back the impressed cylinder. It was this, the act of recognizing familiar voices, that ultimately astonished audiences and persuaded them that the phonograph could reproduce reality as it was.

4   And yet, if we were to listen to some of the surviving examples from this era, we would probably find it hard to believe that anyone could have mistaken what is in them with live sound, even accounting for deterioration of the cylinder. While it is true that some such claims simply echoed Edison's publicity (or transcribed it to the letter), one can imagine that an unfamiliar audience, shocked by the experience of hearing recorded sound for the first time, would be willing to forgive shrillness, blurriness, and lack of definition, and accept what they heard as an accurate representation of reality. Moreover, most audiences would not be particularly interested in hearing a particular recording again and again after they had established that it was, indeed, true to reality. In any case, most would not have been able to do so unless a phonograph was in residence in their town; phonographs were expensive and difficult to manipulate at the time, hardly appropriate as a home appliance. Although some recordings from that era have survived to the present day, most were intended to be as temporary as the sound they recorded: played back in phonographic sessions but seldom treasured in households or collections.

GO ON TO THE NEXT PAGE

5   The phonograph became a domestic appliance with the successive launches of the Spring Motor Phonograph, the Edison Home Phonograph, and the Edison Standard Phonograph between 1896 and 1898. With this came the need for a constant supply of professionally produced, well-crafted recordings that could lure upper- and middle-class phonograph owners back to the shops again and again. The recording as a commodity was born—but it still had to be embedded with values and meanings potential buyers could relate to; values and meanings that resonated with ideas they might have had about themselves, but also that connected them to the powerful narrative of the global revolution brought over by recording technologies. In Constantino's native Spain, the task was undertaken by some forty *gabinetes fonográficos* (phonography studios) scattered across the country—a Spanish phenomenon in some respects, relatively independent of Edison's commercial enterprises in more industrially developed countries. The *gabinetes* sold phonographs imported from the United States, but the wax cylinders were recorded and produced by the *gabinetes* themselves.

6   The *gabinetes* not only produced the first recordings to be made in Spain, they also produced the first Spanish recordings—that is, recordings shaped by the culture they were part of. This is immediately obvious in the choice of repertoire. Theatrical culture thrived in turn-of-the-century Spanish cities. The upper and established middle classes flocked to opera houses; the working and lower middle classes, to *zarzuela* theatres and *café cantantes* where *flamenco* was performed—although the latter two still managed to attract a few members of the wealthier social classes who longed for authenticity. Soon, opera, *zarzuela*, and *flamenco* were filling the *gabinetes'* catalogues.

Breakdown of Thomas Edison's Invention Patents

Patent	Total Percentage
Batteries	13%
Electric	39%
Mining	5%
Others	8%
Phonograph	18%
Telephony	17%

GO ON TO THE NEXT PAGE

20. Which statement best describes the structure of paragraph 1?

(E) It introduces a key figure whose life will be discussed in the rest of the passage.

(F) It recounts an unfounded expectation to introduce an important invention discussed in the rest of the passage.

(G) It makes important claims that will later be proven to be false through a series of evidence-based arguments.

(H) It anticipates the reader's expectation of an invention and proceeds to explain why that expectation is justified.

21. Which statement describes how the author's use of sequencing in paragraph 2 contributes to the overall structure of the passage?

(A) It shows how people from a particular region initially became acquainted with the phonograph.

(B) It shows how the popularity of the phonograph depended on reaching as many people as possible.

(C) It shows how the introduction of the phonograph in America was superior to that in Spain.

(D) It shows why people initially were not interested in the phonograph for business purposes.

22. With which statement would the author of this excerpt most likely agree?

(E) Edison completely abandoned his plans to further develop the phonograph.

(F) The upper classes preferred *café cantantes*.

(G) Most of the recordings from the early phonographs do not exist today.

(H) The sound quality of the phonographs is difficult to judge by today's standards.

23. Which claim is best supported by paragraph 3?

(A) People were not interested in listening to the phonograph recordings of famous musicians.

(B) Recorded local musicians were the most talented and, therefore, the most recorded.

(C) The phonograph did not possess the capabilities to record famous musicians.

(D) The quality of the performances was the primary reason for the audience interest in the phonograph.

GO ON TO THE NEXT PAGE

24. Read the following sentence from paragraph 4.

> **And yet, if we were to listen to some of the surviving examples from this era, we would probably find it hard to believe that anyone could have mistaken what is in them with live sound, even accounting for deterioration of the cylinder.**

How does this sentence contribute to the development of the paragraph?

(E) It emphasizes the surprise most people felt while listening to the recordings.

(F) It suggests that the recordings by today's standards were inferior in quality.

(G) It reveals the fact that most people listening to the recordings were not convinced that they were true representations of reality.

(H) It argues that the deterioration of the cylinder must be prevented in order to produce the best sound quality.

25. Which evidence best supports the author's claim that phonographs "were intended to be as temporary as the sound they recorded"?

(A) the details about the phonograph's price

(B) the details about the phonograph's terrible sound quality

(C) the details about Edison's employees

(D) the details about the phonograph's ability to recreate reality

26. Which sentence is the best summary of the way in which the phonograph became a domestic appliance?

(E) Several companies dedicated themselves to the production of the phonograph, but the phonograph's success depended on the production of recordings that would make a connection with the customers.

(F) Several companies competed against each other to produce recordings that would ultimately help people understand the values that they themselves found interesting and meaningful.

(G) Thomas Edison created several companies to produce both the phonographs and the recordings, and these companies began in Spain.

(H) The emergence of Spanish recording studios called *gabinetes* helped drive the demand for phonographs, which then led to the creation of three phonograph companies: the Spring Motor Phonograph, the Edison Home Phonograph, and the Edison Standard Phonograph.

GO ON TO THE NEXT PAGE

27. Which sentence best conveys the idea that the world began to change its understanding of recorded music?

(A) "the first phonograph parlor opened in San Francisco in 1889, and was soon followed by thousands of others all over the United States." (paragraph 1)

(B) "It was this, the act of recognizing familiar voices, that ultimately astonished audiences and persuaded them that the phonograph could reproduce reality as it was." (paragraph 3)

(C) "one can imagine that an unfamiliar audience, shocked by the experience of hearing recorded sound for the first time, would be willing to forgive shrillness, blurriness, and lack of definition, and accept what they heard as an accurate representation of reality." (paragraph 4)

(D) "The recording as a commodity was born—but it still had to be embedded with values and meanings potential buyers could relate to; values and meanings that resonated with ideas they might have had about themselves, but also that connected them to the powerful narrative of the global revolution brought over by recording technologies." (paragraph 5)

28. With which statement would the author of this excerpt most likely agree?

(E) *Gabinetes* were the most important factor contributing to the growing popularity of phonographs.

(F) *Flamenco* was not favored by the wealthy.

(G) People grew more interested in purchasing phonographs because Edison made them.

(H) The recordings of the *gabinetes* were enjoyed by people from different parts of Spanish society.

29. How does the table showing the breakdown of Thomas Edison's invention patents support the ideas in the passage?

(A) It reveals that electricity was the most important aspect of Edison's invention patents.

(B) It suggests that Edison made considerable investments into developing the phonograph.

(C) It helps explain why the world became more interested in global revolutions.

(D) The recordings of the *gabinetes* were enjoyed by people from different parts of Spanish society.

GO ON TO THE NEXT PAGE

Excerpt from *A Tale of Two Cities*
By Charles Dickens

1   Monseigneur, one of the great lords in power at the Court, held his fortnightly reception in his grand hotel in Paris. Monseigneur was in his inner room, his sanctuary of sanctuaries, the Holiest of Holiests to the crowd of worshippers in the suite of rooms without. Monseigneur was about to take his chocolate. Monseigneur could swallow a great many things with ease, and was by some few sullen minds supposed to be rather rapidly swallowing France; but, his morning's chocolate could not so much as get into the throat of Monseigneur, without the aid of four strong men besides the Cook.

2   Yes. It took four men, all four ablaze with gorgeous decoration, and the Chief of them unable to exist with fewer than two gold watches in his pocket, emulative of the noble and chaste fashion set by Monseigneur, to conduct the happy chocolate to Monseigneur's lips. One lacquey carried the chocolate-pot into the sacred presence; a second, milled and frothed the chocolate with the little instrument he bore for that function; a third, presented the favoured napkin; a fourth (he of the two gold watches), poured the chocolate out. It was impossible for Monseigneur to dispense with one of these attendants on the chocolate and hold his high place under the admiring Heavens. Deep would have been the blot upon his escutcheon if his chocolate had been ignobly waited on by only three men; he must have died of two.

3   Monseigneur had been out at a little supper last night, where the Comedy and the Grand Opera were charmingly represented. Monseigneur was out at a little supper most nights, with fascinating company. So polite and so impressible was Monseigneur, that the Comedy and the Grand Opera had far more influence with him in the tiresome articles of state affairs and state secrets, than the needs of all France. A happy circumstance for France, as the like always is for all countries similarly favoured!—always was for England (by way of example), in the regretted days of the merry Stuart who sold it.

4   Monseigneur had one truly noble idea of general public business, which was, to let everything go on in its own way; of particular public business, Monseigneur had the other truly noble idea that it must all go his way—tend to his own power and pocket. Of his pleasures, general and particular, Monseigneur had the other truly noble idea, that the world was made for them. The text of his order (altered from the original by only a pronoun, which is not much) ran: "The earth and the fulness thereof are mine, saith Monseigneur."

5   A sumptuous man was the Farmer-General. Thirty horses stood in his stables, twenty-four male domestics sat in his halls, six body-women waited on his wife. As one who pretended to do nothing but plunder and forage where he could, the Farmer-General—howsoever his matrimonial relations conduced to social morality—was at least the greatest reality among the personages who attended at the hotel of Monseigneur that day.

GO ON TO THE NEXT PAGE

6   For, the rooms, though a beautiful scene to look at, and adorned with every device of decoration that the taste and skill of the time could achieve, were, in truth, not a sound business; considered with any reference to the scarecrows in the rags and nightcaps elsewhere (and not so far off, either, but that the watching towers of Notre Dame, almost equidistant from the two extremes, could see them both), they would have been an exceedingly uncomfortable business—if that could have been anybody's business, at the house of Monseigneur. Military officers destitute of military knowledge; naval officers with no idea of a ship; civil officers without a notion of affairs; brazen ecclesiastics, of the worst world worldly, with sensual eyes, loose tongues, and looser lives; all totally unfit for their several callings, all lying horribly in pretending to belong to them, but all nearly or remotely of the order of Monseigneur, and therefore foisted on all public employments from which anything was to be got; these were to be told off by the score and the score. Doctors who made great fortunes out of dainty remedies for imaginary disorders that never existed, smiled upon their courtly patients in the ante-chambers of Monseigneur. Exquisite gentlemen of the finest breeding, which was at that remarkable time—and has been since—to be known by its fruits of indifference to every natural subject of human interest, were in the most exemplary state of exhaustion, at the hotel of Monseigneur.

7   Dress was the one unfailing talisman and charm used for keeping all things in their places. Everybody was dressed for a Fancy Ball that was never to leave off. From the Palace of the Tuileries, through Monseigneur and the whole Court, through the Chambers, the Tribunals of Justice, and all society (except the scarecrows), the Fancy Ball descended to the Common Executioner: who, in pursuance of the charm, was required to officiate "frizzled, powdered, in a gold-laced coat, pumps, and white silk stockings." At the gallows and the wheel—the axe was a rarity—Monsieur Paris, as it was the episcopal mode among his brother Professors of the provinces, Monsieur Orleans, and the rest, to call him, presided in this dainty dress. And who among the company at Monseigneur's reception in that seventeen hundred and eightieth year of our Lord, could possibly doubt, that a system rooted in a frizzled hangman, powdered, gold-laced, pumped, and white-silk stockinged, would see the very stars out!

8   Monseigneur having eased his four men of their burdens and taken his chocolate, caused the doors of the Holiest of Holiests to be thrown open, and issued forth. Then, what submission, what cringing and fawning, what servility, what abject humiliation! As to bowing down in body and spirit, nothing in that way was left for Heaven—which may have been one among other reasons why the worshippers of Monseigneur never troubled it.

30. In paragraph 1, how does the phrase "without the aid of four strong men besides the Cook" affect the tone in this part of the excerpt?

(E) It creates an oppressive tone by suggesting that Monseigneur is a demanding man.

(F) It creates a sympathetic tone by showing that Monseigneur is helpless without four people.

(G) It creates a comedic tone by suggesting that Monseigneur prioritizes food over France.

(H) It creates critical tone by showing that the Cook is neglected from an important activity.

GO ON TO THE NEXT PAGE

31. The description of the men in paragraph 2 primarily serves to

    (A) reveal Monseigneur's demanding requirements for his needs.

    (B) highlight the embarrassment of the men.

    (C) promote the importance of luxury in daily activities.

    (D) explain the complexities of eating habits.

32. Read this sentence from paragraph 3.

> **So polite and so impressible was Monseigneur, that the Comedy and the Grand Opera had far more influence with him in the tiresome articles of state affairs and state secrets, than the needs of all France.**

    Which sentence best describes how the sentence fits into the overall structure of the excerpt?

    (E) It signals a change from the positive to the negative effects of Monseigneur.

    (F) It includes a point that builds on passage's focus on the importance of the performing arts.

    (G) It suggests that most people in France are happy because of the performing arts.

    (H) It serves to reinforce a negative characteristic of Monseigneur.

33. Which statement best explains Monseigneur's attitude about his place in the world?

    (A) "It was impossible for Monseigneur to dispense with one of these attendants on the chocolate and hold his high place under the admiring Heavens." (paragraph 2)

    (B) "Monseigneur was out at a little supper most nights, with fascinating company." (paragraph 3)

    (C) "Monseigneur had the other truly noble idea, that the world was made for them." (paragraph 4)

    (D) "A sumptuous man was the Farmer-General." (paragraph 5)

34. Which of the following statements best supports the description of the Farmer-General in paragraph 5?

    (E) He preferred reality over fantasy.

    (F) He preferred fantasy over reality.

    (G) His favorite animals were horses.

    (H) He had more servants than his wife did.

GO ON TO THE NEXT PAGE

35. Read the following sentence from paragraph 6.

For, the rooms, though a beautiful scene to look at, and adorned with every device of decoration that the taste and skill of the time could achieve, were, in truth, not a sound business.

Which of the following sentences from the passage best reflects the ideas from the sentence above?

(A) "Monseigneur was in his inner room, his sanctuary of sanctuaries, the Holiest of Holiests to the crowd of worshippers in the suite of rooms without." (paragraph 1)

(B) "Deep would have been the blot upon his escutcheon if his chocolate had been ignobly waited on by only three men; he must have died of two." (paragraph 2)

(C) "Exquisite gentlemen of the finest breeding, which was at that remarkable time—and has been since—to be known by its fruits of indifference to every natural subject of human interest, were in the most exemplary state of exhaustion, at the hotel of Monseigneur." (paragraph 6)

(D) "Dress was the one unfailing talisman and charm used for keeping all things in their places." (paragraph 7)

36. What statement about Monseigneur's guests is best supported by the passage?

(E) Most of them were outstanding individuals, but they often tired easily.

(F) Some of them were highly educated individuals who did not have the resources to improve themselves.

(G) Most of them did not possess the qualities expected of them.

(H) None of them preferred to be in the company of Monseigneur.

37. In paragraph 6, how do the descriptions of the "military officers," "ecclesiastics," and "doctors" contribute to the central idea?

(A) They highlight the importance of diversity in government.

(B) They illustrate that some people make more important contributions to society than others.

(C) They reveal the professional desire to appear important.

(D) They emphasize the absence of integrity and substance in Monseigneur's court.

GO ON TO THE NEXT PAGE

38. Read this sentence from paragraph 7.

> **Dress was the one unfailing talisman and charm used for keeping all things in their places.**

Which statement best describes how the sentence fits into the overall structure of the excerpt?

(E) It indicates a shift to the importance of clothing that people place over food.

(F) It reveals a shift from an analysis of an attitude to the actions underlying those attitudes.

(G) It illustrates an aspect of the party that reflects the narrator's negative attitude toward Monseigneur.

(H) It advocates the need for reform in a society that the author finds to be problematic.

39. How does paragraph 7 contribute to the plot of the excerpt?

(A) It foreshadows a looming problem that no one in the party could foresee.

(B) It illustrates the power of Monseigneur's imagination and love for luxury.

(C) It shows that many people have different views about life and the future.

(D) It provides additional insight about Monseigneur's habits.

40. Read this sentence from paragraph 8.

> **Monseigneur having eased his four men of their burdens and taken his chocolate, caused the doors of the Holiest of Holiests to be thrown open, and issued forth.**

How does the sentence contribute to the development of the plot?

(E) It shows how the Monseigneur's reliance on others leads the reader to sympathize with the court.

(F) It reveals how the Monseigneur's kindness leads to an external conflict.

(G) It illustrates the Monseigneur's influence on other characters.

(H) It emphasizes the Monseigneur's generosity in taking over the responsibilities of his workers.

GO ON TO THE NEXT PAGE

Annabel Lee

By Edgar Allan Poe

It was many and many a year ago,
In a kingdom by the sea,
That a maiden there lived whom you may know
Line By the name of Annabel Lee;—
(5) And this maiden she lived with no other thought
Than to love and be loved by me.

I was a child and she was a child,
In this kingdom by the sea;
But we loved with a love that was more than love—
(10) I and my Annabel Lee—
With a love that the wingéd seraphs in Heaven
Coveted her and me.

And this was the reason that, long ago,
In this kingdom by the sea,
(15) A wind blew out of a cloud, chilling
My beautiful Annabel Lee;
So that her high-born kinsmen came
And bore her away from me,
To shut her up in a sepulchre,
(20) In this kingdom by the sea.

The angels, not half so happy in Heaven,
Went envying her and me—
Yes!—that was the reason (as all men know,
In this kingdom by the sea)
(25) That the wind came out of the cloud by night,
Chilling and killing my Annabel Lee.

But our love it was stronger by far than the love
Of those who were older than we—
Of many far wiser than we—
(30) And neither the angels in Heaven above
Nor the demons down under the sea
Can ever dissever my soul from the soul
Of the beautiful Annabel Lee;

For the moon never beams, without bringing me dreams
(35) Of the beautiful Annabel Lee;
And the stars never rise, but I feel the bright eyes

Of the beautiful Annabel Lee;
And so, all the night-tide, I lie down by the side
Of my darling—my darling—my life and my bride,
(40) In her sepulchre there by the sea—
In her tomb by the sounding sea.

GO ON TO THE NEXT PAGE

41. The phrase "many and many" in line 1 conveys a sense of

    (A) curiosity.
    (B) contentment.
    (C) remoteness.
    (D) despair.

42. Which statement best describes the repetition of the phrase "kingdom by the sea"?

    (E) It creates an atmosphere of nobility and power throughout the poem.
    (F) It highlights the description of the various kingdoms throughout the poem.
    (G) It repeats hypnotically as each stanza grows in emotional intensity.
    (H) It emphasizes Annabel Lee's aristocratic lineage.

43. The description of the "winged seraphs" (line 11) emphasizes the speaker's

    (A) sense of religious devotion.
    (B) strength of conviction.
    (C) fear of a suggestive symbol.
    (D) desire for an enchanting dream.

44. In lines 17–20, it can be inferred that the speaker

    (E) buried Annabel with her kinsmen.
    (F) did not bury Annabel's body.
    (G) fell out of love with Annabel.
    (H) carried Annabel to the sea.

45. It can be inferred that "the angels" in line 21 also refer to

    (A) "a maiden" (line 3)
    (B) "seraphs" (line 11)
    (C) "kinsmen" (line 17)
    (D) "the wind" (line 25)

46. How do the details in lines 21–26 contribute to the development of the poem?

    (E) They use exaggeration to reveal that the speaker is joking.
    (F) They attempt to create a reason to explain the situation.
    (G) They warn the reader about the dangers of the environment.
    (H) They ask a higher power to answer the speaker's questions.

GO ON TO THE NEXT PAGE

47. The speaker blames which one of the following for Annabel's death?

    (A) "a kingdom by the sea" (line 2)
    (B) "winged seraphs" (line 11)
    (C) "high-born kinsmen" (line 17)
    (D) "sepulchre" (line 19)

48. Which line from the poem best expresses the speaker's eternal connection to Annabel Lee?

    (E) "To shut her up in a sepulchre" (line 19)
    (F) "Went envying her and me" (line 22)
    (G) "Can ever dissever my soul from the soul" (line 32)
    (H) "For the moon never beams, without bringing me dreams" (line 34)

GO ON TO THE NEXT PAGE

Decoding the Morse: The History of 16th-Century Narcoleptic Walruses

The following passage has been adapted from Natalie Lawrence's essay *Decoding the Morse: The History of 16th-Century Narcoleptic Walruses*. It appears in *The Public Domain Review*.

1   The walrus was a relatively unfamiliar creature in sixteenth-century Europe, despite the fact that walrus parts had been circulating for hundreds of years through trade with Greenland, Iceland, and Russia. Tusked amphibious beasts, that may or may not have been based on walruses, existed in various sixteenth-century scholarly works. Some of these harked back to classical authorities: Pliny had described a "sea-elephant," with which the Arctic beast sometimes became identified. The elephant-like "morsus," represented on the 1516 world map of Martin Waldseemüller, was most probably the result of such confusing names and a mainland trade of mammoth teeth through Russia.

2   Once Europeans began hunting walruses in the Arctic themselves in the late sixteenth century, however, undeniably walrus-like creatures began to appear in natural histories. This wasn't a simple process of "discovery" of walruses. Nobody except the hunters who killed walruses on the Arctic ice saw living walruses: carcasses were immediately channeled through the marketplaces of northern European shores into apothecary shops, curiosity cabinets, and natural histories. Walrus hides were carted off to the tanners and the ivory and bone sent for carving into combs and knife handles or ground up. The blubber was rendered into soaps, lamp fuel, or cooking oil. Tusks and bones were sometimes gilded, carved, and polished for luxury sales to curiosity collectors.

3   Apothecaries placed ground-up walrus tusk for sale alongside other exotic and costly medicinal substances. Walrus ivory was often billed as possessing similar qualities to "unicorn horn," a traditional panacea[1] against all poisons. "Unicorn horn" could itself, in reality, be any of a number of powdered, osseous[2] things, from narwhal or walrus tusks to elephant bone. As long as the apothecary was of good repute, nobody would be any the wiser. They certainly weren't going to be protected from poison, whatever species the powder contained.

4   Walruses were physically and metaphorically dismantled and reassembled; they were cut up into transportable parts by hunters and put back together in various guises by scholars who constructed their very own walrus-creatures from walrus artifacts and older textual accounts. These quasi-mythical images had lives of their own. Olaus Magnus's image of narcoleptic[3] cliff hangers was particularly long-lived. Parts of walrus images were also broken up and scattered into other depictions. Imposing, walrus-like tusks or bristly manes were featured by many cartographic denizens of treacherous oceans. Elements of the *morse* were used in depictions of monstrous sea-beasts such as the "sea-pig," "sea-boar," "sea-wolf" and "sea-lion" in various books of monstrosity.

5   There were, in fact, a number of first-hand accounts from hunters published in this period describing the slaying of hundreds of "see-horses" on the Arctic ice, heroic battles with enraged and red-eyed creatures in the waters, followed by the heavy work of flensing (skinning) and dismantling the slain beasts. But very few intellectuals seemed interested in these kinds of images of what a walrus was, preferring the monsters depicted in more authoritative, scholarly accounts.

GO ON TO THE NEXT PAGE

6   It was only in 1612 that a whole, living walrus was brought to mainland Europe. A walrus pup arrived in Amsterdam, along with the stuffed skin of its mother, on a Dutch hunting ship. It was described by Dr. Everhard Vorstius of Leiden University, as a "sea-beast...much like a seal" with holes for ears and a bristly beard. This small animal "roared like a boar" and was placed in a barrel of water to relax. He was fed porridge oats, at which he sucked slowly and grunted as he ate. Vorstius finished with the ominous mention that the walrus's fat was rather "toothsome."[4]

7   This porridge-slurping pup was adopted into the roster of morse images in later descriptions, but sat awkwardly with the fierce-toothed behemoths. It certainly did not replace them: they were far too powerful and too resonant with traditional preconceptions of what the Arctic must be like. The walrus remained a mysterious beast from a wonder-filled north, long after Magnus purported to reveal its secrets.

[1] **panacea:** a medicine that cures everything
[2] **osseous:** consisting of or turned into bone
[3] **narcoleptic:** characterized by sudden attacks of sleepiness
[4] **toothsome:** tasty

49. Read this line from paragraph 1.

     Some of these harked back to classical authorities: Pliny had described a "sea-elephant," with which the Arctic beast sometimes became identified.

     How does this sentence fit into the overall structure of the paragraph?

     (A) It provides the least credible description of the walrus.
     (B) It provides the most credible description of the walrus.
     (C) It serves to emphasize the claim about walruses made earlier in the paragraph.
     (D) It serves as the main thesis to be discussed throughout the passage.

50. Which of the following statements best summarizes paragraph 2?

     (E) Although Europeans had been using walruses for a variety of goods, they were mostly unaware of their existence.
     (F) The popularity of goods based on walruses was recorded in 16th-century natural histories.
     (G) The walrus was hunted almost into extinction until natural histories brought awareness of the problem.
     (H) Europeans began to hunt more walruses because of advances in knowledge about walruses.

GO ON TO THE NEXT PAGE

51. Which statement best describes the way walrus tusks were sold?

    (A) They were sold at a higher price than the tusks of narwhals or elephant bones.
    (B) Many customers insisted that walrus parts be included in a wide variety of products.
    (C) They were used mostly for luxury products.
    (D) They were packaged as something other than what they really were.

52. Which statement best explains how walruses were "metaphorically dismantled and reassembled"?

    (E) "Walrus hides were carted off to the tanners and the ivory and bone sent for carving into combs and knife handles or ground up." (paragraph 2)
    (F) "Apothecaries placed ground-up walrus tusk for sale alongside other exotic and costly medicinal substances" (paragraph 3)
    (G) ". . . they were cut up into transportable parts by hunters and put back together . . ." (paragraph 4)
    (H) "Elements of the *morse* were used in depictions of monstrous sea-beasts such as the 'sea-pig,' 'sea-boar,' 'sea-wolf' and 'sea-lion' in various books of monstrosity." (paragraph 4)

53. With which statement about the "scholarly accounts" in paragraph 5 would the author most likely agree?

    (A) Scholarly accounts were the best way to learn about walruses.
    (B) Other accounts might have provided more accurate images of the walrus.
    (C) Most people preferred the scholarly accounts because they were more reliable.
    (D) It was not the preferred account for most intellectuals.

54. Read the following sentence from paragraph 6.

    He was fed porridge oats, at which he sucked slowly and grunted as he ate. Vorstius finished with the ominous mention that the walrus's fat was rather "toothsome."

    What does Dr. Vorstius's comment reveal about his initial reaction to the walrus?

    (E) It evoked wonder and amazement.
    (F) Its appetite caused Dr. Vorstius much distress.
    (G) Dr. Vorstius might have had more than an intellectual interest in the walrus.
    (H) Dr. Vorstius felt sadness and sympathy for the poor pup.

55. What does paragraph 7 suggest about the "porridge-slurping pup"?

    (A) Most people did not believe in its existence.
    (B) Its description was insufficient to dispel existing biases.
    (C) It changed the way people thought about the walrus.
    (D) Its true representation remains a mystery.

GO ON TO THE NEXT PAGE

56. Which statement about Magnus is best supported by the passage?

  (E) He provided the most accurate depiction of the walrus.
  (F) He was a hunter who witnessed the killings of walruses.
  (G) He wrote several accounts of the walrus.
  (H) He worked in an apothecary to make unicorn horn.

57. Which sentence best supports the claim that most 16th-century accounts were largely fictional?

  (A) "Some of these harked back to classical authorities: Pliny had described a 'sea-elephant,' with which the Arctic beast sometimes became identified." (paragraph 1)
  (B) "These quasi-mythical images had lives of their own." (paragraph 4)
  (C) "It was described by Dr. Everhard Vorstius of Leiden University, as a 'sea-beast . . . much like a seal' with holes for ears and a bristly beard." (paragraph 6)
  (D) "This porridge-slurping pup was adopted into the roster of morse images in later descriptions, but sat awkwardly with the fierce-toothed behemoths." (paragraph 7)

GO ON TO THE NEXT PAGE

PART 2—MATHEMATICS

SUGGESTED TIME: 90 MINUTES, 57 QUESTIONS

IMPORTANT NOTES: (1) Formulas are not provided. (2) Figures other than graphs are not necessarily drawn to scale. (3) Diagrams are in one plane unless stated otherwise. (4) Graphs are drawn to scale. Unless stated otherwise, all relationships on graphs are according to appearance. (5) Simplify all fractions.

Grid-In Questions

QUESTIONS 58–62

Directions: Solve each problem. On the answer sheet, write your answer in the boxes at the top of the grid. Start on the left side of each grid. Print only one number or symbol in each box. Under each box, fill in the circle that matches the number or symbol you wrote above. **DO NOT FILL IN A CIRCLE UNDER AN UNUSED BOX. DO NOT LEAVE A BOX BLANK IN THE MIDDLE OF AN ANSWER.**

58. $$\frac{229 - x}{14} = 15$$

What value of x makes the above equation true?

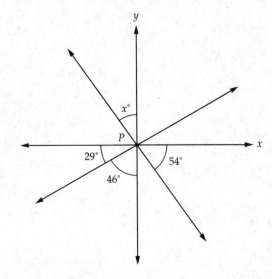

59. How many 4-digit numbers can be created using the digits 1, 3, 5, 7, and 9 without repeating any digits within that 4-digit number?

61. Four straight lines intersect at point P, as shown above. What is the value of x?

60. Solve: $\left| (-7) - (-2) + 2.8 \right| - \left| 2 - 6.8 \right|$

62. Terrance has completed 72 pages in his Chinese workbook. This is 18% of the total number of pages in the workbook. How many pages are in the workbook?

GO ON TO THE NEXT PAGE

Directions: Solve each question. Select the best answer from the choices given. Mark the letter of your choice on the answer sheet.

63. If $\dfrac{72}{y} = 4x$, what is the value of x when $y = 6$?

(A) 3
(B) 6
(C) 9
(D) 12

64.

Dessert	Number of Times Ordered
Cookies	28
Pie	32
Cake	44
Ice Cream	56

The above table shows how many times different desserts were ordered at a restaurant. Based on this data, what is the probability a customer orders pie as a dessert?

(E) 20%
(F) 26%
(G) 32%
(H) 40%

65. At 11:00 A.M. one day, the temperature was 10 degrees above zero. The temperature fell 3 degrees per hour for the rest of the day. What was the temperature at 7:00 P.M. that day?

(A) $-2°$
(B) $-11°$
(C) $-14°$
(D) $-17°$

66.

On the above number line, $MN = 4\dfrac{5}{6}$. What is the position of point M?

(E) $-4\dfrac{1}{2}$

(F) $-3\dfrac{1}{2}$

(G) $3\dfrac{1}{2}$

(H) $6\dfrac{1}{6}$

67. What is the least common multiple of 9, 18, and 6?

(A) 18
(B) 24
(C) 36
(D) 72

68.
$$2X = 3Y = \frac{Z}{5} = W + 3 = \frac{V}{2} > 0$$

Based on the statement above, which variable has the greatest value?

(E) X
(F) Z
(G) W
(H) V

GO ON TO THE NEXT PAGE

69. A pizza shop offers 3 sizes (small, medium, and large) and 5 different toppings for their pizzas. Different pizzas can be made by choosing different sizes and toppings. If Chris wants to order a pizza with exactly 2 different toppings, how many different pizzas can he create?

(A) 6
(B) 10
(C) 30
(D) 60

70. Beverly went to a fabric store and bought $1\frac{1}{4}$ yards of cloth at $8.00 per yard. Sales tax on the cloth was 8%. What was the total cost of the cloth?

(E) $9.76
(F) $10.08
(G) $10.80
(H) $18.00

71. A house painter uses 4 cans of paint for every 108 square feet of wall painted. At this rate, how many cans of paint will she need in order to paint 405 square feet of wall?

(A) 4
(B) 15
(C) 16
(D) 17

72. How many positive even numbers satisfy the inequality $3x + 10 \leq 97$?

(E) 14
(F) 15
(G) 28
(H) 29

73. The Good Morning Restaurant uses 25 dozen eggs for 200 breakfast customers. At this rate, approximately how many dozen eggs are needed for 300 breakfast customers?

(A) 30
(B) 35
(C) 38
(D) 40

74. A small circular dinner plate is placed in the center of a larger circular dinner plate. The large circular plate has a radius of 20 centimeters, and the small circular plate has a circumference of 10π centimeters. What is the area of the part of the larger dinner plate that is not covered by the smaller dinner plate?

(E) 10π sq cm
(F) 300π sq cm
(G) 390π sq cm
(H) 375π sq cm

75. In his first 4 basketball games, Andre scored a mean of 12 points per game. He scored 32 points in his 5th game. What is his mean score for the first 5 games?

(A) 12
(B) 16
(C) 20
(D) 22

76. A cooler contains three types of beverages: 6 bottles of apple juice, 3 bottles of grape juice, and 5 bottles of orange juice. What is the probability that a bottle chosen at random from this cooler is *not* apple juice?

(E) $\frac{1}{8}$
(F) $\frac{3}{7}$
(G) $\frac{4}{7}$
(H) $\frac{2}{3}$

GO ON TO THE NEXT PAGE

77. If $x = 6$ and $y = -9$, what is the value of $x(2x + y)$?

(A) -18

(B) 18

(C) 54

(D) 126

78.

Newspaper Advertising Prices	
Page Space	Price
$\frac{1}{4}$ page	$200
$\frac{1}{2}$ page	$350

The table above shows prices for newspaper advertising. A store purchased $\frac{1}{4}$ pages and $\frac{1}{2}$ pages in equal numbers for a total of $5,500. What is the total amount of page space the store purchased?

(E) $\frac{3}{4}$ pages

(F) $7\frac{1}{2}$ pages

(G) 10 pages

(H) 15 pages

79. Margie is throwing a party. To make invitations, she could buy a package of paper for $10.10, or she could buy x individual sheets of the same paper for $0.12 each. What is the largest value of x that would make buying the individual sheets *less* expensive than buying the package?

(A) 75

(B) 80

(C) 84

(D) 85

80.

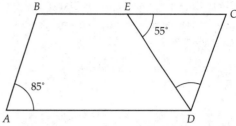

In the figure above, *ABCD* is a parallelogram. The measure of $\angle BAD$ is $85°$ and the measure of $\angle CED$ is $55°$? What is the measure of $\angle CDE$?

(E) $40°$

(F) $55°$

(G) $85°$

(H) $95°$

81. A United States nickel coin is made from an alloy of two metals—nickel and copper—with weights in the ratio of 25 : 75, respectively. The coin weighs a total of 5 grams. What is the weight of the nickel in this coin?

(A) 0.25 g

(B) 0.50 g

(C) 0.75 g

(D) 1.25 g

82. Points *X*, *Y*, and *Z* are on a straight line, and *Y* is between *X* and *Z*. Length $YZ = \frac{4}{5} XY$ and length $XY = 20$ centimeters. What is the length of *XZ*?

(E) 16 cm

(F) 32 cm

(G) 36 cm

(H) 45 cm

83. When completely full, a cylindrical oil drum can hold $5,130$ liters. If the drum is $\frac{2}{3}$ full of oil, how many kiloliters of oil need to be added in order to fill the drum completely?

(A) 1.71

(B) 3.42

(C) 5.13

(D) 17.10

GO ON TO THE NEXT PAGE

84. Albert's age now is three times Clara's age. If Clara was 17 three years ago, how old was Albert five years ago?

(E) 37
(F) 50
(G) 55
(H) 60

85.
$$1 \text{ krutz} = 4.5 \text{ werbs}$$
$$1 \text{ krutz} = 10.8 \text{ flacks}$$

Using the conversion above, how many flacks are equal to 1 werb?

(A) 0.42
(B) 2.4
(C) 6.3
(D) 15.3

86. If w is an odd integer, which one of the following must be an even integer?

(E) $w + 2$
(F) $2w + 3$
(G) $2w + 5$
(H) $w - 3$

87. A bookshelf can hold a total of 42 books. There are now x books on the shelf. If 3 of these books are removed, the shelf will be two-thirds full. What is the value of x?

(A) 17
(B) 24
(C) 28
(D) 31

88. Simplify this expression:

$$4(5 - 3x) - (7 - x)$$

(E) $20 - 11x$
(F) $20 - 12x$
(G) $13 - 13x$
(H) $13 - 11x$

89.

Number of Pets	Number of Students
0	13
1	17
2	7
3 or more	3

Aaron surveyed students at his school about the number of pets they have. What is the probability that a student who participated in the survey has at most 1 pet?

(A) $\dfrac{1}{4}$

(B) $\dfrac{17}{40}$

(C) $\dfrac{27}{40}$

(D) $\dfrac{3}{4}$

90. A large container is partially filled with n liters of water. Irene adds 12 liters of water to the container, making it 60% full. If Isaac adds 6 more liters of water, the container will be 75% full. What is the value of n?

(E) 12
(F) 14
(G) 28
(H) 40

91.
$$2x^3 + 6x^2 + x + 3 + \frac{1}{x^2}$$

If $x = 10$, what is the value of the expression above?

(A) 2,613.01
(B) 2,613.1
(C) 2,614
(D) 2,713

GO ON TO THE NEXT PAGE

92. Which number line below shows the solution set for $x - 3 \leq y \leq 2x + 5$ when $y = 1$?

(E)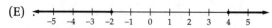

(F)

(G)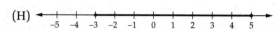

(H)
<image-placeholder number line from -5 to 5 with segment from -2 onward>

93. The Greens spend $5 of every $8 they earn on planned expenses. If the family spent $32,400 on planned expenses last year, how much did they earn that year?

(A) $26,470
(B) $51,840
(C) $97,200
(D) $162,000

94. A bag contains 75 marbles that are red, blue, or green. The ratio of red to blue marbles is 14 : 9, and the ratio of blue marbles to green marbles is 9 : 2. If 2 blue marbles are removed and replaced with 2 green marbles, what will be the new ratio of red to green marbles?

(E) 21 : 3
(F) 7 : 1
(G) 7 : 2
(H) 21 : 4

95.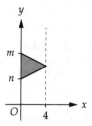

What is the area of the shaded triangle shown above?

(A) $2(m - n)$
(B) $m - n$
(C) $\frac{1}{2}(m - n)$
(D) $4(m - n)$

96. A wooden box has a square base. The height of this box is 2 times the length of one side of the base. If the volume of the box is 128 cu ft., what is the height of this box?

(E) 4 ft.
(F) 8 ft.
(G) 16 ft.
(H) 64 ft.

97. $$\frac{21}{28} = \frac{p}{7}$$

In the equation above, what is the value of p?

(A) $\frac{3}{4}$
(B) 4
(C) $\frac{21}{4}$
(D) 21

98. Points P, Q, R, and S represent -5, -1, 0, and 4, respectively, on a number line. How many units is the midpoint of PQ from the midpoint of RS?

(E) 2
(F) 3
(G) 4
(H) 5

GO ON TO THE NEXT PAGE

99. There are 1,000 cubic centimeters in 1 liter, and 1,000 cubic millimeters in 1 milliliter. How many cubic millimeters are there in 1 cubic centimeter?

(A) 1
(B) 100
(C) 1,000
(D) 1,000,000

100.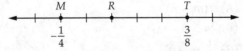

The hatch marks on the number line above are evenly spaced. What is the coordinate of point R?

(E) $-\dfrac{1}{8}$

(F) 0

(G) $\dfrac{1}{8}$

(H) $\dfrac{1}{4}$

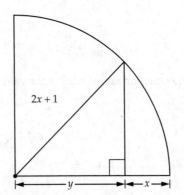

101. In the quarter circle above, what is y in terms of x?

(A) $2x$
(B) $x + 1$
(C) $\dfrac{(2x+1)}{2}$
(D) $\sqrt{\dfrac{(2x+1)^2}{2}}$

102.

Number of Cats	Number of Families
0	21
1	41
2	33
3 or more	5

The table above shows the number of cats per family in 100 households in the Central district. By what percentage is the number of families with 1 cat greater than the number of families with 2 cats?

(E) 8%
(F) 12%
(G) 18%
(H) 22%

103. In a sample of 50 cars at a local dealership, there are 18 gray cars and 10 cars with heated seats. Of the 18 gray cars, 5 have heated seats. If a car is selected at random from the given sample, what is the probability that both of the following are true: the car is not gray and does not have heated seats?

(A) $\dfrac{17}{50}$

(B) $\dfrac{23}{50}$

(C) $\dfrac{27}{50}$

(D) $\dfrac{33}{50}$

104. The decimal 0.14 can be written as the fraction $\dfrac{x}{50}$. What is the value of x?

(E) 7
(F) 14
(G) 28
(H) 70

GO ON TO THE NEXT PAGE

105. Janelle chose an Internet service that charges $16.00 per month plus $0.024 per minute. Declan chose an Internet services that charges $28.00 per month for unlimited usage. At the end of the month, Janelle's and Declan's charges were identical. For how many minutes did Janelle use the Internet service last month?

(A)   50
(B)   60
(C) 100
(D) 500

106.

Number of Cards	Color on Card
6	Blue
5	Red
8	Green
2	Yellow
7	Purple

The cards represented in the above table are mixed together in a box and a card is picked at random. Which color has exactly a 1 in 4 chance of being on the card?

(E) Blue
(F) Red
(G) Green
(H) Purple

107. Ahmed tossed a paper cup in the air 50 times and discovered that it landed on its side 64% of the time. If he tosses the cup in the air 150 more times, what is the total number of times he can expect the cup to land on its side?

(A)   64
(B) 100
(C) 128
(D) 144

108. On a bike trip, Mohammed traveled 72 kilometers in 4 hours, while Harpreet traveled 72 kilometers in 3 hours. How much less was Mohammed's mean speed, in kilometers per hour (kph), than Harpreet's?

(E)   1 kph
(F)   6 kph
(G)   8 kph
(H) 12 kph

109. A ball is selected at random from a box that contains 7 black balls, 12 green balls, and 9 red balls. What is the probability that the ball selected is black?

(A) $\frac{1}{7}$

(B) $\frac{1}{4}$

(C) $\frac{6}{14}$

(D) $\frac{3}{4}$

110. A product survey asked two yes-no questions, Question A and Question B. Of the 600 people who responded to the survey, 430 answered "yes" to Question A, and 380 answered "yes" to Question B. What is the least possible number of these people who could have answered "yes" to both questions?

(E) 170
(F) 210
(G) 220
(H) 380

111. Richard is at least 5 years older than Veronica. Which of the following inequalities gives the relationship between Richard's age (r) and Veronica's age (v)?

(A) $r - v \geq 5$
(B) $r - v \leq 5$
(C) $5 - v \leq r$
(D) $5 - r \leq v$

GO ON TO THE NEXT PAGE

112. A chemical decays in such a way that the amount left at the end of each week is 30% less than the amount at the beginning of that same week. What percent of the original amount is left after two weeks?

(E) 30%
(F) 40%
(G) 49%
(H) 70%

113. Three students stand at the starting line of a running track and begin running laps at the same time. Andy completes 1 lap every 2 minutes, Jazmine completes 1 lap every 4 minutes, and Lev completes 1 lap every 5 minutes. How many laps does Andy complete before all three runners are once again at the starting line at the same time?

(A) 4
(B) 5
(C) 10
(D) 20

114.

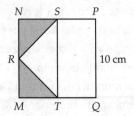

R, S, and T are midpoints of the sides of square $MNPQ$, as shown above. What is the sum of the areas of the shaded triangles?

(E) 12.5 sq cm
(F) 25 sq cm
(G) 50 sq cm
(H) 100 sq cm

ANSWER KEY
Practice Test 2

English Language Arts

1. **B**	16. **G**	31. **A**	46. **F**
2. **E**	17. **C**	32. **H**	47. **B**
3. **D**	18. **F**	33. **C**	48. **G**
4. **G**	19. **D**	34. **H**	49. **C**
5. **D**	20. **F**	35. **D**	50. **E**
6. **F**	21. **A**	36. **G**	51. **D**
7. **C**	22. **G**	37. **D**	52. **H**
8. **F**	23. **A**	38. **G**	53. **B**
9. **A**	24. **G**	39. **A**	54. **G**
10. **H**	25. **D**	40. **G**	55. **B**
11. **D**	26. **E**	41. **C**	56. **G**
12. **F**	27. **D**	42. **G**	57. **B**
13. **C**	28. **H**	43. **B**	
14. **H**	29. **B**	44. **F**	
15. **D**	30. **G**	45. **B**	

Mathematics

58. **19**	73. **C**	88. **H**	103. **C**
59. **120**	74. **H**	89. **D**	104. **E**
60. **−2.6**	75. **B**	90. **E**	105. **D**
61. **51**	76. **G**	91. **A**	106. **H**
62. **400**	77. **B**	92. **G**	107. **C**
63. **A**	78. **F**	93. **B**	108. **F**
64. **E**	79. **C**	94. **H**	109. **B**
65. **C**	80. **E**	95. **A**	110. **F**
66. **F**	81. **D**	96. **F**	111. **A**
67. **A**	82. **G**	97. **C**	112. **G**
68. **F**	83. **A**	98. **H**	113. **C**
69. **C**	84. **G**	99. **A**	114. **F**
70. **G**	85. **B**	100. **F**	
71. **B**	86. **H**	101. **B**	
72. **E**	87. **D**	102. **E**	

ANSWER EXPLANATIONS

English Language Arts

1. **(B)** Examine the pairings of <u>antecedents</u> and **pronouns** below.

(1) Many holidays today can be traced to pagan <u>holidays</u>, **which** were often celebrated to welcome seasonal changes. (2) Christmas, for example, was celebrated as Saturnalia by the <u>Romans</u>, **which** feasted on the surplus from their harvests. (3) Valentine's Day replaced <u>Lupercalia</u>, **which** was celebrated in the spring to welcome the start of a new year. (4) Finally, Halloween took over <u>Lemuria</u>, **which** took place in the fall.

Sentence 1: The correct antecedent to the relative pronoun **which** is <u>holidays</u>.

Sentence 2: The relative pronoun **which** inappropriately replaces the word <u>Romans</u>. Romans refers to people, so the pronoun should be revised to **who**.

Sentence 3: The correct antecedent to the relative pronoun **which** is <u>Lupercalia</u>.

Sentence 4: The correct antecedent to the relative pronoun **which** is <u>Lemuria</u>.

2. **(E)** Sentence 1 contains an independent clause, a modifier, and an independent clause. This is a run-on.

Times Square today isn't what it used to be,	in the past,	it was a very dark, lawless place.
Independent Clause	Modifier	Independent Clause

Correction: Times Square today isn't what it used to be. **In** the past, it was a very dark, lawless place.

Sentence 2 contains a modifier, an independent clause, and an independent clause. This is not a run-on.

In the 1990s	crime rates dropped drastically,	and tourist-friendly establishments sprouted all along the streets.
Modifier	Independent Clause	Independent Clause

Sentence 3 contains an independent clause and a dependent clause. This is not a run-on.

Many credit Mayor Rudy Giuliani,	who decided to make the area more friendly by passing harsh laws and by increasing the number of police officers patrolling the area.
Independent Clause	Dependent Clause

Sentence 4 contains an independent clause and a dependent clause. This is not a run-on.

Critics, however, point to an overall decline in crime rates all across the United States and suggest	that Giuliani's policies were insignificant.
Independent Clause	Dependent Clause

3. **(D)**

Least Precise (cross out)	Most Precise
physical activities	cardio exercises
eating right	limiting caloric intake

4. **(G)**

(E) The killer whale feeds on most marine animals, and some of these are sea birds, cephalopods, turtles, sharks, and fish, but it avoids dolphins and manatees.

Grammatically, the sentence is sound. However, it combines three clauses. Since there is an option with a shorter alternative, this choice should be eliminated.

(F) The killer whale feeds on most marine animals, *of the types to be included being* sea birds, cephalopods, turtles, sharks, and fish, with some avoidance of dolphins and manatees.

The italicized portion of the sentence above is considered an awkward construction.

(G) The killer whale feeds on most marine animals, such as sea birds, cephalopods, turtles, sharks, and fish, but avoids it dolphins and manatees.

This choice best combines the information in one grammatically correct sentence.

(H) The killer whale feeds on most marine animals, sea birds, cephalopods, turtles, sharks, and fish, it avoids dolphins and manatees.

This sentence is a run-on.

5. **(D)** The purpose of this paragraph is to introduce the importance of the gastrointestinal tract. Choice D best serves that purpose.

6. **(F)** Sentence 5 provides more information about the gastrointestinal tract. Choice F combines the additional detail most concisely.

Choices E and H are wrong because they use causal connections.

Choice G is wrong because the transition word *Whereas* is used for comparisons.

7. **(C)** The purpose of this paragraph is to discuss problems in the GI tract. Sentence 13 makes a claim about how people feel about IBS and is therefore not important to this paragraph.

8. **(F)** Sentence 15 provides concrete examples of the *factors* mentioned in sentence 14, so a transition word to introduce examples is most appropriate.

9. **(A)**

Least Precise (cross out)	Most Precise
decide to live a healthy life focus on many habits decide to create a life	create a more routine schedule, eat a healthy diet and smaller more frequent meals, add in some exercise, and get a good amount of sleep

10. **(H)** Connect the phrase *those issues* to *lifestyle-related GI issues* in sentence 16.

11. **(D)** The paragraph discusses the impact of stress on the development of IBS. Choice D introduces that idea.

12. **(F)** The main purpose of this passage is to highlight the importance of the GI tract and to recommend healthy habits. Choice F captures that idea.

13. **(C)** Choice A is wrong because it is a minor detail that helps the reader understand how Europeans were introduced to cacao. Choice B is wrong because the author never makes this point. Choice D is wrong because the passage does not discuss the meaning of cacao.

14. **(H)** The lines *they wrote home about to describe the new world bounty* introduces the series of responses to the drink. Choice E is wrong because it doesn't provide a reason for popularity, just a mention of it. Choice F is wrong because the paragraph focuses primarily on Europeans. Choice G is wrong because there is no comparison.

15. **(D)** Choice A is wrong because the passage states Mesoamericans used it for currency. Choice B is wrong because there is no reference to *the ease* of making money. Choice C is wrong because it is a distortion of the meaning of the line *fortifying drink and the money that grew on trees*.

16. **(G)** The preceding sentence states that the cacao *perplexed early-modern humoral science*. This supports *the mysterious characteristics* in choice G. Choices E and F are wrong because the paragraph doesn't discuss origins or recipes. Choice H is wrong because the author never judges the Spanish colonists and their behaviors.

17. **(C)** The question asks you to find information about cacao's *commercial interests*. This links with *economic exploitation* in paragraph 3.

18. **(F)** The preceding sentence claims that *few Europeans had, however, seen the plant*. The sentence provided indicates that interested individuals had to gain information from an intermediary source, such as clerics and scientists. Choice E is wrong because it distorts the comment about clerics and scientists producing knowledge about cacao. Choice G is wrong because the paragraph mentions the detail about armchair philosophers to make a broader point about the availability of information. Choice H is wrong because there is no discussion of landscape.

19. **(D)** Paragraphs 3 and 4 suggest that cacao generated scientific interest. Choice A is wrong because although cacao was important, the passage never indicates that it is the *most important*. Choice B is wrong because although paragraph 3 suggests that cacao was *addictive*, it never specifies that this is because of *chemicals*. Choice C is wrong because the Spanish colonists' importance is implied in paragraph 2.

20. **(F)** Paragraph 1 discusses how Edison's expectation for the phonograph didn't turn out to be the reason for its popularity. Choice E is wrong because although Edison, an important figure, is introduced, he is not discussed in the rest of the passage. Choice G is wrong because there are no claims that are proven false. Choice H is wrong because the readers' expectations are not justified.

21. **(A)** The paragraph shows how people from a particular place, Spain, showed interest in the phonograph. Choice B is wrong because although reaching many people to enhance popularity logically makes sense, it is not explicitly stated in the text. Choice C is wrong because the paragraph isn't making a comparison. Choice D is wrong because it does not explain why people were *not* interested in business. The paragraph shows that they *were* interested.

22. **(G)** The last sentence of paragraph 4 makes it clear that *most were intended to be temporary.* Choice E is wrong because paragraph 1 notes that the two companies that popularized the phonograph were owned by Edison. Paragraph 2 notes that Edison encouraged his workers to continue marketing the phonograph. Choice F is wrong because paragraph 6 states that the working class, not the upper class, preferred the *café cantantes.* Choice H is wrong because paragraph 4 clearly shows that people could make a judgment on the sound quality.

23. **(A)** The first sentence of paragraph 3 summarizes the claim in choice A, *It was not the thrill of listening to internationally famous performers and speakers that drew audiences to these phonographic sessions.* Choice B is wrong because there is no indication of who was most recorded and whether local musicians were most talented.

24. **(G)** The line *hard to believe that anyone could have mistaken what is in them with live sound* reflects the phrase *not convinced that it was a true representation of reality.* Choice E is wrong because it distorts the phrase *hard to believe.* Choice F is wrong because the opposite is true. Choice H is wrong because the paragraph states that *even accounting for the deterioration of the cylinder,* the quality would still be pretty bad.

25. **(D)** In paragraph 4, the author states *most audiences would not be particularly interested in hearing a particular recording again . . . after they had established that it was, indeed, **true to reality**.*

26. **(E)** The first three sentences in paragraph 5 support choice E. Choice F is wrong because there is no suggestion of competition. Choice G is wrong because Thomas Edison is never said to have created recording studios in Spain. Choice H is wrong because the relationship between the *gabinetes* and Edison's phonograph companies is never made clear.

27. **(D)** Choice D mentions *the global revolution brought over by recording technologies*, which best fits the question stem's *the world began to change its understanding of recorded music.* Choice A is wrong because it only mentions the number of studios opening in San Francisco. Choice B is wrong because it is in reference to the Spanish audiences. Choice C is wrong because it refers to a hypothetical audience that might have been responding to the phonograph.

28. **(H)** Paragraph 6 says that people from different classes enjoyed different types of music. They were also found in *gabinete* catalogues, which suggests that people of different classes would enjoy the music from the *gabinetes.* Choice E is wrong because although *gabinetes* were important, there is no suggestion that they were the *most important.* Choice F is wrong because paragraph 6 states that *flamenco . . . managed to attract a few members of the wealthy.* Choice G is wrong because this is never suggested anywhere in the passage.

29. **(B)** The table presents a breakdown of Thomas Edison's patents. The phonograph is the second highest, which suggests that Edison made investments in the phonograph. Choice A is wrong because although it is an accurate description of the table, it does not support any idea in the passage. Choice C is wrong because the table is about Edison, not the world. Choice D is wrong because the table has no relationship to anything in Spain.

30. **(G)** The image of a person requiring four men for something so simple as chocolate is an absurdity that is supposed to poke fun at Monseigneur. Choice E is wrong because although the statement suggests that he is a demanding man, this doesn't create an oppressive tone. Choice F is wrong because there is no evidence to suggest that Monseigneur is helpless. Choice H is wrong because the phrase *besides the Cook* does not indicate that the Cook is excluded from the activities.

31. **(A)** Each description outlines the detailed requirements that Monseigneur expects for the people serving his chocolate. Choice B is wrong because there is no indication that the men are embarrassed. Choice C is wrong because the author is not promoting any cause. Choice D is wrong because although the paragraph illustrates the complexity of Monseigneur's eating habits, it does not explain the complexities of eating habits in the general sense.

32. **(H)** The sentence here suggests that Monseigneur is concerned more with the needs of entertainers than the country. Choice E is wrong because the entire passage characterizes Monseigneur in a negative light. Choice F is wrong because the passage suggests that the performing arts have an important influence on Monseigneur, not that the performing arts are important. Choice G is wrong because there is no indication that the people of France are happy.

33. **(C)** The sentence from paragraph 4 reflects Monseigneur's attitude: that the world was made for them. Choice A is wrong because the sentence is concerned more with the value Monseigneur places on chocolate. Choice B is wrong because it describes Monseigneur's habits. Choice D is wrong because it describes another character.

34. **(H)** The second sentence makes it clear that he had more servants than his wife; he had 24 and his wife had 6. Choices E, F, or G are not supported anywhere in the passage.

35. **(D)** The idea here is that the beauty of the rooms were *not a sound business*, meaning that things were not the way they appeared. Choice D reflects this idea by suggesting that the way people dressed reinforced the illusion that things were fine. Choice A is wrong because the statement reflects Monseigneur's room. Choice B is wrong because it reflects the importance that Monseigneur places on chocolate. Choice C is wrong because this describes people in Monseigneur's party.

36. **(G)** Paragraph 6 describes *Military officers destitute of military knowledge; naval officers with no idea of a ship; civil officers without a notion of affairs* and others that lack the required expertise. Choice E is wrong because it is a misinterpretation of the last sentence in paragraph 6. Choice F is wrong because there is no reference to resources or the idea that they prevented the guests from improving themselves. Choice H is wrong because the description of the party actually suggests the opposite: that most wanted to be near Monseigneur.

37. **(D)** The line *all totally unfit for their several callings* reflects the description of the guests that suggest that they all lack integrity and substance. Choice A is wrong because although there may be a diversity of characters at the party, the description is not intended to emphasize the variety of characters. Choice B is wrong because there is no comparison between these people in the paragraph. Choice C is wrong because the descriptions serve to undercut the character of the men, not to highlight their attempts to look important.

38. **(G)** The sentence suggests that Monseigneur's court is all about appearances and that the party is intended to create the image that things are not as they appear. This shows the narrator's negative attitude toward Monseigneur. Choice E is wrong because there is no comparison between food and clothes. Choice F is wrong because the passage is less an analysis than it is a description. Choice H is wrong because the narrator is not trying to persuade the reader to reform anything in society.

39. **(A)** The last sentence *And who among the company at the Monseigneur's reception . . . could possibly doubt that a system rooted in a frizzled hangman . . . would see the very stars out* suggests that the people could not foresee a problem in the future. Choice B is wrong because the paragraph does not reveal anything about the Monseigneur's imagination. Choice C is wrong because the paragraph introduces what the people did not expect, not what they expected. Choice D is wrong because the paragraph reveals more about the guests' assumptions rather than the insights about Monseigneur.

40. **(G)** The phrase *caused the doors . . . to be thrown open* illustrates the power that Monseigneur commands in the room. Choice E is wrong because there is no indication that the reader should sympathize with the court. Choice F is wrong because nothing in the passage supports the idea that Monseigneur is kind. Choice H is wrong because it is a misinterpretation of the wording in the first sentence.

41. **(C)** The phrase serves to heighten the following phrase *a year ago* to suggest a time far away.

42. **(G)** In each repetition, the speaker's emotions get more intense. The first and second create a tender tone, the third creates an ominous tone, and the fourth a maniacal tone. Choice E is wrong because power is never suggested. Choice F is wrong because the phrase refers to only one kingdom. Choice H is wrong because although it may suggest it, the phrase is certainly not used to emphasize the fact that Annabel is of aristocratic lineage.

43. **(B)** The repetition of the word *love* in line 9 serves to emphasize their love. The phrase in line 12, *Coveted her and me*, also serves to emphasize the speaker's conviction that their love was so strong that the seraphs of Heaven were jealous of the speaker's relationship with Annabel. Choice A distorts the word *Heaven*. There is no religious connotation associated with it. Choice C is wrong because the speaker does not reveal any fear. Choice D is wrong because the speaker finds the event neither enchanting nor dreamlike.

44. **(F)** Line 19 says that the kinsmen wanted to *shut her up in a sepulchre*. This suggests that Annabel was not properly buried. Choice E is wrong because the kinsmen are not dead. Choice G is wrong because the speaker clearly still believes he is in love with Annabel. Choice H is wrong because the phrase *kingdom by the sea* never suggests that Annabel was carried to the sea.

45. **(B)** The phrase *in Heaven* connects back to the *seraphs in Heaven* of line 11. The winged seraphs are the angels.

46. **(F)** Line 23, *that was the reason*, supports choice F. Choice E is wrong because there is no attempt at humor. Choice G is wrong because this is not a warning. Choice H is wrong because he speaker never asks questions.

47. **(B)** In line 21, the speaker mentions the angels, which are the seraphs. These angels were envious and brought the wind that killed Annabel.

48. **(G)** The phrase *dissever* means to divide or cut. The phrase *can ever dissever my soul from the soul of the beautiful Annabel Lee* suggests that nothing can cut the connection between his soul and her soul.

49. **(C)** The details about Pliny serve to support the sentence preceding it. Choices A and B are wrong because they suggest extremes. Nowhere in the passage does it suggest that Pliny's description is the most or the least credible. Choice D is wrong because it is a minor detail that builds on the previous sentence.

50. **(E)** Two sentences support choice E: *Nobody except the hunters who killed. . .* and *Walrus hides were carted off to the . . . .* Choice F is wrong because it is a misinterpretation of the first sentence of paragraph 2. The first sentence says that the *walrus-like creatures began to appear in natural histories,* not that the popularity of the goods were recorded in those histories. Choice G is wrong because there is no mention of walrus extinctions. Choice H is wrong because it attributes knowledge as the cause for increased hunting. There is no such causation discussed.

51. **(D)** Paragraph 3 says that walrus tusks were presented as other things, such as *unicorn horns.* Choice A is wrong because prices are never mentioned in comparison to those of narwhals or elephant bones. Choice B is wrong because the paragraph never discusses what customers demanded. In fact, they were not even aware of what was in unicorn horns. Choice C is wrong because paragraph 2 suggests that walrus products were included in common household items and not exclusively luxury products.

52. **(H)** Choices E, F, and G all refer to physical dismantling or reassembling of the walrus. Choice H refers to the names and depictions, a metaphorical dismantling.

53. **(B)** The first sentence of paragraph 5 introduces the existence of first-hand accounts. The last sentence indicates that intellectuals preferred other types of accounts that contained images of walruses as "monsters." These two sentences suggest that the scholarly accounts were not very accurate. Choices A and C are wrong because the author suggests that the scholarly accounts were inferior to the first-hand accounts. Choice D is wrong because the paragraph suggests the opposite.

54. **(G)** *Ominous* suggests that something bad is going to happen. *Toothsome* means tasty. Put together, the words *ominous* and *toothsome* suggest that the walrus might have been eaten. Therefore, the idea that the walrus might have represented something more than an intellectual interest best fits. Choice E is wrong because although it may be true, the sentence does not suggest that impression. Choice F is wrong because the word *ominous* applies to the walrus not Vorstius.

55. **(B)** The second sentence supports this choice. Choice A is wrong because there is no discussion of what most people believed. Choice C is wrong because the second sentence says that people's ideas were not replaced. Choice D is wrong because the word *mystery* misrepresents how the author uses the word *mysterious.* The author means that the walrus remained mysterious for the people of the 16th century.

56. **(G)** Paragraph 4 suggests that there are several *images . . . broken up and scattered into other depictions.* This best supports choice G. None of the other answer choices are supported.

57. **(B)** The pronoun *These* refers to the images of the walrus made up *by scholars who constructed their very own walrus-creatures.* Choice A is wrong because the previous sentence says it *may or may not have been based on walruses*, which means that the account may not have been fictional. Choices C and D are wrong because they refer to a factual description of Dr. Vorstius's interaction with the walrus.

Mathematics

58. **(19)** Multiply both sides of the equation by 14 to get $229 - x = 15 \times 14$. So $229 - x = 210$, and $x = 19$. A guess-and-check approach could also be applied. Notice that the numerator of $\frac{229 - x}{14}$ must be an integer, so try some values of x that make $229 - x$ a multiple of 14 (like 140, 280, etc.) and see what happens.

59. **(120)** This is a standard permutation problem. There are five choices for the first digit, four choices for the second digit, three choices for the third digit, and then two choices for the fourth digit. By the FCP, the total number of options is thus $5 \times 4 \times 3 \times 2 = 120$. Notice this is the same answer you would get if you were making five-digit numbers from these five digits, because once you choose the first four digits, you have only one choice for the fifth!

60. **(−2.6)** Simplify each absolute value expression by working from the inside out:

$$\left|(-7) - (-2) + 2.8\right| = \left|(-7) + 2 + 2.8\right| = \left|(-7) + 4.8\right| = \left|-2.2\right|$$

and

$$\left|2 - 6.8\right| = \left|-4.8\right|$$

Now take the absolute value of each and subtract:

$$\left|(-7) - (-2) + 2.8\right| - \left|2 - 6.8\right| =$$
$$\left|-2.2\right| - \left|-4.8\right| =$$
$$2.2 - 4.8 = -2.6$$

61. **(51)** Notice the angle vertical to the angle with measure $x°$ combines with the other three given angles to form a straight line with measure 180°. And since vertical angles are congruent, we can write the equation $29° + 46° + x° + 54° = 180°$. Solving for x yields $x = 51°$.

62. **(400)** Let N be the number of pages in the workbook. Since 72 is 18% of N, we can write the equation $0.18 \times N = 72$ and solve for N:

$$N = \frac{72}{0.18} = \frac{7200}{18} = \frac{72 \times 100}{18} = \frac{72}{18} \times 100 = 4 \times 100 = 400$$

A similar approach starts with the proportion $\frac{72}{N} = \frac{18}{100}$. Also, notice that if 18% of the book is 72 pages, then 1% of the book is $\frac{72}{18} = 4$ pages, which means 100% of the book would be 400 pages.

63. **(A)** Substitute $y = 6$ into the equation to get $\frac{72}{6} = 4x$, so $12 = 4x$ and $x = 3$. Note that $\frac{72}{6} = 12$ is an answer choice, so be careful not to choose the first number you see as the answer!

64. **(E)** Recall that probability is favorable outcomes divided by total outcomes. There are 32 favorable outcomes (numbers of pies ordered) and $28 + 32 + 44 + 56 = 160$ total outcomes (total number of desserts ordered). The desired probability is thus $\frac{32}{160} = \frac{16}{80} = \frac{8}{40} = \frac{1}{5}$, and $\frac{1}{5}$ is 20%.

65. **(C)** Since eight hours elapsed from 11:00 A.M. to 7:00 P.M., the temperature dropped $8 \times 3 = 24$ degrees, and $10 - 24 = -14$. Be careful to avoid the "off by 1" error of calculating the temperature after 7 hours or 9 hours, which are both answer choices. To be sure, you can make a simple chart for each hour between 11 A.M. and 7 P.M. and decrease the temperature 3 degrees each step.

66. **(F)** We know that the position of M plus the length of MN is the position of N. This makes the position of M equal to $1\frac{1}{3} - 4\frac{5}{6}$. To compute this, first convert both numbers to "improper fractions," then find a common denominator:

$$1\frac{1}{3} - 4\frac{5}{6} = \frac{4}{3} - \frac{29}{6}$$
$$= \frac{8}{6} - \frac{29}{6}$$
$$= -\frac{21}{6}$$

Now reduce to find the final answer:

$$-\frac{21}{6} = -\frac{7}{2} = -3\frac{1}{2}$$

Practice your arithmetic with fractions! **Note:** Since M is left of N on the number line, its coordinate must be less than N's. This immediately eliminates two of the answer choices.

67. **(A)** The LCM of three numbers is the smallest number that has each number as a factor. Notice that all three numbers are factors of 18, and since 18 is the smallest answer choice, it must be the correct answer. **Remember:** A number is a factor of itself!

68. **(F)** This is a good problem to "make a wish": What values of X, Y, Z, W, and V make every expression equal to 1? Notice by making $X = \frac{1}{2}$, $Y = \frac{1}{3}$, $Z = 5$, $W = -2$, and $V = 2$, our equation becomes $1 = 1 = 1 = 1 = 1 > 0$, and Z has the greatest value.

69. **(C)** Choosing toppings here is the special case of choosing a pair of objects. Since there are 5 toppings to choose from, there are $\frac{5 \times 4}{2} = 10$ ways to choose a pair of those toppings. We also have three choices of size, so altogether there are $3 \times 10 = 30$ different pizzas.

70. **(G)** The cost of the cloth alone is $10.00, since one yard costs $8.00 and $\frac{1}{4}$ of a yard costs $2. The 8% tax is $0.08 \times 10 = 0.8$, or 80 cents, making the total cost $10 + \$0.80 = \$10.80$. We could also compute the full price directly as $1.08 \times 10 = 10.80$. **Note:** Be careful not to interpret 8% as 0.8; 8% is 0.08!

71. **(B)** The answer can be found by solving the proportion $\frac{4}{108} = \frac{x}{405}$ for x, the number of cans of paint needed to paint 405 square feet of wall. Alternately, notice that 1 can of paint covers $\frac{108}{4} = 27$ square feet, so to cover 405 square feet, she would need $\frac{405}{27} = \frac{135}{9} = \frac{45}{3} = 15$ cans.

72. **(E)** Solve the inequality for x. Subtract 10 from both sides to get $3x \leq 87$, and then divide both sides by 3 to get $x \leq 29$. There are 14 positive even numbers less than or equal to 29, namely: 2, 4, 6 ... 28. A quick way to count them is to notice that the numbers are $2 \times 1, 2 \times 2, 2 \times 3, \ldots 2 \times 14$, so there are as many of these numbers as there are numbers from 1 to 14, which is 14. **Note:** The word *even* here is critical! There are 29 positive integers less than or equal to 29, and 29 is one of the answer choices.

73. **(C)** Solve the proportion $\frac{25}{200} = \frac{x}{300}$ to get $x = \frac{3}{2} \times 25 = \frac{75}{2} = 37.5$, then round to get the correct answer. Or notice that 100 customers require 12.5 dozen eggs, so 300 customers require $3 \times 12.5 = 37.5$ dozen eggs.

74. **(H)** The answer is the difference in areas of the two plates. The formula for the area of a circle is $A = \pi r^2$. This means the area of the larger plate is $\pi \times 20^2 = 400\pi$. The formula for the circumference of a circle is $C = 2\pi r$, and since the circumference of the smaller circle is 10π, it has a radius of 5 centimeters, so its area is $\pi \times 5^2 = 25\pi$. The answer is thus $400\pi - 25\pi = 375\pi$. **Note:** The radius of one circle is given, but the circumference of the other is given. Always read the question carefully!

75. **(B)** The mean, or average, of n numbers is the sum of the n numbers divided by n. Andre scored an average of 12 points per game is his first 4 games, which means he scored 48 total points in those first 4 games, since $\frac{48}{4} = 12$. So he scored $48 + 32 = 80$ points in his first 5 games, making his average over those 5 games $\frac{80}{5} = 16$.

76. **(G)** There are $3 + 5 = 8$ favorable outcomes (non-apple juices) and $6 + 3 + 5 = 14$ total outcomes, for a probability of $\frac{8}{14} = \frac{4}{7}$. **Note:** Watch out for the word *not* in probability problems! If you solved the problem without the *not*, the answer is $\frac{3}{7}$, which is one of the choices.

77. **(B)** Substitute $x = 6$ and $y = -9$ into the expression $x(2x + y)$ to get the following:

$$6(2 \times 6 + (-9)) =$$

$$6(12 - 9) =$$

$$6(3) = 18$$

78. **(F)** Since the store is buying $\frac{1}{4}$ page and $\frac{1}{2}$ page ads in equal numbers, you can think of the store as simply buying some number of $\frac{1}{4} + \frac{1}{2} = \frac{3}{4}$ page ads, each for $200 + \$350 = \$550$. Since $10 \times \$550 = \$5,500$, this means the store bought ten $\frac{3}{4}$ page ads, and $10 \times \frac{3}{4} = \frac{30}{4} = \frac{15}{2} = 7\frac{1}{2}$ pages.

79. **(C)** Trying each answer is a good strategy here. Notice that since $8 \times 12 = 96$, we have $80 \times 0.12 = 9.60$. Four more sheets of paper would cost $\$0.48$, so 84 sheets would cost $\$9.60 + \$0.48 = \$10.08$, and 85 sheets would cost $\$10.20$. You could also solve the inequality $0.12x < 10.10$ for x, and get that $x < 84\frac{1}{6}$.

80. **(E)** In a parallelogram, opposite angles are congruent; this makes $m\angle ECD = 85°$. In a triangle, the measures of the angles sum to $180°$, so $m\angle DEC + m\angle ECD + m\angle CDE = 180°$. Substituting in the known angle measures gives us $55° + 85° + m\angle CDE = 180°$, which makes $m\angle CDE = 40°$. Alternately, $\angle ACD$ is supplementary to $\angle DAB$, so $m\angle ACD = 180° - 85° = 95°$. And since $\angle ADE$ and $\angle CED$ are alternate interior angles, they are congruent.

$$m\angle CDE = m\angle ADC - m\angle ADE$$
$$= m\angle ADC - m\angle DEC$$
$$= 95° - 55°$$
$$= 40°$$

81. **(D)** Since nickel and copper are in a $25 : 75$ ratio, this means that 25% of the 5 g coin is nickel, and $0.25 \times 5\,\text{g} = 1.25\,\text{g}$.

82. **(G)** If the length of $YZ = \frac{4}{5}XY$, then $YZ = \frac{4}{5}XY = \frac{4}{5} \times 20 = 16$. Since Y is between X and Z, we know $XZ = XY + YZ$, so $XZ = 20 + 16 = 36$ centimeters. **Note:** The hardest part of this problem is decoding the various lengths and relationships. Make sure you draw a diagram!

83. **(A)** Since the drum is $\frac{2}{3}$ full, an additional $\frac{1}{3}$ is needed to fill it. One-third of 5,130 liters is $\frac{5,130}{3} = 1,710$ liters. Since 1,000 liters is equal to 1 kiloliter, 1,710 liters is equal to 1.710 kiloliters. **Note:** The fact that the drum is cylindrical is irrelevant in this problem! Don't waste time thinking about circles or cylinders here.

84. **(G)** If Clara was 17 three years ago, she is 20 now, which makes Albert $3 \times 20 = 60$ now. Five years ago he was 55. You can also simply check each possible answer. First, add 5 to the answer choice to find Albert's age right now, then divide by 3 to find Clara's age right now, then subtract 3 to find Clara's age three years ago. Only one of the answers will produce 17 through this process, and that is the correct answer.

85. **(B)** Since 10.8 flacks and 4.5 werbs both equal a krutz, then 10.8 flacks = 4.5 werbs. This means 1 werb $= \frac{10.8}{4.5}$ flacks. Long division gives you $\frac{10.8}{4.5} = 2.4$, or you can just notice that $\frac{10.8}{4.5}$ is approximately 2, and only one answer choice is approximately 2. **Note:** Remember to always be estimating! It can save you time.

86. **(H)** A simple approach to this problem is to "make a wish": Since w is an odd integer, let $w = 7$. Now see which one of the answer choices is an even integer: not choice E, since $w + 2 = 7 + 2 = 9$; not choice F, since $2w + 3 = 2 \times 7 + 3 = 14 + 3 = 17$; not choice G, since $2w + 5 = 2 \times 7 + 5 = 14 + 5 = 19$; but $w - 3 = 7 - 3 = 4$ is even, so choice H is the correct answer.

87. **(D)** One-third of 42 is 14, so two-thirds of 42 is 28. This means there are $28 + 3 = 31$ books currently on the shelf.

88. **(H)** Use the distributive property to simplify the expression:

$$4(5 - 3x) - (7 - x) = 20 - 12x - 7 + x$$
$$= 13 - 11x$$

Note: Be very careful with negative signs and parentheses! This is one of the most common algebraic mistakes, so be prepared for it.

89. **(D)** *At most* 1 pet means 0 or 1 pets. Since $13 + 17 = 30$ students have 0 or 1 pets, and there are $13 + 17 + 7 + 3 = 40$ total students, the probability that a student who participated in the survey has at most 1 pet is $\frac{30}{40} = \frac{3}{4}$. **Note:** Watch out for phrases like *at most* and *at least*. If you had read this question as "students who have 1 pet," the answer to that question, $\frac{17}{40}$, is one of the choices.

90. **(E)** Let A be the amount of water in the tank. We can write the two equations $n + 12 = 0.60A$ and $n + 18 = 0.75A$, and then solve this system of equations to find that $6 = 0.15A$. So $A = \frac{6}{0.15} = \frac{600}{15} = 40$. When 60% full, there will be $0.60 \times 40 = 24$ liters in the tank, and since $n + 12 = 0.60A$, we get $n + 12 = 24$, and so $n = 12$.

91. **(A)** Plug in 10 for x in the expression and evaluate:

$$2(10)^3 + 6(10)^2 + (10) + 3 + \frac{1}{(10)^2} =$$

$$2000 + 600 + 10 + 3 + \frac{1}{100} = 2613.01$$

Note: Watch out for fraction to decimal conversions. If you had erroneously written 0.1 for $\frac{1}{(10)^2}$, your incorrect answer of 2,613.1 would be one of the choices.

92. **(G)** Substituting $y = 1$ yields the compound inequality $x - 3 \leq 1 \leq 2x + 5$, which is equivalent to the two inequalities $x - 3 \leq 1$ and $1 \leq 2x + 5$ (note the importance of the word *and* here, not *or*). Simplifying these two inequalities yields $x \leq 4$ and $-2 \leq x$. The numbers that are both less than or equal to 4 and greater than or equal to -2 are represented graphically by choice G. Alternately, you could test values in the given ranges of the answer choices. For example, testing $x = -3$ from choice H yields $-3 - 3 \leq 1 \leq 2(-3) + 5$, which simplifies to $-4 \leq 1 \leq -1$. This is false, so choice H cannot be the correct answer.

93. **(B)** Let X be the amount the Green's earned last year: $\frac{5}{8} = \frac{\$32,400}{X}$. Then cross-multiply and solve for x:

$$\frac{5}{8} = \frac{\$32,400}{X}$$
$$X = \frac{8}{5} \times \$32,400$$
$$= 8 \times \frac{\$32,400}{5}$$
$$= 8 \times \$6,480$$
$$= \$51,840$$

You could also solve this by estimating. Spending $5 out of every $8 on planned expenses means roughly around half of their income is spent on planned expenses. The only answer choice for which half is roughly $32,400 is choice B.

94. **(H)** Notice that the ratio of red to blue to green marbles is $14 : 9 : 2$. As is often the case in these problems, the sum of the marbles in the ratio is a convenient number. Here, $14 + 9 + 2 = 25$, and 25 is one-third of 75, the total number of marbles in the bag. So we can triple the ratio to find the exact number of marbles of each color. There will be 42 red, 27 blue, and 6 green. Removing 2 blue and adding 2 green means there will now be 42 red, 25 blue, and 8 green, making the ratio of red to green marbles $\frac{42}{8} = \frac{21}{4}$, or $21 : 4$. **Note:** Don't fall for the trap of subtracting 2 blue and adding 2 green to the ratio $14 : 9 : 2$. The marbles are removed and added to the total number of marbles in the jar.

95. **(A)** The area of a triangle is $\frac{1}{2}bh$, where b is the length of the base and h is the height. The trick in this problem is to identify the vertical segment of length $m - n$ as the base, which makes the height the horizontal distance of 4. So the area of the triangle is $\frac{1}{2}(m - n)4 = 2(m - n)$.

96. **(F)** Let s be the side length of the square base of the box. This makes the height of the box $2s$, and thus the volume of the box is $s \times s \times 2s = 2s^3$. Then $2s^3 = 128$, and $s^3 = 64$, therefore $s = 4$. Since the height is $2s$, this is 8. **Note:** Always make sure you answer the question that was asked! The question is not asking for s, but the value of s is an answer choice.

97. **(C)** Multiply both sides of the equation $\frac{21}{28} = \frac{p}{7}$ by 7 to solve.

$$p = 7 \times \frac{21}{28}$$
$$= \frac{7}{28} \times 21$$
$$= \frac{1}{4} \times 21$$
$$= \frac{21}{4}$$

98. **(H)** The midpoint of two points on the number line is the average of their coordinates. Thus, the midpoint of PQ is $\frac{(-5) + (-1)}{2} = \frac{-6}{2} = -3$, and the midpoint of RS is $\frac{0 + 4}{2} = \frac{4}{2} = 2$. The distance from -3 to 2 is 5 units.

99. **(A)** There are 1,000 milliliters in 1 liter. But 1 liter is also 1,000 cubic centimeters. This means 1,000 milliliters is equal to 1,000 cubic centimeters, and so 1 cubic centimeter is equal to 1 cubic milliliter.

100. **(F)** The four evenly spaced hatch marks on the number line divide MT into five equal parts.

$$MT = \frac{3}{8} - \left(-\frac{1}{4}\right)$$
$$= \frac{3}{8} + \frac{1}{4}$$
$$= \frac{3}{8} + \frac{2}{8}$$
$$= \frac{5}{8}$$

Each of the five equal parts has length one-fifth of $\frac{5}{8}$, which is $\frac{1}{5} \times \frac{5}{8} = \frac{1}{8}$. R is therefore two-eighths to the right of M, so you can solve for the coordinate as follows:

$$-\frac{1}{4} + \frac{1}{8} + \frac{1}{8} =$$
$$-\frac{1}{4} + \frac{2}{8} =$$
$$-\frac{1}{4} + \frac{1}{4} = 0$$

101. **(B)** In a circle, all radii are the same length. In this diagram, that means $2x + 1 = y + x$, which makes $y = x + 1$. **Note:** Sometimes elements of the diagram are meant to distract you. Here, the right triangle has nothing to do with finding the value of x!

102. **(E)** Since a total of $21 + 41 + 33 + 5 = 100$ families were surveyed, the percentage of families with 1 cat is 41% and the percentage of families with 2 cats is 33%. The difference is $41\% - 33\% = 8\%$.

103. **(C)** The 50 cars can be divided into three disjointed groups, as illustrated in the following Venn diagram:

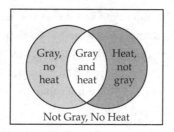

There are 5 gray cars with heated seats, which means there are $18 - 5 = 13$ gray cars without heated seats, and $10 - 5 = 5$ non-gray cars with heated seats. This accounts for $13 + 5 + 5 = 23$ of the total cars, which means the other $50 - 23 = 27$ cars are not gray and do not have heated seats. This makes the probability of a selecting a car that is not gray and does have heated seats $\frac{27}{50}$.

104. **(E)** The decimal number 0.14 is *fourteen hundredths*, which means $0.14 = \frac{14}{100}$. We can reduce this to $\frac{14}{100} = \frac{7}{50}$.

105. **(D)** If Janelle's monthly charges totaled $28.00, then she used $28 − $16 = $12 worth of minutes. If m is the total number of minutes she used, then $0.024 \times m = 12$. Solve for m:

$$m = \frac{12}{0.024}$$
$$= \frac{12{,}000}{24}$$
$$= \frac{12 \times 1{,}000}{12 \times 2}$$
$$= \frac{1{,}000}{2}$$
$$= 500$$

You could also answer this questions using guessing and checking and estimating. Notice that at \$0.024 per minute, 100 minutes would cost \$2.40. The only reasonable answer choice is 500 minutes.

106. **(H)** There are $6 + 5 + 8 + 2 + 7 = 28$ total cards in the box. Since $\frac{1}{4}$ of 28 is 7, we are looking for the color with exactly 7 cards, namely purple.

107. **(C)** If the cup lands on its side 64% of the time, then in 100 tosses the cup would land on its side 64 times. Ahmed tosses the cup a total of 200 times, so the cup lands on its side $2 \times 64 = 128$ times.

108. **(F)** Mohammed's mean speed is $\frac{72}{4} = 18$ km/hour, and Harpreet's mean speed is $\frac{72}{3} = 24$ km/hour. So Mohammed's mean speed is $24 - 18 = 6$ km/hour less than Harpreet's.

109. **(B)** There are $7 + 12 + 9 = 28$ total balls. Since 7 are black, the desired probability is $\frac{7}{28} = \frac{1}{4}$.

110. **(F)** Notice that the sum of the number of people who said yes to A and the number of people who said yes to B is $430 + 380 = 810$. This is more than 600, the total number of people asked, because those who said yes to both are double-counted in this calculation. Thus, at least $810 - 600 = 210$ people would have to have said yes to both. This is an example of the principle of inclusion/exclusion, covered in the chapter on probability.

111. **(A)** If Richard were 5 years older than Veronica, we would write $r = v + 5$. Since Richard is *at least* 5 years older than Veronica, we rewrite this as an inequality: $r \geq v + 5$, which is equivalent to $r - v \geq 5$. You can also test the various answer choices to find the correct answer. Notice that (B), (C), and (D) are all true if Richard and Veronica are both, say, 20: that is, if $r = v = 20$. Since Richard is not 5 years older than Veronica in this case, these choices can't model the relationship between their ages.

112. **(G)** Imagine starting with 100 g of the chemical. After one week, 30%, or 30 g, decays, and that leaves 70 g of the chemical. After the second week, 30% more decays, but this is 30% of the 70 g that remains. Since 30% of 70 is $0.30 \times 70 = 21$, another 21 g is lost, so the amount remaining after two weeks is $70 - 21 = 49$ g. **Note:** Don't make the mistake of thinking that losing 30% over two weeks is a loss of 60%! To quickly see how this can't make sense, notice that if you lost 30% every three weeks, by this reasoning you would lose 120% in four weeks, which is more than you have to lose!

113. **(C)** The runners will all be at the starting line at the same time at every common multiple of 2 minutes, 4 minutes, and 5 minutes. The least common multiple of 2, 4, and 5 is 20, which means they will all be at the starting line again after 20 minutes. At this point, Andy will have run 10 laps. A chart showing each runner's progress over time could also be used here.

114. **(F)** Because T, R, and S are midpoints, we know that $NS = NR = MR = MT = 5$. Notice that the shaded triangles RNS and RMT are congruent right triangles, which means the area of each shaded triangle is $\frac{1}{2} \times 5 \times 5 = \frac{25}{2}$. Since there are two shaded triangles, their total area is $2 \times \frac{25}{2} = 25$ sq cm. Alternately, notice that you could slide the two shaded triangles together to make a square that occupies one-fourth of the larger square with side length of 10 cm. The area of the larger square is 100 sq cm, and one-fourth of that is 25 sq cm. Also notice that the area of rectangle $MNST$ is half the area of square $MNPQ$, so it has an area of 50 sq cm. Since the shaded regions are contained in rectangle $MNST$, their area must be less than 50 sq cm, eliminating answer choices G and H.

ANSWER SHEET
Practice Test 3

Part I: English Language Arts

1. Ⓐ Ⓑ Ⓒ Ⓓ	16. Ⓔ Ⓕ Ⓖ Ⓗ	31. Ⓐ Ⓑ Ⓒ Ⓓ	46. Ⓔ Ⓕ Ⓖ Ⓗ
2. Ⓔ Ⓕ Ⓖ Ⓗ	17. Ⓐ Ⓑ Ⓒ Ⓓ	32. Ⓔ Ⓕ Ⓖ Ⓗ	47. Ⓐ Ⓑ Ⓒ Ⓓ
3. Ⓐ Ⓑ Ⓒ Ⓓ	18. Ⓔ Ⓕ Ⓖ Ⓗ	33. Ⓐ Ⓑ Ⓒ Ⓓ	48. Ⓔ Ⓕ Ⓖ Ⓗ
4. Ⓔ Ⓕ Ⓖ Ⓗ	19. Ⓐ Ⓑ Ⓒ Ⓓ	34. Ⓔ Ⓕ Ⓖ Ⓗ	49. Ⓐ Ⓑ Ⓒ Ⓓ
5. Ⓐ Ⓑ Ⓒ Ⓓ	20. Ⓔ Ⓕ Ⓖ Ⓗ	35. Ⓐ Ⓑ Ⓒ Ⓓ	50. Ⓔ Ⓕ Ⓖ Ⓗ
6. Ⓔ Ⓕ Ⓖ Ⓗ	21. Ⓐ Ⓑ Ⓒ Ⓓ	36. Ⓔ Ⓕ Ⓖ Ⓗ	51. Ⓐ Ⓑ Ⓒ Ⓓ
7. Ⓐ Ⓑ Ⓒ Ⓓ	22. Ⓔ Ⓕ Ⓖ Ⓗ	37. Ⓐ Ⓑ Ⓒ Ⓓ	52. Ⓔ Ⓕ Ⓖ Ⓗ
8. Ⓔ Ⓕ Ⓖ Ⓗ	23. Ⓐ Ⓑ Ⓒ Ⓓ	38. Ⓔ Ⓕ Ⓖ Ⓗ	53. Ⓐ Ⓑ Ⓒ Ⓓ
9. Ⓐ Ⓑ Ⓒ Ⓓ	24. Ⓔ Ⓕ Ⓖ Ⓗ	39. Ⓐ Ⓑ Ⓒ Ⓓ	54. Ⓔ Ⓕ Ⓖ Ⓗ
10. Ⓔ Ⓕ Ⓖ Ⓗ	25. Ⓐ Ⓑ Ⓒ Ⓓ	40. Ⓔ Ⓕ Ⓖ Ⓗ	55. Ⓐ Ⓑ Ⓒ Ⓓ
11. Ⓐ Ⓑ Ⓒ Ⓓ	26. Ⓔ Ⓕ Ⓖ Ⓗ	41. Ⓐ Ⓑ Ⓒ Ⓓ	56. Ⓔ Ⓕ Ⓖ Ⓗ
12. Ⓔ Ⓕ Ⓖ Ⓗ	27. Ⓐ Ⓑ Ⓒ Ⓓ	42. Ⓔ Ⓕ Ⓖ Ⓗ	57. Ⓐ Ⓑ Ⓒ Ⓓ
13. Ⓐ Ⓑ Ⓒ Ⓓ	28. Ⓔ Ⓕ Ⓖ Ⓗ	43. Ⓐ Ⓑ Ⓒ Ⓓ	
14. Ⓔ Ⓕ Ⓖ Ⓗ	29. Ⓐ Ⓑ Ⓒ Ⓓ	44. Ⓔ Ⓕ Ⓖ Ⓗ	
15. Ⓐ Ⓑ Ⓒ Ⓓ	30. Ⓔ Ⓕ Ⓖ Ⓗ	45. Ⓐ Ⓑ Ⓒ Ⓓ	

ANSWER SHEET
Practice Test 3

Part II: Mathematics

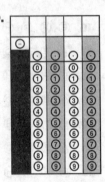

58. 59. 60.

61. 62.

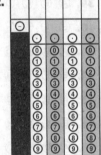

63. Ⓐ Ⓑ Ⓒ Ⓓ
64. Ⓔ Ⓕ Ⓖ Ⓗ
65. Ⓐ Ⓑ Ⓒ Ⓓ
66. Ⓔ Ⓕ Ⓖ Ⓗ
67. Ⓐ Ⓑ Ⓒ Ⓓ
68. Ⓔ Ⓕ Ⓖ Ⓗ
69. Ⓐ Ⓑ Ⓒ Ⓓ
70. Ⓔ Ⓕ Ⓖ Ⓗ
71. Ⓐ Ⓑ Ⓒ Ⓓ
72. Ⓔ Ⓕ Ⓖ Ⓗ
73. Ⓐ Ⓑ Ⓒ Ⓓ
74. Ⓔ Ⓕ Ⓖ Ⓗ
75. Ⓐ Ⓑ Ⓒ Ⓓ

76. Ⓔ Ⓕ Ⓖ Ⓗ
77. Ⓐ Ⓑ Ⓒ Ⓓ
78. Ⓔ Ⓕ Ⓖ Ⓗ
79. Ⓐ Ⓑ Ⓒ Ⓓ
80. Ⓔ Ⓕ Ⓖ Ⓗ
81. Ⓐ Ⓑ Ⓒ Ⓓ
82. Ⓔ Ⓕ Ⓖ Ⓗ
83. Ⓐ Ⓑ Ⓒ Ⓓ
84. Ⓔ Ⓕ Ⓖ Ⓗ
85. Ⓐ Ⓑ Ⓒ Ⓓ
86. Ⓔ Ⓕ Ⓖ Ⓗ
87. Ⓐ Ⓑ Ⓒ Ⓓ
88. Ⓔ Ⓕ Ⓖ Ⓗ

89. Ⓐ Ⓑ Ⓒ Ⓓ
90. Ⓔ Ⓕ Ⓖ Ⓗ
91. Ⓐ Ⓑ Ⓒ Ⓓ
92. Ⓔ Ⓕ Ⓖ Ⓗ
93. Ⓐ Ⓑ Ⓒ Ⓓ
94. Ⓔ Ⓕ Ⓖ Ⓗ
95. Ⓐ Ⓑ Ⓒ Ⓓ
96. Ⓔ Ⓕ Ⓖ Ⓗ
97. Ⓐ Ⓑ Ⓒ Ⓓ
98. Ⓔ Ⓕ Ⓖ Ⓗ
99. Ⓐ Ⓑ Ⓒ Ⓓ
100. Ⓔ Ⓕ Ⓖ Ⓗ
101. Ⓐ Ⓑ Ⓒ Ⓓ

102. Ⓔ Ⓕ Ⓖ Ⓗ
103. Ⓐ Ⓑ Ⓒ Ⓓ
104. Ⓔ Ⓕ Ⓖ Ⓗ
105. Ⓐ Ⓑ Ⓒ Ⓓ
106. Ⓔ Ⓕ Ⓖ Ⓗ
107. Ⓐ Ⓑ Ⓒ Ⓓ
108. Ⓔ Ⓕ Ⓖ Ⓗ
109. Ⓐ Ⓑ Ⓒ Ⓓ
110. Ⓔ Ⓕ Ⓖ Ⓗ
111. Ⓐ Ⓑ Ⓒ Ⓓ
112. Ⓔ Ⓕ Ⓖ Ⓗ
113. Ⓐ Ⓑ Ⓒ Ⓓ
114. Ⓔ Ⓕ Ⓖ Ⓗ

Practice Test 3

PART 1—ENGLISH LANGUAGE ARTS

SUGGESTED TIME: 90 MINUTES, 57 QUESTIONS

Revising/Editing

QUESTIONS 1–10

> **IMPORTANT NOTE:** The Revising/Editing section (Question 1–10) is in two parts: Part A and Part B.

REVISING/EDITING PART A

> **Directions:** Read and answer each of the following questions. You will be asked to recognize and correct errors in sentences or short paragraphs. Mark the best answer for each question.

1. Read this paragraph.

> (1) A contagious respiratory infection, people infected with the seasonal flu virus feel miserable with fever, chills, muscle aches, and fatigue. (2) Within two weeks, the symptoms of the flu disappear, and most people get better. (3) However, some people may develop serious complications, such as pneumonia. (4) Each year, seasonal influenza sickens millions and causes thousands of hospitalizations and flu-related deaths.

Which sentence should be revised to correct an error?

(A) sentence 1
(B) sentence 2
(C) sentence 3
(D) sentence 4

GO ON TO THE NEXT PAGE

2. Read this sentence.

> The heavy, bulky box contained an invaluable relic that could be traced to the ancient Egyptians but John, unaware of its contents, broke it by sitting on the box.

Which edit should be made to correct this sentence?

(E) Delete the comma after *heavy*.

(F) Insert a comma after *relic*.

(G) Insert a comma after *Egyptians*.

(H) Delete the comma after *John*.

3. Read this paragraph.

> (1) Redfish Lake is located in central Idaho, where the majestic Sawtooth Range provides beautiful scenery. (2) The shores of Redfish Lake are filled with picnic areas and campsites, with beach access and fantastic views. (3) The Redfish Lake Lodge offers overnight lodging, cabin options, a dining facility, bike and canoe rentals, public showers, and more, making this a great mountain beach destination. (4) You deserve some peace, this is the best place to get it.

Which sentence contains an error in its construction and should be revised?

(A) sentence 1

(B) sentence 2

(C) sentence 3

(D) sentence 4

4. Read this paragraph.

> (1) With a rover named Curiosity, Mars Science Laboratory is part of NASA's Mars Exploration Program. (2) They are a part of a long-term effort of robotic exploration of the red planet. (3) Curiosity was designed to assess whether Mars ever had an environment able to support small life forms called microbes. (4) In other words, its mission is to determine the planet's "habitability."

Which sentence should be revised to correct an inappropriate shift in pronoun?

(E) sentence 1

(F) sentence 2

(G) sentence 3

(H) sentence 4

GO ON TO THE NEXT PAGE

5. Read this paragraph.

> (1) Jupiter is the fifth planet from our Sun and the largest planet in the solar system. (2) Its stripes and swirls are cold windy clouds of ammonia and water. (3) The atmosphere is mostly hydrogen and helium, and its iconic Great Red Spot is a giant storm bigger than Earth that has raged for hundreds of years. (4) Scientists have observed, however, that the Great Red Spot is shrinking in length but growing in height.

Which edit should be made to correct this sentence?

(A) Add a comma after **Sun** in sentence 1.
(B) Add a comma after **cold** sentence 2.
(C) Delete the comma after **helium** in sentence 3.
(D) Delete the comma after **however** in sentence 4.

GO ON TO THE NEXT PAGE

> **Directions:** Read the passage below and answer the questions following it. You will be asked to improve the writing quality of the passage and to correct errors so that the passage follows the conventions of standard written English. You may reread the passage if you need to. Mark the best answer for each question.

Managing Wasted Food

(1) Wasted food is a growing problem today. (2) In 2014 alone, over 40 million tons of food waste was produced. (3) The Food and Agriculture Organization estimates that approximately a third of all food produced for human consumption worldwide is wasted. (4) Reducing waste can trim our waistlines and bulk up our wallets.

(5) When we waste food, we're not just creating a problem, we're also missing an opportunity to save money. (6) First, by keeping wasted food out of the garbage, homeowners may be able to save money by paying less for trash pickup. (7) Secondly, donating healthy, safe, and edible food to hungry people can have tax benefits in the form of charitable deductions. (8) Thirdly, many people, not only the well-to-do, but those in moderate circumstances, throw out a ridiculous amount of food. (9) Finding ways to prevent waste in the first place can lead to money saved, as well as reduction of energy and labor costs associated with food waste.

(10) Reducing wasted food can also be good for the environment. (11) When food goes to the landfill, it's no different than throwing out food into a plastic bag. (12) The nutrients in the food never return to the soil. (13) The wasted food rots and produces methane, which contributes to climate change. (14) Reducing food waste can not only mitigate global warming, but also save water, gasoline, energy, labor, pesticides, land, and fertilizers used to grow the food.

(15) If you can't prevent, reduce, or donate wasted food, consider composting. (16) Composting is an eco-friendly alternative to throwing out food. (17) By sending food scraps to a composting facility instead of to a landfill, you're helping make healthy soils. (18) Compost processing typically costs less than recycling plastics or cans. (19) Properly composted organics improve soil health and structure, improve water retention, support more native plants, and reduce the need for fertilizers and pesticides.

(20) This is not to say that composting is a magic bullet, but it is one out of many tools that we must use in order to conserve and reuse our resources.

6. Which sentence should replace sentence 4 to best introduce the main claim of the passage?

   (E) One of the largest waste management companies derives a large part of its revenue from restaurant waste disposal.

   (F) It is important to note that with wasted food also comes wasted opportunity.

   (G) The problem of food waste is compounded by our demand for ethanol, a corn-based fuel.

   (H) While the USDA recommends that we watch we eat, the EPA tells us to watch what we don't eat.

GO ON TO THE NEXT PAGE

7. Which of the following revisions should be made to sentence 5?

   (A) When we waste food, we're not only creating a problem but also missing an opportunity to save money.

   (B) When we waste food, we are not just creating a problem but also an opportunity to save money.

   (C) We waste food, we create a problem, and we save money.

   (D) Wasting food, we are not just creating a problem, but we miss opportunities to save money also.

8. Which revision to sentence 8 best maintains the formal style of the passage?

   (E) Thirdly, many people, not only the well-to-do, but those in moderate circumstances, waste tons of food.

   (F) Thirdly, many people, not only the well-to-do, but those in moderate circumstances, blow all their dough on food.

   (G) Thirdly, many people, not only the well-to-do, but those in moderate circumstances, use needless quantities of food.

   (H) Thirdly, many people, not only the well-to-do, but those in moderate circumstances, eat like savages.

9. Which transition word or phrase should be added to the beginning of sentence 9?

   (A) Due to this fact,
   (B) In contrast,
   (C) More importantly,
   (D) Finally,

10. What is the best way to combine sentences 11 and 12 to clarify the relationship between the ideas?

   (E) When food goes to the landfill, it's no different than throwing out food into a plastic bag since the nutrients in the food never return to the soil.

   (F) When food goes to the landfill, it's no different than throwing out food into a plastic bag, but the nutrients in the food never return to the soil.

   (G) Despite the food going into the landfill, it's no different than throwing out food into a plastic bag because the nutrients in the food never return to the soil.

   (H) While food goes to the landfill, it's no different than throwing out food into a plastic bag, and the nutrients in the food never return to the soil.

11. Which sentence is irrelevant and should be removed?

   (A) sentence 8
   (B) sentence 13
   (C) sentence 16
   (D) sentence 17

GO ON TO THE NEXT PAGE

Reading Comprehension

QUESTIONS 12–57

> **Directions:** Read each of the following six passages, and answer the related questions. You may write in your test booklet as needed to take notes. You should reread relevant parts of each passage before marking the best answer for each question. Base your answers only on the content within the text.

The Many Lives of Wound Man

The following passage has been adapted from Jack Hartnell's essay *The Many Lives of Wound Man*. It appears in *The Public Domain Review*.

1   Staring impassively out of the page, he bears a multitude of graphic wounds. His skin is covered in bleeding cuts and lesions, stabbed and sliced by knives, spears, and swords of varying sizes, many of which remain in the skin, protruding porcupine-like from his body. Another dagger pierces his side, and through his strangely transparent chest we see its tip puncture his heart. His thighs are pierced with arrows, some intact, some snapped down to just their heads or shafts. A club slams into his shoulder, another into the side of his face.

2   His neck, armpits, and groin sport rounded blue buboes, swollen glands suggesting that the figure has contracted plague. His shins and feet are pockmarked with clustered lacerations and thorn scratches, and he is beset by rabid animals. A dog, snake, and scorpion bite at his ankles, a bee stings his elbow, and even inside the cavity of his stomach a toad aggravates his innards.

3   Despite this horrendous cumulative barrage of injuries, however, the Wound Man is very much alive. For the purpose of this image is not to threaten or inspire fear, but to herald potential cures for all of the depicted maladies. He contrarily represents something altogether more hopeful than his battered body: an arresting reminder of the powerful knowledge that could be channeled and dispensed in the practice of late medieval medicine.

4   The earliest known versions of the Wound Man appeared at the turn of the fifteenth century in books on the surgical craft, particularly works from southern Germany associated with the renowned Würzburg surgeon Ortolf von Baierland. Accompanying a text known as the "Wundarznei" (The Surgery), these first Wound Men effectively functioned as a human table of contents for the cures contained within the relevant treatise. A remarkable image of the Wound Man from Wellcome library depicts a figure that is penetrated not only by weapons but also by text.

GO ON TO THE NEXT PAGE

5   Scattered around him are numbers and phrases, indicating where in the text a particular cure might be found. Next to the spider, crawling up the Wound Man's thigh, a phrase directs the reader to the appropriate paragraph for a cure: "Wo eine spynne gesticht, 20" ("When a spider bites, 20"). By the figure's right hand: "10, Boss negeli" ("10, Bad nails"). Inside his left thigh: "38. Ein phil do der schaft notch ynne stecket" ("38. An arrow whose shaft is still in place").

6   The Wound Man image was a convenient way for medieval surgeons to navigate their texts, but it was also an arresting reminder for both practitioners and patients of the vital knowledge contained within such manuscripts. It was living proof of the efficacy of the surgical enterprise, and a popular inclusion in medical works alongside a wide variety of related images that plotted diseases, the zodiac signs, bloodletting points, and anatomical schemes onto a similarly arranged human body.

7   Living on today in libraries from Copenhagen to Munich, the strange figure of the Wound Man gives modern viewers a glimpse of the worrying injuries that the medieval body could receive through war, accident, and epidemic. But at the same time, it shows that medieval people did not think of themselves as helpless victims in the face of these assaults. Far from reinforcing the common perception of the European Middle Ages as a backwards and bloody period of human history, the Wound Man reminds us that it was in fact a period busy with innovative medical treatments, a vital link between the long-standing cures of the classical world and developments that were to follow in early Renaissance medicine.

12. Which statement best describes the central idea of the passage?

(E) Technology is the primary driver of human knowledge.

(F) The Wound Man was a mysterious figure whose origin and purpose remains unknown.

(G) The Wound Man reveals the lack of knowledge that people in the Middle Ages possessed.

(H) The Wound Man was a useful tool that aided both medical procedures and medical knowledge.

13. Which of the following statements best describe the function of paragraphs 1 and 2?

(A) They provide an image of the Wound Man to help the reader visualize the object to be discussed in detail.

(B) They convey the idea that the Wound Man was a terrible representation of life in the Middle Ages.

(C) They highlight the grotesque monstrosity that reflected the brutal life of the Middle Ages.

(D) They introduce the idea that life in the Middle Ages was difficult and filled with violence.

GO ON TO THE NEXT PAGE

14. Which sentence from paragraph 1 and 2 best supports the idea that the series of descriptions are not those of a real human being?

(E) "Staring impassively out of the page, he bears a multitude of graphic wounds." (paragraph 1)

(F) "His skin is covered in bleeding cuts and lesions, stabbed and sliced by knives, spears, and swords of varying sizes, many of which remain in the skin, protruding porcupine-like from his body." (paragraph 1)

(G) "His neck, armpits, and groin sport rounded blue buboes, swollen glands suggesting that the figure has contracted plague." (paragraph 2)

(H) "A dog, snake, and scorpion bite at his ankles, a bee stings his elbow, and even inside the cavity of his stomach a toad aggravates his innards." (paragraph 2)

15. In paragraph 3, the word "alive" is used to highlight

(A) how realistic the illustration appears to the viewer.

(B) how dynamic and exciting life was in the Middle Ages.

(C) how important the image is to medieval medicine.

(D) how fortunate a person can be despite all the wounds.

16. Read the following sentence from paragraph 4.

A remarkable image of the Wound Man from Wellcome library depicts a figure that is penetrated not only by weapons but also by text.

How does this sentence fit into the overall structure of the passage?

(E) It emphasizes the brutality of war in the Middle Ages.

(F) It presents an explanation for the importance of the Wellcome Library.

(G) It supports a previously made assertion about the role of the Wound Man.

(H) It indicates that the Wellcome Library is the only place one can see the remarkable image of the Wound Man.

17. Paragraph 5 contributes to the development of the topic mainly by

(A) listing the most typical disorders and physical problems encountered by most people in the Middle Ages.

(B) providing examples of the ways in which Wound Men appeared in publications.

(C) revealing that the Wound Men were at first limited to cures for spiders and treatment of arrow wounds.

(D) demonstrating how limited the early Wound Men were in comparison to modern medical texts.

18. The author mentions the Wound Man's "popular inclusion" in paragraph 6 mainly to

(E) criticize the failure of most people to recognize the Wound Man's importance.

(F) support the claim that the Wound Man was well known to people of the Middle Ages.

(G) emphasize the idea that the Wound Man was perceived to be a useful tool.

(H) highlight the fact that the image of the Wound Man grew more complex over time.

GO ON TO THE NEXT PAGE

19. Which sentence is the best summary of the impact the Wound Man had on helping us understand the Middle Ages?

   (A) By carefully listing all the types of cures, the Wound Man helped us modify our own medical practices.
   (B) It reminds us that war and violence has no place in the modern world.
   (C) Because of its specific references to various types of wounds and diseases, the Wound Man enabled us to gain a greater understanding of war.
   (D) It helps us to gain a greater appreciation of the technological advancements of the Middle Ages.

20. Which sentence best supports the idea that the Wound Man continues to have an important influence in society today?

   (E) "Despite this horrendous cumulative barrage of injuries, however, the Wound Man is very much alive." (paragraph 3)
   (F) "Accompanying a text known as the 'Wundarznei' (The Surgery), these first Wound Men effectively functioned as a human table of contents for the cures contained within the relevant treatise." (paragraph 4)
   (G) "It was living proof of the efficacy of the surgical enterprise, and a popular inclusion in medical works alongside a wide variety of related images that plotted diseases, the zodiac signs, bloodletting points, and anatomical schemes onto a similarly arranged human body." (paragraph 6)
   (H) "Living on today in libraries from Copenhagen to Munich, the strange figure of the Wound Man gives modern viewers a glimpse of the worrying injuries that the medieval body could receive through war, accident, and epidemic." (paragraph 7)

GO ON TO THE NEXT PAGE

When Chocolate Was Medicine

The following passage has been adapted from Christine Jones's essay *When Chocolate was Medicine: Colmenero, Wadsworth, and Dufour*. It appears in *The Public Domain Review*.

1   In the seventeenth century, Europeans who had not traveled overseas tasted coffee, hot chocolate, and tea for the very first time. For this brand-new clientele, the brews of foreign beans and leaves carried within them the wonder and danger of far-away lands. They were classified at first not as food, but as drugs—pleasant-tasting, with recommended dosages prescribed by pharmacists and physicians, and dangerous when self-administered. As they warmed to the use and abuse of hot beverages, Europeans frequently experienced moral and physical confusion brought on by frothy pungency, unpredictable effects, and even (rumor had it) fatality.

2   These mischievously potent drugs were met with widespread curiosity and concern. In response, a written tradition of treatises was born over the course of the seventeenth and eighteenth centuries. Physicians and tradesmen who claimed knowledge of fields from pharmacology to etiquette proclaimed the many health benefits of hot drinks or issued impassioned warnings about their abuse. The resulting textual tradition documents how the tonics were depicted during the first century of their hotly debated place among Europe's delicacies.

3   Chocolate was the first of the three to enter the pharmaceutical annals in Europe through Antonio Colmenero de Ledesma. Colmenero's work dates from the era when Spain was the main importer of chocolate. Spain had occupied the Aztec territories since the time of Cortés in the 1540s—the first Spanish-language description of chocolate dates from the 1552—whereas the British and French were only beginning to establish a colonial presence in the Caribbean and South America during the 1620s and 30s. Having acquired a degree in medicine and served a Jesuit mission in the colonies, Colmenero was as close as one could come to a European expert on the pharmaceutical qualities of the cacao bean. Classified as medical literature in libraries today, Colmenero's work introduced chocolate to Europe as a drug by appealing to the science of the humors, or essential bodily fluids.

4   "Humoralism," a theory of health and illness inherited from Hippocrates and Galen, was still influential in 1630. It held that the body was composed of four essential liquids: black bile, blood, yellow bile, and phlegm. Each humor echoed one of the four elements of nature—earth, air, fire, and water—and exhibited particular properties that changed the body's disposition: black bile was cold and dry, blood was hot and wet, yellow bile felt hot and dry, and phlegm made the body cold and wet. Balanced together, they maintained the healthy functioning of an organism. When the balance among them tipped and one occurred in excess, it produced symptoms of what we now call "disease" in the body. While common European pharmaceuticals had long been classified as essentially cooling or heating, cacao presented both hot and cold characteristics. Later treatises faced the same conundrum[1] regarding coffee. Depending on how it was administered/ingested, hot chocolate's curative effects also crisscrossed the humoral categories in unexpected ways.

GO ON TO THE NEXT PAGE

5　　By applying the dominant theory of the body to chocolate's uncommon powers—was it sorcery, magic, alchemy?—Colmenero endeavored to make its mystery at least debatable in terms readily accessible across the countries of Western Europe. Because Colmenero was a doctor and surgeon who was said to have traveled to the West Indies, his work was received as medical lore and remained an important reference throughout the early history of writing on hot beverages. It also supplied the very first recipe for hot chocolate on the European continent to the delight of the less learned who encountered his expertise in a mug.

[1]**conundrum:** a confusing or difficult problem

21.　In paragraph 1, the phrase "rumor had it" is used to highlight

(A) the dangers of consuming chocolate in the seventeenth century.
(B) the miraculous effects chocolate was supposed to possess.
(C) the unfounded claims that were not based on facts.
(D) the belief that chocolate was considered food and not drugs.

22.　The seventeenth-century European attitude toward chocolate was most influenced by

(E) "the brews of foreign beans."
(F) "wonder and danger of far-away lands."
(G) "pharmacists and physicians."
(H) "the abuse of hot beverages."

23.　Which statement best describes professional reactions to chocolate?

(A) They were generally positive, proclaiming its many health benefits.
(B) They were generally negative, warning consumers about its potential for mischief.
(C) They were mixed, resulting in competing evaluations about its usefulness.
(D) They were generally ignored by the public, which prioritized taste over benefits to health.

24.　How did Colmenero's work "enter the pharmaceutical annals" in Europe?

(E) by using the descriptions of chocolate made by Cortés
(F) by acquiring his degree in medicine from a Jesuit mission in the colonies
(G) by contextualizing his work in a specialized branch of science
(H) by acting as the main importer of chocolate

25.　It can be inferred that Hippocrates would agree with which of the following statements?

(A) Chocolate presents both the hot and cold characteristics.
(B) Humoralism can be applied to the study of chocolates.
(C) An excess of phlegm can lead to a sickness.
(D) Fire is the strongest of all elements.

GO ON TO THE NEXT PAGE

26. The author includes the details about "humoralism" in order to

   (E) describe the origin of European medicine.
   (F) explain how people develop sicknesses.
   (G) highlight the problems in the logic behind ancient medicinal theories.
   (H) reveal why ideas about chocolate were subject to disagreements.

27. Which statement best supports the idea that Colmenero had a large role in shaping the way people viewed chocolate?

   (A) "Colmenero's work dates from the era when Spain was the main importer of chocolate." (paragraph 3)
   (B) "Colmenero's work introduced chocolate to Europe as a drug by appealing to the science of the humors, or essential bodily fluids." (paragraph 3)
   (C) "Colmenero endeavored to make its mystery at least debatable in terms readily accessible across the countries of Western Europe." (paragraph 5)
   (D) "Because Colmenero was a doctor and surgeon who was said to have traveled to the West Indies, his work was received as medical lore." (paragraph 5)

28. Which sentence from the excerpt best shows that Colmenero's contributions were not limited to medicine?

   (E) "Chocolate was the first of the three to enter the pharmaceutical annals in Europe through Antonio Colmenero de Ledesma." (paragraph 3)
   (F) "Colmenero's short treatise dates from the era when Spain was the main importer of chocolate." (paragraph 3)
   (G) "Colmenero endeavored to make its mystery at least debatable in terms readily accessible across the countries of Western Europe." (paragraph 5)
   (H) "It also supplied the very first recipe for hot chocolate on the European continent." (paragraph 5)

29. Read the following sentence from paragraph 5.

   Colmenero endeavored to make its mystery at least debatable in terms readily accessible across the countries of Western Europe.

   How does the sentence contribute to the development of the central idea?

   (A) It reveals Colmenero's argumentative personality that set off many debates in Western Europe.
   (B) It suggests that Colmenero wanted higher supplies of chocolate available to the people of Western Europe.
   (C) It identifies one impact of Colmenero's research.
   (D) It highlights the mystery chocolate caused among the people of Western Europe.

GO ON TO THE NEXT PAGE

John L. Sullivan Fights America

The following passage has been adapted from Christopher Klein's essay *John L. Sullivan Fights America*. It appears in *The Public Domain Review*.

1   A dense ocean of humanity lapped up to the doorstep of John L. Sullivan's gilded liquor palace. Heads craned and tilted as hordes of Bostonians attempted to steal a passing glance of their hometown hero through the open doorway. Inside, a ceaseless flow of well-wishers offered their farewells to America's reigning heavyweight boxing champion.

2   Sullivan's dark, piercing eyes gleamed with the reflections of the flickering gaslights. His clean-shaven chin glistened like polished granite, although darkness hid in the recesses of a deep dimple and in the shadow of his glorious handlebar mustache. Sullivan's pristine skin, full set of even teeth, and straight nose belied his profession and visibly testified to the inability of foes to lay a licking on him. Muscular without being muscle-bound, the "Boston Strong Boy" was constructed like a pugilistic product of the Industrial Age, a "wonderful engine of destruction" manifest in flesh and blood.

3   After guzzling the praise inside his saloon on the evening of September 26, 1883, the hard-hitting, hard-drinking Sullivan waded through the throng of fawning fans outside and stepped into a waiting carriage that sprinted him away to a waiting train. The man who had captured the heavyweight championship nineteen months prior had departed on many journeys before, but no man had ever set out on such an ambitious adventure as the one he was about to undertake.

4   For the next eight months, Sullivan would circle the United States with a troupe of the world's top professional fighters. In nearly 150 locales, John L. would spar with his fellow boxers but also present a sensational novelty act worthy of his contemporary, the showman P.T. Barnum. The reigning heavyweight champion would offer as much as $1,000 ($24,000 in today's dollars when chained to the Consumer Price Index) to any man who could enter the ring with him and simply remain standing after four three-minute rounds.

5   The "Great John L." was challenging America to a fight. Sullivan's transcontinental "knocking out" tour was gloriously American in its audacity and concept. Its democratic appeal was undeniable: any amateur could take a shot at glory by taking a punch from the best fighter in the world. Furthermore, the challenge, given its implicit braggadocio that defeating John L. in four rounds was a universal improbability, was an extraordinary statement of supreme self-confidence.

6   Accounts of the financial receipts from the tour vary, but Sullivan likely pocketed tens of thousands of dollars, and his earnings probably approached or surpassed the $50,000 annual salary earned by President Chester A. Arthur. While the exact size of his financial windfall may not be known, it's certain that Sullivan earned an incredible level of superstardom by traversing the continent. The "Boston Strong Boy" proved to be a drawing card around America due to both his prowess in the ring and his personal magnetism. Americans paid money not just to see John L. Sullivan box, but just to see John L. Sullivan. On Sullivan's tour stop in St. Louis, five thousand people paid just to see him pitch five lackluster innings in an exhibition game for baseball's St. Louis Browns.

GO ON TO THE NEXT PAGE

7   Thanks to the "knocking out" tour, Sullivan became the most famous athlete in the United States—and one of the most famous Americans in any walk of life. Through railroads and newspapers, Sullivan was able to reach hundreds of thousands of people across America, something that wasn't possible just years before. He became an American celebrity of the highest order as well as the first sports superstar, and his fame would endure even after he lost the heavyweight championship to "Gentleman Jim" Corbett in 1892.

30. Which statement best describes the central idea of this passage?

   (E) John L. Sullivan was a muscular boxer who rarely lost a boxing match.
   (F) John L. Sullivan lost to Corbett because he was unprepared for the fight.
   (G) John L. Sullivan was one of the most popular Americans in history whose popularity continued to last even after his loss.
   (H) John L. Sullivan became a rich boxer because of all the money he had won from his fights.

31. In paragraph 1, how do the words "horde" and "steal" affect the tone of the first part of the excerpt?

   (A) It creates a threatening tone by suggesting that many people with to hurt John L. Sullivan.
   (B) It introduces an aggressive tone by showing that people were initially hostile to John L. Sullivan.
   (C) It suggests an excited tone by highlighting the anticipation for John L. Sullivan.
   (D) It establishes an angry tone by pointing out problematic behaviors of mobs.

32. Read the following sentence.

   Muscular without being muscle-bound, the "Boston Strong Boy" was constructed like a pugilistic product of the Industrial Age, a "wonderful engine of destruction" manifest in flesh and blood.

   What do the quoted references in this sentence emphasize?

   (E) Sullivan's arrogance by highlighting the qualities that enabled it
   (F) descriptions of Sullivan's physique to characterize him within his time period
   (G) the materialistic shallowness of the Industrial Age
   (H) the notion that violence and boxing were a product of the Industrial Age

GO ON TO THE NEXT PAGE

33. Which sentence from the excerpt best supports the claim that Sullivan was a remarkable boxer?

   (A) "Heads craned and tilted as hordes of Bostonians attempted to steal a passing glance of their hometown hero through the open doorway." (paragraph 1)
   (B) "Sullivan's pristine skin, full set of even teeth, and straight nose belied his profession and visibly testified to the inability of foes to lay a licking on him." (paragraph 2)
   (C) "After guzzling the praise inside his saloon on the evening of September 26, 1883, the hard-hitting, hard-drinking Sullivan waded through the throng of fawning fans outside and stepped into a waiting carriage that sprinted him away to a waiting train." (paragraph 3)
   (D) "For the next eight months, Sullivan would circle the United States with a troupe of the world's top professional fighters." (paragraph 4)

34. Read the following sentence from paragraph 4.

   In nearly 150 locales, John L. would spar with his fellow boxers but also present a sensational novelty act worthy of his contemporary, the showman P.T. Barnum.

   How does this sentence contribute to the development of the narrative?

   (E) It shows that Sullivan sparred with both boxers and other showmen like P.T. Barnum.
   (F) It reveals that Sullivan wanted to spar with anyone he could fight.
   (G) It highlights the entertaining aspect of Sullivan's exhibitions.
   (H) It suggests that boxing exhibitions of the time required novelty acts.

35. Which sentence is the best summary of paragraph 5?

   (A) Defeating Sullivan was an impossible dare that no one ever took up.
   (B) John Sullivan was being unpatriotic by challenging Americans to a fight.
   (C) John Sullivan challenged the ideals of what it meant to be American.
   (D) John Sullivan's tour reflected the ideas about himself as well as those about America.

36. In paragraph 6, how does the phrase "drawing card" contribute to the development of the paragraph?

   (E) It acknowledges the great contributions that illustrative talents made in promoting Sullivan's fights.
   (F) It emphasizes the random nature of Sullivan's fame.
   (G) It supports the idea that Sullivan was extremely popular wherever he went.
   (H) It highlights the fact that Sullivan was a difficult man to beat in the ring.

GO ON TO THE NEXT PAGE

37. In paragraph 7, which sentence best supports the idea that some of Sullivan's fans were more interested in Sullivan the man and not Sullivan the boxer?

(A) "Accounts of the financial receipts from the tour vary, but Sullivan likely pocketed tens of thousands of dollars, and his earnings probably approached or surpassed the $50,000 annual salary earned by President Chester A. Arthur."

(B) "While the exact size of his financial windfall may not be known, it's certain that Sullivan earned an incredible level of superstardom by traversing the continent."

(C) "The 'Boston Strong Boy' proved to be a drawing card around America due to both his prowess in the ring and his personal magnetism."

(D) "On Sullivan's tour stop in St. Louis, five thousand people paid just to see him pitch five lackluster innings in an exhibition game for baseball's St. Louis Browns."

38. Which sentence from the passage best conveys the author's perspective regarding the legacy of Sullivan's accomplishment?

(E) "A dense ocean of humanity lapped up to the doorstep of John L. Sullivan's gilded liquor palace." (paragraph 1)

(F) "The man who had captured the heavyweight championship nineteen months prior had departed on many journeys before, but no man had ever set out on such an ambitious adventure as the one he was about to undertake." (paragraph 2)

(G) "Americans paid money not just to see John L. Sullivan box, but just to see John L. Sullivan." (paragraph 7)

(H) "He became an American celebrity of the highest order as well as the first sports super-star, and his fame would endure even after he lost the heavyweight championship to 'Gentleman Jim' Corbett in 1892." (paragraph 8)

GO ON TO THE NEXT PAGE

Excerpt from "Hop-Frog"
By Edgar Allan Poe

1   At the date of my narrative, professing jesters had not altogether gone out of fashion at court. Several of the great continental 'powers' still retain their 'fools,' who wore motley, with caps and bells, and who were expected to be always ready with sharp witticisms, at a moment's notice, in consideration of the crumbs that fell from the royal table.

2   Our king, as a matter of course, retained his 'fool.' The fact is, he required something in the way of folly—if only to counterbalance the heavy wisdom of the seven wise men who were his ministers—not to mention himself.

3   His fool, or professional jester, was not only a fool, however. His value was trebled in the eyes of the king, by the fact of his being also a dwarf and a cripple. Dwarfs were as common at court, in those days, as fools; and many monarchs would have found it difficult to get through their days (days are rather longer at court than elsewhere) without both a jester to laugh with, and a dwarf to laugh at. But, as I have already observed, your jesters, in ninety-nine cases out of a hundred, are fat, round, and unwieldy—so that it was no small source of self-gratulation with our king that, in Hop-Frog (this was the fool's name), he possessed a triplicate treasure in one person.

4   I believe the name 'Hop-Frog' was not that given to the dwarf by his sponsors at baptism, but it was conferred upon him, by general consent of the several ministers, on account of his inability to walk as other men do. In fact, Hop-Frog could only get along by a sort of interjectional gait—something between a leap and a wriggle—a movement that afforded illimitable amusement, and of course consolation, to the king, for (notwithstanding the protuberance of his stomach and a constitutional swelling of the head) the king, by his whole court, was accounted a capital figure.

5   But although Hop-Frog, through the distortion of his legs, could move only with great pain and difficulty along a road or floor, the prodigious muscular power which nature seemed to have bestowed upon his arms, by way of compensation for deficiency in the lower limbs, enabled him to perform many feats of wonderful dexterity, where trees or ropes were in question, or anything else to climb. At such exercises he certainly much more resembled a squirrel, or a small monkey, than a frog.

6   I am not able to say, with precision, from what country Hop-Frog originally came. It was from some barbarous region, however, that no person ever heard of—a vast distance from the court of our king. Hop-Frog, and a young girl very little less dwarfish than himself (although of exquisite proportions, and a marvelous dancer), had been forcibly carried off from their respective homes in adjoining provinces, and sent as presents to the king, by one of his ever-victorious generals.

7   Under these circumstances, it is not to be wondered at that a close intimacy arose between the two little captives. Indeed, they soon became sworn friends. Hop-Frog, who, although he made a great deal of sport, was by no means popular, had it not in his power to render Trippetta many services; but she, on account of her grace and exquisite beauty (although a dwarf), was universally admired and petted; so she possessed much influence; and never failed to use it, whenever she could, for the benefit of Hop-Frog.

GO ON TO THE NEXT PAGE

39. In the first paragraph, how does the phrase "in consideration of the crumbs" contribute to the plot?

(A) It highlights the importance of being observant of the smallest details at a royal table.

(B) It points out the conditions under which jesters were expected to perform.

(C) It emphasizes the point that jesters were growing more fashionable.

(D) It indicates the times at which jesters were expected to be witty.

40. Paragraph 2 suggests that the king believed his ministers were

(E) hopelessly foolish.

(F) artistically grim.

(G) relatively popular.

(H) overly serious.

41. How does paragraph 3 contribute to the development of the plot?

(A) It shifts the focus of the narrative.

(B) It provides a historical background.

(C) It discusses a possibility to be dismissed.

(D) It builds on an idea touched upon in the previous paragraph.

42. Read the following statement from paragraph 3.

(days are rather longer at court than elsewhere)

How does this statement contribute to the plot?

(E) It illustrates an abstract concept.

(F) It offers an explanation.

(G) It defines a term.

(H) It challenges an assumption.

43. The effect of the sentence beginning with "But although" in paragraph 5 is to

(A) lighten the tone by introducing the cheery aspect of the character.

(B) express an opinion that is not supported by facts.

(C) provide a clue to the narrator's bias.

(D) balance a description of limitations with one of positive attributes.

44. In paragraph 7, the phrase "close intimacy" can best be described as

(E) avoidable.

(F) admirable.

(G) expected.

(H) horrifying.

45. Which of the following best describes Trippetta's attitude toward Hop-Frog?

(A) cold

(B) disgusted

(C) kind

(D) respectful

GO ON TO THE NEXT PAGE

It Is Not Growing Like a Tree
By Ben Jonson

It is not growing like a tree
In bulk doth make Man better be;
Or standing long an oak, three hundred year,
Line To fall a log at last, dry, bald, and sere:[1]
(5) A lily of a day
Is fairer far in May,
Although it fall and die that night—
It was the plant and flower of light.
In small proportions we just beauties see;
(10) And in short measures life may perfect be.

[1] **sere:** dry and withered

46. Read lines 1 and 2.

    It is not growing like a tree
    In bulk doth make Man better be;

    How do the lines contribute to the central idea of the poem?

    (E) They dismiss one criterion used to evaluate humanity.
    (F) They suggest that growing large makes a man better.
    (G) They reveal that men do not grow like trees.
    (H) They reveal that men are better than trees.

47. Read lines 3 and 4.

    Or standing long an oak, three hundred year,
    To fall a log at last, dry, bald, and sere:

    How do the lines contribute to the ideas in lines 1 and 2?

    (A) They suggest that growing older is better than growing bigger.
    (B) They suggest that growing bigger is better than growing older.
    (C) They point out the negative aspects of living a long time.
    (D) They point out that oaks live up to about three hundred years old.

48. Lines 5 to 8 convey the central idea of the poem by

    (E) implying that everything must ultimately come to an end.
    (F) illustrating the temporary nature of beauty.
    (G) emphasizing the power of nature to command respect.
    (H) highlighting the diversity of nature in the world.

GO ON TO THE NEXT PAGE

49. Read lines 9 and 10.

In small proportions we just beauties see;
And in short measures life may perfect be.

Which of the following supports what is implied in these lines?

(A) "It is not growing like a tree/In bulk doth make Man better be" (lines 1−2)

(B) "Or standing long an oak, three hundred year,/To fall a log at last, dry, bald, and sere" (lines 3−4)

(C) "A lily of a day/Is fairer far in May" (lines 5−6)

(D) "Although it fall and die that night—/It was the plant and flower of light." (lines 7−8)

50. How does the form of the poem contribute to its meaning?

(E) The number of words in each line depends on the importance of the image.

(F) The lack of regular rhyme reflects the lack of regularity in life.

(G) The contrasting characteristics between a tree and a flower serve to emphasize a key point.

(H) It uses unusual capitalization to suggest the unusual nature of life.

GO ON TO THE NEXT PAGE

Sir Arthur and the Fairies

The following passage has been adapted from Mary Losure's essay *Sir Arthur and the Fairies*. It appears in *The Public Domain Review*.

1   In the winter of 1920, readers of the popular British magazine the *Strand* found a curious headline on the cover of their Christmas issues. "*FAIRIES PHOTOGRAPHED*," it said. "*AN EPOCH-MAKING EVENT DESCRIBED BY A. CONAN DOYLE*." The *Strand*'s readership was well acquainted with Sir Arthur Conan Doyle; most of his wildly popular Sherlock Holmes stories had appeared for the first time in its pages. The great man's claim that fairies—real fairies—had been photographed in the north of England by two young girls was greeted with wonder, but unfortunately for Conan Doyle, most of it was of the "what can he be thinking?" variety. How could the creator of the world's most famous, least-fool-able detective have convinced himself that "fairy" photographs were real? Let us proceed, Holmes-like, to examine the question.

2   To his credit, Conan Doyle made what was (to him) a thorough, scientific, step-by-step investigation of the "fairy" photographs. For his first step, he consulted experts at the London offices of the George Eastman Kodak Company. They examined prints of the first two "fairy" photos and told Conan Doyle they could find no evidence of photo-doctoring; still, they insisted someone who knew enough about photography could have faked them. In Conan Doyle's mind, that ruled out the two Yorkshire village girls who had taken the photographs, Elsie Wright and Frances Griffiths. Working class girls, surely, would not be able pull off such a hoax.

3   Conan Doyle's next step was an on-the-scene investigation—but Conan Doyle himself did not go. Instead, he enlisted a far-from-impartial surrogate[1]—an ardent believer in fairies named Edward Gardner—to carry out the mission. Gardner had already talked to several people who had assured him the girls had played with fairies and elves since babyhood. He had already written to Elsie Wright's mother begging her to get her "little girl" to take more photos. Gardner explained to Elsie's mother that he had long been anxious to obtain photos of "fairies, pixies, and elves, and if possible of brownies and goblins."

4   During his visit to Cottingley, Gardner implored Elsie's parents to get her to take more fairy photos. Elsie insisted that wasn't possible because Frances had to be there, too, for the fairies to appear. (By that time, Frances had moved away from Cottingley to the seaside town of Scarborough.) Undeterred, Gardner arranged with Frances's parents for Frances to spend part of her summer holidays in Cottingley. There was nothing either girl could do—the pressure was on. So when Frances arrived in Cottingley and the two were alone, Elsie told her she'd prepared two more cutout fairies, one for each girl. In the hidden valley, the two girls took two more photos. Then they both agreed, in secret, they would never take another fairy photo.

5   Gardner was delighted to get the two new photos, but even more thrilled with a third photo, one which Elsie had not faked. Both girls thought at the time it was just a bird's nest, some rainwater, some shapes and shadows—but Gardner insisted it showed fairies. Conan Doyle thought so, too.

GO ON TO THE NEXT PAGE

6   A second *Strand* article, published in March of 1921, announced "The Evidence for Fairies by A. Conan Doyle, With New Fairy Photographs." In the article, Conan Doyle quoted Gardner's assertion that the third and most amazing photo was a "fairy bower." Conan Doyle also included Gardner's remark that "We have now succeeded in bringing this print out splendidly." The article did not say what Gardner meant by "bringing out" the print. The man who had created the world's greatest detective never knew how badly astray his own investigation had gone. In part to avoid embarrassing him, Elsie and Frances did not reveal the secret of the paper cutouts until long after his death.

[1]**surrogate:** a substitute

51. Which sentence from paragraph 1 best illustrates the response to Doyle's claim about fairies?

(A) "In the winter of 1920, readers of the popular British magazine the *Strand* found a curious headline on the cover of their Christmas issues."

(B) "The *Strand*'s readership was well acquainted with Sir Arthur Conan Doyle"

(C) "most of it was of the 'what can he be thinking?' variety."

(D) "Let us proceed, Holmes-like, to examine the question."

52. Why did Doyle believe that the two girls were not responsible for creating a fake photo of fairies?

(E) The photo company told him that girls would not be able to master such skills.

(F) The girls did not possess a camera.

(G) Their social class suggested that they would not have the necessary abilities.

(H) Doyle believed that the girls were incapable of dishonesty.

53. Which of the following lines from paragraph 3 most strongly suggests that Gardner was not the ideal person for the "mission"?

(A) "Conan Doyle's next step was an on-the-scene investigation . . . "

(B) "Instead, he enlisted a far-from-impartial surrogate . . . "

(C) "Gardner had already talked to several people who had assured him the girls had played with fairies and elves since babyhood."

(D) "He had already written to Elsie Wright's mother begging her to get her 'little girl' to take more photos."

54. Paragraph 4 contributes to the development of the narrative of the passage by

(E) revealing a promise that the two girls would later break.

(F) providing an explanation for the girls' actions.

(G) demonstrating the idea that most people will lie when they are forced to.

(H) highlighting the evil nature of even the purest people.

GO ON TO THE NEXT PAGE

55. Which statement best describes Doyle's and Gardner's response to the third photo?

   (A) They were convinced that the girls faked the image.
   (B) They were motivated by a desire for fame that the photo would bring.
   (C) They were not convinced by the girls' thoughts about the photo.
   (D) They were not thrilled to learn that it was not a fake.

56. Which of the following sentences most strongly supports the idea that the girls did not want to take additional fairy pictures?

   (E) "He had already written to Elsie Wright's mother begging her to get her 'little girl' to take more photos." (paragraph 3)
   (F) "Elsie insisted that wasn't possible because Frances had to be there . . . " (paragraph 4)
   (G) "Both girls thought at the time it was just a bird's nest, some rainwater, some shapes and shadows . . . " (paragraph 5)
   (H) "The man who had created the world's greatest detective never knew how badly astray his own investigation had gone." (paragraph 6)

57. With which statement would the author most likely agree?

   (A) Since Doyle wrote about mysteries, he was the best person to solve them.
   (B) Doyle never realized the truth about the photos.
   (C) Elsie and Frances never revealed the truth about the photos.
   (D) Gardner figured out that the photos were fake.

GO ON TO THE NEXT PAGE

PART 2—MATHEMATICS

57 QUESTIONS, SUGGESTED TIME: 90 MINUTES

IMPORTANT NOTES: (1) Formulas are not provided. (2) Figures other than graphs are not necessarily drawn to scale. (3) Diagrams are in one plane unless stated otherwise. (4) Graphs are drawn to scale. Unless stated otherwise, all relationships on graphs are according to appearance. (5) Simplify all fractions.

Grid-In Questions

QUESTIONS 58–62

DIRECTIONS: Solve each problem. On the answer sheet, write your answer in the boxes at the top of the grid. Start on the left side of each grid. Print only one number or symbol in each box. Under each box, fill in the circle that matches the number or symbol you wrote above. **DO NOT FILL IN A CIRCLE UNDER AN UNUSED BOX. DO NOT LEAVE A BOX BLANK IN THE MIDDLE OF AN ANSWER.**

58. A muffin shop bakes chocolate and blueberry muffins in a ratio of 7 : 8. If the muffin shop has 210 chocolate muffins, how many blueberry muffins does the muffin shop have?

59.
$$\frac{100}{12 - x} = 8$$

What is the value of x in the equation shown above?

60. A survey asked students what pets they have. Based on the results, the following statements are all true:

- 41 students have cats.
- 36 students have dogs.
- 12 students have both cats and dogs.
- 14 students have no dogs or cats.

How many students were surveyed?

61.

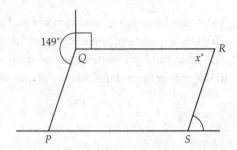

In the parallelogram above, what is the value of x?

62. The sum of two consecutive odd integers is −16. If 3 is added to the smaller integer and 1 is subtracted from the larger integer, what is the product of the two resulting integers?

GO ON TO THE NEXT PAGE

PRACTICE TEST 3

Multiple-Choice Questions

QUESTIONS 63–114

> **DIRECTIONS:** Solve each question. Select the best answer from the choices given. Mark the letter of your choice on the answer sheet.

63. $8 + (4n + 5) - (5n + 7) =$

    (A) $6 - n$
    (B) $6 + n$
    (C) $20 - n$
    (D) $20 + n$

64. A bottle contains 250 milliliters of water. How many liters of water are there in 24 of these bottles?

    (E) 6 L
    (F) 60 L
    (G) 600 L
    (H) 60,000 L

65. If $x = -5$ and $y = 7$, what is the value of $x(x - 2y)$?

    (A) -95
    (B) -45
    (C) 45
    (D) 95

66.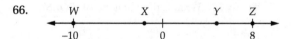

    On the number line above, points W, X, Y, and Z are integers, and $WX : XY : YZ = 4 : 3 : 2$. What is the length of WY?

    (E) 4
    (F) 7
    (G) 14
    (H) 18

67. At West Lake High School, course grades range from 0 to 100. Ahmed took 5 courses and his average course grade was 72. Rita took 4 courses and had the same sum of course grades as Ahmed. What was Rita's average?

    (A) 72
    (B) 84
    (C) 90
    (D) 98

68.
$$\frac{q}{r} = \frac{s}{t}$$

    In the equation above, q, r, s, and t are all positive numbers. Which of the following expressions is equal to r?

    (E) $\dfrac{s}{q}$
    (F) t
    (G) $\dfrac{s}{qt}$
    (H) $\dfrac{qt}{s}$

69. There are 183 teachers and 512 first-year students at East State College. The student-to-faculty ratio for the entire college is 15 to 1. What is the total number of second-, third-, and fourth-year students?

    (A) 2,233
    (B) 2,432
    (C) 2,730
    (D) 2,745

GO ON TO THE NEXT PAGE

70. The width of a rectangle is 114 cm. The ratio of the length to the width is 3 : 2. What is the perimeter of the rectangle?

(E) 190 cm

(F) 285 cm

(G) 380 cm

(H) 570 cm

71. If $3n$ is a positive even number, how many odd numbers are in the range from $3n$ up to and including $3n + 6$?

(A) 2

(B) 3

(C) 4

(D) 5

72.

Number of People in Vehicle	Percent of Vehicles
1	47%
2	28%
3	15%
4	8%
5 or more	2%

At a state park, a researcher recorded the number of people in each vehicle that passed through the park entrance. The table above shows the percent distribution for the 400 vehicles that passed through the park entrance yesterday morning. How many of the vehicles contained at least 3 people?

(E) 25

(F) 60

(G) 100

(H) 300

73. Using the approximation 2.54 centimeters = 1 inch, how many centimeters are in 3 feet 9 inches?

(A) 17.72

(B) 99.06

(C) 114.30

(D) 137.16

74. The set of possible values of m is {2, 3, 4}. What is the set of possible values of k if $k = m^2 - 4$?

(E) {0, 2, 4}

(F) {0, 5, 12}

(G) {8, 10, 12}

(H) {−2, −1, 0}

75.
$$1 \text{ dollar} = 6 \text{ jerms}$$
$$1 \text{ dollar} = 0.4 \text{ zeeb}$$

Kyle has 120 jerms and 20 zeebs. If he exchanges the jerms and zeebs for dollars according to the rates above, how many dollars will he receive?

(A) $28

(B) $70

(C) $86

(D) $100

76.

In the figure above, $PQRS$ is a parallelogram. The measure of $\angle PQT$ is 45° and the measure of $\angle PTQ$ is 75°. What is the measure of $\angle QRS$?

(E) 60°

(F) 75°

(G) 80°

(H) 120°

77. The decimal 0.12 can be written as the fraction $\frac{x}{25}$. What is the value of x?

(A) 3

(B) 6

(C) 12

(D) 18

GO ON TO THE NEXT PAGE

78. In a sample of 10 cards, 2 are red and 8 are blue. If 2 cards are selected at random from the sample, one at a time without replacement, what is the probability that both cards are not red?

(E) $\dfrac{14}{25}$

(F) $\dfrac{28}{45}$

(G) $\dfrac{16}{25}$

(H) $\dfrac{4}{5}$

79. The height of a square-based wooden box is 2 times the length of one side of the base. If one side of the base is 4 feet long, what is the volume of this box?

(A) 8 cu ft.

(B) 32 cu ft.

(C) 128 cu ft.

(D) 196 cu ft.

80. Malik and Shana went biking. Malik traveled 63 kilometers in 3 hours while Shana traveled 72 kilometers in 3 hours. How much less was Malik's mean speed, in kilometers per hour (kph), than Shana's?

(E) 1 kph

(F) 3 kph

(G) 5 kph

(H) 9 kph

81. What is the least common multiple of 24, 20, and 15?

(A) 60

(B) 120

(C) 180

(D) 360

82. The sum of the numbers x, y, and z is 60. The ratio of x to y is 2 : 4, and the ratio of y to z is 2 : 3. What is the value of y?

(E) 4

(F) 12

(G) 20

(H) 30

83.

Test Sore	Number of Students
90	4
80	4
70	2

What is the mean test score of the 10 students in the table above?

(A) 80

(B) 82

(C) 85

(D) 87

84.
$$1 \text{ flooz} = 4.5 \text{ slanks}$$
$$1 \text{ flooz} = 12.15 \text{ gribs}$$
Using the conversion above, how many gribs are equal to 1 slank?

(E) 0.37

(F) 2.7

(G) 6.3

(H) 15.3

85. Today, Jack's age is $\dfrac{1}{4}$ of Molly's age. In seven years, Jack's age will be $\dfrac{3}{5}$ of Molly's age. How old is Molly today?

(A) 5 years old

(B) 8 years old

(C) 9 years old

(D) 15 years old

GO ON TO THE NEXT PAGE

86. A paste used for highway billboards is made by mixing the following ingredients by weight: 3 parts powder, 3 parts water, 3 parts resin, and 1 part hardener. To cover 1 billboard requires 30 pounds of the paste. How many total pounds of the resin are required to cover 4 billboards?

(E) 9
(F) 18
(G) 27
(H) 36

87.

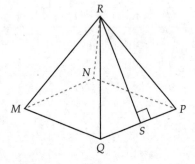

The base of the pyramid above is a square and each triangular face has the same area. The side length of the base *MNPQ* is 8 centimeters. If the surface area of the pyramid, including the base, is 160 sq cm, what is the length of *RS*?

(A) 4 cm
(B) 6 cm
(C) 8 cm
(D) 10 cm

88. There are 5 different cookies on a plate. Amin will choose 2 of these cookies to pack in his lunch. How many different pairs of 2 cookies can he choose from the 5?

(E) 10
(F) 12
(G) 20
(H) 25

89. Working on a class presentation, Darla can create 4 slides in 20 minutes working at a constant rate. Kaito can create 3 slides in 10 minutes working at his own constant rate. What is the total number of slides the two of them can create in one hour?

(A) 14
(B) 18
(C) 30
(D) 60

90. The least of 5 consecutive integers is *h* and the greatest is *g*. Which of the following is equal to $\dfrac{(g - h)}{2}$?

(E) 1
(F) 2
(G) $h - 2$
(H) $h - 4$

91. A rectangular box that is currently $\dfrac{1}{4}$ full of gravel can hold 3,240 liters of gravel when completely full. How many kiloliters of gravel need to be added in order to fill the box completely?

(A) 0.81
(B) 2.43
(C) 3.24
(D) 8.10

92. In the town of Plainview, 40% of the population is female and 65% of the population commutes to work daily. Of the total Plainview population, 23% are females who commute to work daily. What percentage of the total Plainview population are males who do not commute to work daily?

(E) 17%
(F) 18%
(G) 25%
(H) 42%

GO ON TO THE NEXT PAGE

93. Which number line below shows the solution set for $2x - 4 \leq y \leq 4x + 6$ when $y = 1$?

(A)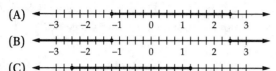

(B)

(C)

(D)

94. Ms. Clark went to the store where she bought eight bottles of water for $0.80 each, 3 pounds of cheese at $2.40 per pound, and 6 pounds of meat. She paid a total of $45.40 for these items, not including tax. What was the price per pound of the meat?

(E) $5.30
(F) $6.10
(G) $6.70
(H) $7.05

95. A box of colored pencils contains exactly 12 red pencils. The probability of choosing a red pencil from the box is $\frac{3}{5}$. How many of the pencils in the box are not red?

(A) 2
(B) 8
(C) 48
(D) 60

96. Which of the following numbers has factors that include the smallest factor (other than 1) of 221?

(E) 33
(F) 34
(G) 35
(H) 39

97.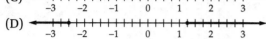

$7\frac{3}{8}$

On the number line above, $JK = 3\frac{1}{4}$, $JM = 9\frac{7}{8}$, and $LM = 2\frac{3}{8}$. What is the position of point K?

(A) $3\frac{1}{8}$

(B) $3\frac{5}{8}$

(C) $4\frac{1}{4}$

(D) $4\frac{5}{8}$

98. A bag contains 75 marbles that are yellow, purple, and white. The ratio of yellow to purple marbles is $6:5$, and the ratio of purple marbles to white marbles is $5:4$. If 1 purple marble is removed and replaced with 1 white marble, what will be the new ratio of yellow to white marbles?

(E) $4:5$
(F) $6:5$
(G) $15:11$
(H) $10:7$

99. If $6x + 4y = 12$, what is x in terms of y?

(A) $x = -\frac{2}{3}y + 2$

(B) $x = \frac{2}{3}y + 12$

(C) $x = \frac{2}{3}y + 2$

(D) $x = -\frac{2}{3}y + 12$

GO ON TO THE NEXT PAGE

100. On Monday, the Sunny Day Restaurant used 35 loaves of bread for 200 breakfast customers. Assuming they use bread at the same rate, approximately how many loaves of bread will be needed on Tuesday when 300 breakfast customers visit the restaurant?

(E) 45

(F) 53

(G) 61

(H) 70

101.

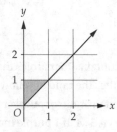

What is the area of the shaded region in the graph above?

(A) 0.25 square units

(B) 0.5 square units

(C) 1 square units

(D) 1.5 square units

102. A box contains three types of cookies: 11 chocolate, 7 vanilla, and 6 strawberry. What is the probability that a cookie chosen at random from this box is *not* strawberry?

(E) $\dfrac{1}{4}$

(F) $\dfrac{11}{24}$

(G) $\dfrac{2}{3}$

(H) $\dfrac{3}{4}$

103. Jill scored a mean of 13 points per game in her first 3 basketball games. After her 4th game, her mean score was 15 points per game. How many points did she score in her 4th game?

(A) 15

(B) 17

(C) 21

(D) 27

104. A bag contains 7 lemon cookies, 5 vanilla cookies, and 3 chocolate cookies. If Martha selects 2 candies at random from this bag, without replacement, what is the probability that both cookies are not vanilla?

(E) $\dfrac{2}{21}$

(F) $\dfrac{4}{21}$

(G) $\dfrac{3}{7}$

(H) $\dfrac{4}{9}$

105. Three students all start running laps at a track at the same time. Alfonso finishes 1 lap every 2 minutes, Jeremy finishes 1 lap every 2.5 minutes, and Luther finishes 1 lap every 3 minutes. How many laps does Alfonso complete before all three runners are once again at the starting line at the same time?

(A) 10

(B) 12

(C) 15

(D) 30

GO ON TO THE NEXT PAGE

106.

Number of Pens or Pencils	Number of Students
0	1
1	5
2	8
3	4
4	1
5	0
6	1

There are 20 students in a class. The frequency table above shows the number of students in this class who brought 0, 1, 2, 3, 4, or 5 pencils or pens to school yesterday. What is the mean number of pencils or pens brought to school yesterday per student in this class?

(E) 2

(F) $2\frac{3}{20}$

(G) $2\frac{7}{18}$

(H) $2\frac{1}{2}$

107. A certain chemical decays so that there is 10% less of the chemical at the end of each week. What percent of the original amount is left after two weeks?

(A) 20%

(B) 80%

(C) 81%

(D) 90%

108. How many positive odd numbers satisfy the inequality $5x - 21 \leq 2x + 36$?

(E) 9

(F) 10

(G) 19

(H) 29

109.

Beverage	Number of Times Ordered
Water	63
Milk	42
Tea	36
Juice	39

The table above shows the number of times that different beverages were ordered in a cafeteria. Based on this information, what is the probability of a customer ordering water as a beverage?

(A) 14%

(B) 28%

(C) 35%

(D) 63%

110. At a certain sandwich shop, you can choose between 3 sizes (small, medium, and large) and 7 different toppings. If Laura wants to order a sandwich with exactly 2 different toppings, how many different sandwiches can she create?

(E) 6

(F) 21

(G) 63

(H) 126

111. Points X, Y, and Z are on a straight line, and Y is between X and Z. Length $XZ = \frac{5}{3}XY$ and length $XY = 24$ centimeters. What is the length of YZ?

(A) 16 cm

(B) 20 cm

(C) 32 cm

(D) 40 cm

GO ON TO THE NEXT PAGE

112. If $w - 1$ is an even integer, which one of the following must be an odd integer?

(E) $2w + 4$

(F) $2w - 2$

(G) $3w + 2$

(H) $4w + 2$

113.

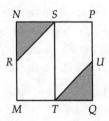

R, S, T, and U are midpoints of the sides of square $MNPQ$, as shown above. If $PQ = 6$ cm, what is the sum of the areas of the shaded triangles?

(A) 4.5 sq cm

(B) 9 sq cm

(C) 18 sq cm

(D) 36 sq cm

114. A large tub is partially filled with n liters of water. If Karen adds 16 liters to the n liters, the tub would be 80% full. But if Maya drains 10 liters of water from the n liters, the tub would be 60% full. What is the value of n?

(E) 26

(F) 47

(G) 88

(H) 104

English Language Arts

1. **A**	16. **G**	31. **C**	46. **E**
2. **G**	17. **B**	32. **F**	47. **C**
3. **D**	18. **G**	33. **B**	48. **F**
4. **F**	19. **D**	34. **G**	49. **D**
5. **B**	20. **H**	35. **D**	50. **G**
6. **F**	21. **C**	36. **G**	51. **C**
7. **A**	22. **F**	37. **D**	52. **G**
8. **G**	23. **C**	38. **H**	53. **B**
9. **D**	24. **G**	39. **B**	54. **F**
10. **E**	25. **C**	40. **H**	55. **C**
11. **D**	26. **H**	41. **D**	56. **F**
12. **H**	27. **D**	42. **F**	57. **B**
13. **A**	28. **H**	43. **D**	
14. **E**	29. **C**	44. **G**	
15. **C**	30. **G**	45. **C**	

Mathematics

58. **240**	73. **C**	88. **E**	103. **C**
59. **−0.5**	74. **F**	89. **C**	104. **G**
60. **79**	75. **B**	90. **F**	105. **C**
61. **59**	76. **E**	91. **B**	106. **F**
62. **48**	77. **A**	92. **F**	107. **C**
63. **A**	78. **F**	93. **A**	108. **F**
64. **E**	79. **C**	94. **E**	109. **C**
65. **D**	80. **F**	95. **B**	110. **G**
66. **G**	81. **B**	96. **H**	111. **A**
67. **C**	82. **G**	97. **A**	112. **G**
68. **H**	83. **B**	98. **H**	113. **B**
69. **A**	84. **F**	99. **A**	114. **G**
70. **H**	85. **B**	100. **F**	
71. **B**	86. **H**	101. **B**	
72. **G**	87. **B**	102. **H**	

ANSWER EXPLANATIONS

English Language Arts

1. **(A)** Examine the pairings of <u>modifiers</u> and *modified objects* below.

    Incorrect: <u>A contagious respiratory infection,</u> *people infected with the seasonal flu virus*

    Correct: <u>A contagious respiratory infection,</u> *the seasonal flu virus*

2. **(G)** Rule number 1: FANBOYS clause. *but John, unaware of the box's contents, broke it by sitting on the box* is a FANBOYS clause. Therefore, a comma is necessary to separate it from the independent clause before it.

3. **(D)** Sentence 1 contains an independent clause and a dependent clause. This is not a run-on.

Redfish Lake is located in central Idaho	where the majestic . . .
Independent Clause	Dependent Clause

   Sentence 2 contains an independent clause and a prepositional phrase. This is not a run-on.

The shores of Redfish . . . campsites	with beach access . . .
Independent Clause	Prepositional Phrase

   Sentence 3 contains an independent clause and a modifier. This is not a run-on.

The Redfish Lake Lodge offers . . . and more	making this a great . . .
Independent Clause	Prepositional Phrase

   Sentence 4 contains two independent clauses joined by a comma. This is a run-on.

You deserve some peace	this is the best place to get it
Independent Clause	Independent Clause

   Correction: You deserve some peace, *and* this is the best place to get it.

4. **(F)** Examine the pairings of <u>antecedents</u> and *pronouns* below.

   (1) With a rover named Curiosity, <u>Mars Science Laboratory</u> is part of NASA's Mars Exploration Program. (2) *They* are a part of a long-term effort of robotic exploration of the red planet. (3) <u>Curiosity</u> was designed to assess whether Mars ever had an environment able to support small life forms called microbes. (4) In other words, *its* mission is to determine the planet's "habitability."

   Sentence 1: Does not contain a pronoun.

   Sentence 2: The plural pronoun *They* is an inappropriate replacement for the antecedent

   <u>Mars Science Laboratory</u>. *They* should be revised to *It*.

   Sentence 3: Does not contain a pronoun.

   Sentence 4: The singular pronoun *its* properly replaces the antecedent <u>Curiosity</u>.

5. **(B)** The adjectives cold and windy are coordinate adjectives, meaning they can be used interchangeably with the word *and* to describe clouds. A comma is necessary to indicate that.

   Choice A is wrong because there are only two characteristics that the word *and* connects: the fifth planet . . . and the largest planet.

   Choice C is wrong because the comma is necessary for the FANBOYS clause. And yes, you can have two *and*s in a sentence. The first *and* is used to complete a list. The second *and* is used to start a FANBOYS clause.

   Choice D is wrong because the commas are necessary around the word *however* to indicate a pause.

6. **(F)** The phrase *wasted opportunity* best links with the phrase *an opportunity to save money* in sentence 5.

7. **(A)** The sentence is a run-on consisting of a dependent clause, independent clause, and independent clause. To fix this, one of the independent clauses needs to be changed to a dependent clause or phrase.

   Choice B is wrong because *not just . . . but also* is awkward. Typically, the phrase should be *not only . . . but also*. Secondly, the wording after *not just* should be similar to the wording after *but also*. For example, *not just <u>creating a problem</u> but also <u>solving a problem</u>* would be similar.

   Choice C is wrong because there are three independent clauses in an unnecessary list.

   Choice D is wrong because the wording after *not just* and *but* are not similar.

8. **(G)** The passage uses formal language (like a textbook). Wording that uses informal choices (words and phrases you would normally see in casual conversation) should be removed.

   Choice E is wrong because *tons of food* is informal.

   Choice F is wrong because *blow all their dough* is informal.

   Choice H is wrong because *eat like a savage* is informal.

9. **(D)** Sentences 6 through 8 all introduce their ideas in order. The transition word *Finally* best fits in with *First* of sentence 6, *Secondly* of sentence 7, and *Thirdly* of sentence 8.

10. **(E)** Choices F, G, and H are wrong because they all create contrasts with the words *but*, *Despite*, and *While*.

11. **(D)** The passage discusses the eco-friendly alternative and not so much the cost benefits.

12. **(H)** Paragraphs 7 and 8 support the answer choice. Choice E is wrong because it is too general. The passage is specifically about the Wound Man, not technology. Choice F is wrong because paragraph 4 clearly shows its origin and its purpose. Choice G is wrong because paragraph 8 explains that the *Wound Man reminds us that it was in fact a period busy with innovative medical treatments.*

13. **(A)** Paragraphs 1 and 2 provide visual details about the Wound Man and nothing more. Choices B and C are wrong because the author's judgment about the Wound Man representing life in the Middle Ages is not discussed until paragraph 8. Even here, the author contradicts those answer choices. Choice D is wrong because in paragraph 3, the last sentence dismisses that idea to introduce the usefulness of the Wound Man.

14. **(E)** The first phrase *Staring impassively out of the page* indicates that the Wound Man is an illustration in a book. None of the other choices make such a suggestion.

15. **(C)** The last sentence of paragraph 3, *He . . . represents . . . the powerful knowledge . . . of late medieval medicine,* best supports the idea that the Wound Man was an important image to medieval medicine. Choice A is wrong because there is no reference to the viewer in the paragraph. Choice B is wrong because the paragraph makes no mention of what life was like for people of the Middle Ages. Choice D is wrong because the paragraph makes no mention of any hypothetical person who might be fortunate.

16. **(G)** The previous sentence claims that *Wound Men effectively functioned as a human table of contents for cures.* The quoted sentence from paragraph 3 is used to support the idea by making a reference to the *text* that is shown next to the Wound Men.

17. **(B)** The author provides direct quotations next to parenthetical translation to exemplify the *numbers and phrases* on the Wound Men. Choice A is wrong because there is no indication that the disorders mentioned are the most typical ones. Choice C is wrong because it mistakenly assumes that the disorders listed are the only ones that appear on the Wound Man. Choice D is wrong because the author makes no comparison between the technologies of the Middle Ages and those of today.

18. **(G)** The previous sentence claims that the Wound Man *was . . . an arresting reminder . . . of the vital knowledge.* The phrase "popular inclusion" serves to emphasize its importance in many manuscripts. Choice E is wrong because there is nothing critical in the entire paragraph. Choice F is wrong because although the Wound Man may have been recognizable to many people, this is never mentioned in the paragraph. Choice H is wrong because this idea is never supported.

19. **(D)** Paragraph 8 clearly supports this idea by claiming that *the Wound Man reminds us that it was in fact a period busy with innovative technological treatments.* Choice A is wrong because although it might seem logically true, nothing in the passage recognizes this connection. Choice B is wrong because the author never makes a value judgment about war and violence. Choice C is wrong because of the word *war.* It is too specific and there is nothing in the text that makes that connection.

20. **(H)** The phrase *Living on today in libraries . . .* clearly notes its importance to society today. Choice E is wrong because the sentence links the importance of the Wound Man to the Middle Ages. Choice F is wrong because it is an introduction to a description of the medical text. Choice G is wrong because the sentence explains what the Wound Man represented to the people of the Middle Ages.

21. **(C)** The first sentence states that chocolate and other substances *carried within them the wonder and danger of far-away lands.* This sentence supports the idea that the *fatality* was based on speculation and wonder rather than on facts. Choice A is wrong because the passage makes no mention of the dangers or fatalities that actually occurred as a result of chocolate consumption. Choice B is wrong because *fatality* is not associated with miracles. Choice D is wrong because the passage states the opposite.

22. **(F)** The second sentence of paragraph 1 links 17th-century Europeans, *this brand-new clientele,* with chocolate and the *wonder and danger of far-away lands.* Choice E is wrong because it refers to chocolate products. Choice G is wrong because it refers to pharmacists and physicians who administered the drugs. Choice H is wrong because it refers to people drinking chocolate products.

23. **(C)** The first and third sentences of paragraph 2 show that chocolate was met with *curiosity and concern*. The author also states that *Physicians and tradesmen . . . proclaimed the many health benefits . . . or issued impassioned warnings*. Choices A and B are wrong because the author never evaluates which position was more preferred. Choice D is wrong because the author never references the public's preference for taste over health.

24. **(G)** This choice is supported by the last sentence of paragraph 3, which states that *Colmenero's work introduced chocolate to Europe as a drug by appealing to the science of the humors*. Choice E is wrong because the author never connects Cortés to Colmenero's work. Choice F is wrong because although it is true that he acquired his degree in medicine, this fact is never acknowledged as the way by which Colmenero introduced his work. Choice H is wrong because the passage never claims that Colmenero imported chocolate. The passage claims that Spain imported chocolate, not Colmenero.

25. **(C)** This choice is supported by paragraph 4, which states that when *one occurred in excess, it produced symptoms of what we now call "disease."* Choices A and B are wrong because the passage only discusses what Hippocrates said about the humors and makes no reference to what Hippocrates would have said about chocolate. Choice D is wrong because Hippocrates never evaluates the strength of the humors.

26. **(H)** The first sentence of paragraph 5 shows that the contextualization of chocolate made it *at least debatable in terms readily accessible*. Choice E is wrong because humoralism is never treated as the origin of European medicine. Choice F is wrong because the author discusses how humoralism explains sicknesses, not how people develop sicknesses. Choice G is wrong because the author never claims that humoralism is a problem.

27. **(D)** The phrase following *medical lore* supports the idea that his work *remained an important reference*, which emphasizes the impact that his work had. Choice A is wrong because it only mentions the dating of Colmenero's work. Choice B is wrong because it only describes how Colmenero introduced the work and not that it had a large impact. Choice C is wrong because it only notes what Colmenero tried to do and not the impact it had on Europeans.

28. **(H)** This sentence suggests that Colmenero's work also included a recipe, which was intended to enhance the consumption and not just the medical aspect of chocolate.

29. **(C)** There were several impacts of his work. The quoted sentence indicates one impact, which was to enable people to talk about it intelligently. Choice A is wrong because Colmenero's personality is never addressed. Choice B is wrong because Colmenero was not concerned with chocolate supplies. Choice D is wrong because the sentence actually helps dispel, not encourage, the mystery of chocolate.

30. **(G)** The last paragraph summarizes the main point, which is reflected in choice G. Choice E and F are wrong because although they contain true details mentioned in the text, they do not reflect the main idea. Choice H is wrong because paragraph 6 states that he made money from not just boxing: *Americans paid money not just to see John L. Sullivan box, but just to see John.*

31. **(C)** The phrase in the last sentence *ceaseless flow of well-wishers* supports the point that the words are intended to contribute to a tone of excitement.

32. **(F)** The phrase *constructed like a pugilistic product of the Industrial Age* makes the connection between physical characteristics and Sullivan's time period. Choice E is wrong because although arrogance is implicitly connected to the knock out tour described in paragraph 5, the author never attributes Sullivan's arrogance to his physique. Choice G is wrong because the author never even mentions materialism. Choice H is wrong because the author does not say anything about violence and boxing in this paragraph.

33. **(B)** In choice B, the phrase *testified to the inability of foes to lay a licking on him* suggests that Sullivan could not be beat in boxing. Choices A and C are wrong because they describe people's desire to see Sullivan. Choice D is wrong because it only provides information about the tour and not Sullivan's boxing skills.

34. **(G)** The phrase *sensational novelty act* suggests that his fights were similar to shows that were *worthy of . . . the showman*. Choice E distorts the meaning of the sentence. Choice F is wrong because the statement says Sullivan sparred with his fellow boxers, not anyone. Choice H is wrong because the sentence states that his fights were like novelty acts, not that he included novelty acts.

35. **(D)** The third sentence supports *those about America* and the last sentence supports *ideas about himself*. Choice A is wrong because the paragraph talks about his tour where anyone could challenge him. Choices B and C are wrong because they are contrary to the author's claim that the tour was American.

36. **(G)** The quoted phrase makes a reference to his *personal magnetism*. Then the following sentence exemplifies the popularity that Sullivan enjoyed. Choices E and F are wrong because they misinterpret the word *drawing*. Choice H is wrong because although it is true, the phrase *drawing card* is not used to emphasize Sullivan's skill in the ring, but his popularity.

37. **(D)** This sentence suggests that they were willing to pay just to see John and not to see him box.

38. **(H)** The question asks you to find information about Sullivan's *legacy*, which refers to something that lasts. Choice H contains the word *endure*, which makes the link that the question is looking for.

39. **(B)** The first part of the sentence before the quote states that jesters *were expected to be always ready with sharp witticisms . . . .* In other words, since there was not a lot of food for the performers, jesters had to be quick to entertain so that they would be fed the little food available. Choice A is wrong because they were not asked to focus on the quantity or the quality of the crumbs. Choice C is wrong because the first sentence states the opposite—that they have *gone out of fashion*. Choice D is wrong because the sentence says *always be ready*; it does not refer to specific times.

40. **(H)** The second sentence of paragraph 2 states that the *folly* was necessary to *counterbalance the heavy wisdom of the seven wise men*. This means that the king felt that the ministers were being overly serious and a fool was necessary. Choice E is wrong because they were not foolish enough. Choice F is wrong because the word *artistically* does not properly describe the ministers' grimness. Choice G is wrong because their popularity is never mentioned.

41. **(D)** This paragraph builds on the parenthetical statement *(this was the fool's name)* by providing additional information that explains the name. Choice A is wrong because the narrative is still focused on Hop-Frog. Choice B is wrong because it provides the background of Hop-Frog's name, not any type of history. Choice C is wrong because there is no claim in the paragraph that is later dismissed.

42. **(F)** The parenthetical comment explains why *many monarchs would have found it difficult to get through their days*. Choice E is wrong because the comment clarifies a description of a monarch's day, not an abstract concept. Choice G is wrong because there is no term that it defines. Choice H is wrong because the comment adds to the preceding statement; it doesn't challenge it.

43. **(D)** The previous paragraph explains that Hop-Frog's name was based on *his inability to walk*. Paragraph 5 explains that the inability led to an impressive development of Hop-Frog's upper body, which *enabled him to perform many feats of wonderful dexterity*. Choice A is wrong because *cheery* is not an accurate description of the characterization. Choice B is wrong because the paragraph is not intended to provide an argument supported by facts. Choice C is wrong because the narrator's bias or objectivity is not intended to be a part of the story.

44. **(G)** The phrase *it is not to be wondered* suggests that the *close intimacy* was an expected one. Choice E is wrong because the phrase suggests the opposite. Choice F is wrong because although it may be true, there are no words that directly support *admirable*. Choice H is wrong because, again, there are no words that describe the intimacy as *horrifying*.

45. **(C)** The line in the last sentence *never failed to use it, whenever she could, for the benefit of Hop-Frog* suggests that Trippetta tried to help Hop-Frog whenever the opportunity arose.

46. **(E)** The lines suggest that possessing one attribute doesn't lead to a better quality in man. Choice F is wrong because the lines suggest the opposite. Choice G is wrong because it misinterprets the wording. Choice H is wrong because the comparison is not between men and trees.

47. **(C)** The word *Or* provides a second instance in which a commonly viewed criteria for a good life is rejected. Growing old, according to the poem, is characterized with being dry, bald, and withered. Choices A and B are wrong because the poem never suggests one is better or worse than the other. Choice D is wrong because it may be true, but the fact is irrelevant to the development of the poem.

48. **(F)** The phrases *of a day* and *die that night* serve to emphasize the beauty of the lily, whose *fair* state does not last very long.

49. **(D)** The quoted lines suggest that beauty is temporary and that a perfect life can be seen in short instances. Choice D best supports that point because it emphasizes the short time in which the beauty and power of the flower exists. Choices A and B are wrong because they focus on what a good life isn't. Choice C is wrong because it supports line 9 but not line 10.

50. **(G)** Choice E is wrong because there are no criteria to determine the importance of any given line. Choice F is wrong because the rhyme is regular. Choice H is wrong because even if the poem is unusual, the capitalization is not.

51. **(C)** *Most of it* refers to the *wonder* mentioned in the same sentence. That wonder refers to the audience's reaction.

52. **(G)** The last sentence of paragraph 2 reflects Doyle's opinion. Choice E is wrong because the company never connected the girls to the skills. Choice F is wrong because this is never stated in the passage. Choice H is wrong because the girls' honesty is never mentioned.

53. **(B)** The phrase *far-from-impartial* means that Gardner was already biased in his belief about fairies and therefore could not conduct an objective investigation.

54. **(F)** Paragraph 4 reveals that the girls were reluctant, but Gardner made arrangements to somewhat corner the girls into producing the photos. Choice E is wrong because there is no indication in the remainder of the passage that suggests that the girls took more photos. Choices G and H are wrong because the purpose here is to reveal information about the two girls and not about human nature.

55. **(C)** Paragraph 5 shows that the girls tried to explain that the photo had nothing to do with fairies, but Doyle and Gardner *insisted* that it did. Choice A is wrong because they believed the photos were real. Choice B is wrong because it may be logically true, but the paragraph never supports this indication. Choice D is wrong because the first sentence says that they were thrilled.

56. **(F)** This sentence shows that Elsie tried to create an excuse so that she wouldn't have to take another photo. Choice E is wrong because this sentence only shows what Gardner wanted. Choice G is wrong because it refers to their observation about the third photo. Choice H is wrong because it is a description of Doyle, not an observation about the girls.

57. **(B)** The last sentence of paragraph 6 supports this statement. Choice A is wrong because paragraph 6 states that even though Doyle *created the world's greatest detective*, his investigations were a complete dud. Choice C is wrong because the last paragraph shows that the girls did reveal the truth. Choice D is wrong because this is never mentioned in the passage.

Mathematics

58. **(240)** Let b be the total number of blueberry muffins. Set up the proportion $\dfrac{7}{8} = \dfrac{210}{b}$, and solve for b. Cross-multiply to get $7b = 8 \times 210$, divide by 7, then simplify: $b = \dfrac{8 \times 210}{7} = 8 \times \dfrac{210}{7} = 8 \times 30 = 240$. **Note:** Since there are 8 blueberry muffins for every 7 chocolate muffins, the number of blueberry muffins should be more than the number of chocolate muffins, which is true since $240 > 210$.

59. **(−0.5)** Multiply both sides of the equation by $12 - x$ to get $100 = 8 \times (12 - x)$. Simplify to get $100 = 96 - 8x$, and solve for x: $4 = -8x$, so $x = \dfrac{4}{-8} = -\dfrac{1}{2} = -0.5$. Some number sense can help guide our search for the solution as well. Notice that if $x = 0$:

$$\frac{100}{12-x} = \frac{100}{12-0}$$
$$= \frac{100}{12}$$
$$= 8.5$$

This is close to 8. So our answer is probably close to 0.

60. **(79)** A Venn diagram is helpful in these kinds of problems.

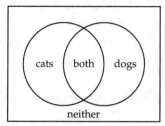

The total number of students surveyed is equal to the number of students who have cats or dogs plus the number of students who have neither. A common mistake is to compute the number of students who have cats or dogs as (number who have cats) + (number who have dogs); this counts those who have both pets twice. To compensate, we must subtract from this the number who have both. Thus, the number of students who have cats or dogs is: (number who have cats) + (number who have dogs) − (number who have both). Adding to this the number who have neither gives us a final answer of $41 + 36 − 12 + 14 = 79$.

61. **(59)** Since the measure of a right angle is $90°$ and the sum of the measures of all the angles around a point is $360°$, we have $149° + m \angle Q + 90° = 360°$, and so $m \angle Q = 360° − 90° − 149° = 121°$. And since $PQRS$ is a parallelogram, adjacent angles are supplementary, making $m \angle Q + m \angle R = 180°$. Thus, $m \angle R = 180° − m \angle Q = 180° − 121° = 59°$.

62. **(48)** To find the two consecutive odd integers, use the fact that consecutive odd integers differ by 2 to set up and solve the equation $x + (x + 2) = −16$. Or you can just guess and check to determine that the consecutive odd integers $−7$ and $−9$ sum to $−16$. Adding 3 to the smaller integer gives us $−9 + 3 = −6$; subtracting 1 from the larger integers gives us $−7 − 1 = −8$. The product is thus $(−6) \times (−8) = 48$. **Note:** Be careful when comparing negative numbers, as $−7$ is greater than $−9$.

63. **(A)** Use the distributive property to remove parenthesis, being especially careful with distributing negative signs: $8 + (4n + 5) − (5n + 7) = 8 + 4n + 5 − 5n − 7$. Then combine like terms to get $6 − n$. **Note:** The other answer choices follow from common mistakes. For example, if you do not distribute the $−1$ to the 7, you'll end up with $20 − n$, which is choice C. Be careful when you distribute!

64. **(E)** At 250 milliliters per bottle, 4 bottles contain 1,000 milliliters, which is equivalent to 1 liter. Thus, $6 \times 4 = 24$ bottles contain 6 liters of water.

65. **(D)** Substitute $x = −5$ and $y = 7$ into the expression $x(x − 2y)$ to get:

$$(−5)((−5) − 2(7)) =$$

$$(−5)(−5 − 14) =$$

$$(−5)(−19) = 95$$

Be careful with the signs: $−95$ is an answer choice as well!

66. **(G)** The length of WZ is $8 - (-10) = 18$. If WZ were 9 units long, the ratio $WX : XY : YZ = 4 : 3 : 2$ would give us that $WX = 4$, $XY = 3$, and $YZ = 2$. Since WZ is 2×9 long, each of WX, XY, and YZ will be 2 times as long. Thus, in our diagram, $WX = 8$, $XY = 6$, and $YZ = 4$. (Check that these sum to 18 and are in the $4 : 3 : 2$ ratio.) Thus, $WY = 14$. Notice that the *position* of Y on the number line, namely $-10 + 14 = 4$, is choice E.

67. **(C)** Let S be the sum of Ahmed's course grades scores. If Ahmed had an average of 72 in 5 courses, then $\frac{S}{5} = 72$, and so $S = 5 \times 72 = 360$. So the sum of Rita's four course grades is 360, and her average is $\frac{360}{4} = 90$.

68. **(H)** Isolate r in the equation $\frac{q}{r} = \frac{s}{t}$ by cross-multiplying: $qt = sr$, and so $r = \frac{qt}{s}$. You could also "make a wish" here: Let $q = 4$, $r = 2$, $s = 10$, and $t = 5$, which makes $\frac{q}{r} = \frac{s}{t}$ true. Since we are looking for the answer choice that is equal to r, plug $q = 4$, $r = 2$, $s = 10$, and $t = 5$ into the answer choices and see which one equals 2. This is choice H.

69. **(A)** With 183 teachers and a 15 to 1 student-to-teacher ratio, there are $183 \times 15 = 2{,}745$ total students. Subtracting off the first-year students gives us $2{,}745 - 512 = 2{,}233$ students. Be careful not to answer 2,745 just because that number appears in your calculations; 2,745 is the number of total students, and the question asked for only the number of second-, third-, and fourth-year students. Always read carefully.

70. **(H)** Find the length, L, of the rectangle by solving the following proportion:

$$\frac{L}{114} = \frac{3}{2}$$
$$2L = 3 \times 114$$
$$L = \frac{3 \times 114}{2} = 3 \times 57 = 171$$

The perimeter, P, of a rectangle is given by $P = 2L + 2W$, which we compute as follows:

$$P = 2 \times 114 + 2 \times 171$$
$$= 228 + 342$$
$$= 570$$

Notice that $L + W = 285$ is an answer choice—remember that the perimeter of a rectangle is *twice* the sum of the length and width.

71. **(B)** The numbers in the given range are $3n$, $3n + 1$, $3n + 2$, $3n + 3$, $3n + 4$, $3n + 5$, and $3n + 6$. If $3n$ is even, then $3n + 1$, $3n + 3$, and $3n + 5$ will all be odd, so the answer is 3. This is also a good opportunity to "make a wish": If $n = 2$, then $3n = 6$, which is a positive even number. The numbers in the given range are thus 6, 7, 8, 9, 10, 11, and 12, three of which are odd.

72. **(G)** The total percentage of vehicles containing at least 3 people is $15\% + 8\% + 2\% = 25\%$, and 25% of 400 is one-quarter of 400, or 100. You could also find 25% of 400 by computing $0.25 \times 400 = 100$. **Note:** The number of vehicles that contained exactly 3 people is one of the answer choices. Remember to be on the lookout for phrases like "at least" and "at most."

73. **(C)** Since there are 12 inches in 1 foot, there are $12 \times 3 = 36$ inches in 3 feet, and thus $36 + 9 = 45$ inches in 3 feet 9 inches. The answer is then $2.54 \times 45 = 114.3$. A common error is to convert 1 foot into 10 inches. In this problem, that would give you choice B.

74. **(F)** We compute the value of k for each value of m. When $m = 2$, $k = 2^2 - 4 = 4 - 4 = 0$; when $m = 3$, $k = 3^2 - 4 = 9 - 4 = 5$. We actually now know the answer is choice B, since that is the only set that contains both 0 and 5. But we check that when $m = 4$, $k = 4^2 - 4 = 16 - 4 = 12$.

75. **(B)** At 6 jerms per dollar, 120 jerms is $20. If 0.4 zeeb is 1 dollar, then 4 zeebs is $10, making 20 zeebs equal to $50. Thus, the total value is $70. A common mistake in this situation is to convert 20 zeebs into $20 \times 0.4 = 8$ dollars, which gives choice A. As a quick check, notice that 1 zeeb is more valuable than 1 dollar, so 20 zeebs should be worth more than $20.

76. **(E)** In a triangle, the measures of the angles sum to $180°$, so $m \angle PQT + m \angle QTP + m \angle TPQ = 180°$. Substituting in the known angle measures gives us $45° + 75° + m \angle TPQ = 180°$, which makes $m \angle TPQ = 60°$. In a parallelogram, opposite angles are congruent, which makes $m \angle QRS = m \angle TPQ = 60°$.

77. **(A)** The decimal number 0.12 is *twelve hundredths*, which means $0.12 = \dfrac{12}{100}$. We can reduce this to $\dfrac{12}{100} = \dfrac{6}{50} = \dfrac{3}{25}$.

78. **(F)** The probability that the first card drawn is not red is $\dfrac{8}{10}$. Since the card is not replaced, the probability that the second card drawn is not red is $\dfrac{7}{9}$ (there is one less non-red card and one less card overall). To find the probability of both of these events, we multiply their probabilities:

$$\frac{8}{10} \times \frac{7}{9} = \frac{56}{90}$$
$$= \frac{28}{45}$$

79. **(C)** Since the height of the box is twice the side length of the base, the height of the box is 8 feet long. This makes the volume $4 \times 4 \times 8 = 128$ cu ft.

80. **(F)** Malik's mean speed is $\dfrac{63}{3} = 21$ kph, and Shana's mean speed is $\dfrac{72}{3} = 24$ kph. So Malik's mean speed is $24 - 21 = 3$ kph less than Shana's.

81. **(B)** The least common multiple (LCM) of three numbers is the smallest number that has each number as a factor. Trying out all the answers is a good strategy here. Notice that 24 is not a factor of 60, so choice A is not the answer. Since all the numbers are factors of 120, choice B is the answer. Notice that 24 is not a factor of 180, so choice C is not the answer. Although all three numbers are factors of 360, making 360 a common multiple, it is not the *least* common multiple, so choice D is not the answer. **Note:** When looking for the *smallest* number that has a property, be sure to test the smaller answer choices first!

82. **(G)** Notice we can also write the ratio of x to y as $1:2$, which allows us to write the single ratio $x:y:z = 1:2:3$. Since $1 + 2 + 3 = 6$, we quickly see that $10 + 20 + 30 = 60$, and so $x = 10$, $y = 20$, and $z = 30$ is a solution to our problem.

83. **(B)** The frequency of each number is important here. You must count four 90s, four 80s, and two 70s. Thus, the mean is computed as follows:

$$\frac{4 \times 90 + 4 \times 80 + 2 \times 70}{10} = \frac{360 + 320 + 140}{10}$$
$$= \frac{820}{10}$$
$$= 82$$

84. **(F)** We know that 4.5 slanks is equal in value to 12.15 gribs, since they are both equivalent to 1 flooz. So 1 grib is equal to:

$$\frac{12.15}{4.5} = \frac{1215}{450}$$
$$= \frac{243}{90}$$
$$= \frac{81}{30}$$
$$= \frac{27}{10}$$
$$= 2.7 \text{ slanks}$$

Estimation is also a good approach here. A grib is worth more than twice a slank, but less than 3 slanks, thus F is the only reasonable answer.

85. **(B)** Using a chart and testing all answers is a good approach to this problem.

Today		In 7 Years	
Molly's Age	Jack's Age	Molly's Age	Jack's Age
5	1.25	12	8.25
8	2	15	9
9	2.25	16	9.25
15	3.75	22	10.75

You can check that the only situation where, in 7 years, the ratio of Jack's age to Molly's age is $3:5$ is when Jack is 9 and Molly is 15.

86. **(H)** Notice that 3 parts of the 10 parts making up the paste is the resin. That is, the resin constitutes $\frac{3}{10}$ of the paste. Since 1 billboard requires 30 pounds of paste, 1 billboard requires $\frac{3}{10}$ of 30 pounds, or 9 pounds, of resin. Thus, 4 billboards would require $4 \times 9 = 36$ pounds of resin. Notice that 9 is an answer choice, which is the amount of resin required for 1 billboard.

87. **(B)** To find the length of *RS*, we need to find the area of a triangular face. The surface area *including* the base is the area of the four triangles on the sides of the pyramid plus the area of the square base. This is given to be 160 sq cm. Since the square has side length 8 cm, the area of the square is 64 sq cm, which means the area of the four triangles is $160 - 64 = 96$ sq cm. The area of one of these triangles is thus $\frac{96}{4} = 24$ sq cm. Since the area of each triangle is $\frac{1}{2}$ the base times the height, we have $24 = \frac{1}{2}bh$. But the length of the base is 8 cm, since it is a side of the square. This gives us $24 = \frac{1}{2} \times 8h$, and so $24 = 4h$, and $h = 6$. **Note:** If you *exclude* the area of the base, you'll get $h = 10$, which is an answer choice. Always read carefully!

88. **(E)** There are 5 choices for the first cookie. Once that cookie is selected, there are 4 choices for the second cookie. The fundamental counting principle tells us to multiply the number of options for each choice, giving us $5 \times 4 = 20$. But this is not the correct answer, because the order in which the cookies are selected makes no difference. Choosing cookie A first, then cookie B gives us the same pair of cookies as choosing cookie B first, then A. Thus, our calculation above double counts the number of pairs of cookies, and so the correct answer is $\frac{20}{2} = 10$.

89. **(C)** Since Darla can make 4 slides in 20 minutes, she can make 1 slide in 5 minutes, which means she can make 12 slides in 1 hour. Kaito can make 3 slides in 10 minutes, so he can make $6 \times 3 = 18$ slides in 60 minutes. Thus, the two of them can make $12 + 18 = 30$ slides in one hour.

90. **(F)** If h is the least of 5 consecutive integers, the 5 consecutive integers are h, $h + 1$, $h + 2$, $h + 3$, and $h + 4$. This means that $g = h + 4$. Then solve the following:

$$\frac{(g - h)}{2} = \frac{(h + 4 - h)}{2}$$
$$= \frac{4}{2}$$
$$= 2$$

You could also "make a wish" here: Let $h = 10$, then $g = 14$, so $\frac{(g - h)}{2} = 2$. Only choice F can be the correct answer.

91. **(B)** Since the box is $\frac{1}{4}$ full, an additional $\frac{3}{4}$ is needed to fill it. One-fourth of 3,240 liters is $\frac{3240}{4} = 810$ liters, and so three-fourths of 3,240 is $3 \times 810 = 2430$ liters. Since 1,000 liters is equal to 1 kiloliter, 2,430 liters is equal to 2.43 kiloliters. **Note:** The shape of the box is irrelevant in this problem! Don't waste time thinking about volume formulas.

92. **(F)** We can use a Venn diagram to represent our situation:

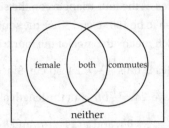

Notice that "neither" here means "a person who is not a female and who doesn't commute," which we take to mean "males who don't commute." Let x be the number of men who don't commute. We have the equation $0.40 + 0.65 - 0.23 + x = 1.00$, with the 1.00 on the right representing 100% of the population. Solving gives us $x = 0.18$, or 18%. Trying each answer choice in the standard inclusion-exclusion formula would also be a good approach.

93. **(A)** Substituting $y = 1$ yields the compound inequality $2x - 4 \leq 1 \leq 4x + 6$, which is equivalent to the two inequalities $2x - 4 \leq 1$ and $1 \leq 4x + 6$. (Note the importance of the word *and* here, not *or*.) Simplifying these two inequalities yields $x \leq 2.5$ and $-1.25 \leq x$. The numbers that are both less than or equal to 2.5 and greater than or equal to -1.25 are represented graphically by choice A. Alternately, you could recognize that only choices A and C represent *and* inequalities, and then test a value to determine which one to choose.

94. **(E)** Let $m =$ the price per pound of meat. Then $0.80 \times 8 + 2.40 \times 3 + m \times 6 = 45.40$. Solving for m gives us the following:

$$0.80 \times 8 + 2.40 \times 3 + m \times 6 = 45.40$$
$$6.4 + 7.2 + 6m = 45.40$$
$$13.6 + 6m = 45.40$$
$$\underline{-13.6 \qquad\quad -13.6}$$
$$6m = 31.8$$
$$m = 5.3$$

Since $m = 5.3$, the answer is $5.30. Alternately, the price of the meat is the total price minus the price of the water ($0.08 \times 8 = $6.40) and the price of the cheese ($2.40 \times 3 = $7.20):

$$\$45.40 - \$0.80 \times 8 - \$2.40 \times 3 =$$
$$\$45.40 - \$6.40 - \$7.20 = \$31.80$$

Divide by 6 pounds to get the price per pound of meat: $31.80 \div 6$ pounds $= $5.30.

95. **(B)** The probability of drawing a red pencil is equal to $\dfrac{\text{\# of red pencils}}{\text{\# of total pencils}}$, which is $\dfrac{3}{5}$. Let p be the total number of pencils. Since there are 12 red pencils, we have $\dfrac{3}{5} = \dfrac{12}{p}$. Solving, we get $3p = 60$, and so $p = 20$. Since p is the total number of pencils, the number of non-red pencils is $20 - 12 = 8$.

96. **(H)** To solve this problem, you must know the prime factorization of 221, namely $221 = 13 \times 17$. If you don't see it immediately, try dividing 221 by primes (2, 3, 5, 7, 11, 13, etc.) until something evenly divides it. Once you find that 13 is the smallest factor of 221, the question now is which answer choice has 13 as a factor, and that is H. Notice that answer choice F, 34, shares a factor with 221 (namely 17), but it doesn't share 221's smallest factor.

97. **(A)** The position of L minus the length KL is the position of L. To find KL, we use the fact that $JM = JK + KL + LM$, substitute known values, and simplify:

$$9\frac{7}{8} = 3\frac{1}{4} + KL + 2\frac{3}{8}$$
$$9\frac{7}{8} = 5\frac{5}{8} + KL$$
$$4\frac{2}{8} = 4\frac{1}{4} = KL$$

This means the position of K is:

$$7\frac{3}{8} - 4\frac{1}{4} =$$
$$7\frac{3}{8} - 4\frac{2}{8} = 3\frac{1}{8}$$

98. **(H)** Notice that the ratio of yellow to purple to white marbles is $6 : 5 : 4$. As is often the case in these problems, the sum of the marbles in the ratio is a convenient number. Here, $6 + 5 + 4 = 15$, and 15 is one-fifth of 75, the total number of marbles in the bag. So we can multiply the ratio by 5 to find the exact number of marbles of each color. There will be 30 yellow, 25 purple, and 20 white. Removing 1 purple and adding 1 white means there will now be 30 yellow, 24 purple, and 21 white, making the ratio of yellow to white marbles $\frac{30}{21} = \frac{10}{7}$, or $10 : 7$.

99. **(A)** Solve the equation for x: $6x = -4y + 12$, then divide both sides of the equation by 6 to get the following:

$$x = \frac{-4y + 12}{6}$$
$$= -\frac{4y}{6} + \frac{12}{6}$$
$$= -\frac{2y}{3} + 2$$
$$= -\frac{2}{3}y + 2$$

100. **(F)** Solve the following proportion:

$$\frac{35}{200} = \frac{x}{300}$$
$$x = \frac{3}{2} \times 35$$
$$= \frac{105}{2}$$
$$= 52.5$$

Then round to get the correct answer. Or notice that 100 customers require 17.5 loaves of bread, so 300 customers require $3 \times 17.5 = 52.5$ loaves of bread.

101. **(B)** The area of a triangle is equal to $\frac{1}{2}$ the product of its base and height. In the diagram, the shaded triangle is a right triangle with a base of 1 unit and a height of 1 unit. Its area is therefore: $\frac{1}{2} \times 1 \times 1 = \frac{1}{2} = 0.5$ square units. Alternately, note that the shaded region is half of a square of area 1.

102. **(H)** There are $11 + 7 + 6 = 24$ total cookies in the box. Since 18 of them are not strawberry, the probability of choosing a non-strawberry cookie from the box is $\frac{18}{24} = \frac{3}{4}$.

103. **(C)** The mean, or average, of n numbers is the sum of the n numbers divided by n. Jill scored an average of 13 points per game is her first 3 games, which means she scored 39 total points in those first 3 games, since $\frac{39}{3} = 13$. Let P be the number of points she scored in her 4th game. Since her average after 4 games is 15, we have $\frac{39 + P}{4} = 15$. Solving for P gives us $39 + P = 60$, and so $P = 21$.

104. **(G)** To start, there are 15 cookies total and 10 non-vanilla cookies. The probability that the first cookie is not vanilla is $\frac{10}{15} = \frac{2}{3}$. Since the first cookie is not put back, there are now 14 total cookies and 9 non-vanilla cookies, which makes the probability that the second cookie selected is not vanilla $\frac{9}{14}$. To find the probability of both cookies not being vanilla, we multiply the following:

$$\frac{2}{3} \times \frac{9}{14} = \frac{18}{42}$$
$$= \frac{9}{21}$$
$$= \frac{3}{7}$$

Note: If you consider the problem *with replacement*, you get answer choice H. And if you find the probability that both candies *are* vanilla, you'll get choice E.

105. **(C)** Notice that Alfonso and Luther will meet at the starting line every 6 minutes—after Alfonso has completed 3 laps and Luther has completed 2 laps. Jeremy will return to the starting line every 2.5 minutes, but since neither of the other students will be at the starting line at a non-integer time, it's better to think of Jeremy as being at the starting line every 5 minutes after completing two laps. The LCM of 6 and 5 is 30, which means the first time all three students will meet again at the starting line is after 30 minutes, at which point Alfonso will have completed $\frac{30}{2} = 15$ laps. **Note:** 30 is the amount of minutes it takes for all runners to meet up and is an answer choice, but 30 is not the answer to the question that was asked.

106. **(F)** Note that this is a frequency chart. You are not finding the mean, or average, of 0, 1, 2, 3, 4, 5, and 6 (choice H). Instead, you are finding the average of one 0, five 1s, eight 2s, four 3s, one 4, zero 5s, and one 6, representing the 20 total students in the class. Solve as follows:

$$\frac{1 \times 0 + 5 \times 1 + 8 \times 2 + 4 \times 3 + 1 \times 4 + 0 \times 5 + 1 \times 6}{20} =$$
$$\frac{0 + 5 + 16 + 12 + 4 + 0 + 6}{20} =$$
$$\frac{43}{20} = 2\frac{3}{20}$$

107. **(C)** Imagine starting with 100 g of the chemical. After one week, 10%, or 10 g, decays, leaving 90 g. After the second week, 10% more decays, but this is 10% of the 90 g that remains. Since 10% of 90 is $0.10 \times 90 = 9$, another 9 g is lost, so the amount remaining after two weeks is $90 - 9 = 81$ g. **Note:** Don't make the mistake of thinking that losing 10% over two weeks is a loss of 20%! If this were true, in 15 weeks you'd lose 150%, or more than you have to lose!

108. **(F)** Solve the inequality for x. Subtract $2x$ from both sides to get $3x - 21 \leq 36$, then add 21 to both sides to get $3x \leq 57$. Now divide both sides by 3 to get $x \leq 19$. There are 10 positive odd numbers less than or equal to 19, namely: 1, 3, 5 . . . 19. A quick way to count them is to notice that half of the 20 numbers from 1 to 20 are odd, and these are exactly the numbers you are counting here.

109. **(C)** Recall that probability is favorable outcomes divided by total outcomes. There are 63 favorable outcomes (number of times water is ordered) and $63 + 42 + 36 + 39 = 180$ total outcomes (total number of beverages ordered). The desired probability is thus the following:

$$\frac{63}{180} = \frac{9 \times 7}{9 \times 20} = \frac{7}{20}$$

Since $\frac{7}{20} = \frac{35}{100}$, this is 35%.

110. **(G)** Choosing toppings here is the special case of choosing a pair of objects. Since there are 7 toppings to choose from, there are $\frac{7 \times 6}{2} = 21$ ways to choose a pair of those toppings. We also have 3 choices of size, so altogether there are $3 \times 21 = 63$ different sandwiches.

111. **(A)** Since $XY = 24$ and $XZ = \frac{5}{3}XY$, we know $XZ = \frac{5}{3} \times 24 = 40$. Since Y is between X and Z, we know $XZ = XY + YZ$, so $40 = 24 + YZ$, which makes $YZ = 16$.

112. **(G)** A simple approach to this problem is to "make a wish." Since $w - 1$ is an even integer, let $w - 1 = 10$, which makes $w = 11$. Now see which one of the answer choices is an odd integer when $w = 11$. It's not choice E, since $2w + 4 = 2 \times 11 + 4 = 26$. It's not choice F since $2w - 2 = 2 \times 11 - 2 = 20$. But with choice G, we have $3w + 2 = 3 \times 11 + 2 = 35$, an odd integer. For completeness, note that in choice H we have $4w + 2 = 4 \times 11 + 2 = 46$, an even integer.

113. **(B)** Because T, R, S, and U are midpoints, we know that $NS = NR = QT = QU = 3$ cm. This makes the area of each shaded right triangle $\frac{1}{2} \times 3 \times 3 = \frac{9}{2}$, and since there are two shaded triangles, their total area is $2 \times \frac{9}{2} = 9$ sq cm. Alternately, notice that you could slide the two shaded triangles together to make a square that occupies one-fourth of the larger square with side length 6 cm. The area of the larger square is 36 sq cm, and one-fourth of that is 9 sq cm.

114. **(G)** Let A be the amount of water in the tub. We can write the two equations $n + 16 = 0.80A$ and $n - 10 = 0.60A$, and then solve this system of equations to find that $26 = 0.20A$. So $A = \frac{26}{0.20} = \frac{260}{2.0} = 130$. When 80% full, there are $0.80 \times 130 = 104$ liters in the tub, and since $n + 16 = 0.80A$, we have $n + 16 = 104$, or $n = 88$. **Note:** The tub holds 130 liters, which is an answer choice, but that is not what the question is asking for.